KUNGL. VITTERHETS

HISTORIE OCH ANTIKVITETS AKADEMIENS

HANDLINGAR

Antikvariska serien

Trettiosjätte delen

Rome in the Age of Bernini

VOLUME II

*From the Election of Innocent X
to the Death of Innocent XI*

BY

TORGIL MAGNUSON

The Swedish Institute in Rome

ALMQVIST & WIKSELL
INTERNATIONAL
STOCKHOLM, SWEDEN

HUMANITIES PRESS
N.J., U.S.A.

Cover design, Alan Adler

Printed with grants from
Humanistisk-samhällsvetenskapliga forskningsrådet
Konung Gustaf VI Adolfs fond för svensk kultur
Längmanska kulturfonden
Berit Wallenbergs fond

Translated from the Swedish manuscript by Nancy Adler
Technical editor: Gunnel Sjörs

ISBN 91-7402-170-2
ISSN 0083-6761
U.S.A. ISBN 0-391-03448-0

Printed in Sweden by
Bohusläningens Boktryckeri AB, Uddevalla 1986

Contents

Foreword

The first volume of *Rome in the Age of Bernini* (1585–1644) was published in 1982. In the present volume I continue the story of the artistic and cultural life of seventeenth-century Rome up to the turn of the century. It is of course impossible to give any definite date for the end of "the age of Bernini", as the influence of the artist and his associates and pupils persisted in Rome for some time after his death in 1680. For this reason I close my account with a brief epilogue, in which I look at some of the subsequent developments. As in the first volume, I have tried to view events in the arts in a broader context, linking them with the patronage of the papal families and with the political, economic and urbanistic environment in which they occurred.

I should like to express my warmest thanks to Sten Karling for his generous support and unwavering encouragement, which together with advice from the late Aron Andersson helped me through many of the sticky patches inevitably bound up with the publication of a book of this kind. Once again I would also like to thank Nancy Adler, who not only translated my Swedish manuscript but also helped to adapt it to the slightly different requirements of an English-speaking readership. She has never failed to encourage me when the fate of this second volume seemed uncertain. Collaboration with her has always been a pleasure.

The Swedish Institute in Rome has long been my second home in the Eternal City, and I am glad to have this chance of expressing my gratitude to its staff, in particular to Kerstin Bellerba who with patience and competence has checked the bibliographical notes and helped to solve many of the knotty problems that arose.

Most of the research for this second volume has been done in the Biblioteca Apostolica Vaticana and the Bibliotheca Hertziana, and I am happy to record my thanks to the staffs of these libraries. As the most important Italian photographic archive (the Istituto Centrale del Catalogo e della Documentazione) has been closed for many years, the photographic department of the Hertziana has instead been my main source of illustrations. My thanks go to its staff and in particular to Verena Luchsinger. I also gratefully acknowledge the help I have received from Christoffer Gatiss and other members of the Courtauld Institute in London, from the Gabinetto Nazionale delle Stampe and the Gabinetto Comunale delle Stampe in Rome, from the Graphische Sammlung Albertina in Vienna, from the Heim Gallery, London, the Conway Library, Courtauld Institute of Art, London, and from the Nationalmuseum in Stockholm.

I would also like to thank Charles Burns, Birgitta Jordell, Richard Krautheimer, Laura Laureati, Eduard Safarik, Karl Gustaf Tapper and Oscar Savio.

Last but not least warm thanks are due to Stefan Hammenbeck for generously offering to help me with the index covering both volumes of this work, and to Myra Frigieri who with speed and accuracy has typed the final version of the translation from a thoroughly tangled manuscript.

Rome, December 1984

Torgil Magnuson

Coat of arms of Pope Innocent X (From Filippo Juvarra, *Raccolta di targhe*, 1732).

CHAPTER I

Innocent X
(1644–1655)

Introduction: Mazarin and the Holy See

Towards the end of Urban VIII's pontificate an important event occurred in France, which was to have repercussions also in Rome. On his death in 1642 Cardinal Richelieu was succeeded as ruling minister of France by the 40-year-old Cardinal Jules Mazarin or, more properly, Giulio Mazzarino. Born in Pescina in the Abruzzi, the cardinal had grown up in Rome and been educated by the Jesuits at the Collegio Romano.[1] As a young man he entered the service of the pope, first as an officer in the papal army and later as a diplomat, acting as secretary to the papal legate in Valtellina. His talents soon gained him the confidence of Urban VIII, who sent him on a variety of special diplomatic missions, mostly involving negotiations with the French. This brought him to the attention of Richelieu, who was quick to note the young man's gifts. It was not long before Mazarin entered the service of the French, rapidly becoming Richelieu's right-hand man. And Richelieu thought so highly of his new aide that in 1641 he contrived to have him raised to the cardinalate. Mazarin never came to Rome in this capacity, however, not even for the bestowal of the red hat as custom required, and for this reason was never granted a titular church. Unlike Richelieu, who was a bishop, Mazarin had never taken even minor orders; he simply held the title of cardinal. On Richelieu's death Louis XIII made Mazarin his chief minister, and when the king also died a few months later, Mazarin was appointed to Louis XIV's council of regency, on which he worked in intimate collaboration with Anne of Austria, the queen mother.[2] For almost twenty years France was governed to all intents and purposes by the upstart Italian, who was ruler of the nation more indisputably than Richelieu had ever been. Mazarin's claim to authority over bishops and church property soon brought him into conflict with the Holy See, since the minister of France would always allow his personal position and the interests of the French crown to take precedence over his membership of the Sacred College, and he only too readily disregarded the obedience and respect for the pope which this position should have inspired.

The Conclave of 1644

For some days after Urban VIII's death the situation in Rome was extremely critical.[3] Crime increased alarmingly—as always when the papal throne was unoccupied—and every private palace was barred against looters. Bands of French mercenaries who had fought in the Castro War under Taddeo Barberini were still roaming the streets. The Grand Duke of Tuscany and the Viceroy of Naples had drawn up their troops on the borders of the Papal States, threatening to intervene "in order to guarantee the freedom of the conclave" as they put it, unless the French troops were disbanded and Taddeo Barberini dismissed. The emperor, working through his trusted ally Cardinal Savelli, had the same end in view. The College of Cardinals decided to let the troops march away towards Bologna, but they allowed Don Taddeo to remain as commander-in-chief, albeit sharing his authority now with two cardinals. There was certainly every reason to fear that Mazarin would try to influence the papal election and that the presence of the French mercenaries in Rome would suit him very well. In February that year, when Urban VIII was seriously ill, the cardinal had already instructed his envoy in Rome to prepare for the approaching conclave by supporting the election of Guido Bentivoglio or, as a second choice, Giulio Sacchetti.

In the College of Cardinals the French interest was represented by Antonio Barberini. His brother Francesco Barberini was leader of the party, consisting mainly of Urban VIII's cardinals, which supported the gifted and sympathetic Sacchetti, a man considered by many to be the most suitable candidate. Unfortunately he was burdened with one serious handicap: he had been too closely allied with Urban and the Barberini family. Also included among the *papabili* was Giambattista Pamphili, widely recognised as an honest and upright man and a persistent opponent of Urban VIII's nepotism. This last was certainly regarded by many of the cardinals as an unqualified advantage, but it was also one which by its very nature denied Pamphili the support of Francesco and Antonio Barberini. Perhaps, though, the attitude of the two cardinals was not altogether clear, or at least their brother Taddeo Barberini may not have felt sure of them. In any case, just as the conclave was about to start, Don Taddeo sent them a *memoriale*, in which he expressly warned them against Pamphili: if they chose as pope a man who was unfavourably disposed towards the Barberini family, the consequences would be fatal not only to himself but also to them. The economic and political power of the family would be destroyed, he declared. Taddeo's document reveals an astonishing degree of barefaced egoism and greed.[4]

The conclave opened on 9 August.[5] There was great consternation when the Spanish Cardinal Albornoz immediately announced the Spanish king's opposition to the election of Sacchetti, who was considered too pro-French. Francesco Barberini recognised at once the futility of trying to defy this veto, since few of the cardinals would be courageous enough to imperil the papal throne by provoking the hostility of so powerful an enemy as Spain. As a result of the subsequent complicated negotiations, the conclave dragged endlessly on and once again the unhealthy heat of the Roman summer did more to influence the election of a pope than all the manipulations of the Great Powers. Several cardinals fell victim to malaria and had to leave the conclave, and on 7

September Mazarin's chief contender, Cardinal Bentivoglio, died. At this point Pamphili's supporters succeeded in getting his candidature accepted, overcoming the opposition of the two Barberini cardinals and their allies. Pamphili, who had been nuncio in Madrid, was thought to enjoy the confidence of the Spanish king. However, since it was known that for this very reason Mazarin would be against him, the cardinals sent an urgent message to Paris—as Mazarin was not attending the conclave in person—to sound out his attitude to the possible election of Pamphili.[6] Mazarin answered on 19 September, pronouncing his formal veto on Pamphili's election. But it was too late: by the time his answer reached Rome, Pamphili had already been elected on the morning of 15 September. In honour of Innocent VIII (1484–1492), during whose reign his parents had settled in Rome, he took the name Innocent X.

Innocent X and his Entourage

The new pope was seventy years old. A contemporary source tells that he tended to be thin, and that he had large feet, small eyes and a sparse beard—in other words, he was ugly.[7] As a young man Pamphili had trained in canon law, and Clement VIII had made him a consistorial advocate and a member of the Sacra Rota. Gregory XV sent him to Naples as papal nuncio. Urban VIII appointed him counsellor to Francesco Barberini, when the young man was sent to Paris as papal legate in 1625, and during this period Innocent gained Francesco's confidence and friendship by his wisdom and loyalty. The next year Urban entrusted him with the difficult and responsible post of nuncio to Madrid, and when he returned to Rome in 1629 he was elevated to the Sacred College.[8] Pamphili was one of the few members of the College who dared to oppose Urban VIII; among other things he had resolutely opposed the Castro War. He was thus generally recognised as an upright man, strongly disposed towards order and justice, as well as being an indefatigable worker. Further, he was regarded as a man of wide reading and extensive knowledge. As pope he always bore himself with great dignity. His piety was genuine and he was punctual in attendance at all the feasts and ceremonies of the Church where his presence was required. He would even listen with interest to the lengthy sermons so often preached during Lent. His moderate eating and drinking habits were well known, and his health was good.[9] On the other hand he had always been cross-grained and stern. In Paris he had been nicknamed *monseigneur On-ne-peut-pas*, and even in Madrid many heads had been shaken over this taciturn and uncommunicative man; malicious tongues would have it that his silence was to cover up his meagre talents. As pope he soon proved not only hot-tempered but also erratic and unreliable; his anger would flare up unexpectedly and rash decisions could then be made. He was also deeply suspicious of almost everyone, even the people closest to him, and it is hard to escape the impression that these less attractive qualities became increasingly marked with the passing of the years. This is how we see him in Velazquez' famous portrait painted in 1650: suspicious, contrary and morose. On the

Velazquez: portrait of Pope Innocent X. Galleria Doria-Pamphili (Alinari).

other hand, a redeeming feature of Pamphili's nature was his unfailing kindness to the poor.

In Innocent's immediate family there was only one person who might have been expected to achieve a measure of importance, namely the pope's sister-in-law, Olimpia Maidalchini, widow of his elder brother Panfilo Pamphili. She was born in Viterbo in 1594 and was of fairly simple extraction. She was intelligent although not deeply cultivated; her greatest interest was hunting. She was a determined woman, somewhat mannish and possessed of two great faults: she was grasping and ambitious for power.[10] In his earlier career as a diplomat she had helped Giambattista Pamphili by providing him with funds from her personal fortune. The cardinals who elected Pamphili as pope cannot have been altogether unaware of the debt of gratitude which he owed to his sister-in-law and some of them uttered warning words, but they can hardly have envisaged the extent to which this ruthless female would make her influence felt.

To the general surprise Innocent broke with tradition and appointed a cardinal as his secretary of state. He chose a previous colleague of his own, Giovanni Giacomo Panziroli. The new secretary, the son of a poor Roman tailor, was the typical bureaucrat. He continued to live extremely discreetly, but it was believed that behind his civil and courteous manner he concealed a strong personal desire for power. Certainly he was as well-acquainted as Donna Olimpia with Innocent's occasionally freakish temper; he knew how to handle the pope and how to get his own way with him.[11]

Donna Olimpia's son, Camillo Pamphili was appointed commander-in-chief of the papal army, after Taddeo Barberini, and Donna Olimpia was busy planning a dynastic alliance for Camillo with the Barberini family. But her plans on this score were thwarted when the pope changed his mind and raised Camillo to the purple: the support of a cardinal-nephew was felt to be indispensable. Thus as *cardinal padrone* Camillo became an intimate of the pope's on a par with Panziroli. He was immediately given the lucrative but not exactly demanding post of legate to Avignon. He also became *Segretario ai Brevi* in charge of the pope's foreign correspondence and prefect of the *Segnatura di grazia*, one of the papal law courts. Camillo was a handsome man, well liked for his friendly and courteous manner. He was not perhaps highly cultivated; never having studied, he spent most of his time riding and hunting. But he was not devoid of interest in poetry and the arts, and had certain horticultural and even technical gifts.[12] Significantly, though, he had no aptitude at all for an ecclesiastical career—a serious drawback in a cardinal-nephew. Despite his own nature he applied himself diligently to his duties for a while. But when he found that Innocent allowed him no real influence, he soon grew tired of his new position.

Donna Olimpia made up for the thwarting of her plans by arranging another dynastic alliance: in 1665 her daughter Costanza was married to the Prince of Piombino, Niccolò Ludovisi. Already before Pamphili's election an elder daughter, Maria, had made a wealthy marriage to a Marquis Giustiniani. Costanza's husband, who resided in Rome at the papal court, was decidedly pro-Spanish and a personal friend of King Philip IV, but he had never exercised any real influence on papal policy. After 1645 he had been in command of the papal navy during the conflict with France, and had taken part in the Venetian defence of Crete.

A few years after his elevation to the Sacred College, Camillo Pamphili fell in love with the beautiful Olimpia Aldobrandini, previously married to a member of the Borghese family but recently widowed. She was not only beautiful but gifted and witty as well, besides which she had inherited a

Alessandro Algardi:
portrait bust of Donna
Olimpia Maidalchini,
marble. Doria-Pamphili
collection (Alinari).

considerable fortune together with the little principality of Rossano in Calab-
ria. She was always known henceforth as the princess of Rossano. Camillo
succeeded in persuading the pope to allow him to abandon his career in the
Church in order to marry his princess. There was no legal obstacle, although it
was an unusual step, since he had never taken even minor orders.[13] In January
1647 Camillo laid aside the purple. To Donna Olimpia this blow was grievous.
She never forgave the princess of Rossano for capturing her son's heart, but
even more seriously she feared the influence that her intelligent daughter-in-
law might obtain over the pope. When the pair were quietly married a month
or so later Donna Olimpia was not present, and she succeeded in seeing that
the newly married couple left Rome. They settled first in Caprarola and later in
Frascati—not, after all, so very far away.

Now that Camillo had fallen into disfavour, Donna Olimpia's influence
grew apace. Since apart from Panziroli, she was the only person who understood Innocent's reserved and erratic character, anyone seeking a favour or
wanting anything from the pope would turn first to her. And in fact the pope
rarely embarked on any important undertaking without first asking his sister-
in-law's advice. This was regarded as all the more scandalous since Donna
Olimpia was said to be "*di nauseante ingordigia*", disgustingly greedy, never
hesitating to exact substantial payment for the slightest favour obtained from
her brother-in-law the pope. Malicious Romans nicknamed her *olim pia*, the
"once-so-pious". More often she was simply known as *la Dominante*, and the

Anonymous master:
portrait of Donna Olimpia
Aldobrandini-Pamphili,
princess of Rossano.
Doria Pamphili collection
(ICCD).

Venetian ambassador Giovanni Giustiniani openly expressed his hatred of this
"latter-day Agrippina".[14]

Soon after Camillo had renounced the cardinalate the pope elevated Francesco Maidalchini, a boy of only seventeen and a nephew of Donna Olimpia, to
the purple and granted him the official title of *cardinal padrone*. This appointment was the result of one of Innocent's whims and it immediately proved to
have been a capital error, for this unprepossessing young man was both stupid
and indolent. Malicious tongues hinted that he was barely literate and that the
Jesuits had given up hope of instilling any sort of knowledge into him at
school. Rarely has such a nonentity been received into the Sacred College.
Although the aging Panziroli genuinely needed help, it was actually better to
keep Francesco Maidalchini away from anything that mattered, as even the
simplest tasks were beyond him. Innocent was bitterly disappointed but tried
to laugh the whole thing off, declaring that because the young cardinal was so
ugly he did not want to see him.[15]

The Barberini Called to Account; Conflict with Mazarin

No sooner was Urban VIII dead than the storm clouds began to gather over the Barberini family. With their arrogant behaviour and accumulation of wealth the Barberini nephews had incurred hatred and envy on all sides. In September 1645, as Innocent X was preparing to call them to account before a special congregation, Cardinal Antonio Barberini the Younger fled. After many adventures and even shipwreck he arrived in France and betook himself to the court in Paris. In January the following year, equally suddenly, Francesco Barberini took flight together with Don Taddeo and his four children. They, too, found refuge in Paris. Anna Colonna, Taddeo's wife, was the only member of the family courageous enough to stay in Rome, where with great dignity she watched over her husband's interests. Confounded by these sudden disappearances, Innocent could do nought but condemn the Barberini *in contumatiam*; their wealth was confiscated, their fiefs abolished, and their palaces closed.[16]

To Mazarin the election of the Pamphili pope naturally represented a political defeat of some dimensions, and to begin with he vented his wrath on Francesco and Antonio Barberini. But after the two cardinals and Don Taddeo had found refuge at the French court, he forgave them and granted them his official support.[17] He now turned his anger on Innocent X instead, with the result that relations between France and the Holy See, already rather tense, became critical in the extreme.[18] At first Mazarin actually considered refusing to acknowledge the election, and hinted at both schism and the calling of a general council. In the end, however, he refrained from such drastic measures, merely intimating his intention of upholding the "Gallic rights". Such threats had often been heard from France over the last few centuries, and the pope could of course have imposed ecclesiastical sanctions. But Innocent saw the risks this would involve. When Mazarin realised that his threats were making no impression, he had recourse to arms. His action was not directed at the pope himself, however, but at the Spanish *presidios*, the military bases held by the Spanish since 1557 on the Tuscan coast. Thus the military action was a move in his war against Spain, but it was cunningly intended at the same time as a blow at the pope's nephew, Niccolò Ludovisi, whose principality of Piombino on the Tuscan coast was under Spanish overlordship. French troops occupied Talamone and Porto Santo Stefano and began to lay seige to Orbetello, but after a defeat at the hands of the Spanish navy in the summer of 1646 the French were forced to retire.[19]

The hostilities between France and Spain had repercussions also in Rome. Among other things an intermezzo occurred which in many of its ingredients was typical of the times. On his arrival in Rome in the spring of 1646, the Spanish ambassador, Cabrera, Admiral of Castille, behaved both arrogantly and provocatively, declaring at once that he had no intention of paying his respects to Cardinal Rinaldo d'Este or even of greeting him should they meet in their carriages in town. Cardinal d'Este, it should be noted, watched over

Left: A. Clouet: portrait of Cardinal Jules Mazarin, engraving (BAV).
Right: G. Testana: portrait of Cardinal Astalli-Pamphili, engraving (BAV).

the interests of France vis-à-vis the Holy See in the absence of Francesco Barberini. From Naples, where he had previously been viceroy, Admiral Cabrera acquired a doughty guard of 4,000 men. Cardinal d'Este hastily answered by recruiting 2,000 infantry and 200 well-armed knights on his own account. The Romans waited on tenterhooks to see what would happen. And the clash when it came was a violent one. On 29 April Cabrera paid a visit to Cardinal Lante, dean of the Sacred College. Returning home to Palazzo Colonna, where he was staying, his armed guard met the "enemy" head on in the piazza outside the Gesù. Shots were fired, and the curious spectators scattered in panic leaving several dead, among them the wretched beggar who used to stand in the doorway of the church. Cabrera's men dispersed, and the ambassador only managed to escape by the skin of his teeth, first picking up the wounded and fallen in his carriages.[20] Naturally there were diplomatic repercussions, but eventually Innocent succeeded in reconciling the two great lords at a special meeting which he arranged in the Vatican.

It was not long before Mazarin, now all conciliation and courtesy, was reconciled with the pope. The Marquis of Fontenay-Mareuil was sent as ambassador to Rome, where he arrived in May 1647. Over the next few months he attended on the Pope innumerable times, chiefly to negotiate for a cardinal's hat for Mazarin's brother Michel. The official reception was delayed until September, as the marquis' carriages were not yet ready. Gigli tells us that when he finally attended on the pope at the Quirinal Palace he came with five carriages, three drawn by six horses and the others by two; his pages and grooms were clad in green silk with silver braid, and he was accompanied by almost a thousand members of the Roman aristocracy in over 200 carriages.

When he subsequently paid his respects to Donna Olimpia, she received him attended by ten ladies of the highest nobility and conducted herself with the airs of a queen.[21]

This reconciliation prepared the way for the return of the Barberini. Francesco arrived in February 1648, but Antonio waited until the summer of 1653. They were received by the pope with the utmost kindness. But Don Taddeo never saw Rome again. He died in Paris in 1647.

Foreign Policy

More or less against his will Innocent X had become involved in the war between France and Spain as a result of Mazarin's action in support of the Barberini and the attack against the Spanish *presidios*.[22] The struggle for supremacy between the two dominating powers in Europe went back a long time. Innocent X was anxious to remain neutral, however, particularly because he hoped to bring about a united European action against the Turks—something which many popes had been dreaming of for over 200 years. The Turks had taken the offensive by invading Crete, which had been a Venetian possession for the whole of that time. They landed on the island in 1645, captured several coastal towns and laid seige to Candia, the present Heraklion. Venice now appealed for help to the pope, and also to Spain. Innocent provided financial subsidies, and even sent soldiers and several galleys which joined up with the Venetian navy in 1646. The Venetian ambassadors Contarini and Guistiniani pleaded constantly for further supplies of money, but in vain; Innocent told them they were asking the impossible. The pope's own financial difficulties were beginning to assume catastrophic proportions, but in fact Innocent felt in his innermost heart that the Turkish offensive was God's way of punishing the *Serenissima Repubblica* for the many breaches of ecclesiastical privilege in her territories.[23]

In July 1647 a popular insurrection against Spanish repression broke out in Naples, led by a young fisherman named Masaniello.[24] The rebels expelled the viceroy and proclaimed Masaniello *capitano del popolo*. But success went to the young leader's head, and it was not long before he was murdered himself. During the ensuing confusion Mazarin had some vague idea of intervening and making good the ancient claim of the French king to the crown of Naples. But he acted with great caution, not wanting to jeopardise the possibility of peace with Philip IV. The Neapolitans appealed to the French and the pope in turn. But although Innocent X could have claimed his traditional feudal rights, he too preferred to remain neutral. In the autumn of the same year the Spaniards, having concluded their war in the Netherlands, sent a strong detachment to Naples. A French auxiliary corps dispatched by Mazarin was defeated, and the revolt was crushed in blood. Innocent X alone protested at the cruelty of the Spaniards towards the people of Naples, but in vain.[25] And perhaps at the same time he saw some advantage in Philip IV regaining control of his vassal state, since it meant that the French were no longer the immediate neighbours of the

Papal States to the south. Certainly he must have been relieved that the rebellion did not spread to other parts of Italy, as many of the subjects of the Papal States were also complaining vociferously about high taxation and punitive imposts.

On 24 October 1648 the Treaty of Westphalia was signed. The pope had been following every stage in the tough and long-drawn-out negotiations in Osnabrück and Münster in the excellent reports of his nuncio, Fabio Chigi, one of the few people whom he trusted.[26] None of the delegates of the states involved in the negotiations paid any attention to the pope's wishes. Chigi opposed the various clauses of the treaty in vain. In his view far too little account was taken of the interests of the Catholic Church in Germany, where much former ecclesiastical property was lost. But above all Chigi opposed the principle of *cujus regio ejus religio*, implying the rulers' dominion over the religion of their subjects. Chigi's protest was officially confirmed by the pope, and the total disregard of his wishes in this respect was the cause of bitter disappointment to Innocent X, who realised that he was successively losing ground in the political game. His protest took the form of a letter rather than a bull, addressed to all his nuncios and dated 26 November 1648, in which he proclaimed that the clauses in the peace treaty which damaged the Church were to be regarded as invalid.[27]

After settling with the Barberini, Innocent X was forced for various reasons to renew Urban VIII's Castro War, of which he had previously disapproved.[28] Odoardo Farnese died in 1646, and his son Ranuccio II succeeded him as Duke of Parma and Castro. The new duke again refused to pay the interest on his *monti*, just as his father had done before him. At first Innocent was chary of repeating Urban's mistake and was unwilling to resort to arms, but when the Bishop of Castro was murdered by assassins in March 1649 and Ranuccio was suspected on good grounds of knowing more about it than he should, the pope demanded that justice be done. During the spring, as the duke made various threatening moves, the pope felt bound to recruit an army of mercenaries. Fortunately it soon became obvious that Ranuccio was not going to get the same support that his father had formerly received from France, which was involved at the time in its internal struggles with the Fronde. Thus the papal troops were able to lay seige to Castro without any complications and to receive its capitulation at the end of the summer. The pope then gave orders for the evacuation of the population and the total destruction of the town, which was accordingly razed to the ground. It is still possible to discover among the ruins, overgrown with thistles and brambles, a single column inscribed with the words "Here stood Castro". At last, when the important customs station of Ronciglione on the Via Cassia in the Cimini Hills was transferred by treaty to the *Camera apostolica*, the pope was rid of the last vestiges of feudal power within the Papal States. And the whole action had cost him far less than Urban VIII's unsuccessful campaign.

Opposition in France to the pressure of taxes and the absolute royal power residing in Mazarin's hands led to the five-year civil war generally known as the Fronde. In 1649, soon after the insurrection began, Mazarin fled to Germany. Three years later, when the rebellion had been crushed, he returned together with the young King Louis XIV, who at thirteen had been declared of age. Mazarin's position was now stronger than ever, and his only substantial political opponent was the young coadjutor to the archbishop of Paris, Jean François Paul de Gondi. This gifted but very unclerical prelate had been one of the leaders of the Fronde. After Mazarin's return, Gondi manoeuvred Innocent X by skilful intrigue and by bribing the princess of Rossano, to raise him to the cardinalate, after which he was known as the Cardinal de Retz. If he believed that the dignity of his new rank would protect him from Mazarin's revenge, he soon discovered his mistake: on command of the king he was imprisoned. This was a serious infringement of the papal jurisdiction, but the pope's protests fell on deaf ears. Two years later de Retz managed to escape, making his way to Spain and ultimately to Rome. He has described his many adventures in his famous *Memoirs*.[29]

Over the next few years relations between France and the Papal States became increasingly tense, until in 1652 the papal nuncio, Neri Corsini, was actually arrested on Mazarin's orders as he landed at Marseilles. In the meantime the reports which Innocent was receiving from Cardinal de Retz only served to confirm what he already felt about Mazarin.

Innocent was also disturbed by the situation of the Catholics in England, where the Civil War which had been raging since 1642 ended in the total victory of Oliver Cromwell and the execution of Charles I in January 1649. Cromwell certainly introduced religious tolerance, but it did not extend to the supporters of the "popish religion"; Catholics lost most of their civil rights, and all Catholic priest were forced to leave the country on pain of death.

To Ireland with its predominantly Catholic population Innocent X dispatched a nuncio, Rinuccini, and later provided the Irish with substantial financial support. The pope had no political ambitions, but he hoped by means of firm opposition to the English to strengthen the Catholic position. But Rinuccini failed and the Catholic alliance was defeated. After 1652, when all opposition had been crushed, the English subjugated the whole of Ireland and took possession of its land, often showing barbaric cruelty to its people.[30]

Thus, after the Treaty of Westphalia the Roman Catholic Church was in retreat throughout Northern Europe. The Protestant countries—England, the Netherlands and Sweden—were becoming both politically and economically great powers, while in Germany the Catholic Church had again lost ground after the successes at the beginning of the century.

Further Intrigues and Scandals in the Papal Family

Since the elevation of Francesco Maidalchini to the Sacred College had proved such a disaster, and as Panziroli grew increasingly ill and unable to direct the Secretariate of State on his own, it became obvious that the pope would have to find a replacement. Panziroli suggested as his own successor a distant relative of Donna Olimpia Maidalchini's, one Camillo Astalli. Astalli thus belonged to an old Roman patrician family; he was 34 years old, of agreeable appearance and refined manners.[31] There was certainly an element of pure calculation in Panziroli's suggestion, since he expected Astalli's consequent gratitude and loyalty to increase his own influence. In the course of a single day, 19 September 1650, the pope raised Camillo Astalli to cardinal's rank and granted him the titular church of S. Pietro in Montorio, adopted him as a member of the Pamphili family with the right to assume the family name and armorial bearings, and appointed him *cardinal padrone*. Astalli also received the Avignon legation, an ancient sinecure worth about 30,000 scudi a year. In addition to all this he was granted possession of the Palazzo Pamphili in Piazza Navona and the Villa di Belrespiro outside Porta S. Pancrazio. The appointment had all the impact of a bombshell; among foreign observers it was the great sensation of the day. Everyone was amazed by this sudden and unprecedented generosity, which was seen as yet another papal caprice. Many suspected Donna Olimpia's hand behind the whole thing, as they knew she had already helped the young man to his place in the Curia. Others believed the opposite: that the pope was looking for a counterweight to Donna Olimpia's influence. This last may have been nearer the truth, as in fact she had nothing to do with Astalli's elevation. Indeed she felt the threat to her own position, expressing her anxiety to the pope in a violent outburst of anger with the happy outcome that Innocent, sick of *la Dominante's* greed and intrigues, took his courage in both hands and showed her the door. On Panziroli's advice he forbade her ever to set her foot in the papal palace again.

Naturally Donna Olimpia's fall caused a sensation. It was partly due, so the gossip said, to reports from the papal nuncio in Vienna of the emperor's horror at such female influence over the pope, and this in turn had offended Innocent; then, too, Donna Olimpia's power was said to be greatly to blame for the political setbacks suffered by the papacy in recent years and for the ground lost to the Catholic Church in Europe.[33]

Not long after this the pope became reconciled with Prince Pamphili and the princess of Rossano. The mediator here was the pope's sister, Sor Agatha, a nun from the convent of Tor de' Specchi, who despite her more than eighty years was still an energetic and enterprising woman. The princely couple were received in audience in January 1651 together with their young sons, whom the pope embraced with much emotion. Henceforth victory lay with the princess of Rossano, Donna Olimpia Aldobrandini-Pamphili, who soon occupied a position at the papal court almost as important as Donna Olimpia Maidalchini before her, while her more easy-going husband was kept firmly in the background. The young family installed themselves in the Palazzo Aldobrandini on the Corso, next to the church of S. Maria in Via Lata, where they entertained Roman society to a series of banquets and festivities, each more brilliant and costly than the one before.

After Donna Olimpia's fall Panziroli found he had badly misjudged the nature of the new cardinal-nephew. Astalli was by no means content to follow

Anonymous master:
portrait of Donna Olimpia
Maidalchini with her
granddaughter Olimpia
Giustiniani, called
Olimpiuccia. Doria-Pamphili
collection (Alinari).

his benefactor's lead but instead was soon intriguing against him. In the end
Panziroli retired from the Curia, sick and disillusioned, to die a year later in a
state approaching disgrace. When Cardinal Astalli-Pamphili was left alone to
deal with all the work that comes the way of a papal lieutenant, however, his
inadequacy and indolence were mercilessly revealed. Innocent had made
another mistake.

It became necessary to find someone to replace or at least to complement
Astalli-Pamphili. On the advice of that sensible diplomat, Cardinal Bernardino
Spada, the pope sent for Fabio Chigi, former nuncio at the negotiations leading
to the Treaty of Westphalia. Chigi arrived in Rome in November 1651 and was
appointed secretary of state.[34] He was an intelligent and serious-minded man,
possessed of profound humanist learning in the old tradition, combined in his
case with genuine personal piety and a warm, optimistic view of the Christian
life. Chigi was also modest and discreet in manner, living in the greatest
simplicity, at least by the standards of the day.[35] He meditated constantly on
death, always drinking his wine—so it was said—from a goblet engraved with

a skull. Chigi's integrity won the respect and admiration of the pope, who soon gave his new secretary his fullest confidence. Both the princess of Rossano and Cardinal Pamphili tried to gain Chigi's favour, hoping to acquire him as an ally, but he rejected their overtures on the grounds that as secretary of state his duty was to further the interests of the Papal States, not to watch over the economic interests of a single family.[36] In the spring of 1652 Chigi was made a cardinal and given S. Maria del Popolo—where his ancestors where buried—as his titular church.

That same spring a scandal broke upon Rome causing a considerable stir. A member of the Curia, a certain Monsignor Mascambruno employed in *la Dataria*, was found to have been falsifying documents submitted to the pope for his signature, and this had been going on for quite some time. Innocent had trusted his official and signed the papers put before him, which meant that Mascambruno and his friends had been enriching themselves at the expense of the papal coffers. Mascambruno was tried, condemned to death, and executed.[37]

These events were extremely distressing to the pope, who was anyway feeling increasingly isolated and lonely. Panziroli, the only person who knew how to joke with him and could sometimes make him smile, had gone. And Innocent missed Donna Olimpia, the only living being who was really close to him now that he was growing old. He found the ceaseless intrigues of the princess of Rossano and Cardinal Astalli-Pamphili, and their hostility to Donna Olimpia, a constant irritant.

Finally Innocent wearied of his loneliness and longed for a reconciliation with his sister-in-law, taking no notice of Chigi's warnings. Once again the mediator was Sor Agatha, who first arranged a meeting between the princess of Rossano and Donna Olimpia, and on 11 March 1653 the two ladies were reconciled. On 25 March Sor Agatha accompanied Donna Olimpia to an audience in the Quirinal Palace, and the reconciliation was later sealed at a banquet in the Pamphili Palace in Piazza Navona, at which the pope was present in person.[38] At this feast the engagement was announced between Donna Olimpia's twelve-year-old granddaughter Olimpia Giustiniani, known as Olimpiuccia, and young Maffeo Barberini, Don Taddeo's son. The wedding was celebrated with great pomp in the Vatican in June.

This dynastic alliance set the seal on Donna Olimpia's triumph. From the very beginning of Innocent's pontificate she had been striving to unite the Barberini and Pamphili families: she felt that her own family would be in a stronger position by allying itself with the relatives of Urban VIII. The reconciliation with the Barberini was further strengthened when Taddeo's eldest son Carlo was raised to the purple later that year. At the same time he was allowed to keep the title of *prefetto di Roma* which his father had held before him and which was never subsequently used again. On the other hand he abstained from his rights of succession as the first-born son and the title of prince of Palestrina in favour of his younger brother Maffeo.

Once Donna Olimpia Maidalchini had regained favour with the pope, her

Alessandro Algardi:
portrait bust of Innocent X
in bronze and porphyry,
detail. Doria-Pamphili
collection (Alinari).

influence waxed stronger than before, and her greed was as shameless as ever.
Cardinal Astalli-Pamphili's position soon became untenable, and it was not
long before he fell victim to the intrigues so skilfully woven by Donna
Olimpia. The excuse for his demotion was his affiliation with Spain. It so
happened that just at this time, the beginning of 1654, the pope was harbouring
plans together with Donna Olimpia and the Barberini to make a surprise attack
on Naples with a troop of 12,000 men, and to make Maffeo Barberini Prince of
Salerno. Cardinal Pamphili warned Philip IV, who was able to instigate countermeasures and thwart the papal plans. Evidence of the cardinal's involvement
was provided by one of Chigi's young men in the state secretariat, a highly
gifted protégé of Donna Olimpia's named Decio Azzolini.[39]

The pope decided to remove Cardinal Pamphili from the Curia at once by
offering him the episcopate of Ferrara, but the cardinal firmly refused the
appointment and left Rome. As a result of this intractability he fell into
disfavour, was deprived of all his titles except that of cardinal, lost his sources
of income and his membership of the Pamphili family—in future he was
known simply as Cardinal Camillo Astalli—and was exiled to the village of
Sambuci in the mountains beyond Tivoli.

The next victim of Donna Olimpia's intriguing was Prince Nicolò Ludovisi,
who was also exiled from Rome, after which she set about undermining the

pope's confidence in Chigi. In March 1654 a consistory was held for the creation of cardinals—it was to be Innocent's last—and without Chigi even being informed the red hat was given to Decio Azzolini. From then on Donna Olimpia made sure that her protégé occupied a position on a par with Chigi's and it was felt to be only a matter of time before Chigi fell and Azzolini took his place as secretary of state.[40] The aging pope was quite incapable of opposing the intrigues of his dominating sister-in-law, while at the same time he was also becoming increasingly irritable and suspicious of everybody else around him.

Innocent X as Head of the Church

With regard to the internal administration of the Church, Innocent continued his predecessors' work. In this field there was genuine continuity. Despite his many faults Innocent was methodical and orderly, and he devoted himself from the very beginning of his pontificate to reforming the religious orders. He issued a special bull to the effect that monasteries should be closed if it were no longer possible to maintain an ordered monastic life there. Similarly several minor and unimportant congregations were discontinued, while the statutes of some other reformed congregations were confirmed, such as the Benedictine congregation of Monte Cassino.[41]

In 1650 a Holy Year was to be celebrated, and the pope devoted much interest to its preparation. The Holy Year had been proclaimed in a bull on 4 May 1649.[42] The completion of the decoration of the nave of St. Peter's and the almost total restoration of the Lateran Basilica had been commissioned in good time.

On Christmas Eve 1649 Innocent opened the holy door to St. Peter's, while specially delegated cardinals opened the corresponding doors at the Lateran Basilica, S. Paolo fuori le mura, and S. Maria Maggiore. For the last of these the pope had delegated the 17-year-old Cardinal Francesco Maidalchini, who was almost knocked over by the enormous crowd that thronged behind him.

In the course of the year the pope personally visited the four pilgrim basilicas no less than sixteen times, to obtain the indulgences of the Holy Year. Several cardinals undertook the pilgrimage on foot, to set a good example.[43] Easter was celebrated with special solemnity, and it was estimated that no less than 70,000 pilgrims were already in Rome by that time, while 700,000 people visited Rome in the course of the year, every one of them staying for at least fourteen days.[44] Wealthy Romans rivalled one another in collecting benefactions for the poor and caring for impoverished pilgrims; not least among them was Donna Olimpia Maidalchini. For the inhabitants of Rome the great influx of visitors provided a substantial and extremely welcome economic boost.

Although the Catholic Church had suffered severe setbacks in various parts of Europe during the 1640s, Innocent X could at least rejoice in successes in the missionary field beyond the confines of Europe. The Roman Church was

increasingly assuming the role of a universal world church. The most remarkable triumphs had been gained in the decades immediately following the
establishment of the *Propaganda fide*, and Innocent X could now reap the
harvest sown during the pontificates of Gregory XV and Urban VIII.

The Philippines were now almost entirely Christian, and a Catholic university had been founded in Manila. Missionary activities in China were led by the
German Jesuit, Johann Adam Schall, an outstanding mathematician and
astronomist; like his predecessor, Father Ricci, he had attained the rank of
mandarin of the first class. There were now more than 150,000 Christians in
China.[45] The last empress of the recently overthrown Ming dynasty and her
son were both converted and given the names of Helena and Constantine in
baptism. And the new emperor of the Manchurian dynasty also showed great
esteem for the Christian religion without actually undergoing conversion.

Already under Urban VIII the argument about the Chinese rites had begun.
The Jesuits recognised the futility of introducing into China the Latin culture
of the Roman Church, and they had not only translated the liturgy of the mass
into Chinese but had also allowed the baptised to continue under certain forms
to venerate the memory of K'ung Su-tzu, known in the West as Confucius,
and to revere the spirits of their ancestors. But here the Jesuits came up against
opposition from the Franciscans and Dominicans, and the latter reported the
whole issue to the Inquisition. The Inquisition proclaimed 17 points on the
question of the Chinese rites, which were more or less condemned, and the
outcome was confirmed by the *Propaganda fide* in 1645.[46] But this by no
means settled the issue. The Jesuits insisted on certain methods, albeit under
forms acceptable to the Church, and the question was to be debated for almost
another hundred years.

In North America the Catholic Church was gaining ground particularly in
California. Most of the missionaries there came from Mexico, which was
already Christian. In the northern and western states and in Canada, on the
other hand, French Jesuits predominated. In Canada particularly they met
with fierce opposition from the Indians, and many Jesuit fathers suffered
martyrdom there, tortured to death by hostile tribes.[47]

One of the most important events of Church history during Innocent X's
pontificate was the condemnation of Jansenism.[48] The pope began by citing
Urban VIII's bull, *In eminenti*, thus engendering bitter battles between the
Jansenists and the Jesuits, as the Jansenists denied ever having preached the
propositions referred to in the bull. The battle was fought exclusively and
exhaustively on paper. The universities, the bishops, the clergy, and to some
extent the upper social classes as well, were those primarily affected. Several
bishops opposed the bull, but on this issue Innocent X could rely on Mazarin's
support, as the cardinal was as keen an opponent of Jansenism as Richelieu had
been before him. Nonetheless, to his dismay the pope saw Jansenism spreading
not only in France but also in the Netherlands, the Rhineland and even in
distant Poland.

In the end Innocent felt forced to intervene, particularly as the Jansenists

INNOCENTIVS X PONT MAX APERVIT PORTAM SANCTAM
in die Vistra Nativitatis Jesu Christi tunc Jubilei 1650 Pont Anno 6.

G. D. De Rossi: Innocent X opens the Holy Door in St. Peter's on Christmas Eve 1649, engraving (GCS).

questioned the supremacy and apostolic authority of the papacy. In April 1651 he appointed a special congregation of cardinals to study the question. One of the leading members of this group was Fabio Chigi, who had personal knowledge of the Jansenists from his period as nuncio in the Rhineland.[49] French bishops who supported Jansenism personally petitioned the pope, and the French government officially asked him to declare his position. Innocent often participated personally in the deliberations of the congregation, and in 1653 he finally issued an apostolic constitution, *Cum occasione*, drawn up by the two cardinals Chigi and Albizzi. This confirmed the papal authority, and five propositions of the Jansenist doctrine were condemned.[50] They concerned the vexed question of the relation between grace and free will. According to the Jansenists God has chosen a few only for salvation, and these few cannot reject the divine grace; the rest, those not so chosen, cannot keep God's commandments and are thus condemned to perdition, however hard they strive to live a righteous life. Innocent's successors were to find to their cost that Jansenism was far from defeated by this declaration. The struggle was to continue in France throughout the seventeenth and into the eighteenth century. And even today there are traces of the influence of Jansenism in French Catholicism.

Conditions in the Papal States under Innocent X

As temporal head of state, Innocent X was much more interested in the internal administration of the Papal States than in the problems of foreign policy. Formerly an official, he still favoured orderliness and method and was always eager to keep himself informed about everything. But with his suspicious nature he would never rely on a single report, even from his most trusted colleagues; he always had to listen to another party, with the result that important decisions often came too late.[51] Even though Innocent proved scandalously feeble in controlling those around him, particularly as he became older, and although he was incapable of settling the conflicts and intrigues within his own family, he nevertheless insisted that the Papal States were conscientiously administered and that justice was done. The new prison, *Carceri Nuovi*, which he had built by his architect Antonio del Grande on the Via Giulia, is one example of his merits in this respect. The prison was to replace the ancient and terrible dungeons in Tor di Nona; at the time it represented the epitome of humane prison administration. But political offenders were still incarcerated in Castel Sant'Angelo.

Any attempt at restoring the papal finances, which had become completely chaotic during Urban VIII's Castro War, was bound to fail. The savings in the papal court which Innocent introduced had little effect. More important was his reduction of the interest on certain *monti* from 7 to 4½ per cent, but too great a proportion of the income of the Papal States still had to be used for paying interest on earlier loans. New state loans to a sum of 3 million scudi were taken up.[52] In the aftermath of Masaniello's rebellion in Naples a few taxes were reduced and some savings were made. But the *Camera apostolica* was depleted again by the subsidies to support the Venetians in their struggle to save Crete, where the siege of Candia dragged on for years.

Innocent X would have liked to abolish Urban VIII's unpopular tax on flour, but circumstances forced him to keep it. In fact he was compelled to introduce several restrictive measures just in connection with the food trades.[53]

During the severe flooding of the Tiber on several occasions at the beginning of Innocent's pontificate big supplies of grain were destroyed, particularly in December 1647 when all the lower parts of the town from Piazza Navona to *Botteghe oscure* were under water.[54] Gigli complained that bread was so poor after this, and tasted so foul, that even dogs and cats refused to eat it—the result of mixing ground horse-beans with the flour. Any reader of Gigli's *Diario* can see just how much bread meant to the Romans. Complaints are always recurring that the weight of loaves has been reduced and the quality of the bread is getting continually worse. During the famine after the inundation of 1647, Innocent procured grain for bread for the city at his own expense, and opened the stores of the *Camera apostolica* to the people.[55] The following year harvests failed everywhere in Europe, and the pope prohibited the export of grain; further, grain was to be used solely for baking bread, and any grain in storage must be sold before October. Stockpiling was forbidden. Attempts were made to get grain from Danzig and Amsterdam, and negotiations were even held with the Turks. Fortunately the harvest improved in 1649, and it was possible to reduce grain prices. Over the next few years prices continued to vary a good deal, but in 1653 grain was again in short supply, with famine as a result.[56] During these years of scarcity Rome was also afflicted by an epidemic of spotted fever, while endemic malaria reached a peak in the Campagna and along the coast during the same difficult years.

The flooding of the Tiber was caused, of course, by the heavy rains which usually fall particularly in winter in the region of Rome. But Gigli also mentions abnormal weather at other times of the year, for example in 1652 there was too much warm weather in February followed by frost in April and hail in June, and such events contributed to the ruin of the crops[57]—and nobody could blame pollution or nuclear bombs!

The Papal States as a whole were generally regarded as a fertile region, with extensive areas under cultivation particularly in Emilia and Romagna, and even in Umbria as well. Latium was not quite so well off, partly because of its different geological conditions. The soil of Sabina, for example, was too chalky for the successful cultivation of grain or wine on a large scale, whereas olives had been cultivated there from time immemorial. The Campagna, on the other hand, was a wasteland. The area between Rome and Tivoli was almost devoid of habitation or cultivated plots, and towards the sea coast the countryside was mainly deserted. In winter great flocks of sheep would graze there. Most of the cultivated area consisted of *latifundia* belonging to the Church or to the old feudal nobility, and the cultivation of the land was dictated entirely by the economic policy of the city. And so it remained for the whole of the century.

In his *relazione* to the Venetian senate in 1648 Contarini reported that of the 2 million scudi which the Papal States enjoyed in revenues, 1,300,000 went towards paying interest on earlier debts. The pope, he reported, had a personal annual income of 400,000 from *la Dataria*, consisting mainly of the income from vacancies in various bishoprics which accrued to the Holy See, and it was up to the pope himself to decide how this revenue should be used. Contarini also mentioned—and this was the kind of information that interested *La Serenissima*—that plenty of people were available to form an army in the Papal States, but the existing troops lacked training and skilled leadership. The pope always kept 800 mounted men and 1,500 foot soldiers as a kind of police corps *"per le correnti turbolenze"*.[58]

The economic crisis which had overtaken the noble families of Rome at the end of the 16th century still persisted, partly due to their lack of interest in cultivating their inherited lands. The new Borghese and Barberini families, on the other hand, were still thriving and adding to their possessions during the 1640s. And now in the 1650s they were joined by the Pamphili family. In 1651 Camillo Pamphili purchased Valmontone, where he was later to build a large palace.

Throughout the century the middle class in the city of Rome itself represented an economically stable stratum, consisting partly of officials of the Curia—although many of these were priests who could not found families—and partly of merchants with commercial connections throughout the Papal States.[59] But with few exceptions this middle class contributed little to the cultural life of Rome. And, as we have already seen, the new papal families were more important to culture than the old feudal dynasties. The Farnese enjoyed almost the status of a state within the state. But the Aldobrandini family died out in 1637 in the male line—although the name was revived much later by a collateral branch—and the Peretti di Montalto family became extinct in 1656. Of the powerful mediaeval families only the Colonna, the Gaetani and the Orsini still retained their economic power and could still behave with a certain amount of grandeur, although they had lost all political influence. There were also some fairly important newly rich aristocratic families, namely the Sacchetti, the Mattei and the Falconieri.

One of the few representatives of an ancient family which still played a part in the cultural life of the period was Paolo Giordano Orsini, the somewhat eccentric and snobbish duke of Bracciano. In 1649 he started a correspondence with Queen Christina, at the time still in Sweden, feeling cut off from the cultural life of the Continent and eager to hear what was going on in Rome.[60] He told her for instance that Pietro da Cortona was the most regarded painter, while sculpture was represented by the two great names of Bernini and Algardi. In reply the queen told him of the art treasures which the Swedes had taken as booty in Prague and which she had incorporated into her collections. Orsini wrote in considerable detail about the musical life of Rome, as this was a particular interest of his. The queen wanted to know whether any composer could compare with Giacomo Carissimi, and Orsini answered that Orazio Benevoli, who had worked for a time in Vienna, was indeed as great. This was the composer who, as organist of S. Luigi dei Francesi and later of S. Maria Maggiore and leader of the papal Cappella Giulia, had brought polyphonic Baroque music to a peak of contrapuntal finesse in the choral works he composed for these churches.

Camillo Massimo was another Roman noble who particularly a little later became an important connoisseur and patron. In 1640, at the age of 20, he had inherited his family's estate from a cousin, who in turn was a relative of Vincenzo Giustiniani. Camillo Massimo had chosen to make a career in the Church and was for a time Innocent X's nuncio in Madrid. Later, however, he was called home by Alexander VII. He showed evidence of excellent taste at an

Alessandro Algardi,
previously attributed to
Bernini: marble bust of
Innocent X. Doria-Pamphili
collection (Anderson).

early age and was a passionate collector of antique sculptures, books, drawings
and paintings.[61] He was an intimate friend of Nicolas Poussin, buying several
pictures from him and commissioning others. He also became friendly with
Velazquez when the Spanish painter made a second visit to Rome in 1649, and
had his portrait painted by him. After Cassiano dal Pozzo's death Massimo
came to play somewhat the same role in the cultural life of Rome, although he
did not achieve his greatest importance until much later.

Innocent X lacked Urban VIII's intense interest in literature and the fine
arts, and had no distinctive personal taste. For this reason his impact on
cultural life was limited, and he devoted himself mainly to such commissions as
were already under way when he came to power and to others that concerned
the glorification of his own family.

Festivities and Spectacles

Pamphili's pontificate opened with a brilliant spectacle, namely the pope's
possesso which took place on 23 November. Thanks to a couple of contemporary descriptions we can envisage this cavalcade in all its glory; it was one of
the most costly ceremonies of its kind which had ever taken place.[62]

Despite the desperate financial straits of the Holy See at the time, vast sums were paid for decorations and fireworks, as well as for new costumes for all the cortège. Gigli tells us in great detail about the lavish dress donned by his fellow councillors for the occasion.[63] The *conservatori* and the prior of the *caporioni*—the representatives of Rome's 14 districts—were each given 140 scudi to acquire full-length coats of red silk and mantles of gold brocade. The *caporioni* received 70 scudi each, to fit themselves out with knee-length mantles of red velvet, trousers and jackets in silver lamé decorated with gold, stockings of white silk with gold lace, a golden sword with an embroidered belt, and topping it all caps of black velvet plumed in red and white. The 50 pages accompanying them were also clad in silver lamé with white shoes and stockings.

To the sound of bells and salutes from Castle Sant'Angelo the cavalcade left the Vatican. From the Ponte Sant'Angelo it took the Via del Papa past Piazza Pasquino, Palazzo Massimo and S. Andrea della Valle, and on towards the Gesù. From there, instead of passing S. Marco as in earlier times, it proceeded to the Capitol along the straight thoroughfare built by Paul III.

John Evelyn, who came to Rome in the autumn of that year, describes the composition of the cavalcade. First came a division of the Swiss guard, followed by "the Popes Barber, Taylor, Baker, Gardner & other domesticall all on horse back in rich liveries: the Squires belonging to the Guard. Then were lead by 5 men in very rich liverys 5 Neapolitan Horses white as Snow, covered to the ground with trappings gloriously embroidered, which is a Service payd by the King of Spaine for the Kingdomes of Naples & Sicily..." Other dignitaries and nobles with their pages followed, together with officers of the Curia on mules and officials from the Capitol, the governor of Castel Sant'Angelo and the *prefetto di Roma*. "Then next the Pope himselfe carried in a Litter, or rather open chaire of Crimson Velvet richly embrodred & borne by two stately Mules... This was follow'd by the Master of the chamber, Cupp-bearer, Secretary, Physitian. Then came the Cardinal Bishops... all in their several and distinct habits; some in red, others in greene flat hatts with tassles, all on gallant Mules richly trapp'd with Velvet, & lead by their servants in great state & multitudes..."[64]

The cavalcade proceeded up Michelangelo's ramp, where the two porphyry lions spouted wine instead of water, watched over by two stucco statues representing *Roma pacifica* and *Roma trionfante*. On the Capitol, between the trophies of Marius, Carlo Rainaldi had been instructed to build a triumphal arch in wood, stucco and painted canvas.[65] This had one storey in the composite order and a fairly low attic storey in the Ionic, as well as eight allegorical plaster figures representing Innocent's most outstanding qualities. There were *Nobiltà* and *Fatica*—more or less the same as Diligence—*Premio* and *Merito*; along the short sides were *Disciplina reale* and *Politica*, and on the upper floor *Sapienza* and *Vigilanza*. In the porch itself there were paintings depicting Pamphili's diplomatic enterprises. Donna Olimpia watched it all, attended by 25 high-born ladies, from a window in the Palazzo dei Conservatori.[66]

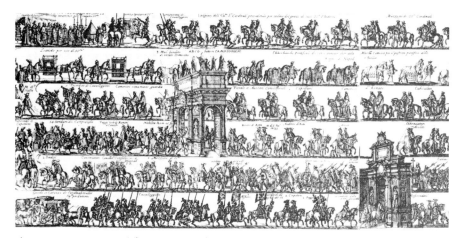

Anonymous master: The *possesso* of Innocent X, detail of engraving, showing the triumphal arches (GCS).

Decoration with fireworks in the Piazza Navona at the *possesso* of Innocent X, representing Noah's ark (From L. Banck, Roma triumphans..., 2nd ed., 1656).

As a novelty for this *possesso* the Duke of Parma's architect—Carlo's father, Girolamo Rainaldi—was commissioned to build a triumphal arch just by the arch of Titus at the entrance to the Orti Farnesiani. It was not possible to complete this in time, and the pope had to return a couple of weeks later to see it, but even so it caused a sensation.[67] It was made to resemble marble, and some parts were gilded. Two allegorical figures represented the Humility and Majesty of the duke, and divers bombastic Latin inscriptions celebrated the peace between the ducal house of Farnese and the popes. According to an ancient tradition the Jewish colony would honour the pope at his *possesso*, in gratitude for the privileges they enjoyed by his favour, and this time they hung up between the Arch of Titus and the Colosseum woven tapestries and paintings on Old Testament themes, most of them illustrating the psalms or the Song of Songs.

The origins of the ceremony in the Lateran Basilica lay in the Middle Ages, but most of the ancient and often extremely strange rites had been discontinued when Sixtus V pulled down the old papal palace and built his new one. The climax was now in the cavalcade itself, and so it would remain as long as the *possesso* continued to be celebrated in this way.

As darkness fell, the pope returned to the Vatican without any further pomp. But during the evening fireworks and festive illuminations appeared all over the city; every house lit its façade with candles and variegated lanterns of waxed paper, all of which Evelyn duly admired.[68] The envoys of the foreign powers strove to outshine one another in the splendour of their decorations. The most magnificent were provided by the Spaniards at their national church, S. Giacomo in the Piazza Navona: there stood Noah in his ark on Mount Ararat, holding out his arms to receive the dove with the olive branch in its beak—the olive branch which also happened to be the heraldic emblem of the Pamphili family. The dove floated gently down on a thread from the Palazzo Pamphili; it then set light to the *macchina* which was loaded with fireworks, and the ear-splitting bangs of the subsequent explosions were received by the populace with delight.[69] John Evelyn also mentions the *macchina* arranged by the French in front of the Palazzo Farnese, with "Diana in her coach drawne in a chariot by her doggs" high on a cliff; this *macchina*, too, was naturally intended to go up in smoke and flames.[70] And Evelyn ends, "Thus were the streetes this night as light as day, full of Bonfires, Canon roaring Musique pla(y)ing, fountaines running Wine in all excesse of joy and Triumph".[71]

The cavalcades accompanying the arrival of foreign ambassadors for their official reception by the pope, would sometimes almost rival the *possesso* in splendour, although they were of course on a smaller scale. But to compensate for this there would generally be a vast array of magnificently decorated coaches provided by the Roman aristocracy. We have already mentioned two such imposing cavalcades, one held by the Spanish ambassador in 1646 and one by the Frenchman, Fontenay Mareuil.[72]

The splendour displayed on such occasions was really more than many of the noble families could afford, but a strong element of rivalry entered into it:

Jan Miel: *Carnival.* Galleria Nazionale d'Arte Antica (ICCDcop).

nobody wanted to be outshone by the others, with their pages in costly garb and their magnificent carriages. And at no time was this so important as at the annual carnival.

Naturally the old popular entertainments, races and burlesque spectacles, were still a part of every carnival. The customary races between Jews, youths, old men, and even between asses, buffaloes and horses, were run along the Corso. Only once in 1648, Gigli tells us, was there no old men's race, as only one competitor appeared.[73] But the greatest popular entertainment was to watch the gentlemen and ladies as they strolled around the city in their masks, usually in brilliant dress; and the climax on one of the last days of the carnival was generally a tournament and cortège with floats.

The theatrical spectacles in the palaces of the noble families were always arranged for a limited audience of invited guests; they were not public theatre performances, as these were not allowed. The Barberini had left Rome, and their theatre was closed. But there was no great difference between the present carnivals and those of the previous pontificate. It was simply that some fresh minds were now behind them; it was no longer the Barberini but Donna Olimpia Maidalchini who set the trend. The spectacles, tournaments, banquets, plays and carnival cavalcades were becoming even costlier than before. The Roman nobility set no limits to the outlay on these occasions, and it was often this expense and the rivalry in magnificence and luxury which led

Carlo Rainaldi: decorations in Piazza Navona at Easter 1650, engraving by D. Barrière, detail (GCS).

to the ruin of many an ancient family. Providing a grand banquet, and above all having a comedy played in the family palace, had become a status symbol as important as possessing a couple of carriages. You simply had to keep up; you must put on a play, regardless of whether you had any genuine interest in drama.

Cardinal d'Este, who realised the importance of winning Donna Olimpia's favour, arranged a *giostra* in her honour during the carnival of 1645. It took place in the garden of his palace, which was illuminated for the occasion by 300 tapers and 130 torches. Donna Olimpia, attended by a company of Rome's highest born ladies, watched the spectacle from a temporary glassed-in dais built especially for the occasion. This was followed by one of the costliest collations ever known, where the guests were served "*molte statue di zuccaro e 60 bacili de canditi*".[74] Spectacular dishes and confectionery were received with the greatest admiration. On a subsequent occasion, when Donna Olimpia was again present with nine cardinals and the cream of Roman society, d'Este had a comedy performed for them with "*scene superbissime*" and followed it by a collation costing over 2,000 scudi.[75]

Later Donna Olimpia, whose interest in literature was extremely limited, had theatrical spectacles—some of them said to be downright frivolous —produced in her own palace. In 1649 Gigli tells us that "marquises and dukes took pleasure in appearing as actors" at her home.[76] The prince of Gallicano, Pompeo Colonna, put on a performance of *Proserpina rapita*, which cost him the tidy sum of 8,000 scudi.[77]

But not all dramatic performances were as costly as this. The Dutch lawyer and Curia official Dirk van Ameyden, known to us for his many comments on the events of the period, also wrote stage dramas, some of them translated from Spanish. He too had a theatre in his home, although it could probably seat no more than 100 people at most. Sometimes, however, his comedies were played in the homes of the greatest nobles such as Cardinal d'Este himself.[78]

In 1646 the carnival was on a more modest scale, because of the hard times and prevailing famine. The following year the processions were almost ruined by persistent rain. But in 1649 no expense was spared, despite famine and despite the sick who overflowed the hospitals. But everyone knew that next year was Holy Year and there could be no carnival in Rome at all. And so, while the going was good, floats paraded with allegorical scenes based on the heraldic emblems or *imprese* of the nobles concerned. Some of these were so complicated, however, that explanatory notes had to be distributed among the spectators.[79] Two years earlier *il Conestabile* Colonna had arranged a float for a musical drama, *Il premio della fatica*, complete with a stage, and another on which young men performed a ballet dressed as girls.

In 1651, when the princess of Rossano and Camillo Pamphili were reconciled with the pope, they had a glass-covered platform built outside their palace on the Corso, so that their guests could watch the races and processions unperturbed by possible rain. But the weather that year was brilliant, right up to Shrove Tuesday when it finally broke.[80] On the last of the fine days the musical drama *S. Agnese*, lit by hundreds of tapers, was performed in the Piazza Navona.[81]

By 1653 the Barberini had returned to Rome, and for the carnival that year their theatre was re-opened. The play was Giulio Rospigliosi's comedy *Dal male il bene*, for which Anton Maria Abbatini and Marco Marazzoli wrote the music.[81] On this occasion tickets were sold to anybody who was interested: Rome had acquired its first public theatre.[83]

The following year the carnival was the most brilliant of Pamphili's pontificate. The Barberini family was once again setting the trend, and Don Maffeo, prince of Palestrina, had designed a float which is described for us in detail by Gigli. Don Maffeo sat on a raised throne dressed as the sun, sceptre in hand and holding the reins of the four horses drawing the float. Beneath the throne was an eagle looking up at the sun, the sun being Barberini's *impresa* and the eagle that of his wife's family, the Giustiniani. Before the float rode young men in fantastic attire representing the four seasons, and behind were 100 servingmen all clad in gold brocade and carrying lighted tapers. They represented the light of the sun itself and, as Gigli notes, they made a "bellissima vista". He also mentioned, however, that it was freezing cold at the time.[84]

To counterbalance these profane and often frivolous performances, the Jesuits would present classical tragedies, always recited in Latin. These were

TEATRO ERETTO NELLA CHIESA DEL GIESV DI ROMA NELLA QVINQVAGESIMA L'ANNO SANTO MDCL

Carlo Rainaldi: decoration in Il Gesù for the *Quarantore* adoration of the Holy Sacrament 1650, engraving (GCS).

performed by the students of the Collegio Romano. One year the students appearing in two different dramas fell out with one another. There was a violent clash, in which even some of the austere Jesuit fathers became involved.[85] In 1649 special festival scenery was prepared for the solemn *quarantore* or Forty Hours Devotions in the Gesù, which Gigli describes as *"una prospettiva di riflessi"*. It was probably an illusionistic view culminating in a garden as the scene of a miracle which was much in the public mind at the time: a greedy apiarist had stolen the consecrated host and concealed it in his bee-hive, hoping to increase his honey supply by white magic; but lo and behold the bees built a temple of wax complete with an altar for the Sacrament.[86]

In the Holy Year of 1650 the Church festivities were celebrated with extra splendour, particularly at Easter. For a procession on the morning of Easter Sunday Carlo Rainaldi had transformed the Piazza Navona to create a great peristyle illuminated by 1,600 lanterns; round the still uncompleted central fountain he built a square wooden enclosure with corner towers like a mediaeval fortress, where musicians could play. At each end of the piazza there were pavilions with domes supported on tall pillars of simulated marble. One pavilion contained a statue of the Risen Christ and the other one of the Virgin Mary, and both had room for a choir. The pavilions were supposed to represent Castille and Aragon. Next to the still quite insignificant little church of S. Agnese a sacramental altar had been erected, resembling a miniature church façade with columns and an entablature, all at the expense of three Portuguese in honour of the Spanish king. As we would expect there was also a firework display, much to the consternation of the spectators as rockets flew off by mistake in all directions and threatened to set fire to the surrounding buildings.[87]

The Pamphili and Architecture

It was only to be expected that Innocent X should carry on his predecessor's commitments to the arts and, in particular, to ecclesiastical architecture. The main task of course was the completion and adornment of St. Peter's, but another extremely demanding enterprise was also calling for attention, namely the restoration of the Lateran Basilica in time for the Holy Year of 1650. But, also like his predecessors, Innocent was interested from the very start of his reign in buildings to enhance the prestige of his own family, an interest which he naturally shared with his nearest kin, Camillo Pamphili and Donna Olimpia Maidalchini. Innocent had little natural or even trained artistic taste, and his interest in architecture and painting was pragmatic rather than aesthetic: to build and adorn Rome to the glory of God and the glorification of the Pamphili family.

At the beginning of his pontificate the pope gave orders for the completion of what came to be known as the Palazzo Nuovo, opposite the Palazzo dei Conservatori on the Capitol, in accordance with Michelangelo's plans; almost nothing had been done since the foundations were laid in 1603. The palace was now built as an exact copy of Michelangelo's Conservatori façade, as completed by Giacomo della Porta. The only change was that the short side of the palace, which according to Michelangelo was to consist of a single window bay, was now given two such bays and the palace opposite was altered to match. Both façades were thus denied the screen-like effect at which Michelangelo had aimed. The Palazzo Nuovo progressed extremely slowly and was not finished until 1654, after almost ten years work.[88] The reason for the delay was shortage of funds: the pope wanted the city of Rome to bear the cost, and not a single scudo was forthcoming from the *Camera apostolica*. To finance this building the city authorities had to make cutbacks within their own administration, and the pope's disobliging conduct of the whole affair aroused considerable irritation.[89]

During the early years of the Pamphili pontificate Bernini, for a time at least, lost most of his standing as the leading artist in Rome, mainly because of his extremely close ties with the Barberini family. Francesco Borromini came to the forefront instead, at any rate in the field of architecture; and for him the pontificate of the Pamphili pope was to be a period of feverish activity. He obtained the prestige-laden commission to restore the Lateran Basilica; moreover, his expertise was consulted for the building of the Palazzo Pamphili in Piazza Navona, where he was later also put in charge of the work on the neighbouring church of S. Agnese. As we shall see later, however, the real architect of these two family buildings was in fact the aging Girolamo Rainaldi together with his son Carlo—a sign that despite everything the pope's own taste remained firmly conservative. During this period the building of the Oratory of St. Philip Neri was still requiring Borromini's active participation, as did the church of S. Ivo della Sapienza. The plans for this church had been largely completed under Urban VIII, but it was built mainly during Pamphili's pontificate. And on top of all this, Borromini found time and energy to work on grandiose plans for private palaces such as the Palazzo Carpegna and the rebuilding and adorning of the Palazzo Falconieri, as well as building the little monastery church of S. Maria dei Sette Dolori. It is astonishing that he was able simultaneously to plan, and discuss, and even involve himself personally in such a variety of building enterprises.

*

When Innocent X became pope, Gian Lorenzo Bernini was still working on the *campanili* for the façade of St. Peter's. For the southern tower he had a full-scale wooden model made in 1641 for a third crowning storey, but since this was not considered satisfactory, it was removed already the same year.[90] The northern bell-tower had barely been begun. Because Bernini's towers had been criticised already during Urban VIII's pontificate, Innocent X decided to consult other experts. Virgilio Spada, the first to be called in, submitted a detailed statement which has been preserved.[91] In Spada's opinion the cracks which had appeared were not too dangerous, and he suggested how the technical weaknesses could be remedied. But in view of the continuing criticism voiced by Bernini's adversaries, the pope instructed the congregation for the *Reverenda Fabbrica* to look into the question more carefully, and a special commission was appointed in the summer of 1645. Among the architects and artists included as experts were Girolamo and Carlo Rainaldi, Francesco Borromini, Paolo Maruscelli and Martino Longhi, as well as Bernini himself, who thus had every opportunity to defend his *campanile*.[92] However, in February 1646 it was decided that the tower must be pulled down, and work on its demolition began in April. It may have been Borromini's criticism which led to this decision. It is said that Bernini managed to avoid paying damages or bearing the cost of the demolition, by sending Donna Olimpia a largish sum of money and giving the then Cardinal Camillo Pamphili a diamond worth 6,000 scudi.[93]

The failure of the bell-tower project was naturally a heavy blow to Bernini's reputation as an architect, but although the pope's confidence in him was shaken, he retained his position as chief architect of the *Reverenda Fabbrica*. Nor was the question of the bell-tower for St. Peter's resolved once and for all after the demolition of Bernini's *campanile*; over the next few years various proposals were submitted by both Bernini and Borromini, as well as by Girolamo and Carlo Rainaldi. A drawing by Borromini shows a much lower and lighter construction, while some drawings from Bernini's studio have more complicated towers. One of Bernini's proposals would have introduced free-standing *campanili*, like those which Antonio da Sangallo had planned.[94] But none of the bell-towers ever came to anything, probably because of financial difficulties.

With the approach of the Holy Year of 1650 the internal adornment of St. Peter's had become an urgent matter. Already in 1645 Bernini had been commissioned to paint the pilasters under the arches between the nave and the aisles and in the chapels. The geometrical marble encrustation of the pilasters by the Cappella Clementina, dating from the beginning of the century, no longer satisfied contemporary taste; moreover the idea was to continue the tradition of Constantine's basilica, which had been decorated with a series of papal portraits in mosaic on the upper walls of the nave. One of Bernini's assistants, Guidobaldo Abbatini, produced full-scale sketches painted on canvas; these were displayed on two pilasters and were then accepted. Between 1647 and 1648 the work was executed by 39 sculptors, most of them Bernini's assistants.[95] Portraits of 56 popes from Peter to Benedict I were made in white marble in medallions carried by *putti*. Other *putti* bear the papal tiaras and keys, while the Pamphili dove is naturally everywhere present. The portraits and other details are all in high relief in white marble on a yellow *giallo antico* or warm red-brown *portasanta* ground, with borders in various kinds of darker marble and the warm red *breccia di Francia*.

A series of allegorical figures, personifications of virtues in almost three-dimensional form, were placed in the spandrels above the arches of the nave.

Gian Lorenzo Bernini:
marble decoration on one
of the pilasters in the nave
of St. Peter's (CI).

They continued the set of allegorical figures already disposed above the arches by the Cappella Gregoriana 50 years before. These figures were executed between 1647 and 1650, again by Bernini's assistants.[96]

While work proceeded on these sculptures, the floor of the nave was being covered with a wealth of multicoloured marble, some of it from the old basilica.[97] A major alteration was made in the aisles, in that Maderno's original travertine piers in the openings between the chapels were replaced by the red-and-white *cottanello* marble[98]—yet another sign of changing taste over the last half-century.

These various activities in St. Peter's all progressed much more rapidly than the Palazzo Nuovo on the Capitol, which had been started at the same time. This did not depend on any greater generosity on the part of Innocent X at St. Peter's, however. It was simply that the *Reverenda Fabbrica* had funds and revenues of its own which could be used.[99]

Naturally as Holy Year approached, the completion of the nave of St. Peter's was a pressing matter. Even more urgent, however, was the restoration of the Lateran Basilica. It had long been a scandal that the pope's own cathedral, *omnium urbis et orbis ecclesiarum mater et caput*, had been allowed to fall into a deplorable state of decay.[100] Very little of Constantine's basilica had in fact survived; the church had been radically restored—perhaps even partly rebuilt—by Sergius III at the beginning of the 10th century after the devastating earthquake of 896. It had been damaged again by an earthquake in 1349 and, probably more seriously, by a fire in 1361 when the roof was destroyed. Under Urban V (1362–1370) a few necessary repairs had been carried out, but to judge from the later state of the building they must have been rushed and were in any case inadequate. Many of the columns in the nave which had been damaged by the fire in 1361 were then encased in or completely replaced by octagonal brick pillars. A more thorough restoration had been carried out under Martin V (1417–1431). This was when the floor was covered in the traditional mediaeval style, the clerestory windows provided with Gothic tracery, and the walls decorated with frescoes by Gentile da Fabriano and Antonio Pisanello.[101] These activities continued under Eugene IV (1431–1447) and it was at this stage that the remaining columns of the nave, apart from four near the main entrance, had been replaced by brick pillars.[102] Between 1564 and 1566 Daniele da Volterra had covered the nave with a coffered ceiling and put in a new roof-truss. As we have already seen, the mediaeval transept had been restored and decorated under Clement VIII. After all these restorations and repairs, with additions and adornments in the styles of many different periods, the interior of the basilica was not particularly attractive; nor was it worthy of its rank as one of the most important shrines in Christendom. And, to make things worse, despite all the work that had been done to it, the nave was in danger of collapsing: its upper wall on the northern side was leaning inwards about 0.80 m out of the true.[103]

Exactly what happened when Francesco Borromini was commissioned to rebuild the nave of the basilica is not known. What is known, however, is that his friend and patron Virgilio Spada, who was now Innocent X's *Elemosiniere segreto* and consequently enjoyed the pope's confidence and a certain amount of influence, was appointed to supervise the rebuilding of the basilica on 15 April 1646.[104] It seems very likely that Spada, before or after his appointment, was the one who advised the pope to send for Borromini. The plans for the restoration required somebody with a high degree of technical knowledge as well as a clear understanding of earlier building techniques; in the discussions about the bell-tower for St. Peter's, Borromini had shown his competence on both these counts. Times had changed since Julius II had allowed Bramante to demolish the Constantinian basilica of St. Peter's barely 150 years earlier, in order to build the new temple. This sort of thing was now unthinkable, and Innocent X stated firmly from the start that as much as possible of the old basilica should be preserved: it was to be restored, not rebuilt. This attitude may have been the fruit of a renewal of interest in the Early Christian Church which had been flourishing among learned laymen and clerics since the end of the 16th century; we need only recall Bosio's exploration of the catacombs, Cesare Baronio's studies of ecclesiastical history and Francesco Barberini's interest in Early Christian and mediaeval monuments.

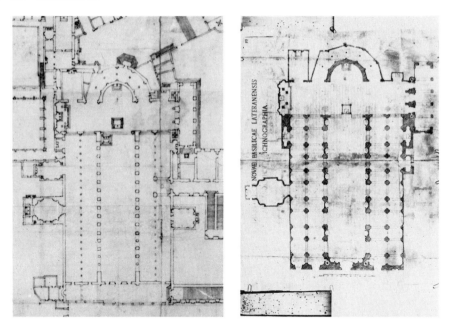

Left: Rainaldi's workshop: plan of the Lateran basilica before Borromini's restoration, detail of drawing. Albertina, Vienna, *IT AZ 373a.*
Right: Plan of the Lateran basilica after Borromini's restoration (From Rasponi, *De basilica Lateranensi...,* 1657).

Borromini immediately set about examining the masonry of the old basilica, to see what could be retained and what must be removed.[105] Several plans and some sections and elevations by Borromini and his assistants have been preserved, most of them in the Albertina collection in Vienna. Later scholars have reviewed these together with other surviving drawings and archeological and structural evidence, in order to reconstruct the earlier appearance of the mediaeval basilica prior to Borromini's alterations.[106]

The Vatican Library also possesses several drawings, plans and sections by Borromini and his studio, representing various suggestions for restoring the nave and aisles.[107] Three longitudinal sections by Borromini's hand have generally been thought to represent three successive stages in the evolution of his ideas, but it is more likely, as Blunt points out, that they were three proposals all submitted at the same time: all three are drawn to the same scale and in the same manner.[108] A comparison with a rival and much more conventional design submitted by Vincenzo della Greca only serves to reveal Borromini's genius all the more clearly. In all three proposals the wall is divided into bays with giant pilasters. In two of the proposals the long wall has three wide arcade openings to the aisles; the end bays and the bays between the openings are treated in the same way. In one proposal—the scheme generally referred to as the first—the bays are all equally wide. The end bays are closed, while the intermediate bays have flat-headed openings with coupled columns. In the second proposal, the arcade bays are very slightly wider, and the columns of the intermediate bays have been set in the wall so that these openings too are a little broader. All three drawings show giant pilasters, but only in the "first" is the distance between them equal. The third proposal, which most closely resembles the final solution, has five arcade openings, and the bays between them have been transformed into solid areas of wall with two giant pilasters closer to one another: there is thus a marked rhythm running the whole length of the wall, emphasised by broader and narrower intervals between the pilasters. All three proposals include an unbroken crowning entablature and clerestory windows with pediments that recall the windows of a palace façade. In the third proposal, however, every other window has been replaced by an oval wreath of leaves, like those which were actually made. A drawing in the National Museum in Stockholm approaches the final scheme even more closely.[109] Here the entablature has been reduced to short sections linking the pilasters in pairs; between these pairs of pilasters it has been eliminated altogether; furthermore the windows are of aedicule type and the central bay is emphasised by the addition of the papal arms and by the free-standing columns and pediment. One of the plans in the Vatican also shows us that in what has been called the third proposal Borromini placed the short bay nearest to the entrance wall across the corner in the manner so typical of his style.[110] In the third proposal, aedicules—generally referred to here as tabernacles—have also been set into the narrow bays. Recent archeological studies show that, contrary to what had always been thought, Borromini took no account in the final building—and probably not in these preparatory studies either—of the pillars and columns of the basilica: all these supports have been eliminated, and it is doubtful whether any remains have been left in the masonry behind Borromini's pilasters—at any rate the pilasters and the gaps between them do not correspond to the old pillars.[111]

In the aisles Borromini had a freer hand. The old double aisles were both divided by a row of fairly short columns—about 3.5 metres high—in *verde antico* and standing on pedestals.[112] The 36 remaining columns of this type were all removed, but 24 of them were used later for the tabernacles in the nave. The old outer aisles were much lower than the inner aisles, and the two together were covered by a lean-to roof. This was taken away and Borromini introduced vaults instead: in the wider bays behind each arcade arch he put flat domed vaults, and in the narrow bays behind the paired pilasters barrel vaults. The openings to the outer aisles and between the bays in these aisles were flat-topped; the bays themselves have flat cavetto ceilings. Borromini was able to introduce dormer windows into the wall above the lower outside aisles; the larger bays of the higher inner aisles are thus brightly lit, while the narrow bays with their barrel vaults are darker with no windows.

According to Borromini's original plan, the nave was to be covered by one great vault, with penetration vaults over the windows.[113] The rising lines of the giant pilasters were to have continued in broad ribs, forming the kind of

Borromini: project for the nave of the Lateran basilica, drawing.
BAV, *Vat. Lat., 11258*, 149r.

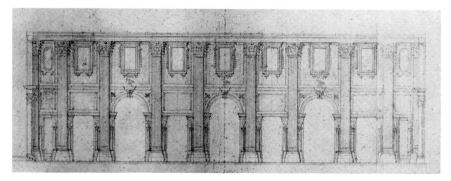

Borromini: project for the nave of the Lateran basilica, drawing.
BAV, *Vat. lat., 11258*, 147r.

Borromini: the third project for the nave of the Lateran basilica, drawing.
BAV, *Vat. lat., 11258*, 166r.

interlacing pattern which Borromini had used in the Oratory of St. Philip Neri and was later to develop in the chapel of the Collegio di Propaganda Fide. The vault was to have an ingenious system of buttressing, with flying buttresses continuing out over the aisles like a Gothic cathedral. We know, too, that Borromini was planning to alter the choir and transepts. The plans have not survived, but the architect Gian Antonio Bianchi Lombardi who saw them among Borromini's papers at the beginning of the 18th century, has left us a brief description.[114] The transepts were to have been provided with apses and the aisles would have continued round the main apse—which at the time was directly connected with the transepts—to form an ambulatory.[115]

Work on the basilica began in the spring of 1646. First of all the foundations had to be strengthened, after which the main walls were reinforced by new walls built along the old ones on the outer side. In this way the leaning northern wall could be corrected.[116] During this period Daniele da Volterra's coffered ceiling remained intact, supported on the remains of the old walls.

The work was organised with remarkable efficiency: the new walls had reached roof height by the end of 1647; by the autumn of the following year the ceilings were finished, and by the end of 1648, in good time for the Holy Year, the stucco ornament in the interior of the basilica was complete.[117] That same year Alvise Contarini reported in his *relazione* to the Venetian senate that the pope was watching over progress with the greatest interest through his agents, who visited the building-site every day; often, too, he would look in personally to see what stage had been reached and to urge the workers on to greater efforts. To finance the project the pope had allocated 70,000 scudi which came from Spain with the so-called *Bolla della Crociata*; he had also allotted part of the sums which could be paid at that time by criminals wishing to avoid imprisonment.[118]

But Borromini was not able to build the basilica as he would have liked. When the walls were on a level with the entablature and work on the vault was about to begin, the pope decided that he did not want to touch the sixteenth-century coffered ceiling; it was to be retained on grounds of piety. In a letter dated 16 March 1647, the pope spoke of retaining as much as possible of the old basilica and of beautifying it: "*mantenerla quanto sarà possibile nella sua primitiva forma e abbellirla*".[119] In fact it is still possible to see above the coffered ceiling where the ribs would have sprung; and, outside, traces of Borromini's buttresses are clearly visible on the walls with their sutures where the flying buttresses would have been placed. None of the plans for altering the transepts and choir came to anything; in the case of the choir economic difficulties may have played a part.

It is important to note here that the respect shown for the mediaeval basilica corresponded not to Borromini's but to the pope's intentions.[120] The pope followed the work at every stage and was anxious to preserve as much as possible of the old church, whereas if Borromini had been given a free hand he would have been much less considerate. It was a source of great disappointment to him not to be able to leave his mark on the Lateran Basilica as clearly

Borromini: the Lateran basilica, interior of nave (Oscar Savio).

Borromini: the Lateran
basilica, corner at east end
of the nave (CI).

as Michelangelo or his own relative Carlo Maderno had been able to do at St.
Peter's.[121] The Lateran Basilica as we see it today is thus the result of an
awkward compromise. We need only look, for instance, at the somewhat
clumsy transition between the nave, in particular the aisles, and the transept,
although Borromini has done his best, not altogether without success, to mask
the different levels and axes which coincide here. But it is mainly the dark
oppressiveness of the gilded and coffered ceiling which disturbs the overall
impression and contrasts unhappily with Borromini's architecture. Innocent
X's insistence on keeping this ceiling may be evidence of piety but it is hardly
proof of good taste.

The tabernacles as built are slightly larger than in the Vatican drawing and a
little more ornate than in the Stockholm version. They bulge out from the wall,
while their bases are concave; at the same time their shallow niches are recessed
into the wall between the giant pilasters. The statues of Evangelists and Church
Fathers which were planned for these niches were never made;[122] not until the
eighteenth century were the present statues placed there and they are only in
stucco. At the same time the iconographical programme was changed and the
statues represent the 12 Apostles. The squares above the tabernacles are
decorated with reliefs, with Old Testament scenes on the left wall and New
Testament on the right. These were completed by the Holy Year of 1650; they
are the work of various artists, including Alessandro Algardi and Antonio

Borromini: the Lateran basilica, view of the middle aisle (Oscar Savio).

Raggi, but they too are in stucco instead of the bronze or marble originally intended.[123]

The oval compartmens between the windows with their wreaths of flowers and leaves are an interesting feature. The present-day paintings, portraits of Old Testament prophets, appeared first during the eighteenth century. To begin with these areas were left empty, so that remains of the old basilica's masonry could be seen framed there. Thus Rasponi described them in 1657 as revealing Constantine's masonry, "to recall their age and the piety shown by later generations towards him".[124] Later scholars have even wondered whether Borromini's building was not meant to represent a kind of reliquary for the remains of the Early Christian basilica, and Fagiolo compares the oval compartments to *fenestella confessionis*.[125] There can be no doubt that Rasponi really did see the old masonry inside the ovals, but Fagiolo's interpretation raises some doubts. Why should these "windows" have been placed so high up when there would also have been remains at more accessible levels, for instance behind the rectangular areas with their reliefs? And can we find a single example in any other building at this time of such "windows" revealing the old

Borromini: the Lateran
basilica, view of the outer
aisle (CI).

masonry underneath? It seems more likely that Rasponi's comment represents
an attempt to decipher an element in the basilica for which he could find no
explanation, since there was nothing like it anywhere else. In fact the ovals
were probably always intended for paintings of prophets.[126] Similar paintings
had after all been executed by Gentile da Fabriano between the clerestory
windows, as can be seen on the Berlin drawing of the basilica wall produced by
Borromini's studio. We know, too, what importance was ascribed at the time
to reviving as much as possible of the earlier iconography in a newly restored
temple. The papal portraits in old St. Peter's were revived by Bernini, for
instance, while the illustrations of the acts of the Apostles in the portico were
repeated in Maderno's stucco decoration.

The window in the central bay on the long wall, as actually built, has been
enhanced by the introduction of double columns, as the Stockholm drawing
already shows, thus repeating the design of the window on the entrance wall.
This last is recessed into the wall above the main door, while the whole central
section of the wall between the canted corner bays projects out into the nave.
Thus once again we have that lively alternation of convex and concave forms
which is so typical of Borromini. It is the design of this short wall that makes
us feel as we turn in the direction of the entrance—which we must do before
we can fully appreciate Borromini's spatial creation—that the room is truly
enclosing us.

Thus, although the basilica still seems in some ways unfinished, it is

Borromini: central
window in the nave
of the Lateran basilica,
engraving (From
Domenico De Rossi,
*Studio d'architettura
civile*).

nonetheless impressive. The rhythmical articulation of the wall and the subtly
balanced illumination of the aisles with their alternating light and dark compartments, combine to produce a pleasing effect. Above all one must admire
Borromini's fine stucco ornamentation, his naturalistic wreaths of leaves and
decorative flowers and fruits, which delightfully ignore the conventional forms
of architectural ornament. In this basilica, as earlier in S. Carlino, all mouldings
and fillets are of a precise design with clearly marked lines of light and shadow.
The flat architrave of the aisles and the stucco wreaths of the vault are carried
by winged cherubs. Fagiolo would have us believe that the ornament is all part
of a special iconographical programme: the basilica was to symbolise the
temple of Jerusalem, as envisaged at that time and as described by Girolamo
Prado and Villalpando in their commentary on the vision of Ezekiel.[127] The
cherubs, the wreaths of foliage, the flowers and fruits—the ovals or eggs in the
egg-and-dart mouldings of the pilaster capitals have been transformed into
pomegranates, for example—are all part of Solomonic decoration and Borromini is supposed to have been trying to create a New Jerusalem.[128] Obviously
Prado's and Villalpando's work must have made an impact during the seven-

Borromini: detail of
stucco decoration in the
Lateran basilica (Oscar
Savio).

teenth century, and we know that the age as a whole was interested in obscure
symbols, hieroglyphs and so on. Nonetheless we should remember
Borromini's general partiality for organic forms in architectural ornament. He
had already demonstrated this fondness in S. Carlino, and there he was
certainly not called upon to create a church in the image of Jerusalem's temple.
Moreover, architectural ornament sometimes assumed naturalistic forms in
Classical Antiquity, and *ovolo* in the shape of pomegranates, for instance,
featured already in Flavian architecture. Furthermore, we should remember
that Borromini cannot himself have had the last word on the iconography and
adornment of the Lateran Basilica; it must have been Innocent X who made
the decisions, and his attitude to these questions has never been studied.

We owe the beautifully balanced colours of the interior largely to Borromini, only allowing for the fact that the colour of the stucco may have changed
in the course of time. It is certainly the original colouring that we can see in the
warm grey *bardiglio* marble of the sockle running round the whole interior,
including the aisles. The same grey marble appears in the tabernacles. Here the
columns in *verde antico* from the old aisles have been used, while the pilasters
inside the niches are of light red *fior di pesco*. Thus, apart from the eighteenth-
century prophets in their oval frames, the tabernacles provide the only touches
of colour in the interior. Apart from the sockle mentioned above and the white
marble bases of the pilasters, stucco has been used for the rest of the interior;
even the giant pilasters are of stucco in imitation of white marble. All the
mouldings, pilasters, archivolts and panels on the walls and in the aisles are in
yellow-grey stucco, resembling the colour of travertine, while the vaults are in
a lighter shade of grey. Against this background the foliage and flowers, the
wreaths, festoons and stucco cherubs all stand out in shining white silhouette.

*

During the autumn of 1644, immediately after Innocent X's election, building
began on the projects which were to glorify the Pamphili family. Although

Francesco Borromini already enjoyed a considerable reputation, the official post as architect was given to the elderly Girolamo Rainaldi. Rainaldi's style continued the tradition of Domenico Fontana and Carlo Maderno, and it was characteristic of Innocent X and his family to choose this conservative architect for most of their family building.

Admittedly Borromini's most important commissions up to now had been in the ecclesiastical sphere, but he had also had a good deal of experience of domestic architecture in which he had shown signs of great originality. Towards the end of the 1630s he had produced several plans for a large palace for Count Ambrogio Carpegna, a wealthy noble belonging to the Barberini circle who had always shown an interest in the arts.[129] In 1638 Carpegna acquired the Palazzo Vaini at the northern end of the block to the east of the present Fontana di Trevi, which is now the seat of the Accademia di S. Luca. A year later he purchased more land, until finally he owned the whole block down to Via del Lavatore to the south. The first project for a new palace simply involved extending the Palazzo Vaini, but over the next few years a series of variants was produced, some on a fairly magnificent scale. The drawings are now in the Albertina Collection in Vienna.[130]

According to these grandiose schemes, the whole site would have been developed and the entrance to the palace located to the south on Via del Lavatore. Inside the entrance a round vestibule was planned, with a great courtyard at the centre of the block. In one of the proposals this last has a rectangular plan and columns in pairs, obviously intended to carry Serlian arches. It is interesting to study the various ways in which Borromini managed to overcome the inherent awkwardness of the trapezoid site. The most interesting scheme shows an oval courtyard with Serlian arches; the stairway at the northern end of the palace, which in the first proposals was oval, is now semicircular with an open centre, and the vestibule has been given an elongated octagonal form.[131]

Count Carpegna died in 1643, and the site and the plans were inherited by his brother, Cardinal Ulderico Carpegna, who arranged for work to start immediately. During the following year, when Urban VIII was ill and men's minds turned to the approaching conclave, Carpegna was reckoned among the *papabili*, those who might be candidates for election. Perhaps he began to wonder whether he would soon be called upon to glorify his family as would befit a pope. For whatever reason, work on the new palace anyway began on 29 October 1643.[132] Some of Borromini's more grandiose plans may perhaps have been produced after building had started. But Carpegna's dreams were disappointed; the splendid projects were abandoned and the cardinal was content with a far more modest palace. Palazzo Vaini was left more or less intact, simply being extended by a *cortile* with a loggia open on one side towards the Fontana di Trevi. On the south side of the *cortile* there is an oval ramp, which together with the original and rather bizarre stucco ornamentation over its entrance, is the only sign of Borromoni's presence in the palace as it now stands.[133]

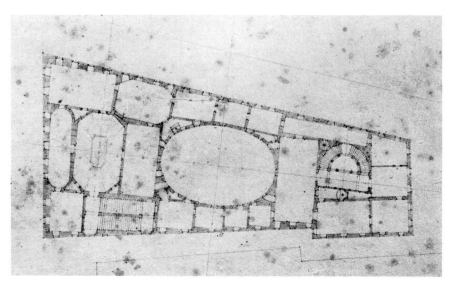

Borromini: plan project for the Palazzo Carpegna with oval courtyard. Albertina.
IT AZ 1019r.

The oval *cortile* was a novelty in Rome where palaces were almost always built round a square or rectangular courtyard. A few circular courtyards had been known, however. Raphael had designed one for the Villa Madama, although only half of it was ever built; also, in the Farnese palace at Caprarola, Vignola had built his circular *cortile* based on the plan of the existing fortress. But Serlio's treatise includes examples of oval courtyards, and Borromini may have been familiar with these. Perhaps he had also seen Piero Ligorio's reconstruction, now known to have been mistaken, of Hadrian's villa.[134]

The original and personal treatment of ornament and architectural detail manifest in the Palazzo Carpegna as well as in Borromini's earlier ecclesiastical buildings are also to be found in the Palazzo Falconieri. In 1646 he was commissioned to enlarge and redecorate a complex of older buildings belonging to the Falconieri family between the Via Giulia and the Tiber.[135] The façade is embellished with the family emblem, the falcon, in the great corner pilasters. In fact these members, widening at the top, are a cross between pilasters of the kind used by Michelangelo in the Medici Chapel and herms with falcons' heads. The palace is best known for its airy loggia—a kind of *belvedere*—with its three serlian arches; the loggia overlooked the garden which originally ran down to the river bank. However, the most remarkable feature of this palace is the stucco-work on several of its ceilings—in what is now the Hungarian Academy—for which Borromini executed the designs. There is an astonishing variety of elaborately curved patterns and ornament with vegetable forms including lilies, sunflowers and laurel wreaths and some strange symbolical emblems, all revealing craftsmanship of the very highest quality.[136] With their

Borromini:
Palazzo Falconieri,
loggia overlooking
the Tiber (MV).

Borromini: Palazzo
Falconieri, ceiling
(ICCDcop).

playful grace these stuccoes almost seem to foreshadow the decorative style of the eighteenth century, but they also bear witness to the taste for enigmatic and esoteric symbolism obtaining in Borromini's Rome.

✻

As a cardinal Innocent had owned a fairly modest *vigna* outside the Porta S. Pancrazio, beyond Urban VIII's new fortified walls on the Janiculum and close to Via Aurelia. This is the site of the present Villa Doria-Pamphili. Camillo Pamphili took over the *vigna*, and in September 1644 even before he had been made a cardinal he began to extend the garden and to acquire building materials for a new villa which he called Villa di Belrespiro.[137] A scheme for the villa was proposed in the autumn of the same year. It has been preserved in a draft letter addressed to Cardinal Camillo Pamphili, and in some drawings among Virgilio Spada's papers in the Vatican Library.[138] Portoghesi, who found these documents and published them in 1954, attributes them to Borromini,[139] but Thelen has subsequently rejected this attribution: the actual description and a simple sketch are in Virgilio Spada's hand, while the ground plan and the elevation of the villa are by Girolamo Rainaldi.[140]

The writer first points out that as so many splendid villas have been built in Rome and Frascati, with extensive parks and costly fountains, it would be no good trying to rival them; rather, it would be better to create something on a smaller scale and yet original, *"pensiero modestissimo, studioso, e curioso"*.[141] The villa was to be provided with four bastion-like corner towers, just as in Spada's sketch, and it was to have a hall with a rectangular plan and canted corners, to form an elongated octagon.[142] It was to have 32 windows corresponding to the points on a wind-rose: the whole thing was to act as a kind of gigantic sun-dial, and expressly to provide a practical application of mathematics, *"uno studio di matematica practica"*. There was to be a statue of Innocent X, positioned in such a way that on 15 September each year—in other words on the anniversary of his election—its foot would be lit by a sun-ray shining through a hole specially made for it, "in the manner of the ancients as Baronio has described it". A circular room in one of the corner towers would have had a starry ceiling shaped like the vault of heaven and able to turn on its own axis, just as Andrea Fulvio describes a hall in Nero's palace from a well-known passage in Suetonius' description of the Golden House.[143] The park was to contain an *Uccelliera* built like a Noah's Ark and provided with many unusual animals, presumably alluding to Pamphili's heraldic emblem of the dove with the olive branch on its return to Noah in the ark.

The villa, which the accounts show to have been started in 1644, was not built according to Spada's and Rainaldi's proposals, although these may have had some influence on its design. The villa as it stands is more or less cube-shaped. Five rooms are grouped symmetrically round a circular hall which rises through two storeys and is covered by a dome. The ground floor has a

Alessandro Algardi: Villa di Belrespiro, now known as Villa Doria-Pamphili
(From G. B. Falda, *Li giardini di Roma*, 1683).

nypheum-like grotto with stucco decoration on the garden side, which is
lower.

Inside the villa many pieces of ancient sculpture are displayed; in the
seventeenth century the collection was larger and included antique reliefs set in
stucco frames. The façade is also rich in reliefs, many of them restored by
Algardi.[144] This way of decorating the façade of a villa had been common in the
sixteenth century. The garden façade of the Villa Medici was adorned in a
similar manner, and so later was the Villa Borghese. It was a type of ornament
expected of a Roman villa. But the reliefs and sculptures are more numerous at
the Pamphili *casino* than anywhere else, and they are also arranged with
remarkable good taste.

Outside lies an unusually large *giardino secreto* designed in the traditional
Italian style with formal parterres and low hedges. This garden terrace commands a view over an extensive park in which a large, wild and pastoral area
was reserved for hunting. On the other hand the English look of the Villa
Doria-Pamphili garden which inspired Corot and many other artists during
the last century, is a creation of the eighteenth century.[145]

Bellori attributed the villa to Alessandro Algardi, who had come to Rome
from his home town of Bologna already in 1625. According to Bellori he
derived the plan from Palladio.[146] If the villa had been completed as shown in a
seventeenth-century engraving, it would have had two low straight wings,
which would have made it even more Palladian. In his *Vite* Passeri also gives
Algardi as the architect, but adds that Algardi, who had no building experience, confided the work of construction to someone else. He mentions no-one
by name.[147]

As a sculptor Algardi enjoyed an excellent reputation. He frequently undertook the restoration of antique works of art; he had also made a famous statue

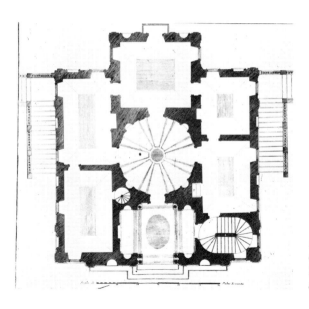

Alessandro Algardi: Villa
di Belrespiro, plan (From
Domenico De Rossi, *Studi
d'architettura civile*).

of St. Philip Neri in the sacristy of the Chiesa Nuova, as well as several funerary monuments and papal portraits. In 1640 he was elected *principe* of the Accademia di S. Luca. Algardi's architectural work, on the other hand, is extremely limited. He cannot have had anything to do with the façade of S. Ignazio, which is sometimes attributed to him, but he did execute the high altar which was set up in S. Nicola da Tolentino in 1654 at Camillo Pamphili's expense.[148] In the accounts relating to the Pamphili villa, Algardi's name appears several times, as Pollak has shown.[149] However, he is mentioned not as an architect but exclusively as a sculptor: he was involved in the stucco ornamentation, some of which is probably his own work, as well as in the restoration of the antique art-works which the cardinal was collecting in large numbers. Instead, the accounts mention Giovanni Francesco Grimaldi as being in charge of the work on the villa. Grimaldi was primarily a painter, and he is responsible for several landscape paintings in the villa. He was also a close friend of Algardi's, and he is presumably the unnamed architect mentioned by Passeri, said to have built the villa in accordance with Algardi's ideas. The two men may perhaps have worked together, starting from Girolamo Rainaldi's proposal which they then altered.[150] Among other things they kept Rainaldi's central *salone*, only making it circular instead of octagonal. Camillo Pamphili's word would certainly have had considerable weight in any discussion on the appearance of the villa. His interest in the art of gardening is both well known and well documented, and it now appears—perhaps rather surprisingly, since he was not a deeply cultivated man—that he was also interested in antique sculpture. But a profound interest in culture was hardly necessary for a man who wanted to collect ancient sculpture in seventeenth-century Rome. Anybody planning a garden in the city more or less had to place antique sculptures in it: they were an important status symbol.

Villa Doria-Pamphili, façade decoration (ICCDcop).

Work on the villa appears to have proceeded very quickly, and the accounts show that already in 1646 the stucco reliefs in the circular *salone* were being executed. Thus the project was well advanced when Camillo Pamphili gave up his cardinal's hat in 1647 and fell into disfavour. When Camillo Astalli became *cardinal padrone* in 1650, he took over the Villa di Belrespiro. The house was completed in 1652, when the final accounts with the master mason were settled, and in the following year the garden was also finished.[151]

⁂

The idea of enlarging the Pamphili palace in Piazza Navona, where Innocent had lived while still a cardinal, also arose at the beginning of the new pontificate. The commission was handled by Girolamo Rainaldi and his son Carlo, as well as by Francesco Borromini.

It was during the autumn of 1644, while the Palazzo Carpegna was being built, that Girolamo Rainaldi began to plan the palace which the pope wanted for his family in Piazza Navona. Since the Pamphili family had come to Rome

Alessandro Algardi:
Apollo, stucco in ceiling.
Villa Doria-Pamphili
(ICCDcop).

from Gubbio, they had owned and resided in a fairly modest palace close to Piazza Navona but facing on to Piazza Pasquino. Here Giambattista Pamphili had been born in 1574. While still a cardinal he had acquired property between his family home and the piazza, and had extended the palace right up to Piazza Navona, where it acquired a façade with ten windows.[152]

To the north of the cardinal's palace lay property belonging to the families of De Rossi and Cibo, while on the other side was the oblong site of the Palazzo Mellini which was later to make way for the new church of S. Agnese. During the autumn of 1644 Camillo Pamphili and Donna Olimpia began to purchase the land immediately next to the cardinal's palace, which according to Rainaldi's plans was to remain more or less intact with its original rooms behind a few façade.[153] In April 1646 they obtained permission to extend their palace as far as the Palazzo Mellini.

In the spring of 1646, on Virgilio Spada's advice, Francesco Borromini was called in for consultation, perhaps because Rainaldi's conservative plans were not entirely satisfactory. Among Spada's papers in the Vatican Library are the minutes of committee meetings held between April and June 1646 under

Girolamo Rainaldi: Palazzo Pamphili in the Piazza Navona, engraving showing Borromini's *Serliana* window of the gallery on the right (From Ferrerio, *Palazzi di Roma*, 1655).

Virgilio Spada's chairmanship.[154] Every Thursday a group consisting of Girolamo and Carlo Rainaldi, Borromini, Ludovico the master mason, and somebody representing Donna Olimpia would meet. After Camillo's marriage in 1647 Donna Olimpia supervised the building on her own. We can see from the minutes of these meetings how buildings at this time would often emerge as a result of discussions, changes and compromises. This particular case was certainly not unique. There were pedantic discussions about the orders to be used in the façade and the design of windows, but fundamental problems connected with the plans were also aired. Here and there in the margin someone has noted that "the pope thought..." or "the pope decided...".[155] The last word on this family palace always lay, as might have been expected, with Innocent X.

Borromini contributed several drawings that have been preserved in the Vatican Library; some show variants of Rainaldi's plan, and some variants of his façade.[156] None of these proposals were realised, but they are nonetheless interesting. Towards Palazzo Mellini, Rainaldi had intended to leave a narrow passage, and it is just there that in one of his earlier proposals Borromini wanted to put a stairway. He had intended to provide Rainaldi's great rectangular *cortile* with apsed ends, creating something of an oval effect, and facing Via dell'Anima he planned a long narrow gallery in the *piano nobile*. Thus, the gallery idea was born at quite an early stage, probably even before Borromini appeared on the scene: at that time a gallery was already being regarded as an essential part of any Roman palace worthy of the name. In addition there was a *sala grande*, which Borromini envisaged together with the gallery as elements in a carefully designed suite of reception rooms.

In his final proposal Borromini retained the *sala grande* in more or less the same position, but he moved the gallery into the passage facing the Palazzo

Mellini.[157] In this way the two palaces would have been built together. In one of his very first schemes, the passage was occupied by a kind of double-aisled hall in two storeys, and only later did Borromini consider placing the gallery in the *piano nobile*, first with a loggia towards the piazza, and later with the Serlian window which was actually built. In the definitive proposal the ground floor has been provided with rustication—which is now no longer there—and this Serlian window together with the rusticated ground floor is reminiscent of Bramante in the Palazzo Caprini or of Raphael's painted loggia in *The Fire in the Borgo*.[158] The architecture of the High Renaissance gave Borromini more inspiration than has often been thought.

Both the *sala grande* and the gallery were built in accordance with Borromini's ideas, and they are his only contribution to the Palazzo Doria-Pamphili as the palace is now called. The façade, on the other hand, with its pilaster strips, its blind arcades, and its rather old-fashioned windows is altogether the work of the two Rainaldis. Borromini's variants were not considered. Borromini had also envisaged an airy belvedere over the centre of the façade and two types of towers or belvedere over the two corner projections.[159] With their light arches supported on columns, they would have helped to lift Rainaldi's heavy and over-long façade.

Building proceeded apace. The palace was more or less finished by 1650, and the question then arose of decorating the gallery with frescoes: who should be given this important commission? We shall return to this point later. When Camillo Astalli was made *cardinal padrone* in 1650, and shortly afterwards Donna Olimpia fell into disfavour, the pope transferred the palace to Astalli as his residence. On Barrière's engraving of the festive decorations for Easter 1650 in Piazza Navona, the palace façade is finished, complete with its Serlian window in Borromini's gallery.

✻

When the Palazzo Pamphili was finished in the Holy Year of 1650, the new church of S. Angese had not yet been started. At some distance from the palace on the other side of Palazzo Mellini, an extremely insignificant little church had been built into the arcades under Domitian's stadium during the 9th century to commemorate Agnes, the local martyr long revered by the Romans with special affection. The magnificent festive decorations made by Carlo Rainaldi for Piazza Navona at Easter 1650 included a sham façade for this church. But we do not know when the idea of building an entirely new church on the site was born; the early history of the plans is shrouded in mystery, and we can only say when work started.[160] The first sign that plans for a new church were under way appears in December 1651, when the architect Giovanni Battista Mola made measurements of the old church. A plan by Mola, now in Oxford, shows that the scheme did not stop at moving the old church; it even included a major alteration in the Piazza Navona itself: the

Girolamo Rainaldi:
projected façade for
S. Agnese in Piazza
Navona, detail of drawing.
Albertina, *IT AZ 50.*

church, which had an oval plan, was to be located at the rounded short end of
the piazza.[161]

However, nothing came of this idea, and by February 1652 at the latest other
architects had been called in. The commission was given, as might have been
expected, to the Pamphili family architect, Girolamo Rainaldi. The plan which
he developed during the spring of 1652, and which was used when building
began, has not survived. However, we can assume from contemporary descriptions that it comprised a centralised church, a simple Greek cross with a dome;
facing the piazza there was a narthex between two towers and a broad stairway
in front.[162] As it was intended to preserve the old church as a kind of crypt, the
new church had to stand high above the level of the piazza. It represented a
conservative type of architecture stemming from the beginning of the century.

In the spring of 1652 it became possible to acquire the old Palazzo Mellini
on the site where the church was to be built. Work could start in August the
same year.[163] The foundation stone was laid by Giovanni Battista, the five-
year-old son of Don Camillo and the princess of Rossano, with whom Innocent had recently been reconciled. The pope wanted to emphasise that the
Pamphili family would in future have S. Agnese in its gift; it was to be regarded
as a family church. Innocent even intended to place his own funerary monument in the church, which would thus replace the rotunda that Borromini had
previously planned next to the Chiesa Nuova. Today the church of S. Agnese
is still owned by the Doria-Pamphili family.

The subsequent building history of S. Agnese seems to have been complicated in the extreme. Several scholars have recently examined the numerous
problems, and a number of previously unknown documents have come to
light. But despite extensive research, the course of events is still very unclear

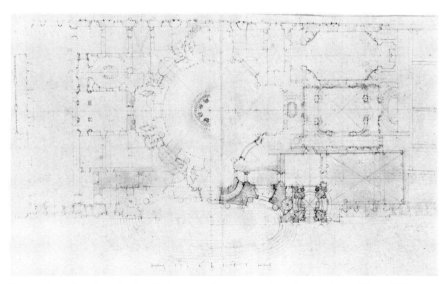

Borromini: plan drawing for S. Agnese, showing projected alteration of Rainaldi's plan on the right. Albertina, *IT AZ 55.*

Borromini: façade for S. Agnese with projected towers, drawing. Albertina, *IT AZ 59r.*

S. Agnese in Piazza Navona, interior (Anderson).

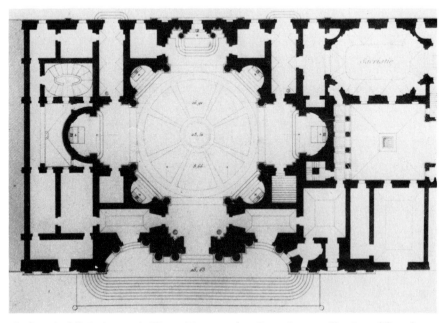

Carlo Rainaldi: S. Agnese in Piazza Navona, plan (From Letarouilly, *Les édifices de Rome moderne*).

Carlo Rainaldi: S. Agnese,
detail of façade
(Author's photo).

and many questions are unresolved or still disputed.[164] A wealth of records has
survived. The documents bear witness to innumerable discussions, compromises and intrigues; drawings and models were made and criticised not only by
architects and a variety of experts and interested parties but also by draftsmen
and masons. But every proposal had to be approved by the member of the
family in charge: first Don Camillo Pamphili and later Donna Olimpia Maidalchini, and after her death by Don Camillo again. But as long as Innocent X was
alive, no decision could be made which had not also been approved by him. He
was keenly interested in this project, frequently visiting the site for purposes of
inspection or encouragement, and often venting his wrath on both architects
and workmen. Foremost among the experts who took part in the many
discussions and deliberations was Virgilio Spada, who apparently sought out
the pope so persistently that Innocent became annoyed. But Spada knew how
to handle Donna Olimpia, and she could then manoeuvre the pope into
agreeing with his suggestions.

Alterations began to be made in the plan as soon as the foundations were
laid—a procedure which seems to have been pretty typical in Roman building.
After only a month or so it became clear that sub-soil water would frustrate
any idea of using the mediaeval church as a crypt, and it was therefore possible

to lower the level of the floor.[165] Various proposals were submitted by Girolamo Rainaldi, but the plans used when work actually began have not survived. It is nevertheless clear that the plans, whatever they were like, were modified as building proceeded. But the ground plan of the interior has in all essentials remained a hybrid between a Greek cross and an octagon.

One of the most serious objections to Girolamo's plan concerned the steps in front of the church, which jutted out too far into the piazza. Research has subsequently revealed that Girolamo's son, Carlo Rainaldi, produced a variation on this theme quite early on, abandoning the vestibule and introducing a concave middle section into the façade, so that the flight of steps could be drawn back from the piazza. This proposal can be seen on a drawing in the Biblioteca Corsiniana.[166] Like later versions of the twin-towered façade and dome solution, this suggests that the various schemes for the *campanili* of St. Peter's which had seen the light of day in the preceding years were providing a source of inspiration.

The aging Girolamo could no longer be expected to produce anything very creative, and he was slowly relegated to the sidelines, although officially he seems to have remained at the head of the team. In the summer of 1653 Carlo Rainaldi was put in sole charge of the building, probably at the suggestion of Virgilio Spada.[167] At this point the idea of the narthex was definitely abandoned, to be replaced by the concave front between two towers,[168] although the actual curve of the façade was later slightly altered. In the summer of 1653 the façade as it stood was pulled down; at the same time the slow progress of the work triggered off one of Innocent's rages.[169]

A number of changes were also made in the interior. The pope's tomb was to be placed at right angles to a line from the doorway to the main altar. At the same time the great columns in red-and-white *cottanello* marble where introduced, flanking the entrance to the transepts.[170] This emphasis on the transverse axis meant that Girolamo Rainaldi's conservative centralised church was gradually being transformed into a more complex spatial unit with a tension between the two axes which was typical of the High Baroque.

But towards the end of the summer of 1653 Carlo Rainaldi was dismissed, apparently falling victim to one of the innumerable Pamphili family intrigues.[171] It was just at this point that Innocent X was reconciled with Donna Olimpia Maidalchini, which meant that Don Camillo—and with him his trusted architect—had to abandon the controls. After a short interregnum under the direction of Cardinal Giacomo Franzone, superintendent of the *Reverenda Fabbrica di S. Pietro*, Francesco Borromini was appointed architect of S. Agnese in August 1653.[172]

Borromini now faced the rather thankless task of building further on Rainaldi's plans, making such alterations as were feasible.[173] He had no reason to change the emphasis on the transverse axis which the younger Rainaldi had introduced; he also retained the great *cottanello* columns, but he freed them from the wall by reducing the pilasters behind them;[174] in this way they achieved greater visual independence, being perceived as plastic elements framing the entrance to the transepts. The actual curvature of the vaulting of the dome was to be remodelled on the lines of the dome of St. Peter's.[175] Borromini made only slight changes in Rainaldi's façade with its concave centre, although he intended to introduce a semi-circular window above the main door. The two towers were to be lowered and given a single open storey. These changes can be seen in Borromini's drawings in the Albertina in Vienna and on a medal for which Borromini made the design.[176] One of the suggested changes which can be seen on one of the Albertina drawings is particularly interesting. The four domes were to be altered so that their sides, complete with the great niches, would jut inwards between the cross-arms; the ground plan would thus have been characterised by a lively alternation between convex and concave elements. The niches were to have been transformed into aedicules. These forms recall the complex spatial solutions of antique architecture, particularly the Piazza dell'Oro in Hadrian's Villa which Borromini would certainly have studied.[177] Borromini's convex pillars in the dome would have involved changing the vaulting, but we do not know what he had envisaged here. He may even have intended a dome with the same complicated forms as S. Ivo's, at least on the inside.

However, most of Borromini's suggested alterations were ignored, partly because of the pope's conservative attitude and his unwillingness to change what had already been begun, and partly because Carlo Rainaldi was still the Pamphili *architetto di casa* with, apparently, a certain amount of influence.

The façade was now built under Borromini's direction but essentially according to Rainaldi's plans. A few details only, such as the size of the main doorway, are Borromini's, while the great window over the central porch was never built. During the summer of 1654 the drum of the dome was raised with remarkable speed.[178] Borromini was extremely particular about the materials; and only the finest brick could be used. But work advanced so rapidly during the autumn of 1655 that even the most elementary safety precautions for the workers were neglected; a collapse occurred which occasioned a considerable stir.[179] The pope visited the site every month to urge the workers on, at the same time often falling foul of Borromini.[180] When Innocent became ill during the autumn of 1654, nobody paid the workmen, who quite naturally left. Work did begin again later, but after Innocent's death in January 1655 it ceased altogether for lack of funds. As we shall see later, building recommenced during the next pontificate, again with Don Camillo Pamphili in control. Once again the situation changed: Don Camillo felt no sympathy for Borromini's architectural style, and further intrigues were to lead to one of the most unhappy episodes in Borromini's career. But to these matters we shall be returning in another context.

With this concave façade flanked by two towers and topped by a dome behind, Carlo Rainaldi had created a type of church front which was to have repercussions north of the Alps. Johann Bernhard Fischer von Erlach, who studied in Rome in 1680, produced the first direct offshoot of his Trinitatis-kirche in Salzburg (1684–1702), and the Swedish architect Tessin the Younger

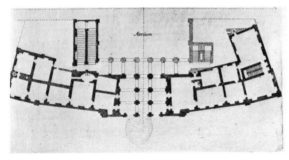

Bernini: Palazzo Ludovisi, now Montecitorio, façade (From Falda, *Il nuovo teatro*, IV) and plan (From Bonanni, *Numismata Pont. Romanorum*, II).

later showed in an unrealised project for a church in Stockholm (1711–1713) that he was directly inspired by S. Agnese in the Piazza Navona in Rome.[181]

*

After his setbacks over the *campanili* of St. Peter's, Gian Lorenzo Bernini was without architectural commissions for several years. But in 1651 he finished the Fountain of the Four Rivers in Piazza Navona, and in doing so regained the confidence of the pope. But it was not until almost the end of Pamphili's pontificate that Bernini emerged again as an architect, with a commission to design a palace for Prince Nicolò Ludovisi. It was an important commission as Ludovisi was the pope's nephew, and the idea may have come from Innocent X

Bernini: Palazzo
Montecitorio, window
and rustication
(Courtesy Dr. Lehmann-
Brockhaus).

himself. It was to be a magnificent palace, to rival the Palazzo Borghese and the Palazzo Barberini in both size and splendour. Work began in the spring of 1653, and there seems little reason to date the plans much earlier than this.[182] It was intimated already at that stage, that Ludovisi was prepared to spend 100,000 scudi on the project.

The nature of the site resulted in an unusual façade: a straight central section with seven windows on each floor is flanked on either side by a section with six windows; at the end of each side there is a further three-window unit, thus giving us an overall rhythm 3-6-7-6-3. But since these units are set at obtuse angles to one another, the façade as a whole is convex. Above the socle, the various sections of the façade are separated by giant pilasters; the lowest storeys of the side sections are rusticated with irregular hewn blocks, while their window sills and mouldings appear to be carved straight out of the naturalistic rocks—there are even weeds carved in the stone. This is a consciously sought-after aesthetic effect corresponding to a similar element in Bernini's sculpture; it also represents an early example of the romantic view of ruins, which we have already seen in the bridge in the Palazzo Barberini garden.[183]

But work on the Palazzo Ludovisi was discontinued after little more than a year, as Ludovisi fell into disfavour, left Rome, and never returned.[184] Nothing

Martino Longhi: Ss. Vincenzo ed Anastasio, engraving by G. B. Falda.

more was done until 1694, when Carlo Fontana was commissioned to trans-
form the palace, which Innocent XII had acquired from Ludovisi's heirs, into
the papal lawcourts known as the Curia Innocentiana. After 1870 it was
restored and remodelled to become the Chamber of Deputies.

At about the same time that Borromini was restoring the Lateran Basilica, a
new façade was being built for the Church of Ss. Vincenzo ed Anastasio by
Martino Longhi the Younger. Martino belonged to a family of architects from
Viggiù in Lombardy.[185] His grandfather Martino Longhi the Elder was active
in Rome after 1569, working for Gregory XIII in the Vatican and the Quirinal.
Later he worked on the Palazzo Borghese, although there is some dispute
about how much he actually did there. Martino's father Onorio Longhi,
together with Martino himself, had made the first plans for S. Carlo al Corso,
and Martino was later a member of the commission concerned with the
campanili of St. Peter's, where he appears to have been fairly mild in his
criticism of Bernini. During the 1630s he had built the charming and elegant
little church of S. Antonio dei Portoghesi, which was left unfinished.

At Ss. Vincenzo ed Anastasio he was to create a façade for an existing
church; the interior was subsequently altered during the 1760s. The façade was
begun in 1646, commissioned by Cardinal Mazarin immediately following his
reconciliation with Innocent X. It was finished during the Holy Year of
1650.[186] Mazarin's arms with the tassled cardinal's hat provide a decorative
feature above the window. This was not Mazarin's titular church; since he
never set foot in Rome as a cardinal, he had never been assigned one. However,
it had been his parish church as a child, and he had been baptised there. It is
easy to see why Mazarin was anxious to create a magnificent church façade just
here—apart, perhaps, from hoping to get into the pope's good books. The
church was close to the Quirinal, although its façade was not actually visible
from the palace, and it could be regarded as part of the setting for the new

FACCIATA DELLA CHIESA DE SANTI VINCENZO ET ANASTASIO ET ALLA FONTANA DI TREVI

Martino Longhi:
Ss. Vincenzo ed Anastasio,
façade (From De Rossi,
*Studio d'architettura
civile*, III).

Fontana di Trevi which Bernini had begun to design. Work on the fountain
had in fact been stopped, but Mazarin and others would be expecting it to start
again in the near future.

The façade of Ss. Vincenzo ed Anastasio differs from other earlier Roman
façades in the great number of columns which it boasts. There are no less than
18 of them, which among the local wits has gained the church the nickname *il
canneto*, the clump of reeds. The central bay has two groups of three columns
on both storeys, flanking the door and the window.[187] They are all fully
detached from the wall behind, projecting even further out towards the centre.
In the upper storey pairs of columns (1 and 6, 2 and 5, 3 and 4) support three
pediments that nestle one inside the other. The lower storey is not equally
logical, however. Here a segmental arch over the door is supported by the
inner columns, while a broken segmental arch above this is supported by the
next pair. Corresponding projections appear in the entablature. The outer
columns in this triad then combine with the first columns in the next set to
support the unbroken entablature over the flanking bays with their wall
panels. The outermost columns on the lower storey together with their match-

Martino Longhi:
Ss. Vincenzo ed Anastasio,
detail of façade
(Author's photo).

ing projections above, should be envisaged rather as sitting at right angles to the sides; the idea is that they should be visible along the two approaching side streets, Via del Lavatore and Via San Vincenzo. It was intended to provide the wall panels with reliefs, but for economic reasons these were never executed.[188] The reliefs would have enlivened the façade in a different way, however, and would have helped us to grasp the role of the columns in the lower storey as elements framing the reliefs.

Pictures of this façade hardly ever reveal that behind every column—and they all stand well forward from the wall—there is a pilaster, such as we see in the architecture of Antiquity when free-standing columns are placed in front of a wall. The arch of Septimius Severus and the arch of Constantine are only two of many examples. The façade thus commands two levels, one with pilasters on the wall plane and one in front of this with its more independent free-standing columns. In this way the façade is also enlivened by the play of subtle forms—an effect which would have been reinforced by the reliefs—as well as light and shade. In fact this church front is essentially three-dimensional.[189]

It is often claimed that the role of the aedicules in this façade and the emphasis on the free-standing columns are north Italian features. But Martino Longhi was born, brought up and trained in Rome, and more recently scholars have in fact pointed out that the aedicular theme can be found in earlier Roman church façades, stemming originally from Vignola's façade proposal for the Gesù, and appearing later in Maderno's work.[190] Perhaps Martino Longhi may have found inspiration for his independent treatment of the columns when visiting the north of Italy. Whatever the truth of the matter may be, he has certainly created a church façade which is both original and interesting and which makes an unparalleled decorative impact. It is difficult not to believe that Carlo Rainaldi found inspiration here for the façade of S. Maria in Campitelli.[191]

Sculpture during Pamphili's Pontificate

For a time at least after the fiasco of the *Campanili* for St. Peter's, Innocent X lost a certain amount of confidence in Bernini. But this disfavour at the beginning of the pontificate, so far as it went, was probably mainly due to Bernini's intimate association with the Barberini during the previous reign. However, none of this caused any stagnation in Bernini's artistic creativity, as the sculpture *Truth Unveiled by Time* and other works commenced in 1646 bear witness. This sculpture group was intended as a silent protest against what Bernini considered to be his unjust treatment, as well as a mark of his conviction that things would right themselves in the future.[192]

The group was never in fact completed; only *Truth* was made and finished in 1652.[193] The statue remained in the artist's own home and was willed to his descendants. It is now in the Galleria Borghese. *Truth* is shown as a naked woman, leaning in a semi-sitting position against a rough-hewn rock. She is holding the sun of justice, *sol iustitiae*, which had been the Barberini pope's *impresa.* She is gazing upwards with a blissful smile, looking at Father Time (who was never made) just as he has removed the veil that covered her. The drapery has been flung off behind her, forming a rising pointed background. *Time* was to have been depicted as an aged man, supported on a heap of broken columns and bits of marble, symbolising the destructive force of time.[194] This part of the work is known to us only from a sketch which has been preserved.[195] The finely polished surface of the woman's flesh reveals once again Bernini's supreme skill in handling marble; the statue is believed to have been carved entirely by him. But Wittkower points out that for the first time Bernini "gave expression to his new conception of womanhood" here, and that "with determination he turned his back on the classical ideal of beauty ... The *Truth* opened the way for his later rendering of the human body, for ... the *Angels with the Instrument of Passion* (on the Ponte Sant'Angelo) as well as for the almost abstract patterning of draperies in his late works".[196]

In the years immediately following Pamphili's election, Bernini received several more or less direct invitations to go to Paris. Cardinal Mazarin

Bernini: *Truth Unveiled by Time*, marble. Galleria Borghese (Alinari).

cherished a dream of launching the Roman Baroque in France, but the artists he sought to entice to his capital did not respond. Thus he failed to get either Pietro da Cortona or Algardi; only Giovanni Francesco Romanelli was later to answer his invitation. Among other things he painted the gallery in Mazarin's palace. But Bernini was the artist Mazarin most admired. He had tried to persuade the Italian to travel to France already in 1644, but on that occasion was thwarted by Urban VIII, who warned Bernini of the changeableness of the French.[197] In the summer of 1647 Paolo Giordano Orsini, who was a close personal acquaintance of Bernini, wrote to Mazarin of the model of *Truth unveiled by Time* which he had seen in the artist's studio, suggesting that the cardinal should acquire it for his private collection. Mazarin replied that Bernini ought in that case to accompany the sculpture, to supervise its transport and to set it up. But he issued no concrete invitation apart from this,[198] and so the idea foundered. Bernini felt uncertain without an offer in hard cash, and in any case he was kept too busy by his Roman commissions, in particular the completion of Urban VIII's tomb. He was probably also anxious to watch

Bernini: the tomb of Maria
Raggi. S. Maria sopra
Minerva (CI).

over his interests in Rome, and above all to try to regain the confidence of the
new pope.

During these years of official semi-disfavour Bernini was able to spend more
time on private commissions, and it was now that he began to work on the
Cappella Cornaro in S. Maria della Vittoria and *The Ecstasy of St. Teresa*—the
marble group which was to be his masterpiece. But before discussing this
work, we should first consider some other funerary monuments which he
created at about this time or a little earlier.

In the tomb of Alessandro Valtrini in S. Lorenzo in Lucina and the memorial to Ippolito Merenda in S. Giacomo alla Lungara Bernini had created a new
type of funerary monument.[199] In both he included winged skeletons—a
macabre theme which had become very popular at the time. Urban VIII's
tomb provides a well-known example. In the first of these monuments the
skeleton carries the portrait of the dead man in relief, and in the second it is
holding up an inscription on a fluttering drapery. What is important, however,
is that in both cases Bernini has abandoned any enframing architecture. Both

tombs were made mainly by Bernini's assistants, but the tomb of Maria Raggi in S. Maria sopra Minerva was made by his own hand and is of very high quality.[200] Here the portrait of the dead woman is carried by two *putti* in front of a softly falling marble drapery.

The Cornaro Chapel had another predecessor in the Cappella Raimondi in S. Pietro in Montorio which is all too often disregarded, as although it was designed by Bernini it was executed entirely by his assistants. It was commissioned by a wealthy priest named Francesco Raimondi, a native of Savona who was both *chierico di camera* and *protonotario apostolico*. Raimondi had stipulated in his will that both he and his uncle Girolamo, who had predeceased him, should be laid to rest in this chapel. The *terminus post quem* for Bernini's design must be 1640, because the heirs did not acquire the chapel until then, two years after Francesco's death.[201] The altar relief of *St. Frances in Ecstacy* was executed by Francesco Baratta probably between 1642 and 1646; the busts of Francesco and Girolamo and the flanking *putti* were made by Andrea Bolgi some time between 1645 and 1648, and the sarcophagi and their reliefs were produced by Nicolò Sale at about the same time.

In his biography of Francesco Baratta, Passeri notes that in this chapel Bernini introduced *"una novità assai curiosa d'Architettura"*.[202] The relief is actually concave, as well as being recessed in an aedicule, recalling the aedicules in the crossing pillars of St. Peter's; it is then illuminated from the side by a concealed window, which heightens the illusory effect as on a stage.

From the end of the sixteenth century it had become more common in Rome to portray the deceased in bust form, but Bernini has here revived the late mediaeval tradition of the double effigy, showing the subject both living and dead: below the busts there are open sarcophagi in which we see the deceased in relief.[203] Bernini has further introduced a psychological ingredient: one figure is engrossed in reading a prayer-book, while Francesco Raimondi, who commissioned the chapel, turns towards the entrance. Thus the spectator is drawn into the chapel, to take part in the drama displayed in the altar aedicule. Such psychological interplay and the inclusion of the spectator, was to become a common theme in the later Roman Baroque.

The Cornaro Chapel in S. Maria della Vittoria was created as the sepulchral chapel of the Venetian cardinal Federigo Cornèr, known in Rome as Cornaro.[204] The cardinal came from an old patrician family, which over the last few hundred years had produced six cardinals and one doge, Giovanni Cornèr the father of Federigo. Giovanni had been patriarch of Venice, but when he came to Rome for the conclave of 1644 he relinquished his patriarchate and remained in the Eternal City, devoting his last years unsparingly to the activities of the *Propaganda Fide*. He had been a popular and respected patriarch, during whose reign the reformed branch of the Carmelite Order, the Discalced Carmelites, was introduced in Venice, where its members became much sought-after as spiritual directors. Later, in Rome, Giovanni Cornèr maintained close relations with the Order, which took an active part in the missionary work of the *Propaganda Fide*. It was only to be expected that Federigo

Cappella Raimondi in S. Pietro in Montorio, designed by Bernini and executed by Francesco Baratta, Andrea Bolgi and Nicolò Sale (Bildarchiv Foto Marburg).

Bernini: Cappella Cornaro in S. Maria della Vittoria (ICCDcop).

Cornèr would also show great devotion to St. Teresa, founder of the reformed Order; Domenico Bernini makes a point of mentioning this in his biography of Gian Lorenzo.[205] It would also seem obvious to the cardinal that his sepulchral chapel should be built in the church of S. Maria della Vittoria adjoining the monastery of the Discalced Carmelites. The distinction of his family was such that a small side chapel would not suffice; instead he occupied an entire transept of the church. A side altar had previously stood there dedicated to St. Paul and adorned with a painting of *St. Paul elevated to the Third Heaven* by Gerhard Honthorst.

It was previously thought that Bernini began to work on the chapel immediately after 1644, and that the actual architecture was finished in 1647. But documents published by Lavin show that Cornaro did not aquire the right to the chapel until 1647,[206] which therefore precludes a start earlier than this date. Work on the decoration of the chapel and on the figures in the Teresa group must have taken a couple of years, and the whole project was not finished until the summer of 1652, although it was opened to the public earlier.

The chapel has been conceived as a single unit, combining sculpture, architecture and painting in a way that no reproduction can properly convey. The effect is best reproduced in an eighteenth-century painting by an unknown artist in the museum in Schwerin. The chapel is flanked by two pilasters, which also belong to the large pilasters in the crossing of the church. They are covered partly in yellow marble and partly in the black marble known as *bianco e nero di Portovenere*. The altar aedicule dominates the chapel. It protrudes into the transept, its two column pairs providing an oval space for the sculpture like a stage or a *tempietto*. The thickness of the wall was not enough to house this deep oval niche, and on the outside of the church we can see a corresponding bow shape, which also allows light to fall on the sculpture from a concealed window above. The base on which the paired columns stand, and the corresponding powerful projections in the architrave which they support, provide a flowing interplay of convex and concave. This movement is repeated in the triangular pediment, creating an effect of three sharp vertical folds jutting up and cutting through the heavy horizontal layers of the transept's own architrave and frieze, and the extension on each side of the tabernacle's architrave. The vertical folds introduce a powerful upward thrust which plays an important part in the composition: the spectator's gaze is directed from the tabernacle to the vault above, where Bernini's assistant Guidobaldo Abbatini has painted the open sky with angels and *putti* surrounding the dove of the Holy Spirit. The celestial light shines down on the group in the tabernacle below, actually appearing behind the figures as extremely substantial gilded rays. The side walls of the chapel are adorned with portraits of Federigo Cornèr and various of his ancestors, namely his father, Doge Giovanni Cornèr, and the family's six cardinals. The effigies are arranged opposite one another on balustraded balconies draped in dark marble.[207] Behind them is an illusionistic perspective in grey marble, conjuring up a fairly deep room with pilasters and barrel vault, almost as though the cross-arm of

Bernini, *et al.:* Cappella Cornaro, figures of the family tomb on the right. S. Maria della Vittoria (Anderson).

the church has acquired a small transept of its own.

The predominant effect of the colours in the chapel, though dark, is also warm. There is the warm black-brown *africano* in the columns of the aedicule and in the socle, there are pilasters in *giallo antico*, the rich yellowish red of *diaspro*, as well as the white marble of the figures and the grey *bardiglio* in the illusionistic architecture of the balconies.[208] And yet, despite this richness and variety, there is a strong impression of unity.

The founder, Federigo Cornèr, is portrayed second from the right among his ancestors in the balcony on the right. He is visible to the visitor entering the church, which was certainly intentional, but he does not turn in that direction like the founder of the Raimondi chapel. According to many scholars this portrait was carved by Bernini himself. It is certainly the best of the portrait busts, but its authorship can be disputed on stylistic grounds as it differs in many respects from other contemporary portraits by Bernini, which tend to be more idealised.[209] The other portraits are certainly the work of assistants, among them perhaps Ercole Ferrata. There are several earlier examples of donor portraits and effigies behind a balustrade on the sides of a chapel. Instances in both Bologna and Venice have been cited, and it is possible that the idea first appeared in the Netherlands.[210] However, whether or not Bernini saw any such prototypes is probably irrelevant, as Federigo Cornèr is sure to have given the artist his own detailed instructions. Similarly, the doors under the balconies are a common motif in funerary settings in Venice, and we can assume that the client would have given his instructions to the artist about these as well.[211]

Federigo Cornèr and his relatives seem to be involved in conversation. Some are reading or are absorbed in prayer; it is often suggested that they are discussing the vision of *The Ecstasy of St. Teresa* above the altar. But, as the room is constructed, they cannot actually see the Teresa group; some of them have turned in that direction, but they are actually looking at the wall next to the altar tabernacle. Anthony Blunt objects to the interpretation that the effigies are spectators sitting in theatre-boxes or loges, watching the action take place on a stage.[212] Such an explanation is contradicted, for instance, by the fact that the illusionistic perspective behind the figures provides a depth quite alien to the theatre-box conception. Perhaps we shall never find a definitive answer as to Bernini's intention here: are the effigies to be seen as spectators in boxes, or in the kind of *coretti* to be found in many Roman churches, and if so did Bernini mean them to be able to see the figures in the tabernacle, although because of the shallowness of the chapel, the composition has been telescoped? Perhaps the most likely explanation, as Blunt suggests, is that the members of the Cornaro family are not actually doing anything in particular; they are simply there as founders of the chapel.[213] This would mean that we should not regard the portraits as intermediaries between two levels of reality, between the visitor to the church and the figures in the Teresa group.

The group in the tabernacle depicts *The Ecstasy of St. Teresa*. A specific passage in the saint's autobiography, the *Libro de su vida*, underlies the portrayal, which reproduces the passion and the strange mystical experience or transverberation which she has described there in detail.[214] This passage was considered so significant that it was quoted in her bull of canonisation in 1622; it also occupies an important place in the history of Catholic mysticism, providing one of the most famous examples of ecstacy. The relevant passage, with which Bernini was obviously familiar, is worth quoting in full.

"It pleased the Lord that I should sometimes see the following vision. I would see beside me, on my left hand, an angel in bodily form—a type of vision which I am not in the habit of seeing, except very rarely. Though I often see representations of angels, my visions of them are of the type which I first mentioned. It pleased the Lord that I should see this angel in the following way. He was not tall, but short, and very beautiful, his face so aflame that he appeared to be one of the highest types of angel who seem to be all afire. They must be those who are called cherubim: they do not tell me their names but I am well aware that there is a great difference between certain angels and others, and between these and others still, of a kind that I could not possibly explain. In his hands I saw a long golden spear and at the end of the iron tip I seemed to see a point of fire. With this he seemed to pierce my heart several times so that it penetrated to my entrails. When he drew it out, I thought he was drawing them out with it and he left me completely afire with a great love for God. The pain was so sharp that it made me utter several moans; and so excessive was the sweetness caused me by this intense pain that one can never wish to lose it, nor will one's soul be content with anything less than God. It is not bodily pain, but spiritual, though the body has a share in it—indeed, a great share. So sweet are the colloquies of love which pass between the soul and God that if anyone thinks I am lying I beseech God, in His goodness, to give him the same experience."[215]

Thus Bernini has represented the Saint's transverberation as she herself describes it. The angel is "...not tall, but short, and very beautiful". In his right hand he holds the arrow which we envisage as having already pierced the heart of the saint, while with his other hand he gently lifts the edge of her robe, preparing to pierce her entrails yet again. His childish yet tender smile seems to show loving pity for the person to whom he is causing such pain.[216] Yet the angel also partakes of the immaterial: we see his head, one shoulder and his arms, but his body is concealed by the thin, rustling folds in his robe. Unlike the saint's highly polished robe, the angel's tunic is ethereal, as though it were part of the cloud or a whisp of smoke. And although we can see one of his feet far down on the left, this would make his leg unnaturally long and only serves to emphasise his immaterial and celestial nature.

St. Teresa is neither sitting nor lying.[217] She is floating above the ground, experiencing one of the levitations which she herself describes, perhaps borne aloft by an irresistible force as on the wings of an eagle.[218] She is outside and beyond the reach of everyday reality. We should remember, too, that the cloud beneath her was a common contemporary symbol, suggesting a celestial level of reality.[219] Teresa's states of ecstacy and levitation often occurred after communion, but they could also come upon her while listening to a homily or reciting the office in the choir or even when she was busy in the monastery kitchen.

The anatomy of her body is concealed by the deep folds of her robe, which seem to billow upwards as though blown by a strong wind. The treatment of the folds serves emotional ends here, as much as or more than in the *Longinus*. Thus it is difficult to establish the exact relation between Teresa's body and limbs. Her left hand hangs loosely down, and we can see one bare foot, perhaps reminding us that the saint belonged to the barefoot or Discalced Carmelites. Her right hand rests just below the angel, palm upwards and fingers bent as though completely relaxed. But the focus of the portrayal is on St. Teresa's face; our eyes return to it continually. It has a classic loveliness, and contemporary portraits and descriptions tell us that St. Teresa was in fact a typically Spanish, southern beauty. Her lips are slightly parted and her eyes half closed, seeing nothing; the whole powerful emotional experience springs from an internal source.[220] We become aware of this as our gaze rises from the two figures: we have already noted the strong upward movement in this composition, emphasised first by the draping of the mantle and the angel's upright pose, but also and even more powerfully by the three pointed upturned

Bernini: *Ecstasy of St. Teresa*, Cappella Cornaro. S. Maria della Vittoria (Alinari).

Bernini: *Ecstasy of St. Teresa*, detail of the angel. Cappella Cornaro in S. Maria della Vittoria (Anderson).

"folds" in the aedicule. The spectator's attention is directed towards the ceiling with its painting of the open heavens, and there we discover what St. Teresa is experiencing within herself: it is God.

The action portrayed here, the piercing of the saint's heart, generates an emotional tension between the angel and the saint, and the action itself is sharply focused by the repeated diagonals—in the direction of the angel's gaze, in the poised arrow, and in the left hand lifting the edge of the mantle. And this brings us to the relationship between the two actors, a subject that has endlessly interested scholars. First there is the contrast between the angel taking dramatic action and the half swooning saint. The angel's smile expresses profound emotion, and here Bernini has followed St. Teresa's own description, endowing the angel with great beauty. There is strong emotion also in the face of the saint, but of an entirely different kind, for her experience is altogether within herself. Bernini's portrayal of the saint's ecstasy has often been called sensual, "almost embarassingly physical" as John Pope-Hennessy puts it.[221] But, as we have seen, there is no physical contact between the two. Bernini has followed St. Teresa's own description of her transverberation in every detail, and as Pope-Hennessy goes on to say, "the analogy with profane love is implicit in the saint's own narrative..."

At this point we must address a problem which may seem irrelevant, but which in fact is important to an understanding of this visual description and indeed of seventeenth-century spirituality as a whole, namely the distinction between the mystical experience itself and the language in which it is described. St. Teresa says in so many words that her own definitions of her ecstasies and other extraordinary spiritual experiences are utterly inadequate. She often tries

Bernini: *Ecstasy of St. Teresa*, detail of the saint. Cappella Cornaro in S. Maria della Vittoria (Anderson).

to describe her experiences in several ways, or to provide what we could call double definitions. She says that she sees Christ or an angel, but with the eyes of her soul rather than her body, and often it is more like an overwhelming sense of their presence.[222] She also describes the experience of sharp pain, but it is a pain that she cannot be without, a purely spiritual pain in which the body yet participates, sometimes very strongly. Thus she uses words borrowed from general human experience, and this sometimes endows her descriptions of passion and ecstasy with a sensual or even erotic tone. St. Teresa is not alone in this: religious psychologists have often pointed out that mystics have no means of reproducing their experiences in adequate linguistic terms, as they are concerned with states completely outside the experiences of everyday life. They resort to phrases describing the union of intimate friends, of parents and children, and of lovers.[223] The Holy Writ is itself full of such analogies. For this reason many saints, not only St. Teresa, can sound deceptively sensual when they try to describe their ecstasies and mystical experiences, but this does not mean that the actual experience partook of any such physical sensuality.[224]

Bernini has sought to create as dramatic and vivid an image as possible. By uniting the arts of architecture, sculpture and painting he has produced a scenographic effect, and certainly his experience of the theatre has been useful to him here. He had approached his earlier work in the Cappella Raimondi in the same way. Whether this striving for almost tangible clarity and dramatic effect depends on the influence of the Spiritual Exercises of the Jesuits, with their emphasis on concentrated visualisation, and with which Bernini was personally familiar, is something which has often been discussed but also disputed.[225] It could simply be an expression of a general trend in contemporary art, which can also be seen in the work of artists who certainly had no personal connection with the Jesuit Order and who had not, like Bernini, taken part in St. Ignatius' *exercitia spiritualia*. But certainly the effect that Bernini has sought to create in this group can still be experienced very strongly today: it seems that a spiritual drama is being performed before our eyes in the aedicule of the altar.

The Cappella Cornaro was greeted with considerable excitement and general approval; contemporary critics as a whole seem to have felt that Bernini had excelled himself. Paolo Giordano Orsini wrote to Queen Christina in Stockholm that he had not yet seen the chapel, but that he would visit it as soon as he got to Rome, because everyone was talking about it.[226] And according to Bernini's son Domenico, the artist is supposed to have said that "this is the least bad work that I have done".[227]

At almost the same time as *The Ecstasy of St. Teresa* in the Cappella Cornaro, another important and well-known example of Bernini's art saw the light of day, namely the *Four Rivers Fountain* in Piazza Navona.[228] As the walls of the great palace grew higher, keeping pace with Innocent's ambition for the glorification of his family, it became obvious that the character of the piazza itself would also have to be altered. From having been a popular market square and the scene of many festive carnival processions, it was to be transformed into a ceremonial place, almost a kind of *cour d'honneur*, worthy of the splendid new Pamphili palace. Nothing could be more appropriate than to build a monumental fountain there. Giacomo della Porta had created a fountain at the southern end of the piazza for Gregory XIII,[229] where the waters of the Acqua Vergine gushed forth from its mascarons, while in the middle of the piazza there was a simple rectangular stone basin intended as a drinking trough for horses and donkeys. Already at the beginning of his pontificate Innocent X had considered replacing this trough by a monumental fountain, but nothing had been done until 1647 when he decreed that most of the water of the Acqua

Vergine was to be diverted here before it reached the Fontana di Trevi.[230] Urban VIII's unfinished scheme for the Fontana di Trevi was no longer of any particular interest, and Innocent X seems to have wanted to place the monumental termination of the aqueduct in the Piazza Navona instead. Borromini was appointed to direct the work of extending the aqueduct, while building materials and lead and tin were allocated to the project, as well as a considerable sum of money from the *Camera apostolica.*

Borromini was also asked to submit a proposal for the fountain itself, which was to incorporate a broken obelisk from the Via Appia at the Circo di Massenzio. A drawing thought to be by Borromini is still in the Vatican Library, but it is such an unimaginative scheme that it is difficult to believe in his authorship.[231] The drawing shows the obelisk on a square, slightly curved base; the water spouts from four large cockle-shells and falls into a basin.

Later in the spring of 1647 the fountain commission was transferred to Gian Lorenzo Bernini. We have two accounts of this development. Domenico Bernini—and this is also Baldinucci's story—tells us that Prince Nicolò Ludovisi, who was married to Donna Olimpia's daughter Costanza and thus had the ear of the pope, called on Bernini and insisted that he make a model for the fountain. The prince was also a personal friend of Bernini's, and his own large palace was currently being designed by the artist. Bernini was agreeable and soon produced a model. Then, on some occasion when the pope was visiting the Palazzo Pamphili and appeared to be in a particularly good mood, Ludovisi made sure that the model should catch his eye. Everything went according to plan and Innocent was enchanted by Bernini's proposal. At last, after examining it carefully, he exclaimed: "We must indeed employ Bernini: although there are many who would not wish it; the only way to resist him is not to see his work." Bernini was sent for and Innocent showed him many tokens of respect, flattering him, almost apologising for any previous neglect, and finally commissioning him to make the fountain.[232] According to the other version, which appears in an undated letter to the duke of Modena from Francesco Mantovani, his ambassador in Rome, Bernini is supposed to have made a model in pure silver which he presented to Donna Olimpia; she became so enthusiastic, just as he had intended, that she used her influence with the pope to acquire the commission for Bernini.[233] Which version is correct cannot now be determined. The first sounds just the sort of story that does get told, and the second could well be mere gossip. But Bernini might easily have sent some sort of bribe or present to Donna Olimpia, and silver models were not all that unusual at the time. Perhaps the truth lies in a combination of the two stories, for it is by no means unlikely that the powerful lady would have had a finger in the pie. But no silver model has survived.

Work on the fountain started during the summer of 1648, when the obelisk was transported into Rome.[234] Apparently, according to Gigli, this journey alone cost 12,000 scudi, although it has to be admitted that this sounds like an exaggeration. The people of Rome grumbled about all the expense, for which the pope imposed a one-off tax on all Roman property. This caused many

Bernini: the *Four Rivers Fountain*. Piazza Navona (Author's photo).

people to complain that enterprises of this kind were out of place when bread, if it were available at all, was black and evil smelling and costing more every week.[235] Somebody even composed a bitter satirical verse and attached it to the obelisk:

> Noi volemo altro che Guglie et Fontane,
> Pane volemo, pane, pane, pane.[236]

And some wit is reported as saying in a travesty of the biblical words: *"Dic ut lapides isti panes fiant."*[237] Innocent X was not a man to accept such criticism, and the guilty party was soon caught by the *sbirri* and sent to prison.

First, the rock base for the obelisk was prepared in travetine by the stonemason Fracchi, whereupon Bernini added the finishing touches. In August 1649 the obelisk was raised on its base, not without some technical complications.[238] We can see how Bernini arrived at the final version of the fountain and the figures round it in several drawings and two *bozzetti* or models which have survived, one in the Giocondi collection in Rome and one in the Pinacoteca in Bologna.[239] Already in the first sketches—e.g. in a drawing in Chigi's collection in Ariccia—the rock is visible, but it grew in the course of the project, as can be seen in a drawing in the Royal Collection at Windsor. Meanwhile the four river gods, who do not seem to have been included at first, gradually became increasingly important.[240] The Roman *bozzetto*, which probably dates from 1648/49, approaches fairly close to the finished work, and a sheet in Leipzig is thought to show how it emerged. The *bozzetto* in Bologna, however, probably dates from 1650. Whether any later models were made is not known.

The obelisk rises high above the crowds that throng the piazza. Indeed, it almost seems to hover there, as the rock on which it stands is far from solid: wherever you stand you can see through openings in the stone. The obelisk is crowned not with a cross but with the Pamphili dove holding a sprig of olive in its beak. On each of the four projecting corners of the rock there sits a male figure, the famous river gods who have given the fountain its name. They personify what were then regarded as the four greatest rivers of the world and thus, as well, the four known continents. On the south side of the fountain the Danube represents Europe and the Ganges Asia, while on the opposite side the Nile represents Africa and the Rio della Plata America. And other attributes, mainly animals and plants, correspond to the different parts of the world. The *Danube* figure, as benefits the personification of the only wholly Christian continent, carries the papal arms beneath the obelisk and beside him a horse stands in the hollowed-out rock. The *Ganges* holds a large oar, perhaps referring to the fact that the river was navigable right across India. The *Nile* has covered his head beneath his mantle, supposedly indicating the river's as yet undiscovered source, and he is accompanied by a palm-tree and a lion in a rocky grotto. The *Rio della Plata* is represented by a negro with thick lips, and the coins scattered on the rock beside him naturally refer to the wealth of the New World. Behind him we can see a long coiled snake and in the basin beneath an armadillo, an animal found only in South America. The negro has

Bernini: detail of the *Four Rivers Fountain*, the *Nile*, executed by Jacopo Antonio Fancelli (Author's photo).

lifted his hand in a gesture of amazement or fear—but not, as is often suggested, expressing horror at S. Agnese's façade, since the church was not even envisaged when the fountain was built. How this gesture should be interpreted will be discussed later.

The river gods recline on their rocks, half sitting and twisting their bodies into a sort of *contraposto* spiral, perhaps intentionally recalling Michelangelo's *Ignudi* in the Sistine Chapel. Their movements are coordinated so that the *Danube's* spiral corresponds to the curve of the *Ganges* on the opposite side, while the same applies to the *Nile* and the *Plata*. Legs, arms and even bodies provide sharp diagonals; the palm-tree and the oar of the *Ganges* are also balanced one against the other; in the rocks, too, diagonal thrusts are strongly marked. The resulting play of opposing yet balancing movements creates a billowing rhythm, flowing round the fountain and enticing the visitor to the piazza to walk round it and study it from all sides. This is generally regarded as a typically Mannerist effect, which here depends on the fountain's location in the middle of an open place: here the spectator cannot be restricted to one fixed viewpoint such as many of Bernini's other sculptures command. The fountain has not been placed in front of the palace, which is closer to the southern end of the square; instead it dominates the entire open space from the middle of the piazza. It has no relation at all to the façade of the church. The fountain thus has several possible viewpoints, but one of these is the most important, namely the one facing south which we see as we approach from the main entrance of the Palazzo Pamphili.

Naturally the *Four Rivers Fountain* has an allegorical content, its own *concetto*. According to the simplest interpretation, advocated by Wittkower, the obelisk, as a symbol of the cross and by extension also of Christendom or the Church, and crowned here by Innocent X's family emblem, proclaims the worldwide power of Christianity under the rule of the Pamphili pope. Like the obelisks raised by Sixtus V, this one symbolises the triumph of the Christian Faith over the heathen. But, as Wittkower also points out, "other more subtle connotations are perhaps implied".[241]

Many scholars have addressed the controversial issue of the *concetto* of the fountain.[242] Opinions differ even on the most fundamental questions, and no interpretation can yet be accepted as definitive. However, on some points most scholars agree. In the case of a monument on a site as important as this one, a monument so dear to the heart of the pope, Innocent X will certainly have said the final word on the iconography as on everything else. But on this point the sources are silent. As far as we can judge, however, the iconography had not yet been worked out in detail when Bernini submitted his first proposal. As work proceeded and the composition was altered and extended, the iconographical scheme also appears to have evolved. It is probably impossible now to determine Bernini's contribution exactly, but we can be almost certain that the iconographical programme would be suggested to him by some learned person, or that he must at least have consulted such a person—probably, according to several scholars, the German-born Jesuit, Father Athanasius

Kircher.[243] One of the many subjects which Kircher studied with profound scholarship was Egyptology, and he had made a particular study of the obelisks in Rome and their inscriptions. In 1650 he published an important work entitled *Obeliscus Pamphilius*, which discusses the obelisk in the Piazza Navona.

People knew that the obelisk had been an important symbol of the sun, *digitus solis*, already in Antiquity. Later, when Sixtus V crowned his Roman obelisks with a cross, the monoliths acquired a new meaning as bearers of the cross and thus by extension as symbols of Christ or even the Christian Faith as a whole. There was also an old tradition which linked the obelisk with princes and princely power.[244] However, the obelisk in the Piazza Navona was crowned not with a cross but with the Pamphili dove, and its link with the person of Innocent X is thus clear; but the dove is simultaneously the symbol of peace, which means that we can be even more precise: the obelisk is Christendom under the peaceful rule of the Pamphili. The coiled snake at the foot of the obelisk appears to belong to the *Rio della Plata*, but the snake is also traditionally regarded as a symbol of evil: here, evil conquered by the Christian Cross. Yet again, the snake can refer, like the Phoenix, to rebirth and renewal.[245] Indeed it can also be interpreted as a kind of hieroglyph for the prince, in particular the vigilant prince,[246] and so the link with Innocent X is clear here too.

It has also been suggested that Father Kircher's inscriptions, which were never actually used, may have provided clues to an understanding of the fountain's *concetto*. One of the inscriptions alluded to the Holy Year of 1650, when the pope had hoped to see the fountain completed. And the Holy Year was to herald a rebirth of the righteousness referred to in the inscription.[247] Another idea has been that the rivers are the four rivers of paradise according to certain mediaeval depictions in which the rivers spring from the mountain where the cross stands.[248] The palm-tree, too, is an allusion to paradise, but it was also believed to be a hieroglyph for the year, since the palm grows by twelve branches every year; and since it was traditionally seen as a symbol of regeneration, it may allude here to the Holy Year.[249] In a contemporary description of the fountain based not on the finished monument but on a *bozzetto* which he claimed to have seen, Michelangelo Lualdi posits that there is also a symbolism inherent in the positions and gestures of the river gods. The *Rio della Plata*, for instance, is leaning backwards to be able to see the Pamphili dove above the obelisk, which he salutes by raising his hand.[250] Lualdi, it has even been suggested, might have been the learned expert whom Bernini consulted about the iconography.

In other words there are nearly as many explanations as there are interested scholars, and it would be almost impossible to pinpoint one interpretation as the right one. Also, of course, two or three different interpretations need not be mutually exclusive.[251] Many works of art in the seventeenth century were based on ambivalent or double *concetti*. In this *Obeliscus Pamphilius* symbols of the cross and the sun may well co-exist alongside the glorification of a

Bernini: detail of the *Four Rivers Fountain*, the *Rio della Plata*, executed by Francesco Baratta (Author's photo).

particular pope. The rivers, two of whom are carrying the papal arms, are obviously paying homage to the pope, but they also personify the continents conquered by the cross. At the same time they are what they are: rivers, influenced by the light of the sun. The plants and animals allude not only to the continents but also to paradise, and perhaps to the golden age.[252] There may well be simultaneous allegories referring to the triumphs of the cross and the wisdom of the pope, to innocence and justice, and to the regenerating consequences of the Holy Year.

A little more than two years after work began, the fountain was finished; it was unveiled on 14 June 1651. The pope had visited the site a couple of days earlier and expressed his admiration, especially as the water gushed forth unexpectedly just as he was about to leave. The accounts establish a cost of over 29,000 scudi, of which Gian Lorenzo Bernini received 3,000 scudi and his collaborators and assistants 10,000.[253] According to early, reliable sources Bernini worked on the rock, the palm-tree, the horse and the lion himself, whereas the accounts reveal that the *Danube* was carved by Antonio Raggi, the *Ganges* by Claude Poussin, the *Nile* by Jacopo Antonio Fancelli and the *Rio della Plata* by Francesco Baratta.[254] The same documents show that many details and attributes were executed by other collaborators of Bernini's: Nicolò Sale, for example, was responsible for the escutcheons and the dove, which was cast in bronze; Guidantonio Abbatini was paid for painting the rock, the plants and some other details, but of this original polychrome effect no trace remains.

The fountain caused an immediate sensation, receiving both praise and criticism. Gigli reports that the sellers who were wont to ply their trade in the piazza were driven out into the surrounding streets, and there was a good deal of ill-feeling about this.[255] For the remainder of Innocent X's lifetime, the piazza was reserved for the carriages of the great and for costly private festivities, but after his death it resumed its earlier popular character.[256] Domenico Bernini tells us that on one occasion rumours began to circulate after a bad storm that the obelisk was about to fall down, and crowds of curious people gathered in the piazza. Bernini then arrived on the scene and, assuming a suitably serious expression, began cautiously inspecting the fountain. Then, amidst general hilarity, he tied the obelisk with twine attached to the neighbouring buildings, as though to give it support.[257]

In his old age Bernini felt dissatisfied with the *Four Rivers Fountain*, and indeed was often critical of his own works once he had finished them. Domenico writes that once when Gian Lorenzo was driving past Piazza Navona he drew the curtains of his carriage and cried out *"Oh come mi vergogno di haver operato così male"*, "How ashamed I am to have done so poorly".[258] Bernini's religious faith became more profound as he grew older, and he may have found this early work too worldly. Certainly the fountain has more than a little in common with the temporary scenographic decorations so beloved of the times. We can easily envisage a *macchina* rather like this, with artificial rocks and allegorical figures, all in plaster and wood and canvas, and complete with fireworks for the final explosion into smoke and flames.[259] The somewhat theatrical effect of the fountain cannot fail to fascinate the modern visitor to the piazza, and perhaps one has to admit that it looks its best after dark under modern flood-lighting and with underwater illumination, which makes every detail glimmer and glitter as the light flickers over the stone. Never before had water and stone been wed in a fountain to form such a dazzlingly coherent effect. One is tempted to say that Bernini has added a new dimension to this work: sound, a continual murmur of water gushing forth in the generous flow that only a Roman fountain can produce.

Now that water was available, the outlet was sometimes closed, particularly on hot August Sundays, so that the water flooded the piazza and transformed it into a shallow lake.[260] It became very popular to seek the coolness of the *Lago di Piazza Navona*, as it came to be known, and the tradition persisted far into the nineteenth century. Several early prints show grand carriages being towed through the water, watched by all kinds of spectators, from romping children to distinguished gentlemen and dignified Roman matrons. As Angelus chimed, the outlet would be opened again, and a feast laid before the ladies and

Bernini: the *Triton* of the
Fontana del Moro. Piazza
Navona, executed by
Giovan Antonio Mari
(Author's photo).

gentlemen visiting the surrounding palaces, while humbler folk bought wine
and *porchetta* from temporary stalls.

When the *Four Rivers Fountain* was finished, Bernini had to refurbish
Jacopo della Porta's fountain at the southern end of the piazza. In the centre of
the polygonal basin he created a *Triton*, here as a negro, and the fountain is
often referred to somewhat misleadingly as the Fontana del Moro. The figure
was carved by Giovan Antonio Mari from Bernini's model and it was finished
in 1655.[261] The *Triton* stands on a large cockle-shell; between his legs he holds
a fish, from which the water gushes forth. The body twists to form a spiral,
seen by some as a return to an earlier Mannerist style. But in fact this fountain
has one obviously "best" viewpoint, namely from a line between the *Four
Rivers Fountain* and the entrance to the Palazzo Pamphili.

Bernini's official commissions were growing increasingly numerous, and
they included several portrait busts of Innocent X in marble and bronze,
although some are not entirely by his hand.[262] Otherwise Bernini has left few
portraits from this period. A brilliant exception is his bust of Francesco I
d'Este, duke of Modena.[263] This was carved by Bernini alone and was completed by the end of 1651. The duke is looking slightly to one side, his wig
falling in long curls that frame his face. Together with the folds of drapery,

which billow around him as though lifted by a strong wind, this gives an incomparable impression of life and movement, in the play of light and shadow and the unexpected forms. Bernini had never met the duke, but has based his portrait on paintings which were sent to him; this may be one reason why the bust appears to be more idealised than his more or less contemporary portraits of the pope. The duke's appreciation of Bernini's work is reflected in the unusually generous fee for this commission, which amounted to no less than 3,000 ducats, or as much as Bernini received for the entire *Four Rivers* project.

It is difficult to imagine how Bernini can have managed to handle so many major works at one time: the Cappella Cornaro and the *Four Rivers Fountain* were created during roughly the same brief period; and, entirely on his own, he produced the *Truth* group and the bust of the duke of Modena within a very short space of time. The explanation is that Bernini knew how to organise and superintend a large team of collaborators and assistants, just as he had done earlier under Urban VIII when he was working on the *baldacchino* and the sculptures in St. Peter's and the pope's sepulchral monument all at once.[264] His oldest assistant was Giuliano Finelli, who had been engaged already in 1622 and who stayed with him for a great many years. Andrea Bolgi and Stefano Speranza, who had collaborated with him at St. Peter's, also continued to work under Bernini for a long time. Around the mid-1640s he was joined by Ercole Ferrata, Lazzaro Morelli, Giovan Antonio Mari, Pietro Paolo Naldini and Antonio Raggi. Both Ferrata and Raggi also worked independently and received several major commissions of their own, but they collaborated with Bernini now and again. From about 1650 onwards there cannot have been many sculptors in Rome who had not at some point collaborated with Bernini; many of them received their training in his studio and almost all of them were variously influenced by his style. Several of them later left Rome, so that during the second half of the seventeenth century the Bernini style gradually spread to the rest of Italy.

*

Alessandro Algardi was the foremost representative of the classical school in sculpture.[265] As a young man in Bologna he had studied painting under Ludovico Carracci, and when he came to Rome in 1625 he attached himself to the Bolognese group of artists, sharing their admiration of Raphael and their interest in classical art; he was closely associated with Domenichino and numbered Andrea Sacchi, who was his exact contemporary, among his closest friends. As we have seen, at the beginning of Innocent X's pontificate he was commissioned to decorate the Villa di Belrespiro for the Pamphili, and he had probably been involved in planning the villa as well. Since the mid-1630s he had been working on the funerary monument of the Medici Pope, Leo XI, which appears to have been finished by 1644, and the following year he obtained a commission for a large pictorial relief of *The Meeting of Pope Leo I and Attila* for the Cappella Leonina in St. Peter's. Thus, while Gian Lorenzo

Alessandro Algardi: the tomb of Pope Leo XI, marble. St. Peter's (Saskia Archive).

Bernini was more or less out of the running for papal commissions, Algardi was the favourite sculptor of Innocent X and his family. There are several portraits by Algardi from this period, of the pope and of other members of the Pamphili family.[266] One of his best portraits is the bust of Donna Olimpia Maidalchini, which clearly reveals the mannish element in this woman's character (see illustration, p. 6).

Leo XI's funerary monument had been commissioned in 1634 by Cardinal Ubaldini, and a preliminary model was probably already in existence in 1637 when the congregation of the *Propaganda Fide* assumed responsibility for the project. The monument was finished three years before Bernini had completed Urban VIII's tomb, but it was not placed in the basilica until 1652.[267] These two almost contemporary papal tombs are often compared—an exercise which

Alessandro Algardi: *Meeting of Pope Leo I and Attila*, marble relief. St. Peter's (Alinari).

is not without interest and which can be enlightening. But that Algardi was influenced by Bernini's solution, as is sometimes suggested, is probably open to question. When Algardi began to plan his own work, all that existed of Bernini's monument was the statue of the pope. However, there was a large model of the tomb, which we know Bernini had already begun to prepare in 1628,[268] and it is not impossible that Algardi may have seen this.

The composition of the two tombs is basically similar. The pope sits above a sarcophagus flanked by two allegorical figures. Bernini's monument is dynamic and full of verve (see illustration, vol. I, p. 358). He has created a roughly pyramidal group, with the pope dominating the composition from his position high above the heads of the virtues beneath him. Urban raises his arm in a gesture that both commands and blesses as it reaches out into the spectator's space. Below there is a clear movement towards the centre in the two virtues, who provide a clear but subtle play of diagonals, with their sweeping draperies. The liveliness is enhanced by the boisterous *putti*, and the range of colour from white and polychrome marble to bronze and gilding. Algardi's composition, on the other hand, is tranquil and compact, built up round predominantly vertical lines. Leo's gesture is discreet and controlled; the two virtues provide a balanced frame and base for the pope, whom they equal in size. The three figures are more nearly on the same level; the virtues remain calm as though lost in thought, and the colour is limited to the white of the marble.

The iconography of Leo's tomb is unusual: according to the contract the virtues were to represent *Magnanimità* and *Liberalità*, but most scholars now refer to the first one, on the left, as *Fortezza*.[269] Both are personifications of Leo XI's most notable qualities, and can only be understood in light of what we know of his character and interests. *Fortezza*, with her helmet, shows a marked affiliation with portrayals of Pallas Athena, perhaps because like Leo X, his predecessor in the Medici family, Leo XI liked to present himself as a patron of the arts. The problem of how much is Algardi's own work, and how much may have been the work of his assistants, and if so which, remains basically unsolved.[270]

The altar relief, *The Meeting of Pope Leo I and Attila*, was one of the most important commissions that a sculptor could hope to receive in 1645 when the project was mooted. Work began in 1646, but the relief was not finished by the Holy Year of 1650 as had been intended; instead a temporary full-scale plaster model was set up in the basilica. This model can now be seen in the stair-well of the Oratory of St. Philip Neri. Work on the relief proper was not finished until 1653.[271] It shows Pope Leo the Great meeting Attila, king of the Huns, outside Rome in 492, when he succeeded in stopping the invader from entering and plundering the city. The same subject had been treated earlier by Raphael in the Stanza d'Eliodoro, and there is a certain resemblance in the two pictures; Algardi has certainly studied Raphael's composition. In face of Leo's calm and commanding gesture Attila falls back, at the same time gesturing as though to ward off the two saints Peter and Paul, who come sweeping triumphantly down from the sky above the pope. Between the two main figures, the pope and Attila, there is an empty space, a sort of visual caesura, which reinforces the drama of the story. While the main actors and one of the lesser figures in the foreground stand out almost three-dimensionally, protruding into the spectator's space and seeming more real, the other minor figures—of whom there are not many, in obedience to classical theory—recede and become successively flatter. Thus Algardi creates an illusion of depth without resorting to the

Alessandro Algardi:
Vision of St. Nicholas of
Tolentino, marble.
S. Nicola da Tolentino
(Max Hutzel).

rules of linear perspective, just as an Early Renaissance master like Ghiberti could create an effect of space in his Paradise doors. Emotional clarity and a concentration to the essential are the hallmarks of this relief, which is one of the masterpieces of High Baroque sculpture in Rome.

While Algardi was completing the altar relief for St. Peter's he was also working on the high altar of S. Nicola da Tolentino, which was begun in 1651 when Camillo Pamphili assumed responsibility for this church, and probably finished just before Algardi died in 1654.[272] Because this work was mainly executed by Algardi's assistants Domenico Guidi and Ercole Ferrata, it has often been neglected by critics and art historians, and yet it is one of the artist's most personal and original contributions to the art of the altar relief, an art form which is predominantly associated with Algardi and his shool. The figures in the group, the Virgin with the two saints Augustine and Monica appearing in a vision to St. Nicholas, are set in a deeply curved round-headed niche between columns supporting an architrave. Thus here, too, relief is combined with almost three-dimensional sculpture.

These altarpieces of Algardi's, particularly the great relief in St. Peter's itself, made a strong impression on the artist's contemporaries, and wherever possible reliefs of this kind were increasingly preferred to painted altarpieces in Roman churches. Later, the interior of S. Agnese in Piazza Navona was decorated consistently in this style. A relief occupies a position somewhere between reality and pictorial representation, and in this way it satisfied the demands of those times for what we now call "audience participation". The borderlines between art and the real world of the spectator are increasingly blurred, and it becomes easier for the spectator to identify with the events portrayed. At the same time there is something very grand about the relief, executed in a hard material which will inevitably last longer than any equivalent work in fresco or oil.

Painting around the Middle of the Century

Ever since the sixteenth century the cosmopolitan city of Rome had been attracting artists from elsewhere, not only from other parts of Italy but also north of the Alps. Some of the artists spent a year or so in the Eternal City and then returned home, while others stayed for the rest of their lives. Some became wholly assimilated in the Roman setting, others—particularly those from other countries—associated exclusively with some particular group of like-minded people, while yet others remained essentially outsiders. We have already come across stone-carvers and architects such as Domenico Fontana, Carlo Maderno and Francesco Borromini from northern Lombardy and Ticino. Many artists came from Lorraine, among them the sculptor Nicolas Cordier who was active in Rome until his death in 1612, and the copper-engraver Israel Silvestre who stayed in Rome for a year or so at the beginning of the 1640s. But Claude, the best known of the artists from Lorraine, became so absorbed into the Roman scene that we have to count him as a member of the Roman school. The Frenchman Nicolas Poussin, on the other hand, followed quite a different line, remaining something of an eccentric throughout his life. German, Dutch and above all Flemish painters had been coming to Rome in considerable numbers ever since the Renaissance. These often strange and unruly northerners lived a somewhat Bohemian life in the area between Piazza del Popolo and Piazza di Spagna, except when they found themselves in jail for drunkenness or fighting.

None of the commissions for frescoes in palaces and churches came the way of these northerners, who had to occupy themselves almost exclusively with other tasks; in the eyes of the academicians they were little more than heathens, barely to be tolerated. While the masters were engaged by the pontifical court and the papal families, by cardinals and princes, the foreign artists were executing *pittura inferiore* or *divertimenti* for the higher bourgeoisie, for members of the nobility, and for foreigners visiting Rome. Many of them made

Michelangelo Cerquozzi: *L'Abbeveratoio*. Galleria Corsini (ICCDcop).

a speciality of landscape painting, a tradition going back to the days of Paul Bril, while others concentrated on flower paintings, still life, or small mythological scenes. Despite the superior attitude of the official art establishment, many of these painters were popular and well paid, enjoying considerable economic success. They, too, had their admirers and collectors, and it was not unusual to find examples of their work, perhaps as something of a curiosity, in the collections of even the grandest palaces.

A definite and clearly defined tendency or school generally known as the *bambocciata*, existed within the bounds of this unofficial Roman art.[273] Its main distinguishing feature was a striving for realism particularly in the choice of subject, and its artists can therefore be regarded in some ways as late successors of Caravaggio. Some of them were in fact directly influenced by his work. This school of Roman painting began to take shape already under Urban VIII in the person of the Dutch artist Pieter van Laer who was active in Rome from 1625 until his return to Haarlem in 1638. Because of his appearance he was nicknamed *il bamboccio*, the ugly and ungainly one. The people in his pictures, who were also regarded as ugly and ungainly and far removed from the ideal beauty portrayed by Carracci and Sacchi, later came to be dubbed

Master of the Small Trades: *The Tooth Puller.* Galleria Nazionale d'Arte Antica (ICCDcop).

bambocci and his paintings were known as *bambocciate.* Thereafter the appellation *i bamboccianti* referred to his successors, who included both Dutchmen and Italians. They were interested exclusively in the depiction of ordinary people and events: inn scenes and carnival frolics, and the soldiers, highwaymen, market sellers and workmen living out their everyday lives in the alleys and ruins of Rome and the Campagna. These artists have thus left us an often fascinating and amusing picture of the life of the simple Roman people of the seventeenth century.

Around the middle of the century one of the foremost *bamboccianti* was Michelangelo Cerquozzi, a Roman born and bred who died in 1660.[274] Cerquozzi used to collaborate with Viviano Codazzi from Bergamo, who was active in Rome from 1647 until his death in 1672. Because of his lively and realistic battle scenes, full of soldiers and prancing horses and the smoke of gunpowder, Cerquozzi was nicknamed *Michelangelo delle battaglie.* His masterpiece is *Masaniello's Rebellion*, now in the Galleria Spada. He has painted a wild tumult in a piazza, full of details and figures from drawings by Codazzi who had visited Naples on his way to Rome.[275] Codazzi also often collaborated with the landscape painter, Angeluccio. Their joint landscapes are constructed on the lines of the classical idealised landscapes of Carracci's school

Nicolas Poussin: *Christ and the Woman Taken in Adultery.* Musée du Louvre, Paris (Villani & Figli).

and show great sensitivity in the depiction of light and atmosphere, but the figures are painted with a realism which Claude, for example, would never have allowed himself, and the events portrayed are trivial. One of the most attractive examples of Cerquozzi's art is *L'Abbeveratoio*, a little picture in the Galleria Corsini in Rome.[276] The few figures show Cerquozzi's skill as a draughtsman; the overall tones are subdued, recalling Caravaggio, but they are enlivened by a few brilliant touches of colour; in the background we see the Campagna landscape and a cloudy sky.

Perhaps the most typical of the *bamboccianti* was Jan Miel of Antwerp, active in Rome from the early 1630s until 1658. In light of recent research he emerges as a key personage in the history of the *bamboccianti*.[277] His paintings possess a remarkable quality, and in spite of Passeri's critical attitude were very popular with seventeenth-century collectors. However, some paintings which used to be considered typical of his work are now attributed instead to an anonymous painter called the Master of the Small Trades.[278] *The Tooth Puller*, for example, is one of the most typical of those scenes of everyday life in seventeenth-century Rome which posses a special charm and interest for us today. This particular painting also shows Bernini's *Four Rivers Fountain* in process of construction and surrounded by scaffolding.

The attitude of the established artists towards the *bamboccianti* is well illustrated in some letters exchanged between Andrea Sacchi and his ageing teacher Francesco Albani during 1651. These are quoted by Malvasia in *Felsina pittrice*, a book about Bolognese painting published in 1678.[279] Sacchi complains that the *bamboccianti* are interested only in the most trivial subjects,

Nicolas Poussin: *Landscape with St. Matthew and the Angel.* Staatliche Museen, Berlin Dahlem (Villani & Figli).

which they depict without either *decoro* or charm. Albani answers in indignant vein, pouring scorn on the painters for dragging Roman art in the dust of the inns and streets.

Nicolas Poussin stands out as the diametrical opposite of the *bamboccianti*, but in his own way he remained an outsider in Rome, particularly after his return from Paris. Although he included Cassiano dal Pozzo, Camillo de' Massimi and Giulio Rospigliosi among his closest friends, and executed several paintings for them,[280] most of his clients were Frenchmen associated with the court in Paris. In the artistic life of Rome it was Poussin's personality rather than his works which had the greatest impact.[281] With his friends he enjoyed learned discussions on art and philosophy, either at home in his studio or strolling on the Pincio or in the Piazza di Spagna. Theory always fascinated him and he was familiar with the treatises on painting of Leon Battista Alberti, Leonardo da Vinci and others.[282] He also made a profound study of Stoic philosophy, whence came his conviction that the artist should not seek to reproduce the impressions of the senses; instead the foundation of all art must be knowledge. In his paintings he sought to express human dignity and human conduct as guided by the virtues, and in accordance with Stoic philosophy he paid particular homage to man's mastery of the passions. What he prized most in the heroes of Antiquity was the courage and patriotism that they so frequently showed.[283]

Nicolas Poussin: *The Ashes of Phocion Collected by his Widow.* Earl of Derby's collection, Knowsley Hall (Villani & Figli).

In the early 1650s Poussin was unusually productive. Many of his paintings on biblical themes date from this time. They include *Christ Healing the Blind Men*, painted for Reynon in 1650 and *Christ and the Woman Taken in Adultery*, painted for André le Nôtre in 1653, both of which are now in the Louvre,[284] as well as the second series of *The Seven Sacraments*, painted for Paul Fréart de Chantelou in 1644–1648. These all belong to that class of solemn—one is tempted to say theatrical—compositions which seems to us today decidedly lacking in warmth. But it was also during this period that Poussin began to produce paintings of a different kind: those magnificent ideal landscapes which are perhaps among his most attractive works. In *Landscape with St. Matthew and the Angel*,[285] an early landscape probably painted for Cardinal Francesco Borromini in 1643 and now in the Staatliche Museum in Berlin Dahlem, we can see how Poussin has built up his picture around various elements which he has studied in the Campagna outside Rome: the river recalls the Tiber where it bends by Acqua Acetosa, the mountains resemble the Sabine Hills, while the tower in the middle ground is actually the Torre delle Milizie in Rome. This tower's position at the centre of the picture recalls Annabile Carracci's compositional system. In the later landscapes similar borrowings from nature can also be found, but now in a more stylised version. The result is the typical "composed", or what is generally called the ideal, landscape.

Among Poussin's most characteristic landscapes are the two Phocion paintings which he executed in 1648 for the French merchant Cérisier.[286] Bernini saw these pictures in Cérisier's collection in Paris in 1665, and expressed his

Nicolas Poussin: *Landscape with Orpheus and Euridice*. Musée du Louvre, Paris (ICCD).

admiration of them to Monsieur de Chantelou. Poussin would probably have read Plutarch's *Life of Phocion*, and this Greek hero is likely to have aroused his particular admiration and sympathy: he was hated by his Athenian countrymen for his moral integrity; he was exiled to Megara and later murdered there. One of the pictures, *The Ashes of Phocion Collected by his Widow*, now in the Earl of Derby's collection at Knowsley Hall, has much in common with other Poussin landscapes from this period, and therefore repays a more detailed scrutiny. The foreground is clearly marked off from the middle ground both by the trees which also frame the picture, and by a wall parallel with the picture plane. A road leads diagonally into the picture, and the main actors are placed exactly below the intersection of the wall and this road. In the middle ground we can see some smaller figures round a calm, smooth lake—a favourite motif in Poussin's landscapes. These people are bathing in the lake apparently without a care in the world. It is an idyllic scene. In the background a Corinthian temple stands exactly above the main actors at the front of the picture, impressive in the nobility and harmony of its architecture. All the buildings round this temple are either parallel or at right angles to the picture plane, thus reinforcing the effect of calm tranquillity. But the deep shadows in the foreground, and the cloud rising threateningly behind the rocks above the temple, offer a sharp contrast to the tranquil mood. It is on this contrast between two moods that the powerful impact of the picture depends. There is also a sense of latent threat, of something sinister, as so often in Poussin's landscapes: the young woman with Phocion's widow has just turned round

Claude Lorrain: *Seaport with the Villa Medici.* Galleria degli Uffizi, Florence
(Villani & Figli).

and caught sight of the youth under the trees who is obviously spying on them.

This sinister element reappears in the *Landscape with Orpheus and Eurydice*
in the Louvre dated about 1652.[287] In contrast with the idyllic subject of
Orpheus playing his lyre, there is the sky in the background foreshadowing a
storm and the smoke rising from the castle. One of the women listening to
Orpheus turns round in terror, seeing behind her the foreground shadows
approaching and already touching the other two listening figures; it is the
shadow of the Kingdom of Death.

Among Nicolas Poussin's friends was the artist Claude, whose real name
was Gellée but who is generally known as Claude Lorrain after his place of
birth. Claude had been in Rome much longer than Poussin, having studied
already as a young man under Agostino Tassi, and he fitted so easily into the
Roman setting that we can count him as a member of the Roman school. Apart
from his French patrons, most of his clients belonged to the Roman nobility
and included both Camillo de' Massimi and Prince Camillo Pamphili.[288] His
style had evolved from the decorative frescoes in Roman palaces during the late

sixteenth century as represented by Girolamo Muziano and others, but his foremost source of inspiration was Tassi.[289] Another element in his artistic background, however, was the influence of the *bamboccianti*, which was particularly noticeable in his figure drawing. During the 1640s he was influenced by Domenichino's landscapes, and it was at this time that he reached full maturity. He became one of Rome's best known and popular landscape painters. Because of his success, forgeries of his work began to appear on the market in increasing numbers. In order to protect his good name he started a kind of catalogue which he called his *Liber veritatis*, in which he made carefully detailed drawings of his works, noting the client's name and the date.[290] This pictorial document provides a complete list of Claude's works from 1637 until his death in 1682. He was now getting commissions from all over Europe and his clientèle included persons of the highest rank. Princes, counts and ambassadors all wanted landscapes by Claude. During the 1640s he produced six landscapes for no less a patron than Philip IV of Spain. These paintings are now in the Prado.

In contrast to Nicolas Poussin's heroic landscapes, Claude's are painted in elegiac and lyrical mood. He was extraordinarily sensitive to atmosphere and light, which he appears to have studied in the Roman Campagna. Light can perhaps be said to be the recurrent theme in his landscapes: early morning light, the brilliant sunshine of midday, the soft tones of dusk, the light over the Campagna or on the coast when the air is damp. In his early landscapes he showed a predeliction for effects against the light, as in his special seaport subjects, almost all of them painted before 1650. These harbour scenes, with the effect of light over the waves and the architectural structures jutting in from the side, represented a special theme which Claude had discovered for himself, but they stemmed in part from Tassi's *quadratura* painting and Brill's marine landscapes.[291] We should not forget that Claude was greatly admired by his contemporaries as an architectural painter.[292] His architectural subjects were often inspired by Classical Antiquity, but perhaps even more frequently by the architecture of the Renaissance or of his own time. Thus we may find the Villa Medici, for example, in one of his imaginary landscapes or the *Campidoglio* at the edge of one of his harbours.

Claude's mature style culminates in the two great paintings in the Galleria Doria Pamphili, *Landscape with Dancing Figures*, also known as *The Mill*, and the *View of Delphi with a Procession*, both painted for Prince Camillo Pamphili and dated 1648–1650.[293] The National Gallery in London has a version of the first of these, known as *The Marriage of Isaac and Rebecca*.[294] The Delphi landscape, which has no connection at all with the real Delphi, is among the most characteristic of Claude's landscapes and deserves a more detailed analysis. The picture "starts" on the left where a group of women sit round what is presumably the Fountain of Castalia. Here the mood is idyllic. One of the women is pointing towards the background, over the bridge and along the road which runs diagonally towards the temple. A few figures appear to be moving in this direction, but nothing is very precise. The tree in the middle

Claude Lorrain: *View of Delphi with a Procession.* Galleria Doria Pamphili
(Villani & Figli).

ground, its crown silhouetted against the luminous sky, divides the background into two views. On the right we see the temple, a great domed building
rather like the Pantheon or Bramante's St. Peter's. On the left we are looking
out over a bay, which in Claude's characteristic way is shown against the light.
He has included the sun, but it is veiled by thin clouds, producing a soft and
shimmering light that suggests the dawn. Before the vastness of the view the
spectator feels small, and on the right the colossal yet classically harmonious
temple dominates the swarm of tiny figures on the terrace before it. Thus both
views express an emotional mood that is different from that of the foreground,
and the atmosphere there approaches the sublime. The *Landscape with Dancing Figures* also expresses two different moods in the foreground and
background, although this time the idyllic mood of the foreground predomi-
nates. But this modulation from one key to another is always, in some
measure, an important element in Claude's landscapes.

Landscape painting as a whole enjoyed a new flowering from about the
middle of the seventeenth century, and fresco landscapes once more became a
common feature in the adornment of palaces and churches, as they had been
earlier at the beginning of the century. Nicolas Poussin's brother-in-law and
pupil, Gaspar Dughet, sometimes known as Gaspar Poussin, belonged to a
French family and was closely associated with his brother-in-law and the

Gaspard Dughet: *View of Tivoli.* King's College, Newcastle (Villani & Figli).

French colony of painters, but he was in fact a Roman born and bred. He specialised in landscape painting to the exclusion of all else, and occupies a more important position in the history of landscape painting than has generally been recognised. Until about 20 years ago it would be fair to say that he was greatly underrated by the historians of art.[295]

Between 1647 and 1651 Dughet painted a fresco cycle depicting the lives of the prophets Elijah and Elisha for the church of S. Martino ai Monti.[296] These paintings are composed in full accord with the classical rules as applied by Carracci and Domenichino, but they also contain much that is new and represent a turning-point in Dughet's production. During the 1650s he seems to have increasingly assimilated Nicolas Poussin's approach to landscape composition, and his style became more idealised. Generally speaking, however, his landscapes are more romantic: the scene is often wilder, full of violence and storm—in Nicolas Poussin's landscapes there is never the slightest flutter of a breeze. Dughet appears to have studied in the open air, even more than his brother-in-law had done, and it is particularly obvious that trees were important in his paintings, often setting the mood of the whole picture. Sometimes he paints landscapes, such as a view of Tivoli with the famous waterfalls, which almost always have their origins in reality: it is just that ravines and precipices are exaggerated, shadows are deeper and trees much thicker than in nature. Already in S. Martino ai Monti he created an effect that nobody before him had dared try, but which he used more than once: he placed a waterfall in the foreground of his picture where it creates a new element of surprise. One of the most remarkable of all his landscapes is the *Flight into Egypt* in the Galleria Doria-Pamphili. The storm-tossed clump of trees occupies the centre of the

Gaspard Dughet: *Flight into Egypt*. Galleri Doria-Pamphili (Alinari).

picture directly over the Holy Family, the sky is full of storm clouds above the mountains, but the usual framing trees are missing. The stormy mood together with the absence of definite boundaries at the side, rouses in the spectator a sense of uncertainty and fear which coincides with the title and subject matter of the picture.

Detailed studies of rocks and trees such as often appear in Dughet's paintings and naturally also his drawings, foreshadow the work of many later painters, Courbet among them, and it is therefore not without justification that Dughet can be called the father of modern landscape painting. And certainly his landscapes, which he painted in large numbers with great flair and often at top speed, were eagerly collected by Roman art lovers and also by foreigners visiting Rome—often by northerners and in particular by the English who fell in love with his romantic and usually idyllic scenes.[297] Gaspar Dughet's influence has thus been greatest outside Italy.

✳

At the beginning of Innocent X's pontificate Pietro da Cortona was still in Florence. When he had visited the city in 1637 the grand duke of Tuscany, Ferdinand II, had already commissioned him to execute frescoes for the Sala della Stufa in the Palazzo Medici.[298] The frescoes which he created there, *The Four Ages of Man*, are among his best works, already revealing the light joyful colours which were so characteristic of his later monumental paintings. In 1641, after finishing these frescoes during a second visit to Florence, he also began to paint the ceilings in the suite of rooms in the Palazzo Pitti which are called after the five planets.[299] Here he collaborated with his pupil, Ciro Ferri, who completed the last room on his own. The paintings consist of lively descriptive scenes, with allegories glorifying the Medici dynasty and an impressive wealth of decorative detail. They differ from Cortona's Roman paintings in being combined with stucco ornament, for which the artist executed the designs himself. It has been claimed on good grounds that *le style Louis XIV* owes more to these frescoes of Pietro da Cortona's than to any other model, as Le Brun's gallery in the Hôtel Lambert and the ceilings in the Louvre and the Hôtel de la Rivière in Paris bear witness.[300]

With his work for the Barberini and Sacchetti families Pietro da Cortona had already gained considerable prestige, but after completing his cycle of frescoes in the Palazzo Pitti he had a reputation as the greatest decorative painter of his time. He returned to Rome in 1647 chiefly to paint the dome in the Oratorians' Chiesa Nuova, to which we shall return later, but he had every reason to expect other commissions from the pope and the Pamphili family as well. Perhaps like Bernini he was a little suspect in the eyes of the new pope at first, since he had been so closely associated with the Barberini. Whatever the reason, a few years were to pass before he received any official papal commands.

During the 1620s Giovanni Lanfranco had already challenged Domenichino's position as the foremost decorative painter in Rome. He subsequently lived for twelve years in Naples, where he was very productive. His works included the great frescoes in the Certosa di S. Martino and in the dome of the S. Gennaro chapel in the cathedral. During the 1640s he easily matched Pietro da Cortona's fame as a fresco painter, but he died in 1647 only a year after returning to Rome. In this last brief Roman period he was able to paint the fresco in the apse of S. Carlo ai Catinari, the *Apotheosis of St. Charles Borromeo*. The composition closely resembles the dome of S. Andrea della Valle, as the conch of the apse is like a semi-dome. Here too the figures appear on clouds; the cardinal is being introduced to the Holy Trinity by the Virgin, with angels and saints in attendance. Those nearest to us are clearly modelled in light and colour, seeming almost tangible, while the figures approaching the background are successively smaller, becoming absorbed into the divine light emanating from the dove of the Holy Spirit at the top of the conch. Two accents of colour dominate the composition: the Virgin's blue cloak and the train of the cardinal's bright red *cappa magna* which trails behind him over the clouds. Thus the artist has achieved the illusion of space without the use of *quadratura*. This fresco, Lanfranco's last work, is often overlooked in the history of art, but in fact it does him more justice than the darkened and damaged frescoes in the dome of S. Andrea della Valle.

During Pietro da Cortona's and Giovanni Lanfranco's absence, Andrea Sacchi was undisputed as the leading artist in Rome. In 1645 he completed the eight paintings for the dome of the Lateran Baptistry, while his pupils, Giacinto Gimignani, Andrea Camassei and Carlo Maratti, painted the frescoes on the walls below. Maratti's *The Destruction of the Idols by Constantine* was painted about 1648 from a cartoon by Sacchi.[301] Camassei was employed for a while by the Barberini on the decoration of their palace, but he never attained any very great success. The third pupil, Gimignani, a native of Pistoia, received

Giovanni Lanfranco: *Apotheosis of St. Charles Borromeo*. S. Carlo ai Catinari (Alinari).

several commissions for altarpieces in Roman churches during the 1640s. In style he has quite strong affiliations with Sassoferrato, but in some ways resembles Romanelli as well.

During the 1650s Sacchi's own production was very limited. One of his most characteristic paintings from this period, and one of the last large paintings which he did, is *The Death of Saint Anne* in S. Carlo ai Catinari, dated 1648–1649.[302] Here his interest in the psychological content and the appropriate attitudes show to great advantage: the old woman's failing gaze is on the Christ child in his mother's arms. The boy leans forward to bless his dying grandmother. The relationship between these two, shown in the direction of their eyes, is the real subject of the painting. It has been pointed out that the composition greatly resembles that of Caravaggio's *The Death of the Virgin* in the Louvre, which might perhaps seem surprising. The difference, however, lies in the perfect decorum of Sacchi's picture. But it is just this insistence on decorum and ideal beauty that can bring Sacchi dangerously close to the excessively sweet.

A similar combination of a classical ideal of beauty and religious sentiment is to be found in the work of that enigmatic painter, Sassoferrato. This artist, whose real name was Giovanni Battista Salvi, was born in the Marches in 1609. He arrived in Rome while still young and probably joined Domenichino's studio before emerging as an independent artist during the 1640s. The

Andrea Sacchi:
Death of St. Anne.
S. Carlo ai Catinari
(ICCD).

Madonna in various poses was his chief subject, and he even made several
copies of his own works. One of his earliest paintings, dated 1643, is the
Madonna del Rosario in S. Sabina which, like most of his pictures, is executed
in an intentionally archaic style approaching the manner of fifteenth century
painting: the forms are powerfully tactile and there is something of the
brilliance of enamel in the colours.[303] Because of these features of his style,
which are very marked, and because so little is known about him, Sassoferrato
was actually believed during the eighteenth century to be a fifteenth-century
master, and many people regarded him as one of the greatest of them all. He
was still extremely popular during the nineteenth century, and not without
reason; many of his paintings call the pre-Raphaelites to mind. His pictures,

Sassoferrato: *Madonna del Rosario*. S. Sabina (Alinari).

often replicas, are to be found in many Italian churches, and there is hardly an
art gallery in Europe without at least one of his works.

   An artist of quite a different temperament was Mattia Preti, one of the more
important of the painters who worked briefly in Rome. He came from Cala-
bria and is generally regarded as belonging to the Neapolitan school. In April
1651 Preti's wall frescoes in the choir of S. Andrea della Valle were unveiled.[304]
The paintings are said to have been received "*con molto applauso universale*" at
the time, but they evoke little enthusiasm in the modern spectator. Perhaps,
though, they are worthy of a little more appreciation than they generally get.
Iconographically they are related to Domenichino's frescoes in the vault,

S. Andrea della Valle, view of apse with Mattia Preti's frescoes (Anderson).

continuing the story of St. Andrew's life to his crucifixion and burial, but in style they are remote from Domenichino's manner. It is very obvious that Preti has borrowed from a wide variety of styles; we can see the influence of Caravaggio—one of the executioners in *The Raising of the Cross* is clearly derived from *The Crucifixion of St. Peter* in the Cappella Cerasi—as well as of Lanfranco and Guido Reni whose works he would have seen during his studies in northern Italy. He was probably also acquainted with the art of Paolo Veronese.[305] The frescoes are monumental, and this is possibly their greatest merit; they combine easily with the architecture of the choir and the great clustered pilasters that surround them, but they are also well coordinated with one another. St. Andrew's dominating cross captures the attention of the spectator from afar and the compositions as a whole are arranged to be viewed from a distance. In colour they are rather subdued, with few touches of brightness: compared with these scenes, Domenichino's paintings in the vault appear almost gaudy. The flickering light in Preti's frescoes evokes a sense of bustle and haste, which makes yet another contrast with Domenichino's calm, well-balanced creations.

These frescoes were the most important work which Preti produced in Rome. Soon after they were finished he left for Modena and thence for Naples.

Mattia Preti: *Saint Andrew Bound to the Cross*. S. Andrea della Valle (Max Hutzel).

Subsequently, apart from a short visit to Rome in 1661, he settled permanently in Malta.

Late in the autumn in 1647 Pietro da Cortona began to work on the frescoes for the dome and choir of the Chiesa Nuova.[306] He began with the dome, and it is obvious that he found inspiration in the dome painting in S. Andrea della Valle which Lanfranco had made twenty years earlier. The subject here is the *Holy Trinity*. The dove of the Holy Spirit is visible in the lantern, while the Father and the Son are sitting on the ring of clouds below. Angels carry the instruments of Christ's passion. Unlike Lanfranco, Pietro da Cortona has painted only one ring of clouds and the main actors are larger and more dominating here, in sharp silhouette against the angelic multitudes in the luminous sky. From Lanfranco the artist has also borrowed the garlands borne by angels around the opening to the lantern, but he has heightened the sense of contrast. Work proceeded slowly and the dome painting was not unveiled until May 1651.[307] Not until the next pontificate did Cortona paint the apsidal conch, and almost ten years were to pass before he decorated the pendentives of the dome and did the fresco in the nave.

The fresco in the dome of the Chiesa Nuova was finished just as plans were

Pietro da Cortona: *The Holy Trinity*, fresco with stuccoes. Chiesa Nuova (BH).

being made to embellish the new gallery in the Palazzo Pamphili in the Piazza Navona. This must have been regarded in artistic circles as the most important commission of the day, and naturally Pietro da Cortona would have cherished a hope of obtaining it. In December the same year his hopes were fulfilled. Unfortunately we do not know what lay behind the decision to appoint him, nor who advised the pope on the matter. But in view of the success of the Barberini ceiling and the prestige Cortona had gained from his work in Florence, the choice cannot have been a particularly difficult one. It is possible that Donna Olimpia may have come into it somehow. She lived in the palace although she was in disgrace at the time, and the choice of this artist, who had been so closely associated with the Barberini, certainly suited her hopes of reconciling the Pamphili with their predecessor's still powerful relatives.[308] On the other hand, Prince Camillo Pamphili and the princess of Rossano had been reconciled with the pope in January that year, and they were in fact the only members of the family who had any real taste or interest in art. Once painting had started on the gallery ceiling, progress was slow and the fresco was not ready until the spring of 1654. In the end the pope became so annoyed by the delay, that he was considering some way of punishing Cortona. But once the

The Gallery in the Palazzo Pamphili with Pietro da Cortona's frescoes (ICCDcop).

frescoes were actually finished and unveiled, his enthusiasm knew no bounds and he made himself unusually gracious to the artist. Cortona received 3,000 ducats for the job, but he refused the ecclesiastical pension offered him by the pope, on the grounds that as a layman he had no right to such an emolument.[309]

The ceiling painting in the Palazzo Barberini's *gran salone* celebrates the virtues and achievements of Urban VIII, and the Pamphili ceiling too is intended as a panegyric in honour of the reigning pope, but the subject this time is taken from Virgil's *Aeneid*. The long narrow gallery did not permit the same grand all-embracing composition that Cortona had used in the Palazzo Barberini; here it is not possible to see the whole ceiling from any one spot, and it was therefore divided into several compartments. A large central *quadro riportato* illustrates the ultimate object of the whole epic, the apotheosis of Aeneas as he is presented by Venus and Cupid to the Olympian gods. In round

Pietro da Cortona: detail of frescoes in the Gallery of Palazzo Pamphili (CI).

medallions at the sides some of the most significant occasions are depicted when the gods intervened in Aeneas' adventures, while the events and trials of his voyage and the landing in Latium are painted immediately above the walls: there we can see the storm-tossed sea, the landing in Latium, the meeting with Evander and the slaying of Turnus. The descent to the underworld and the prophecy of Rome's future greatness appear in the lunettes on the end walls.

Medallions and *quadri riportati* are framed in simulated stucco frames, and are carried by atlantes and maidens. Together with scroll-work and cartouches they are depicted with powerful illusionistic effect, because here—unlike the Palazzo Pitti—there is no real stucco. Everything is painted. Thus the decorative system recalls not only the Barberini ceiling but also, going further back, Carracci's gallery in the Palazzo Farnese as well. The ceiling is loaded with a superabundance of fruit and flower festoons, mascarons, shells, dolphins,

Pietro da Cortona: detail of frescoes in the Palazzo Pamphili Gallery (ICCDcop).

tritons and genii, in a truly astonishing display. Cortona has returned to the palette he used at the Palazzo Pitti, with colours much lighter than those of the Barberini ceiling. These pale, delicate shades speak of a joy and playfulness more reminiscent of the Rococo.

We can assume that the subject was chosen to celebrate the glory of Pope Innocent X,[310] just as Cortona's earlier Roman ceiling sang the praises of Urban VIII. Nevertheless the later work differs from its predecessor in many ways. Here, for instance, the three Olympian goddesses have attributes which coincide with the three heraldic emblems in the Pamphili arms, namely Venus with the dove, Juno with the lily and Minerva with the laurel, and this may have been one reason for choosing an epic in which the three deities appear together. Moreover Aeneas is the legendary father of the Latin people, and therefore the ancestor of Rome itself. Pietro da Cortona and his contemporaries must have been aware that in his epic tale of the wanderings of Aeneas, of the hero's escape from the dangers that beset him, of his descent into Hades and the promise of an endless future dominion, Virgil was looking forward to the Augustan Golden Age, so that Aeneas becomes the *sine qua non* of the world supremecy of the Roman Church.[311] Seventeenth-century scholars would also certainly know that in his *Disputationis camaldulenses* published in 1480, Cristoforo Landino had furnished an allegorical interpretation of the first six books of the Aeneid, in which Rome emerges as the ultimate destination of the soul through the *vita contemplativa*.[312] The expla-

Pietro da Cortona: *Aeneas and Evander*, detail of frescoes in the Palazzo Pamphili Gallery (Thomas Poensgen).

nation of the iconography of the ceiling probably lies not so much in Virgil's actual text as in the traditional humanist interpretation of the story as a moral allegory.

One reason for Cortona's slow progress in the Galleria Pamphili was a simultaneous commission to produce cartoons for the aisle mosaics in St. Peter's.[313] These kept him busy for most of the 1650s, and even during the following pontificate when he was also working on the tribune and pendentives in the Chiesa Nuova. The first mosaic to be made from one of Pietro da Cortona's cartoons was finished in 1653. The mosaics were executed by specialists, among them Abbatini, Fabio Cristofori and Matteo Piccioni.

It was while Pietro da Cortona was occupied in the Chiesa Nuova and the Palazzo Pamphili that Pier Francesco Mola began to work in Rome. Mola had been born in the Swiss canton of Ticino and he arrived in Rome in 1647 at the age of 35. In 1652 he was commissioned to paint *The Preaching of St. Barnabas* for one of the side chapels in S. Carlo al Corso, commissioned by Cardinal Omodei of Milan. With its rich glowing colours and natural-looking cloudy sky, this painting reveals Mola's dependence on North-Italian painting, particularly on Guercino and even Veronese. It is interesting to note that another painting now attributed to Mola, *The Prodigal Son*, which reveals these North-Italian qualities, was earlier believed to be painted by Guercino.

Also in 1652 Carlo Maratti painted episodes from the life of St. Joseph in a side chapel of the church of S. Isidoro, one of the Franciscan churches where

Pier Francesco Mola:
The Prodigal Son.
Unknown location (CI).

Lucas Wadding was active (see vol. I, p. 238). These paintings show that Maratti was still under Andrea Sacchi's influence at this time. It was not until well into the 1660s, after Sacchi's death, that Maratti found his own idiosyncratic style and emerged as one of the great standard-bearers of the classical school. The future thus belonged to him, while the more romantic and painterly Mola never really won the favour of the major official patrons in Rome. For a time he was employed as a kind of court painter by Camillo Pamphili, however, and we shall have reason to return to this episode later.

The End of a Pontificate

Innocent X was 80 years old in the spring of 1654. Towards the end of the year his health began to deteriorate: the senile decay that accompanies arteriosclerosis seems to have become more marked, and he grew increasingly restive and irritable, quarrelling with his nearest and dearest and even dismissing his faithful physician Gabriele Fonseca. In Rome all was confusion, as it was realised that at any moment the throne of St. Peter would be vacant again and

Carlo Maratti:
Flight into Egypt, fresco.
S. Isidoro (ICCDcop).

the almost inevitable disturbances in the city would be breaking out. Wealthy Romans were already barring their doors and putting guards outside their palaces, and nearly all went armed against possible attack.[315]

As the pope lay on his death bed, Donna Olimpia, according to ancient Roman custom, looted the papal apartments of everything she could carry away, leaving the dying man with little more than the shirt on his back. As the end approached the pope sent for his confessor, Father Oliva, and supported by the priest he begged the forgiveness of the assembled company and became reconciled with those he had previously cast off. Chigi, his secretary of state, arrived at the sick bed and drove Donna Olimpia away. As she still continued to hover in the doorway, Father Oliva told her curtly that this was no place for a woman and she would do better to mind her own business. Innocent X died on 7 January 1655.

At the requiem masses or *novemdiales* held in St. Peter's over the next nine days in the presence of the college of cardinals, Cardinal Camillo Astalli demonstrated his feelings by attending, but without assuming the deep violet mourning prescribed for his rank. When the pope was to be buried on the tenth day at a ceremony which according to custom should have been a family affair, it appeared that none of the family was prepared to pay for the customary coffins of wood and lead. Innocent's relatives squabbled about it among themselves in a manner far from edifying: Donna Olimpia pleaded the poverty of the widowed estate, while neither Don Camillo Pamphili nor his brother-in-law Nicolò Ludovisi were prepared to pay a single ducat. And so the pope's corpse lay for weeks behind the sacristy of St. Peter's in a shed which normally served as a storeroom for the masons of the *Reverenda Fabbrica*. One of these men placed a tallow candle by the bier, and another guarded it from rats at night. Finally a canon of St. Peter's, one of the many members of his *famiglia* whom the pope had in fact dismissed, paid for the funeral out of his own pocket as an act of charity.[316] The body was then buried in S. Agnese, but the splendid tomb which Innocent had envisaged for himself never materialised. It was not until 1729 that a rather insipid monument was made by G. B. Maini. It was placed over the main entrance, where it is likely to be mistaken for a balcony if it is noticed at all.

With Innocent X's death Donna Olimpia's influence was definitely a thing of the past. The new pope exiled her to Viterbo, which she had left so many years before. Two years later, while visiting her palace at S. Martino al Cimino in the hope of avoiding the plague, she fell victim to the terrible epidemic that was ravaging the whole of Italy. She left countless valuables and a fortune said to amount to 2 million scudi, an enormous sum for those times.

Coat of Arms of Pope Alexander VII (From Filippo Juvarra, *Raccolta di targhe*, 1732).

CHAPTER II

The Pontificate of Alexander VII (1655–1667)

Introduction—The Seeds of Decline

Nepotism and the Castro War under Urban VIII, followed by the intrigues in the Pamphili family under Innocent X, had combined to undermine the prestige of the papacy and the personal reputation of the popes. The Treaty of Westphalia had shown that in the world of secular politics the Holy See no longer wielded the same authority as before, and had been unable to look after the interests of the Catholic Church with the success it had hoped for. The conclusion of the Peace of the Pyrenees between France and Spain in 1659 put an end to the war which had been going on between these two powers since 1635. As far as Italy was concerned the *status quo* remained the same: Spain still held the Kingdom of Naples as a vassal state and commanded its traditional military bases on the Tuscan coast, while France retained Pinerolo in Piedmont at the foot of the Alps as a military base and assault post in Italy, but refrained from driving the Spanish from their positions. There followed several decades of political inactivity between the Italian states, which also meant a period of peace. But from now on the political and cultural hegemony of Spain in the Italian peninsula was definitely on the decline.

On the religious front Rome was not only the centre of the Catholic world, it was also the foremost place of Christian pilgrimage, since it was not possible to visit the shrines in the Holy Land. At the same time, however, the conflict with the Jansenists and their challenge to the apostolic authority of the pope had a disruptive effect. During the seventeenth century the Roman intelligentsia still had a predominantly ecclesiastical flavour and most of its members were trained in the spirit of the Counter-Reformation. The Council of Trent had called for a deeper and more serious spiritual life, and it cannot be denied that this was accompanied by a certain degree of puritanism and even intolerance—a defensive position on the part of the Roman Church in understandable reaction to the Reformation north of the Alps. As a result of this spiritual climate, scientific endeavour in the world of Roman scholarship was directed almost exclusively towards the fields of history and philology, while the natural sciences—as Galileo had shown—were only too likely to upset the ecclesiastical authorities on grounds of alleged heresy.

Around the middle of the seventeenth century the economic decline which had set in about 50 years earlier reached its lowest level. During the sixteenth century Italy—that is to say, mainly northern and central Italy—was still the most industrially advanced country in Europe, enjoying an unusually high standard of living.[1] But during the second half of the seventeenth century, it was economically backward and impoverished. During the seventy years from 1600 to 1670, Italy's industrial structure fell into almost total decay. The wool industry in particular declined drastically. In Venice, for example, its capacity fell to one-tenth of the level obtaining at the beginning of the century; of the 120 wool companies operating in Florence at the end of the sixteenth century, only 62 were left in 1627; Genoa, whose silk-weaving shops had long been its chief source of wealth, experienced a similar decline as the 18,000 active looms at the end of the sixteenth century were reduced to little more than 2,500 by 1675.[2] The main reason for this decline was the heavy dependence of Italian industry on exports to other countries in Europe and elsewhere. In the course of the seventeenth century the situation changed; Venice lost most of its Asian markets to England, while French silk and woollen cloth came to dominate on the markets in Europe. There was no doubt as to the high quality of the Italian products, but they were no longer modern and above all they were more expensive. Production costs in Italy were high; the guild tradition was too rigid, Italian business and production methods were old-fashioned, and the taxes and dues between the many small states were too high. Wools from England and Holland were actually less durable, but they came in brighter colours and at easier prices. As a result of the continual fighting during the seventeenth century the German, Spanish and Flemish markets lost their purchasing power, which in turn dealt a harsh blow to the metallurgical industry of Milan. Finally, England's shipping and Holland's shipping and banking caused "a complete collapse of those invisible exports which had been one of the pillars of Italian prosperity".[3]

By 1660 Italian industry was suffering a severe depression; its markets had been lost and the population of the country had been drastically reduced by a major epidemic of plague in 1656. From having been a highly industrialised country during the sixteenth century, Italy had thus reverted to an almost exclusively agrarian economy. Consequently, the failure of the popes to establish industries in Rome did not depend on the Romans' alleged laziness and lack of enterprise or on their inadequate work experience, so much as on the unfavourable state of the economy: any attempt to launch a new industry was doomed to failure from the start. The last such experiment was Urban VIII's small-arms factory at Tivoli.

In addition to all this, agriculture in the Campagna ceased almost entirely after the middle of the seventeenth century, mainly because malaria had become firmly established in the area.

The lively activity which had marked the artistic and cultural life of the Barberini epoch had fallen off during the Pamphili pontificate. Established artists naturally continued to work for Innocent X, although in a smaller way, but it was only too clear that art and culture had lost most of the support they had previously enjoyed: in this respect no member of the Pamphili family could measure up to the Barberini.

Rome still occupied a leading role in the cultural life of Europe, but Paris, capital of the new great power, was in the ascendant and was soon to surpass the Eternal City, even if initially it looked towards Rome as the model of all that was best.

Despite the economic depression we have just been describing, the art of the High Baroque reached its culmination in the course of the new pontificate. It was during the 1660s that some of the greatest and most significant monuments of the Roman Baroque were built, and painting and sculpture flourished at least as vigorously as they had done under Urban VIII. What produced this flowering is not altogether clear. Although the economic history of the Papal States has been the subject of some—albeit rather limited—research, we know very little about the finances of the Holy See during the period in question. There are good grounds for supposing that, despite the economic decline, it possessed resources on a scale at which we can now only guess. Moreover the interest and taste of the pope and the papal nephews must have played a decisive part. Just as the spiritual climate of Rome could change radically from one pontificate to the next, so too could the economic situation which provided the necessary base for artistic and cultural life. Immeasurably important was the presence in Rome of a genius of the calibre of Gian Lorenzo Bernini, who was able to combine supreme creative gifts with an ability to organise a large studio and to direct and train a team of artists. The role that Bernini played in Rome would become fully apparent after his death in 1680, when many artists were left without the firm and steady guidance he had so long provided.

The Conclave of 1655

No less than 66 cardinals entered the conclave on 20 January 1655 to elect a successor to Innocent X.[4] It was obvious that now more than ever the chair of St. Peter needed an occupant possessing not only considerable subtlety and diplomatic experience but also a good measure of moral integrity and spiritual depth. Several cardinals could be regarded as fulfilling these requirements, but as on previous occasions political considerations and an excessive regard for the great powers affected the issue, and the conclave dragged on unconscionably. The Spanish-Imperial party in the Sacred College was led this time by the Jesuit Juan de Lugo, while the French party was steered as at the previous conclave by deference to Cardinal Mazarin, who again failed to attend. In fact he could not have attended if he had wanted to; following the flight of the Barberini, Innocent X had decreed that any cardinal living outside Rome without the consent of the pope would automatically lose his right to participate. Mindful of his defeat in 1644, Mazarin had instructed the two cardinals Rinaldo d'Este and Antonio Barberini to promote the election of Giulio Sacchetti. Many people regretted that Innocent X had not worked closely with a chosen cardinal, who could now bring his influence to bear. The cardinals created by Innocent decided to remain neutral and to support the election of the best man, regardless of political pressures. Because of their uncommitted stance, this group in the Sacred College with Decio Azzolino at their head was nicknamed the *squadrone volante* or flying squadron.

During the first few days of the conclave votes were scattered among several candidates. Chief among these were Giulio Sacchetti, Fabio Chigi and Pier Luigi Carafa, who received roughly the same number of votes in several *scrutini*. First after a couple of weeks of fruitless *scrutini* did Sacchetti begin to emerge as the most likely candidate. The Spanish cardinals then exercised their king's veto to block him. The pro-French faction declared itself horrified at this undue interference on the part of a temporal power in the election of the pope and continued to give their votes to Sacchetti, but it was now impossible to achieve the requisite majority. All attempts to collect enough votes for the election of Chigi failed, because it was known that Mazarin resented his anti-French stance at the time of the Treaty of Westphalia and that he therefore opposed his election. Sacchetti regarded Chigi as the worthiest candidate, and so without saying a word or consulting the other cardinals he wrote to Mazarin, listing the arguments in favour of Chigi and seeking to change the French minister's mind.[5] In the weeks that followed, Chigi took no personal action to promote his own election.

The cardinals, locked up as they were, found their patience sorely tried. They all complained of the foul air in the confined space; several of them fell ill and had to leave the conclave, and on 17 February Carafa died. Six weeks passed before Mazarin's reply arrived, permitting the pro-French cardinals to vote for Chigi if the election of Sacchetti really proved impossible. Sacchetti now declared himself unwilling to stand, causing something of a sensation and leaving nothing in the way of Chigi's candidature. On 7 April Chigi was duly elected with only one opposing vote—his own, which he gave to his friend Sacchetti. Chigi assumed the name of Alexander VII in honour of Alexander IV, another Sienese and one of the most powerful of the mediaeval popes. His arms with the sextuple mount and the eight-pointed star—often quartered with Della Rovere's oak—was eventually to become as common in Rome as the bees of the Barberini.

Alexander VII's coronation was celebrated on 18 April. On the same day, so Gigli tells us,[6] an unusually mild spring was followed by a violent storm with hail and an icy north wind causing terrible havoc in the vineyards around Rome.

When the question of Chigi's *possesso* came up, the pope said he wanted everything to be kept as simple as possible and the money thus saved to be given to the poor; he intended to walk barefoot from S. Maria Maggiore to the Lateran, accompanied by all the clergy. But his advisers persuaded him that the Romans would be disappointed to miss the customary spectacle, and the money would anyway benefit the poor since many of the costumes that brightened the cortège were given later to impoverished members of the

Giovanni Battista Gaulli: portrait of Pope Alexander VII, oil on canvas (Courtesy Heim Gallery, London).

nobility. Moreover, they added, the festive decorations would provide work for a multitude of craftsmen and artists. The pope gave in with one reservation: there were to be no triumphal arches as these were a heathen invention. On 9 May his *possesso* took place, with the functionaries of the Capitol in all their usual finery of brocade and velvet, but otherwise things were on a slightly simpler scale than usual.[7] Thus already at the beginning of the new reign it could be seen that Alexander VII had the best of intentions, but he was weak and not always able to impose his will.

Alexander VII—his Personality and Entourage

It was a long time since a new pope had been greeted with such joy and high hopes. The new pontiff was only 56 years old, and there was every reason to look forward to a long and vigorous pontificate.[8]

Already as a cardinal, Chigi had earned general respect for his political experience and wisdom, and admiration for his modesty and integrity. The Romans were familiar with the appearance of this cardinal, with his dark hair and beard and his finely drawn features and somewhat sensitive air.[9] But his pale complexion was evidence of delicate health: since his youth Fabio Chigi had suffered severely from kidney stones, which often caused him considerable pain. His keen intelligence was widely recognised; the range of his learning and culture was extensive, and it is with justification that he has been remembered as one of the last representatives on the throne of St. Peter of the long tradition of Italian humanism from Petrarch onwards.

Alexander VII was distinguished by a profound piety, in which humanist learning was combined with a deeply serious disposition.[10] The extent of his asceticism was revealed to others at the conclave when he assumed the papal robes, and he was seen to be wearing a hair shirt next to the skin. As pope he began each day with a long period of meditation. He said his own mass, and then as a token of thanksgiving attended another.

Fabio Chigi's personal piety had long been influenced by the teaching of St. François de Sales, whose works he had eagerly studied. He was particularly inspired by the *Introduction à la vie dévote*, one of the classics of Catholic spiritual writing, which for years was part of his daily reading. The central theme of this work, which is also known as *Filotea* after the fictitious person whom the author is addressing, is that love between God and the soul is the source of salvation. All are capable of exercising the Christian virtues, whatever their position in life may be; the way of contemplation is thus open to everyone, in professional or domestic life. Anyone who truly desires to achieve salvation can do so, with the aid of divine grace, since through His death and resurrection Christ has opened the path of salvation to all. François de Sales introduced a new type of piety into the Catholic Church. His importance in this respect is inestimable, and his subsequent recognition as *Doctor ecclesiae* in 1877 seems more than justified.

In his own anonymously published writings,[12] Alexander VII adressed himself to the dissemination of François de Sales' teaching, and we cannot really understand him as a pope or as a man, without taking account of this profound commitment. Fabio Chigi saw de Sales' gentle optimistic view of salvation as a wholesome counterweight to the gloomy Jansenist doctrine of predestination.

An important element in Alexander VII's spiritual life was the meditation on death—something which was typical of the spiritual mode of the times. As a cardinal he is said to have drunk from a silver goblet with a skull engraved on the bottom, and he kept on his desk a marble skull which Bernini had carved.

Immediately after he was made pope, he had placed in his bedroom the lead coffin in which he would one day be buried. It is also interesting to note that, unlike Urban VIII, Alexander VII loathed astrology—*"ingannatrice degli uomini"*—which he regarded as a superstition unworthy of a Christian.[13]

One of the leading principles of Alexander VII's spiritual life was his unreserved submission to the will of God,[14] an attitude which was perhaps the ultimate cause of his organisational and disciplinary stance as pope, and of his intransigence towards the Jansenists.

Despite poor health Alexander VII was indefatigable in the execution of his duties, ignoring the advice of his confessor, Father Cancellotti, that he should try to husband his strength. He would spend six or seven hours a day in audience, and every Sunday he held a general audience at which the poor in need of help and comfort were particularly welcome. It was also characteristic of this pope that despite his deep piety and humility he expected people to show him the greatest respect: everyone in audience except cardinals and ambassadors had to kneel to him. But it was not to his own person that this reverence was due; it was to his high office as Christ's representative on earth.

Alexander VII was always prepared to study any issue with the greatest care, but had little inclination to make decisions on his own. After his two some-what autocratic predecessors he went to the other extreme, and often placed too much reliance on the advice of others. All too many tasks were delegated to the officers of the Curia—a tendency which only increased as the years passed and he withdrew more often to be alone, to devote himself to medita-tion, or to spend time in discussion with his friends. His reign is consequently marked by a certain lack of resolution.[15]

Many of the pope's closest advisers were highly intelligent men, and fore-most among them was Giulio Rospigliosi. As papal nuncio in Madrid Rospi-gliosi had proved himself a disinterested and skilful diplomat, but as one of Barberini's closest friends he had fallen into disfavour under Innocent X. At the beginning of his reign, Alexander made Rospigliosi a cardinal and appointed him Secretary of State. Cardinal Corrado was put in charge of the *Dataria*, which gave him a key position with respect to the papal finances; Corrado was a specialist on canon law, but after spending the greater part of his life in a monastery he was not very familiar with secular politics. Cardinal Imperiali became governor of the city of Rome; there was no doubt of his unusual ability, but he was regarded as authoritarian and arrogant.

Important positions among the pope's personal advisers were occupied by the Jesuit Sforza Pallavicino and the Cistercian Giovanni Bona. Pallavicino was professor of theology and philosophy at the *Collegio romano*, and since receiving his cardinal's hat in 1659 he had been the pope's chief adviser on theological questions.[16] Bona was superior general of a reformed Cistercian congregation and a deeply learned liturgical historian and patrist; already as a cardinal, Chigi had been bound to him in personal friendship.[17]

Bernini: portrait of Pope
Alexander VII, engraving
by F. de Poilly (ING:GS,
inv. no. 52311).

Alexander VII's Nepotism

Chigi had always been deeply attached to his relatives in Siena, but everyone
knew that as a cardinal he had spoken with great severity against papal
nepotism, the many disadvantages of which he had seen at close hand. This was
in fact one of the reasons why the *squadrone volante* had favoured his election.
At the beginning of his pontificate he announced a firm determination to keep
his relatives away from Rome, even though many of them were living in fairly
reduced circumstances; the enormous wealth of the famous Agostino had long
since melted away. The pope's elder brother, Mario Chigi, was a diligent and
gifted man of business who had managed with some success the small family
fortune that remained. In vain did cardinals and ambassadors point out to the
pope that it would be quite natural for him to send for his relatives, who ought
now to live in the social and economic circumstances appropriate to them,
without too great a gap between themselves and the pope. Alexander dismissed
all such advice, declaring that he had more important matters to deal with and
that he would wait and see.[18]

In the long run it proved impossible for Alexander VII to stick to the firm
line he had adopted towards his family, and when he had been pope for a year
he began to need their support and to require someone at his side whom he
could trust. But conscientious as ever, and eager not to repeat the mistakes of
Urban VIII, he first consulted the cardinals and his theological advisers about

Giov. Maria Morandi:
portrait of Cardinal Flavio
Chigi, engraving by
G. Testana (BAV).

the proper extent of his generosity. Among those whose advice he sought were
Father Pallavicino and Cardinal Juan de Lugo, both former members of Urban
VIII's special congregation with, at that time, an accommodating attitude
towards nepotism.[19] At the beginning of May 1656 and on Pallavicino's advice
the pope issued an apostolic constitution, *Inter gravissimas*, severely restricting the possibilities for papal nephews to accumulate excessive wealth. Only
then did he send for his relatives. Their response was immediate, and they left
at once for Rome travelling as fast as they could "*in velocissime carrozze*".
They were received by the pope with the greatest simplicity at Castel Gandolfo
on 16 May.[20]

   Don Mario Chigi was granted the honorary titles which traditionally fell to
the pope's closest kin: commander of the papal army and governor of Borgo
Leonino; in addition he was made prefect of the papal *annona* in charge of
food supplies, a job which he managed with great success. Several years later
the Venetian ambassador Sagredo described Don Mario as a wise old man,
chary of words and accustomed to speaking in proverbs as Tuscans often do;
he never told lies, but was said to be grasping.[21] His greatest passion was
hunting. Don Mario may have been greedy but he was not ambitious for
power, and his wife Donna Berenice—as unlike Donna Olimpia Maidalchini as
it was possible to be—stayed in the background. Only exceptionally were the
female members of the family ever received at the papal court.

   It was decided that Agostino Chigi, son of one of the pope's brothers who had died, should become head of the family. He was made *capitano* of Castel Sant'Angelo and head of the two papal lifeguards, as well as governor of Benevento and Civitavecchia and commander of the fortresses of Perugia and Ascoli. He was married to a daughter of the princess of Rossano by her first husband. The pope agreed to officiate at the wedding in 1658, but it was celebrated at an extremely simple ceremony in his private chapel. Agostino and his wife subsequently had seventeen children. At the time of the marriage the pope purchased for Don Agostino the town of Farnese—now a principality —for 275,000 scudi, while out of courtesy to the pope Emperor Leopold I created the young man a prince of the Holy Roman Empire.[22]

Mario's son Flavio Chigi was destined to become cardinal-nephew. He was a gentle young man of 25, with a round face surrounded by dark curly hair. Sagredo described him as balanced and cultivated, always courteous and lacking superfluous mannerisms.[23] The pope expected serious conduct of his nephew, and sent him first to the Jesuits to study and prepare himself for ordination. Only then, in April 1657, was he raised to the cardinalate and given S. Maria del Popolo as his titular church. He thus acquired the official rank of *cardinal padrone*, becoming at least theoretically the equal of Rospigliosi. However, the pope made sure that Flavio's power was strictly circumscribed—a precaution which proved unnecessary as the young man had little interest in anything connected with politics. Sagredo reported that if an ambassador tried to discuss some important matter with Flavio, he would soon see that the new cardinal was not listening but was thinking of something else. His greatest interests were hunting, conversation, drama, and the pleasures of the table. But, Sagredo added, "as far as his morals are concerned, I do not think we can find anything to reproach him with".[24] Some of his other contemporaries spoke with a certain amount of malice about the sensuality shown by the young cardinal and the "venereal impulses which powerfully raged within him"[25]—not, of course, that there is anything very remarkable about this in a young man of 25. But whatever the truth of the matter, Flavio always behaved with dignity, and no scandal ever attached to his name.

Agostino's younger brother Sigismondo was only six years old when Alexander became pope. He showed signs of great gifts at an early age and was allowed to embark upon an ecclesiastical career, although his uncle considered him too young to become a cardinal. Antonio Bichi, a more distant relative who had previously functioned as internuncio in Flanders with great success, was given his cardinal's hat but was never allowed any influence or any opportunities for the acquisition of great wealth.

As the years passed, however, Alexander VII became more generous towards his family. Perhaps it was partly his precarious health which made him unable to maintain the strict attitude he had adopted at first. With the pope's help Agostino Chigi acquired the title of count of Campagnano; the purchase price of the land was 345,000 scudi. In 1659 Mario and Agostino bought the princess of Rossano's palace—the present Palazzo Chigi—on the Corso next to the column of Marcus Aurelius. And in 1662, with financial aid from the pope, Ariccia in the Alban Hills was bought from Giulio Savelli. At this time it was estimated that the pope had spent 620,000 scudi on the acquisition of feudal lands and palaces for his family.[26] But although the papal nephews had thus been tempted to increase their wealth, despite the rules, they never acquired any political influence. Not even Flavio exploited his high position in order to obtain more power. Thus in both the secular and ecclesiastical spheres the conduct of papal policy owed nothing to the influence of the pope's nephews. This did not prevent general complaints towards the end of Alexander's reign that the pope's brother had abused his position to line his own pockets, and when Don Mario died in 1667 the Romans made no secret of their adverse feelings about him.

The Papal States—Economic Problems and Plague

In 1656 a *censimento* gave the number of inhabitants in the Papal States as a little over 1,800,000, of whom 120,596 lived in Rome itself.[27] The numbers are approximate, partly because children under three years of age were not usually included, and in the case of Rome because the inhabitants of the Jewish ghetto were not counted either.

At the time of Alexander VII's accession the financial situation was anything but bright, with a national debt estimated at 48 million scudi.[28] Several attempts were made to reorganise and improve the state of the economy, and one of the pope's foremost financial advisers was Virgilio Spada. The most important step was to reduce the interest on the *luoghi di monti* or state bonds from 4½ to 4 per cent. This was rather an unpopular move, and it also seems to have had the effect of increasing the nominal value of the bonds. Further, certain high-interest-bearing *monti non vacabili* were redeemed, but a new loan then had to be raised in what were known as *monti ristorati* at a cost of over 12 million scudi.[29] However, the overall effect of these measures was fairly limited, and the old economic system complete with its problems remained essentially unchanged. The pope certainly reduced his own court costs, but otherwise little was done to curb expenditure; large sums were lavished on the nephews and on costly building enterprises, as well as on subsidies to the Venetians for the war against the Turks. About one year after Alexander VII's death it was estimated that the national debt had risen to 52 million scudi.[30]

At the beginning of the Chigi pontificate Italy was hit by bad weather and a failed harvest; among other things heavy hail storms inflicted grievous damage particularly on crops in the neighbourhood of Rome. Grain was consequently in short supply. In order not to have to raise the price of bread the authorities imposed an unpopular measure reducing the weight of each loaf from 8 to 6 *oncie*, not only in Rome but also in the immediate surroundings of the city. The pope arranged for grain to be imported by the *Camera apostolica* from Sicily, Sardinia, Provence and Holland. No less than 300,000 scudi, a colossal sum for the times, was set aside for this purpose.[31] In the end, however, the

Bernini: portrait bust of
pope Alexander VII,
terracotta. Palazzo Chigi,
Ariccia (BH).

price of bread had to be raised, and people complained that the loaves smelt
unpleasant and were barely edible.

The food trade was still subject to detailed regulations, and although the
situation was a little easier than under Innocent X most of the earlier controls
were retained. The innumerable restrictions and prohibitions regulating the
trade in grain and extending also to fodder, vegetables, fruit, meat and so on,
were intended to prevent food shortages in Rome—in fact protecting the city
to the detriment of the countryside—as well as to inhibit speculation and
subsequent increases in price. This last applied particularly to the tangle of
stipulations that regulated trade in olive oil.[32] It was forbidden to store grain,
and all grain or bread had to be sold before the end of October; merchants
from the Campagna were forbidden to buy bread in Rome, and the grain
distributed to bakers by the *Camera apostolica* was not to be used to make
vermicelli or other pasta. Severe penalties were naturally imposed on those
who tried to stop the transport of grain into Rome.[33]

In order to improve the financial situation yet more monopolies, including
one on tobacco, were added to the enormous number that already existed. The
pope would have liked to abolish the unpopular tax on ground grain, *la gabella
sul macinato*, but was compelled to raise it instead.

At the beginning of Alexander VII's reign the Venetian ambassador reckoned that the annual revenue of the Papal States was almost 2 million scudi, but
that 1.4 million of this went on paying interest on *monti*.[34] He assumed that the
major source of income was the sale of offices, the sums concerned being
handled by the *Dataria*. Generally speaking, however, we have only fragmen-

tary information about the papal finances at this time; much research remains to be done here.

With his own experiences as a member of the Curia in mind, Alexander VII also set about reforming the administration of the Papal States in various ways. Thus, officials of the papal courts were forbidden to accept gifts or "presents". Nonetheless complaints were heard towards the end of the reign of divers abuses in the legal administration. The nephews in particular were partly to blame for this, and it seems that Don Mario Chigi, so conscientious in other ways, exploited his position in this respect. The system of "perquisites" was probably difficult to uproot, but now it was spreading downwards and even minor officials and *uditori* in the *Sacra rota* were giving way to the temptation.[36]

Shortly before his death in 1663 Giulio Sacchetti submitted a memorandum[37] to the pope pointing out various malpractices in the administration of justice in the Papal States. These had crept into the system despite the good intentions of the pope, mainly due to his lack of firmness and the delicate state of his health. Sacchetti describes in vivid detail how the rights of the poor are more or less non-existent, how bureaucratic quibbling endlessly prolongs cases which could be dealt with in a couple of days, and how ruthlessly the tax collectors proceed against the people. And as a result of all this, Sacchetti declares, it is the pope as head of the state who is becoming the butt of the people's hostility. Sacchetti also suggests ways of increasing the productivity of agriculture; he mentions the shortage of labour and pleads for subsidies: farmers need the incentive of adequate earnings. This paper was in the nature a warning issued by one of the pope's closests friends and colleagues but Alexander seems to have resented the implied criticism. At any rate nothing was done, although some sort of action was certainly needed—but it would have required a man of far greater energy and thrust.

The population of the Roman Campagna was drastically reduced during the 1650s and 1660s, largely due to the ravages of malaria. Some progress was made in tackling this problem, however, as it was about this time that quinine began to be prescribed for the fever. But it was still impossible to take any effective action to halt the spread of the disease, as nobody knew how it was passed on. Attempts to drain the Pontine Marshes and to acquire new tracts for cultivation, did not help. There were still a few cultivated areas in the Campagna, particularly the vineyards along the Aniene, but otherwise the countryside between Rome and Tivoli was almost completely depopulated. From Rome to the Alban Hills it was equally deserted, especially the low-lying marshy areas towards the coast.[38]

In May 1656 when the pope had just moved out to his beloved villa at Castel Gandolfo, the first cases of bubonic plague, which had been ravaging Naples, appeared in Rome. The pope returned to the city at once and together with Don Mario Chigi initiated a series of measures to limit the epidemic.[39] A special health congregation was appointed under Cardinal Sacchetti. First, communications between Rome and the south had to be cut off; only eight of the city gates remained open, and all travellers had to be kept in quarantine. Holy water was no longer used in the churches, and any services such as the *quarantore* which attracted large numbers of people were cancelled. A special plague hospital was established as during the plague of 1630, but this time on Tiber Island. Those discharged from the hospital were sent to Porta San Pancrazio, and those whose homes were shut up following a case of the plague were given temporary lodgings at S. Eusebio in the Monti district. Alexander visited the various parts of the city in person, often on foot and careless of the risk of infection. And in fact the epidemic was held in check: of a population of approximately 120,000 a total of 15,000 deaths were registered between May 1656 and August 1657, which was regarded as something of a miracle. We need only compare this with Naples which lost about half its population of 300,000, or Genoa with roughly half its inhabitants dead.[40] In Rome the population fell to a little over 100,000, but then gradually began to recover. By 1660 the city reported 106,888 registered inhabitants, excluding about 4,500 members of the Jewish colony.[41] The plague was succeeded in 1657 by an epidemic of influenza, possibly the most severe outbreak since the great European epidemic of 1580.

Foreign Policy

In the field of foreign policy Alexander VII was unable to live up to the high hopes that had accompanied his accession, but this was hardly his own fault as events were steered by circumstances beyond his control. His attempts to mediate in the war between France and Spain were without effect. Previously the Holy See would almost certainly have been invited to participate in peace negotiations between any of the great Catholic powers; Fabio Chigi had himself represented the pope at the peace negotiations in Osnabrück for instance. But now in 1659 the Peace of the Pyrenees was concluded without the pope's knowledge, representing a moral defeat for the papacy. Mazarin's unwillingness to cooperate with the Holy See may have depended on the anti-French attitude adopted by Innocent X and Chigi in negotiating the Treaty of Westphalia. Nonetheless Alexander VII did not veer from the earlier policy of looking after the interests of the Catholic Church. When the Emperor Ferdinand III died unexpectedly in 1657 leaving no instructions about the succession, certain forces in Germany sought to promote the election of a Protestant emperor. To the pope such an outcome would have been a disaster and one which had to be prevented at all costs. Alexander therefore launched an intensive campaign of diplomatic activity, which had no effect at all on events. To his great satisfaction, however, Leopold of Hapsburg was elected.

Poland was being attacked at this time by the Swedes under Charles X, and the pope was anxious to support a country which despite political weakness could still be regarded as a bulwark of Catholicism against Russia and the great

Protestant power in the north. For this reason he subsidised Poland's defence.

Alexander VII's foreign policy was entirely dominated by the Turkish danger, which was terrifyingly real.[42] The pope supported Venice, whose traditional maritime supremacy was under threat of collapse. Although she was losing her possessions in the Aegean Sea one after the other, Venice was still holding on in Crete, where Candia—the present Heraklion—had been bravely withstanding siege since 1648. The pope granted substantial subsidies to the Venetians, but he also imposed a condition: that the Jesuits who had been banished from the republic in 1605 for their loyalty to Paul V should be allowed to return, and this was conceded by the Senate in 1657. Alexander even allowed the Venetians to tax the Church, as well as closing down several monasteries and selling their property. The papal galleys under the command of Alexander's relative Giovanni Bichi were sent to support the Venetians with 1,000 men and they took part in the fighting in the Dardanelles. The allies achieved some success, but partly because of disagreement between the Venetians and the Maltese they were unable to exploit their victories. Nonetheless it was the superiority of the Christians at sea which made possible Candia's continued resistance.

On the European continent the Turks were pushing westwards. The imperial forces suffered several serious setbacks, among others at Klausenburg and Granvaradin, which left Hungary defenceless. From 1660 onwards a Turkish offensive against the Danube region was expected. Leopold I sought help from the pope, and like Venice before him he was granted generous subsidies; the pope also allowed the sale of church property in the hereditary Hapsburg possession with the exception of liturgical furniture, and he looked into new ways of obtaining money from the revenues of the clergy and the monastic orders. Further, 200,000 pounds of powder were put at the emperor's disposal from the papal supplies.

At the beginning of the 1660s Alexander VII was busy forging plans for the creation of a Christian league against the Turks, and he conducted energetic diplomacy among the Christian princes with this in mind. But the results were meagre. Some relief came with Leopold's victory over the Turks at the battle of the River Raab in August 1664 and the subsequent peace of Vasvàr. But the danger was by no means over, and the pope continued his efforts. His exhortations for an alliance against the Turks had always been foiled mainly by the opposition of France. It suited Mazarin to undermine the imperial power, and so he was not interested in reducing the pressure exerted by the Turks in Eastern Europe. It is tragic to see how the political egoism and shortsighted ambitions of the Great Powers scotched any effective Western collaboration on this issue that was so vital to them all.

On 9 March 1661 Cardinal Mazarin died. In his will—perhaps in an effort to appease his conscience—he left a sum of 600,000 livres for the prosecution of the war against the Turks. The 22-year-old Louis XIV now took the reins of government into his own hands and pursued the same policy as Mazarin—although, if possible, with even greater cynicism.[44] Among other things he used a variety of pretexts to prevent payment of the money Mazarin had allotted to the struggle against the Turks.

At one point the strained relations between France and the Holy See led to a dangerous crisis and almost to open war. In June 1662 the duke of Créqui accompanied by a large suite arrived in Rome to take up his duties as French ambassador. He was received at the Palazzo Farnese, where the Duke of Parma had put an apartment at his disposal. It was nine years since France had appointed an ambassador to the Holy See. Créqui's immediate predecessor, d'Aubeville, had been merely a subordinate agent. Officially Créqui's task, as d'Aubeville's had been before him, was to conclude a defensive pact between the Christian princes against the Turks. In fact, though, Louis XIV had given him secret instructions not to allow any such alliance to be formed, and the whole thing was simply a cover-up for Louis' anti-imperial policy.[45] Right from the start Créqui behaved with extreme arrogance, and his pretensions on certain points of etiquette could not fail to offend both the pope's nephews and Alexander VII personally.[46] He also wanted the customary diplomatic immunity—the "liberty of quarters"—attaching to his embassy to be extended to the blocks surrounding the palace, a demand to which the pope would not agree on any account. Créqui also complained that the pope's Corsican guard, whose job was the maintenance of order, was marching past the Palazzo Farnese every day. The simple reason for this, of course, was that their barracks were nearby.

On 20 August a fateful intermezzo took place.[47] A Corsican soldier was knocked down and insulted near the Ponte Sisto by some of Créqui's men. The Corsican guard was so infuriated by this treatment of one of their colleagues that, despite the orders of their commanders, they surrounded the Palazzo Farnese and opened fire. Créqui himself barely escaped with his life, while his wife, who was returning home in her carriage, was forced to flee and seek refuge with Cardinal d'Este. Peace was restored when Don Mario Chigi and Cardinal Imperiali, the governor of Rome, hastily dispatched troops to the scene and forced the Corsicans to withdraw.

This intermezzo was indubitably provoked by the French, but the Corsicans had committed a violation of ambassadorial immunity, as well as defying the orders of their officers. The pope recognised these facts and appointed a special commission consisting of three pro-French cardinals under Sacchetti to try to establish exactly what had happened and to punish the culprits, while Cardinal Flavio Chigi in person expressed the pope's regret to the ambassadress. But Créqui would not be mollified by these conciliatory gestures; instead he seized upon the incident as a welcome opportunity for humiliating the pope. First Alexander offered to move the garrison to another part of the town, and later to remove the Corsican guard from the city altogether. At any rate the culprits themselves were to be punished, although several of them fled from Rome before any action could be taken. Insisting that his own personal safety was at risk, Créqui recruited a guard of a 1,000 men, although a few days later he left Rome with a small company together with Cardinal d'Este. From Tuscany he sent his demands: Cardinal Imperiali was to be dismissed from his post as governor, Mario Chigi called to account for the "coup" against the embassy, and 50 Corsicans and their commanders executed in the Piazza Farnese. Naturally the pope would not agree to any part of this.

On reaching Paris, Créqui began to inflame Louis XIV against the pope, at the same time claiming this as an excellent opportunity for depriving the Holy See of Avignon. The Parisian populace was being stirred up by pamphlets and general propaganda, and the papal nuncio was forced to flee the country in undignified haste. At the beginning of 1663 Avignon was occupied, and an army of 20,000 men was ready to march against the Papal States from Savoy and Pinerolo, the French enclave in Piedmont. Meanwhile, however, negotiations had started, and a year later through the mediation by the grand duke of Tuscany a settlement was reached in Pisa between Louis XIV and Alexander VII, on conditions humiliating to the pope.[48] Flavio Chigi was to be sent to Paris as papal legate to submit an official apology to the king, and only after that would Avignon be returned. Once Flavio had arrived in Paris, he found some compensation for the humiliations heaped upon himself and the pope by exploiting a potent weapon of those times—etiquette. He insisted successfully that the French court show him all the respect due to the pope's recognised representative, thus making it quite clear to the Parisians that in rank and dignity their king was inferior to the Roman pontiff.

Créqui returned to Rome as ambassador in 1664, which was further evidence if any were needed of Louis XIV's lack of interest in conciliating the pope. If possible the duke behaved with even greater arrogance than before, and when it became obvious that he was doing more harm than good as the representative of his king he was at last recalled.

Louis XIV recognised in the end that his anti-papal policy was causing bad blood in many parts of Catholic Europe, and so for the sake of appearances he sent a small French contingent to Crete to help in the defence of Candia, but as he did not want to provoke the sultan his men had to fight under the Venetian flag. At the same time Avignon was restored to the pope. When the Turks invaded Hungary and Vienna was threatened, Louis dispatched troops to the front and then took part—still unofficially—in the Christian victory at Raab in 1664. But Louis was always careful not to damage his good relations with the Sublime Porte.

Alexander VII Pontifex Maximus

In the sphere of internal ecclesiastical affairs Alexander VII's pontificate was more important than it has sometimes been given credit for. He began by introducing several reforms in the papal court and the Curia. But with typical tact and consideration he was always anxious to move cautiously, so as not to cast an unfavourable light upon his predecessor.[49]

Alexander VII demanded irreproachable moral conduct of his family, and at the beginning of his reign dismissed several court officials and servants because their personal conduct was deemed unworthy of men working close to the pope. He insisted that all ceremonial at the papal court should be followed down to the smallest detail, and he was particularly anxious that the *cappella pontificia*, those liturgical ceremonies which he attended in person, should be conducted in a worthy manner. Even the cardinals were subject to the pope's strictures: he disapproved profoundly, he told them, of their participation in the wordly delights of the carnival, which were inappropriate to the dignity of their position. On this point, however, his exhortations were not obeyed.

Alexander VII drew up new rules regulating the *prelatura*, i.e. recruitment to the Curia and advancement to the higher curial offices. He stipulated certain moral and educational requirements, such as university qualifications in law, all of which seem perfectly appropriate to the selection of judges for the papal courts. But how can we explain the condition that appointees should command an annual income of their own amounting to at least 1,500 scudi?[50] Did the pope hope to ensure that the members of his Curia should belong to a particular social stratum? If this was his idea, then the minimum income required was certainly too low, and could hardly have affected the social composition of the Curia. A more probable explanation is that the possession of a fixed income would eliminate the temptation to accept those illegal perquisites and bribes that were still so widespread and persistent; nor was it intended that the Curia should be regarded as a kind of maintenance system for intellectuals, as was so often the case before the Reformation.

Several of Alexander VII's predecessors had undertaken the apostolic visitation of churches, monasteries and hospitals in the Vicariate of Rome. The names of Clement VIII and Urban VIII in particular come to mind. Alexander VII now established a special *Congregazione della Sacra Visita Apostolica* for the purpose. A wealth of documentary material in the *Archivio Segreto* of the Vatican can throw a good deal of light on the spiritual life of the period, but scholars have done little hitherto to tap this source of information. Massimo Petrocchi is one of the few exceptions.[51]

During 1656 the pope participated personally as bishop of Rome in the visitation of the four papal basilicas. During the subsequent visitation of parishes, monasteries and other ecclesiastical institutions, many abuses —mainly economic—were revealed and subsequently corrected.[52] Among other things it appeared that excessive or even quite illegal fees were sometimes being charged. Also it turned out that the ancient custom, which was almost an institution, of begging at the church door was not safe from abuse: complaints were made that beggars were in league with the police, *gli sbirri*, and that the two groups together often made merry in the hostelries of Rome at night. There was frequent mention of the noise during church services: people talked and gossiped during mass and even during the papal ceremonies. In the monastery churches discipline was often poor during divine office, which was recited carelessly or too quickly, and people complained that monks were failing to attend or, if they did so, that they talked all the time. A terrible scandal had once occurred at the Lateran Basilica, when the canons started quarrelling during a ceremony and ended by throwing their breviaries at one another's heads. But, as Petrocchi points out, a list of abuses alone gives us a distorted picture of the true spiritual life. Where are the descriptions of the humble priests who devoted themselves to their apostolic calling in silence and self-denial? What do we know of the deep and genuine piety of the ordinary people of Rome? We can learn more about this from the *statu animarum* or reports which the parish priests had been instructed to keep since the beginning of the century, and which brought them into personal contact with all their parishioners in the course of the year. In these archives, too, much material remains to be uncovered.

Rome also had its saints whose deeds and example exercised a benevolent influence on the spiritual life of the city. One of these was Chiara Maria della Passione, a Carmelite nun at S. Egidio in Trastevere. On one occasion she received a visit from no less a person than Queen Christina of Sweden seeking advice about the path of contemplation. More important, although later almost forgotten and now little known at any rate outside Rome, was St. Carlo da Sezze,[53] who died in 1675 and was canonised in 1956. He worked mainly at S. Francesco a Ripa and S. Pietro in Montorio, where his influence was considerable. He also wrote a treatise on the three ways of meditation which is a major source of knowledge about seventeenth-century mysticism.[54] It is interesting that he advocated frequent confession and daily communion, which was very unusual at that time. Above all St. Carlo da Sezze emphasised the importance of prayer, and for all these reasons came to be the foremost representative of Franciscan piety of his day.

The process of beatification of François de Sales, in which the pope took a personal interest, began under Alexander VII and was completed in 1661. Already by 1665 this spiritual leader whom the pope held in such great devotion was canonised.

One of Alexander VII's first acts as pope was to declare his position on Jansenism, for feeling in France had certainly not been quelled by his predecessor's measures.[55] The severity and gloom of the Jansenists' approach was totally alien to the pope's personality; he had become familiar with their teaching when he was nuncio in Cologne and his personal views are clearly stated in letters he wrote at that time.[56] The French Jansenists did not want to back down, insisting that their view of the relation between divine grace and salvation, and above all of predestination, fully agreed with orthodox Catholic tradition and the teaching of the early Church Fathers. As the spiritual rift in France was growing sharper, the pope was compelled to issue an apostolic constitution, *Ad sanctam beati Petri sedem* in 1656, confirming the official condemnation of the five propositions in Jansen's controversial book *Augustinus* and arousing further opposition in France. The Port Royal group, headed by Arnauld, fanned the flames of the struggle and renewed old Gallican ambitions of independence from Rome. Their new arguments were investigated by the Holy Office and subsequently answered by the pope in 1665 in a second bull, *Regiminis apostolici*, which with minor modifications upheld his previous firm opposition to the Jansenists. Although Alexander VII had the unreserved support of Louis XIV here, nothing could prevent increasing opposition to the pope both at the Sorbonne and in the *parlement* of Paris. The pope decided that four French bishops who refused to submit should be heard by a commission of their colleagues, but the case was discontinued at the pope's death in 1667.

While Alexander VII was moving against the Jansenists with unbounded severity, he also turned his face against its very opposite, the kind of moral laxity to which the Jesuit doctrine of probabilism was apt to give rise.[57] The Jesuits had always been interested in aspects of moral theology relevant to personal conduct and the Christian life, but the probabilism propounded by some members of the Order caused a good deal of confusion and could, when pushed to the extreme, smack of laxism—a situation which the opponents of the Jesuits were not slow to criticise. Blaise Pascal, who became an enthusiastic supporter of the Jansenists after his conversion, was the author of several fierce attacks on the Order. In the last of his *Provincial Letters*, published between 1656 and 1657 as an apology for Jansenism, he attacked the moral theological teaching of the Jesuits and in so doing caused a sensation throughout Europe. What Pascal had really produced was a caricature of Jesuit morality, painted with subtle sarcasm and stylistic elegance; but those hostile to the Jesuits and the Catholic Church, particularly in the Protestant countries, accepted his picture without reservation. In Rome Pascal's *Provinciales* were placed on the Index of forbidden books already in their year of publication. Some of the moral theses attacked by Pascal had already been criticised by the Holy Office, and a new Jesuit defence of the more extreme manifestations of probabilism was also put on the Index. On Pallavicino's advice, however, Alexander refrained from condemning probabilism altogether; instead he warned against the moral laxity to which it could lead.[58] Later he was counselled by Giovanni Bona and the learned Dominican Girolamo Casanate who was secretary general of the Holy Office, to condemn 45 probabilistic propositions which were too extreme. Father Oliva, general of the Jesuit Order since 1664, ranged himself loyally on the side of the pope.

Alexander VII showed a remarkable degree of tolerance in connection with Church missionary activity. He approved the missionary methods of the Jesuits, which as far as possible respected the culture of the various countries, and on the thorny question of the Chinese rites he agreed to certain compromises. But some of the more important problems connected with this issue remained unsolved, and the principle advocated by the Jesuits whereby the Roman liturgy could be adapted to the language and civilisation of the Chinese, met with harsh criticism from the other religious orders.[59]

Alexander VII's devotion to the Virgin should also be mentioned here, particularly as it came to be reflected in contemporary art. Since the Middle Ages various theological schools had been debating the doctrine of the immaculate conception of the Virgin, according to which Mary was exempt

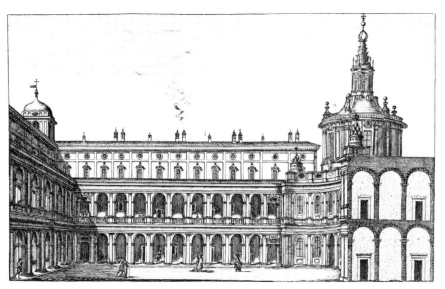

Rome's university, *La Sapienza*, with Borromini's church S. Ivo, engraving by
G. B. Falda (From *Il Nuovo teatro delle Fabbriche di Roma*).

from original sin from the first moment of her existence in the womb, due to
the special intervention of God.[60] This doctrine was particularly dear to the
Franciscans, and since the Early Middle Ages Mary's feast had been celebrated
in many parts of the Catholic Church on 8 December. The pope supported and
confirmed the doctrine in a special bull, *Sollicitudo omnium ecclesiarum* of 8
December 1661. At the same time he forbade further discussion of the issue
among theologians, pending a dogmatic promulgation which in fact came first
in 1854.

Science and Art

Conditions in the world of culture were more favourable during Chigi's
pontificate than they had been under his predecessor; the sciences which had
flourished during the Barberini era had not of course been lying fallow, but
now the atmosphere changed and scholars again enjoyed support and encouragement in the highest quarters.

Two men were working at the University of Rome, *la Sapienza*, at this time
whose names have passed into linguistic history, namely Abraham Ecchellense
and Ludovico Marracci. Ecchellense, an Arab, was born Ibrahim ibn ibrahim
ibn Dawud Haquili; he was professor of Arabic and Syriac and was responsible for the Arabic texts in the famous Paris edition of *Biblia polyglotta*,
published by M. Le Jay in 1645. Marracci devoted himself to a profound study
of the Koran. He published a Latin translation with a full commentary, on
which the first translation of the Koran into a living Western language—Sales'
English version of 1734—was later based.

The historical sciences were also well represented in Rome at this time. One of the pope's close friends was the learned Cistercian abbot Ferdinando Ughelli, who had started on his great work *Italia sacra* under Urban VIII and who now received help with the publication of the last volume from Alexander VII.[61] The pope would have liked to acknowledge this feat of scholarship by raising its author to the cardinalate, but the modest Ughelli firmly declined the offer.

The Cistercian abbot Giovanni Bona was an old friend of Chigi's.[62] The pope now called him to Rome, where he twice renewed Bona's mandate as abbot-general in order to keep him nearby. Bona was one of the first scholars to make a systematic study of liturgical history, and as a liturgical expert he was given a post in the Curia. His spiritual treatise *Manuductio ad coelum*,[63] published in Rome in 1658, was widely read and even compared with Thomas a Kempis, *Imitation of Christ*; no less than seventeen editions were published in various languages during Bona's own lifetime. He also played an important part as the pope's adviser during the controversy with the Jansenists.

Another personal friend of the pope and one of his closest advisers was the Jesuit Father Sforza Pallavicino, whom Alexander raised to the cardinalate in 1659. Pallavicino was not only a pre-eminent theologian and professor at the *Collegio Romano*, but also a historian. His most substantial work, *Istoria del concilio di Trento*, appeared in two volumes between 1656 and 1657 as an apology for the Roman Curia in response to Paolo Sarpi's attacks at the beginning of the century.[64] Pallavicino also wrote a biography of Alexander VII, which although it was never completed and was not even published until the nineteenth century, is nevertheless an important work based mainly on notes provided personally by the pope. Pallavicino's book on Queen Christina of Sweden's first journey to Rome, which also remained unpublished until the nineteenth century, is another very valuable source of material.[65]

One of the most interesting people in the learned world of Rome at this period was Father Athanasius Kircher, another Jesuit attached to the *Collegio Romano*.[66] Kircher was born near Fulda in Germany in 1601 and had been professor of mathematics and ethics and teacher in Hebrew and Syriac at Würzburg. He and his colleagues were later forced to flee in confusion from their university life as the Swedish army under King Gustavus Adolphus drew near, since "we had heard that the Swedes showed no mercy to Jesuits".[67] Kircher eventually arrived in Rome and became professor at the *Collegio romano* where he taught mathematics, physics and Oriental languages. This notable combination of subjects was typical of the phenomenally wide range of Kircher's scholarship, nor did it restrict his continuing study of medicine, astrology and alchemy or the publication of an astonishing number of papers in all these fields. As an Orientalist he was also interested in the mystery of the hieroglyphs and wrote a treatise on the obelisk which was raised in the Piazza Navona during Innocent X's pontificate, believing that he had succeeded in interpreting the inscriptions.[68]

In the *Collegio Romano* Athanasius Kircher had started a museum, a remark-

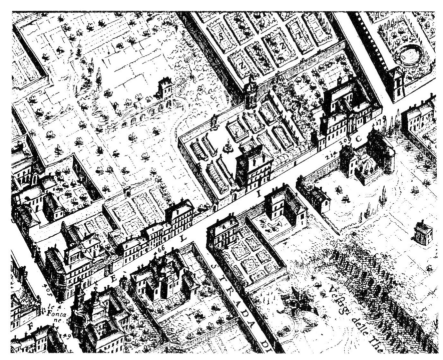

Detail of Falda's map of Rome 1676, showing the villa of Cardinal Chigi on the Strada Felice, the present Via delle Quattro Fontane; the premises are now intersected by the Via Nazionale.

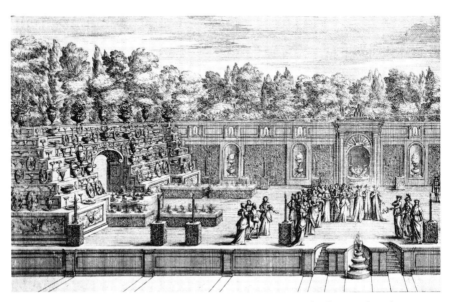

Feast arranged by Cardinal Flavio Chigi in his villa 1668 on the design of Carlo Fontana, left half of engraving (GCS).

able collection of objects of all possible sorts and kinds.[69] They included portraits of famous contemporaries and innumerable samples of the crafts of many—mainly Eastern—countries, as well as stuffed crocodiles, exotic birds and Egyptian mummies, alongside a variety of weapons, optical instruments including a microscope made by Kircher himself, and scientific models and chemical instruments, many of them for use in experiments in alchemy. The *Musaeum Kircherianum* was founded with a definite scientific purpose in mind, namely to display rarities of the natural world and the works of the human hand. It reflected its creator's incredible versatility and encyclopaedic knowledge as well as the strange complexity of seventeenth-century Rome, where art and technology, rationalism and esotericism blended into a synthesis almost without equal elsewhere. In the eighteenth century the *Musaeum Kircherianum* was still regarded as one of the great sights of Rome which no visitor should neglect. But when the Jesuit Order was suppressed in 1773 the collections began to be dispersed; they were finally scattered in 1870. Many items were incorporated into other Roman museums, but the original collection is known to us only from the catalogue published by Filippo Buonanni in 1709.[70]

The building which housed the university of Rome was completed under Alexander VII. In one of the long wings flanking the courtyard a library was founded on the pope's initiative and named *Biblioteca Alessandrina* in his honour. It included the approximately 13,000 printed books which had once been part of the duke of Urbino's library. Since the death of the last duke, Francesco Maria Della Rovere, the library had been divided between the town of Urbino and a monastery in Urbania. To prevent the final dispersal of this valuable library the pope had been advised by Cardinal Luigi Omedei, the legate in Urbino, to move it to Rome, which for a redemption fee of 100,000 scudi was now done. The rent paid by the *botteghe* located on the ground floor of the university building was set aside for further acquisitions. Also for the benefit of the university the pope founded a botanical garden next to the Acqua Paola on the Janiculum. This soon boasted over 3,000 systematically classified plants and ranked as one of the best gardens in Europe.[72] The university also acquired several new professorships under Alexander VII, particularly in the faculty of laws. Several famous natural scientists were also associated with the *Sapienza*, however, including the mathematician Vitale Giordani, famous for his Euclidean studies and his theories on the proportions.

In the autumn of 1659 the pope personally inspected the *Sapienza's* new premises, and in September the following year he attended the university's solemn inauguration and said mass in Borromini's recently completed chapel, S. Ivo.

The Greek and Latin manuscripts from the Urbino library were incorporated into the Vatican library,[73] where from 1653 until his death in 1661 Lucas Holstenius was *custode*. This learned man, whose greatest joy was the study of the Greek Church Fathers, was also in charge of Alexander VII's personal library, now one of the most notable in Rome. It appears that Chigi had been systematically collecting manuscripts and books—not, like most contemporary book collectors, buying at random whatever came his way.[74] The library remained in the possession of the Chigi family until 1918, when it was bought by the Italian state and in 1922 donated to the Vatican library.

As a young man, like his predecessor Urban VIII, Alexander VII had written poetry. He produced Latin verses in the style of Horace, some of them quite personal in content and full of the usual ornaments of a man of humanist education. As imitations they are considered not without value. Particularly during the somewhat difficult years he spent in Germany, Fabio Chigi found comfort in writing these "carmina animo deducta sereno".

When he was studying in Siena, Chigi had been greatly inspired by the learned Celso Cittadini, from whom he inherited not only his love of history and literature but also his beautiful Italian prose style. His literary interests went beyond books to include archives of all kinds. From the notes which the pope dictated to Pallavicino for his account of Fabio Chigi's youth,[76] we learn that Chigi had studied Euclid and geometry, that he was particularly interested in architecture, that he read the works of Vitruvius and had trained himself to perceive the proportions of a building.[77] He also enjoyed drawing and was interested in painting; for his own pleasure he had made an inventory of the works of art in Siena's churches.[78] Thus not only had he a lively interest in art, but his taste was also cultivated. Gian Lorenzo Bernini could hardly have acquired a more enthusiastic patron, and the collaboration between the two men was to bear abundant fruit.

Because of his position as the pope's nephew Flavio Chigi also had ample opportunities for patronage, but in comparison with his uncle his interest in the arts was modest and his taste undeveloped.[79] He was concerned mainly with architecture, employing first Gian Lorenzo Bernini and later Carlo Fontana to work on the palace which he had bought opposite SS. Apostoli and for which Bernini designed a new façade. For the interior adornment of the palace, however, the cardinal engaged several artists of little or no repute.

The cardinal had also acquired a villa on Sixtus V's great thoroughfare leading from S. Maria Maggiore to Pincio, at the point where Via Nazionale crosses Via Depretis today. He later had the garden extended and it is described by contemporaries as well-kept and planned at great cost with fountains and an abundant variety of blooms, particularly carnations. Nothing of this now remains. The *casino* housed a collection not unlike Kircher's museum,[80] including exotic stuffed animals, costly oriental costumes, the horn of a unicorn, mummies and much else. But this collection lacked the scientific aims and methods that informed the *Musaeum Kircherianum*, having more in common with the cabinets of curiosities to be found in many places in Europe.

Flavio Chigi's collection of antiquities, mainly displayed in the palace by SS. Apostoli, was of greater significance. The cardinal had purchased a number of works found in Rome and in the surrounding region. They were all much restored in accordance with current taste; one of the restorers who worked for him was Baldassare Mari, to whom we will return later. The collection was famed, perhaps not altogether justifiably, as one of the foremost of its kind in Rome. It was purchased in 1728 and removed to Dresden, where it came to play an important role for the young Winckelmann, who judged it to be the best collection of antiquities in Germany.[81]

Perhaps to console himself, the young cardinal often organised feasts, banquets and concerts at his villa or his palace. In the palace which he later acquired in Ariccia, he had a collection of 36 portraits of the most beautiful ladies of his day[82]—not an unusual feature in the palaces of many secular princes, but perhaps a little surprising in a cardinal and only too likely to provoke malicious comment on the part of later historians.

Among the chief cultural personalities of this pontificate—apart from Queen Christina to whom we shall soon return—Camillo Pamphili and his wife the princess of Rossano occupied an important place. They continued to hold brilliant parties, particularly at carnival time, and to commission painters and sculptors to adorn the family church of S. Agnese and their many palaces inside and outside Rome.

Camillo de' Massimi, prelate and former nuncio in Madrid under Innocent X, returned to Rome in 1658. Since he held no active ecclesiastical post he was able to devote himself without interruption to his art collections, his library and his friends.[83] Nicolas Poussin was a frequent guest at his home and in his library; the two men often passed the time happily together discussing art and Antiquity, the two subjects that fascinated them both. Massimi was Poussin's foremost Roman patron, and each exerted great influence on the other; they shared the same rigorous, austere taste for the classical style.[84] During this period Massimi to some extent assumed the mantle of Cassiano dal Pozzo as the arbiter of taste, and he too commissioned young artists to make copies of antique works of art. His gallery of paintings included several works by Poussin and Claude, as well as portraits of the Spanish royal family and of himself, painted for him by Velázquez. This modest and deeply learned man was to fill an even more important role under later popes.

Paolo Giordano Orsini, the friend of Christina of Sweden, died six months after the queen's arrival in Rome. His brother Alessandro Orsini also had cultural interests and belonged to Cassiano dal Pozzo's circle, but he never occupied such an influential position as his brother. Instead, another noble family now took its place in the limelight alongside the Pamphili, namely the Colonna, despite the financial straits which had led them to sell several of their ancient estates to the Barberini and others. The scholarly and serious-minded Cardinal Girolamo Colonna possessed several large art collections in the family palace which his brother Filippo enlarged. When he died in 1666 his collections went to his nephew, Lorenzo Onofrio. In 1659, when Lorenzo was 22, he had inherited the title of Grand Constable of the Kingdom of Naples, and in 1661 he married Cardinal Mazarin's niece, Maria Mancini, a celebrated beauty with whom Louis XIV had been passionately in love. It is said that only Mazarin's opposition had prevented Louis from marrying Maria himself.[85]

Together with the princess of Rossano this cheerful, sophisticated, and vivacious woman was one of the leaders of Roman society during the 1660s, and Queen Christina had to call on all her royal dignity in order to compete. In the Colonna Palace festivities succeeded one another with dancing, singing and merrymaking; plays, concerts, and brilliant feasts were arranged at every possible opportunity,[86] although Lorenzo Onofrio himself was often away from Rome either in Spain or Naples.

Arrival of Queen Christina

One of the major events of Alexander VII's pontificate was the arrival in Rome of Queen Christina of Sweden. Christina, daughter of King Gustavus Adolphus, famous champion of the Protestant cause in the Thirty Years War; Christina, once regent of a powerful country and signatory to the Treaty of Westphalia—this was the woman who now arrived in Rome, a convert to the Roman Catholic Faith.[87] For Rome this was more than a sensation, it was a triumph; and naturally the queen's arrival was celebrated with a series of festivities more splendid than the Eternal City had ever known. After renouncing the crown and leaving Sweden in the summer of 1654, Christina stopped for a time in the Spanish Netherlands, where she was received in secret into the Roman Catholic Church on Christmas Eve the same year.[88] She had originally intended to travel on to Rome as soon as possible, but by bringing a certain amount of pressure to bear, Philip IV of Spain constrained her to postpone her departure. He did not want her arriving in Rome while Innocent X was still alive: there was a real danger, it was felt, that the newly converted queen would be scandalised by conditions at the present papal court. Innocent was already seriously ill and could not be expected to live much longer. But naturally it would also be unsuitable for the queen to arrive in Rome during conclave, when no-one would be available to arrange a reception worthy of her rank. And so the journey to Rome began at last in the autumn of 1655. At Innsbruck Christina was met by Alexander VII's internuncio, Lucas Holstenius, who had been specially appointed for the task. Holstenius was himself a convert and a man of great learning, well able to converse with this queen who was famous for her intellectual powers and her scholarly interests. On 3 November he officially received the queen into the Roman Catholic Church. On 21 November Christina crossed the border into the Papal States near Ferrara, where she was greeted by four papal nuncios and the cardinal legate of Ferrara.

The queen reached the last stage of her journey to Rome on 20 December.[89] At the Villa Olgiata a few kilometres north of Rome on the Via Cassia, she was met by two papal legates and cardinals Carlo dei Medici and Frederick of Hessen, a distant relative of hers. The villa had been decorated specially for the occasion with allegorical figures painted in *trompe-l'oeil* on canvas. Christina was conducted into Rome in one of the pope's own carriages, and since her official entry was to be held a few days later she was taken straight to the Vatican palace, where Alexander VII received her in private audience. For the next few days the queen was the guest of the Vatican, an extremely rare honour for a woman. A fitting apartment had been prepared for her in the Torre dei Venti, which rises above one long side of the Cortile del Belvedere next to the Vatican library.

The following day Christina inspected in the Cortile the papal gifts which would later be presented to her officially: a carriage and six horses, a litter and two mules, a smaller sedan chair and a palfrey with a beautiful saddle and trappings. The carriage and chairs had been made under the supervision of the great Bernini himself in his own workshop, where Giovanni Paolo Schor had made the working drawings and assumed the practical direction of the construction.[90] The carriage was covered in silver with finely carved decorations, and adorned with the queen's arms and other heraldic motifs and silver statuettes. Inside it was lined with sky-blue velvet and silver braid. Bernini was presented to the queen on this occasion,[91] which must have been their first meeting. Christina had naturally heard a great deal about the artist, and she was henceforth to be one of his most devoted admirers.

On 23 December Queen Christina made her state entry into Rome, in a cortège described as one of the most splendid of its kind that the century had witnessed.[92] In the morning she rode in one of the pope's carriages to Ponte Milvio, where she was received by the senator of Rome, with a company of nobles, trumpeters and cavalry. The cavalcade continued to Julius III's *vigna* on the Via Flaminia, in pouring rain. In the villa Christina was served a light collation, "una varietà di rinfreschi, di vini, acque, et abbondantissime confetture", while the company waited for the rain to stop. At last the clouds cleared a little, and it was possible to present the papal gifts. Although the weather was still bad, Christina decided to ride into Rome on her new palfrey.

The day had been declared a public holiday and the entire populace was out on the streets to gape at the display, or at least "everyone except nuns and the sick" it was said. Naturally the Romans were anxious to see this eminent guest, about whom the strangest rumours had been heard: the queen was a hermaphrodite, she spoke with a man's voice, she rode astraddle like a man.[93] Inside the Porta del Popolo Christina was welcomed by representatives of the Sacred College; headed by Francesco Barberini and Giulio Sacchetti were 24 cardinals riding on mules and wearing the dark purple robes prescribed for Advent. In honour of the day the gate had been decorated according to drawings made by Bernini of the Vasa sheaves of corn, while the pope had himself composed the inscription FELICE FAUSTOQUE INGRESSUI ANNO 1655.

The procession continued along the Corso to Palazzo Venezia, past the church of the Gesù and along the winding Via del Papa to Ponte Sant'Angelo, where Christina was greeted by a thundering salute from the cannon of the fort. Everywhere people had decorated their houses with tapestries and hangings from windows and balconies. First in the cavalcade rode trumpeters, heralds and papal cuirassiers, followed by the queen's personal guard in scarlet coats with the black gold-edged crosses of the House of Vasa; next came twelve mules in the queen's baggage train. The carriage, the litter and the sedan

MARIA ALEXANDRA CHRI ... STINA .SVECIÆ REGINA 1656

Queen Christina entering Rome, engraving (BAV).

chair which the pope had given to his royal guest were carried in the procession to receive the admiration of the crowd. Heralding the most splendid section of the whole cortège went the papal drummers and mace-bearers; they were followed by the captain of the Swiss guard in his magnificent costume and the papal master of ceremonies immediately preceding the cardinals. The queen rode between the two eldest cardinal deacons, Orsini and Costaguti, followed by the gentleman of her chamber, Ippolito Bentivoglio, on foot. Last, behind the pope's light cavalry, came many representatives of the Roman nobility, the gentlemen on horseback and the ladies in their coaches. Foremost among them was Prince Camillo Pamphili, who was still in mourning for Innocent X; but his black velvet clothing was studded with diamonds valued at 100,000 scudi, and he wore three diamonds in his hat so splendid as to be beyond price. His wife, the princess of Rossano, wore a dress covered in precious stones from top to toe, said by the gossip of the day to be worth seven times as much as her husband's. Their pages were clad in costly black livery, sown in great haste over the last few days. All in all, the noble cortège provided an incredible display of magnificence, colour and costly splendour.

At last the Romans were able to satisfy their curiosity about this queen, the most notable convert of her day. She rode side-saddle, her horse draped in blue embroidered velvet with decorative *putti* and the Vasa sheaves. Christina herself wore a simple grey dress sparsely embroidered in gold, and a black shawl over her shoulders in the French fashion. As was customary at the time, she also wore a wig and a simple black hat. She wore no jewels, which was perhaps just as well as she could never have even remotely competed with the princess of Rossano. To the Romans she appeared a strange queen, whose simplicity contrasted sharply with the peacock splendour of the Roman princes. But Christina loved to present herself in simple attire, while still insisting on her royal dignity and rank. It seemed perfectly natural to her that others should clothe themselves in expensive finery and arrange magnificent receptions in her honour. People who witnessed her arrival commented on her short stature, which was noted even in Italy, and no-one could fail to see that she had a deformed shoulder. But there was also comment—both now and later—on the fascination of her large expressive eyes.

As the salute boomed out from Castel Sant'Angelo and the church bells rang, the cortège reached the piazza in front of St. Peter's, where even the idea of Bernini's colonnades had not yet been born. In the basilica the best voices in the whole of Rome had been assembled to sing a solemn *Te Deum*, and Francesco Barberini, archpriest of the basilica, had caused the nave to be hung with his family's unique collection of tapestries and draperies in gold brocade, and the church was also adorned with emblems combining the royal crown and the Vasa sheaves in honour of the day.[94] After she had prayed before the Blessed Sacrament, the queen was led to the Sala Regia, where the pope received her in a public consistory in a manner worthy of her rank.

On Christmas day Christina attended high mass celebrated by the pope in St. Peter's, where a special box had been prepared for her next to the papal throne. On this occasion she received communion and the sacrament of confirmation from the pope himself. She took the name of Alexandra and also, at the express wish of the pope, the name of Maria. She subsequently signed herself Christina Alexandra.

On St. Stephen's day the queen was invited to dine publicly at the pope's table, an honour which was only afforded to royal persons.[95] But according to the rigid protocol the pope had to sit alone at table, and when his honoured guest was a woman the problem was particularly awkward. However, with exquisite tact, the pope had organised everything down to the smallest detail himself. A special table had been laid next to the pope's, about four inches lower but under the same canopy; the queen's chair was also slightly smaller than the pope's and had no arm-rests. Before them were placed a variety of *trionfi* or spectacular dishes such as were always provided at solemn banquets; they consisted of miniature sculptures in sugar, painted and gilded. Among them were representations of the Vasa sheaves, *Abundance*, and *Minerva* surrounded by the seven liberal arts as a graceful compliment to this highly cultivated queen. The *trionfi* had been designed and executed in Bernini's studio.[96] During the meal Father Oliva preached a sermon, and sacred music was performed by the orchestra and a choir.

The same evening Christina was conducted in cavalcade by the light of torches to the Palazzo Farnese, which had been temporarily placed at her disposal by the duke of Parma. Carlo Rainaldi had erected a false façade in front of the five central windows of the real palace front, adorned with the customary allegorical figures including Christian humility and Royal Dignity, Wisdom and Generosity; the arms of Sweden and the personal arms of the queen were there, together with famous biblical heroines such as Judith and Esther.[97] It is said that when Christina saw this façade, she commanded the cortège to stop; she then paused for at least fifteen minutes to admire it.

Festivities and Carnivals

The Romans still loved to arrange brilliant feasts and spectacles as they had always done. These included secular entertainments as well as solemn Church ceremonies. A carnival or a cavalcade, a papal *possesso* or the *Orazione delle Quarantore* in one of the churches—any of these could provide a reason for arranging a feast. Temporary decorations would be set up, giving artist like Bernini, Carlo Rainaldi or Paul Schor splendid opportunities to improvise in a riot of imaginative extravaganzas. A wealth of material, mainly drawings and engravings, waits to be explored by scholars, much of it bearing witness to the current taste for the bombastic and astonishing, sometimes even the over-decorated and bizarre.[98] Many of these Baroque decorations are hardly in what we would call good taste today. On the occasion of the birth of a French heir to the throne, for example, Bernini and Schor erected a vast festive decor in front of the church of Trinità dei Monti, concealing the entire façade of the church and enhanced—naturally—by a brilliant display of fireworks. And when Philip IV of Spain died, a solemn requiem featuring a magnificent and costly catafalque was held for him in the Spanish national church. The impos-ing decorations made for the Forty Hours Devotion in many Roman churches represented bold experiments in the art of perspective and lighting, and owed much to the influence of stage decor.[99] It is sometimes difficult for us to understand how such decorations could have been accepted as sacred art, and in particular how they could be associated with the Eucharist. They became even more popular after Bernini had designed his colossal *apparato* in 1628 for the Cappella Paolina in the Vatican. A famous *apparato* had been made by Carlo Rainaldi for the Gesù in 1650, and the efforts of the artists culminated in the constructions of Andrea Pozzo towards the end of the century.

   The carnival held in Rome in 1656 was dedicated to Queen Christina, and was therefore known as *il carnevale della regina*. It included a series of brilliant and costly spectacles and festivities in the quintessential spirit of the Roman Baroque, although Alexander VII was strict regarding matters of this kind and had accordingly limited the period of carnival to the ten days immediately preceding Ash Wednesday. The usual horse races which so enraptured the Romans were held on the Corso, as they had been ever since the fifteenth century. Prince Camillo Pamphili, whose palace on the Corso provided a fine view, had arranged a special balcony from which Queen Christina was invited

Gian Lorenzo Bernini & Paul Schor: decoration with fireworks in front of SS. Trinità dei Monti at the birth of the French Dauphin in 1661, engraving by D. Barrière (GCS).

to watch the races. At the same time other festivities were arranged in the palace to honour and amuse the celebrated guest. On the first evening *un dramma in musica* was performed by some of the princess's ladies. The words were by Giovanni Lotti and the music by Tenaglia.[100] On another evening Christina was conducted to a room which had been made into a theatre for the occasion. Without warning the room was transformed and the spectators found themselves gazing out to sea—an effect that amazed them all with its convincing realism. Venus and Amor could be seen in the sky in a chariot drawn by doves. They were singing a duet with words composed by Prince Camillo Pamphili himself. The sea then vanished, to be replaced by eight of the princess' ladies performing a ballet with torches in their hands.[101]

The Barberini family caused two operas to be performed in their palace theatre in honour of the queen. One of them, *La vita humana ovvero il Trionfo della Pietà*, had been composed for this occasion with music by Marco Marazzoli and a libretto by Giulio Rospigliosi.[102] The title role was sung by the *castrato* singer Bonaventura, whom Christina particularly admired. Under Urban VIII women had been permitted to appear on the stage, but Alexander VII reaffirmed the earlier prohibitions, so that the female roles usually had to be sung by *castrati*.

The Barberini theatre had been partly rebuilt for this carnival, but surviving information about its actual appearance is fragmentary.[103] Giovanni Francesco Grimaldi not only designed the costumes and decorations for the *Trionfo della Pietà*; he also rebuilt the proscenium. Surviving engravings show that lamps and mirrors on the ramp were concealed by a row of small fountains from which real water flowed. The reflections caused by this water must have added a glow of magic illumination to the stage. As the curtain rose for the first act, the stage was in darkness and the audience could see daylight gradually dawning—a lighting effect for which Bernini had long before designed special machinery. Aurora then appeared in the sky strewing flowers over the land and awakening the shepherds to their labours. This was followed by the kind of garden scenes that were so popular at the time, with gods and goddesses descending to earth on clouds. The decor for the last act was a view of Rome over the Tiber, with Castel Sant'Angelo and St. Peter's in the background. The finale included a display of fireworks, which must have been a masterpiece of theatrical illusion in lighting and sound effects. Queen Christina was in the audience together with eighteen cardinals, and her enthusiasm was so great that she returned incognito to see the opera again.

To the annoyance of the pro-Spanish party, Christina insisted on paying a visit to the French envoy who did not have the standing of an ambassador to the Holy See. Hugue de Lionne was living in Mazarin's palace on the Quirinal, the present Palazzo Pallavicini-Rospigliosi, where he provided a superabundance of astonishing dishes and *confetture* and put on a performance of Corneille's heavy and complicated drama *Héraclius*.[104]

Naturally Christina did not neglect to attend the more solemn performances which the Jesuits used to arrange during carnival. The interior of the Gesù was

Giovanni Francesco Grimaldi: the proscenium and curtain of Barberini's theatre in 1656, engraving by G. B. Galestruzzi (From M. Marazzoli, *La vita humana . . .*, 1656. BAV).

transformed as usual for the *Quarantore*, the forty hours of veneration of the Sacrament, with the help of cleverly simulated architecture. Complicated stage arrangements included allegorical figures, and the varied lighting effects have been enthusiastically described by Gualdo Priorato.[105] One wonders whether people came to gape at this display rather than to pray before the Sacrament, which may well have vanished altogether in the confusion. Perhaps Christina was more appreciative of a performance in the *Collegio Germanico* of Jacopo Carissimi's oratorio *Abramo et Isaac*.[106] We know that Christina was a great admirer of Carissimi's powerful and expressive music, which is rich in themes and rhythms and succeeds in being dramatic and moving at the same time.

   The climax of the *carnevale della regina* was the *Giostra delle Caroselle* arranged by the Barberini. This surpassed anything of the kind previously seen in Rome.[107] An arena had been specially erected immediately north of the palace, where the Via Barberini runs today. The galleries erected round the arena could seat at least 3,000 spectators, while a box for the guest of honour was built on one long side, opposite the entrance. The arena was designed by Giovanni Francesco Grimaldi, who had also been responsible for the costumes

Giovanni Francesco Grimaldi: stage set for *La vita humana ovvero Il Trionfo della Pietà*, engraving by G. B. Galestruzzi (BAV).

and the triumphal chariots—no small achievement, since he also had the theatre to think about. The joust itself consisted of a kind of ballet, in which 12 knights clothed in blue and silver, Christina's colours, together with 128 yeomen, fought a battle with 12 Amazons in red and gold, the colours of Rome, accompanied by their band of followers, also 128 strong. In the course of the struggle a gigantic fire-breathing dragon entered the arena, only to be defeated by Apollo in his four-horse chariot with a company of personified Seasons and Hours. In conclusion the performers all joined in songs composed for the occasion in honour of the queen. The costumes were extravagant beyond belief; some of the cavaliers wore headdresses topped with ostrich feathers as tall as themselves. The two artists Gagliardi and Lauri have preserved the memory of the performance in a large painting now in the Museo di Roma. The accounts for the whole entertainment have also been preserved in the Barberini archives.[108]

These spectacles proved to be the swan song of the Barberini theatre. The following year the carnival was cancelled because of plague, and for many years after that it was on a far more modest scale. Nor was the Barberini family

Giovanni Francesco Grimaldi: stage set for *La vita humana* representing fireworks at Castel Sant'Angelo, engraving by G. B. Galestruzzi (BAV).

still in undisputed command. Their role was taken over by Colonna and his princess, Maria Mancini. For a good many years Rome lacked a permanent theatre and performances could only be held in private palaces.

Christina, Alexander VII and Azzolino

Alexander VII soon discovered that his royal convert was by no means the obedient daughter of the Church he had hoped for. Wilful and eccentric as she could be, both her conduct and her dress provoked him. She would often shock people with her comments, not always unintentionally, and her political intrigues gave rise to a good deal of anxiety. Up to a point Christina was disappointed too. She had expected to find in Rome the kind of tolerance she had met in Descartes and the other men who had represented her first contacts with Catholicism. Instead she came up against a spirit of Counter-Reformation puritanism almost as harsh as the puritanism she had left behind in Lutheran Stockholm. The intelligentsia of Rome had to follow the lines laid down by the Church, and there was no question at all of free thought. Toleration of deviating views was as rare in Rome as in Stockholm.

Giostra delle Caroselle at Palazzo Barberini during carnival 1656, painting by
F. Gagliardi and F. Lauri. Museo di Roma (Museum photo).

Already during her first year in Rome Queen Christina established bonds of
friendship with Azzolino, who was later to occupy a very important place in
her life. Of their correspondence only Christina's letters have survived, but
these show clearly the strength of her feelings for the cardinal.[109] She speaks of
love, but how much of this love was genuinely erotic on her part is not for us
to judge, although a certain scepticism is perhaps justified in view of her
undoubted Lesbian leanings. At any rate Azzolino appears to have remained
much cooler. But he certainly wielded great influence over Christina, and was
left in charge of her business affairs in Rome when she was away for a period of
several years. His intelligence merged well with her brilliant intuition, while
his Latin acuity and moderation contrasted with her often malicious regal
arrogance. In any case he remained an unswervingly loyal friend until her
death, even if this is perhaps the only wholly attractive thing that can be said
about him.

Christina left Rome in the summer of 1656 when plague broke out, and
betook herself to the court of France. While there she sought Mazarin's and
France's support for her aspirations to the crown of Naples, which must have
seemed within easy reach at a time of Spanish weakness. But her plans were
revealed by Monaldesco, who paid for this betrayal with his life.[110] By the

Bernini's workshop:
portrait bust of Cardinal
Decio Azzolino.
Nationalmuseum,
Stockholm (Museum photo).

spring of 1658 Christina was back in Rome. Mazarin put his palace on the Quirinal at her disposal, and there she continued to devise plans for becoming queen of Naples. The pope was not at all pleased to have as his nearest neighbour this strange woman, "born a barbarian, barbarously brought up and living with barbarous thoughts", as he is supposed to have told the Venetian ambassador.[111] Her political intrigues were extremely embarassing, since they jeopardised the good relations between Spain and the Holy See. Moreover the pope was concerned about the apparently desperate state of the queen's finances, while the Monaldesco affair had helped to discredit her in the eyes of the Roman people. The pope let his disapproval of his new neighbour be known, and had her informed that he would like her to leave the Eternal City. Christina was profoundly insulted. However, her Neapolitan plans soon collapsed, and by bringing all his tact to bear Azzolino managed to patch up relations between the queen and the pope. And in July 1659 he also arranged for her to leave Mazarin's palace and move to the Palazzo Riario on Via della Lungara.

In the summer of 1660, on hearing of the death of King Charles Gustavus X, Christina departed precipitately for Sweden. This visit to her own country was dominated by the eternally embarassing question of her finances. She would now have to negotiate with Charles XI's regency council. After an absence of two years Christina returned to Rome. Alexander VII was gradually becoming reconciled to her, particularly as Christina was wise enough to treat the pope's nephews with the greatest courtesy. On all questions of etiquette the queen was an expert, and absolutely uncompromising as regards her own royal rank and dignity, prerogatives and privileges. In this she was a true daughter of her

Abraham Wuchters:
portrait of
Queen Christina 1661,
oil on canvas.
Private collection (NMS).

time, but she was intelligent enough to exploit the rules of etiquette as a weapon—the only one she had at her disposal. In seventeenth-century Rome, however, it could be a powerful one indeed.[112]

Queen Christina in the Palazzo Riario

The Palazzo Riario, which was restored and enlarged to almost twice its original size in the 1730s to become the present Palazzo Corsini, was henceforth to be Christina's permanent home. Here her art collections would ultimately be displayed in full, here her library was housed, here she would receive authors, scientists and scholars of all kinds, and here her many concerts would be held.

But it took a long time before the palace was ready for her. Before Christina's departure from Rome in 1660 she had been living in the *casino* belonging to the palace on the Janiculum, and it was only on her return that she was at last able to arrange the art collections which had accompanied her from Stockholm and which had been waiting for so long in their packing cases.

Once her collections were on display and her library arranged, Christina's palace became one of the sights of Rome. Nicodemus Tessin the Younger, who visited the city for the second time in 1678, has given us one of the few detailed descriptions which we have of any Roman palace.[113] On the ground floor a suite of ten rooms was mainly devoted to sculptures, some genuine antiquities and some the works of contemporary artists. In the *Stanza delle Muse* there were sculptures of the nine muses, while the most outstanding sculptures in the following rooms included a *Clythia*, a *Venus Bathing*, the *Faun with Kid*, and—most famous of all—the *San Ildefonso Group*, known then as *Castor and Pollux*.[114] These were all antique works which the queen had bought since arriving in Rome, and they were all rather heavily restored in the taste of the times by Ercole Ferrata and others. There were two large rooms on the *piano nobile*, one of which was the audience room where the queen's throne stood. The second room was known as the *Stanza dei Quadri* containing Christina's great collection of pictures which covered the walls from floor to ceiling,[115] mainly representing booty taken by the Swedes from Prague during the Thirty Years' War. Christina regarded these pictures as the royal family's private property which she had every right to bring with her to Rome. They included several masterpieces of sixteenth-century Italian art by artists such as Raphael and Correggio, Titian and Veronese. The queen also possessed works by Guido Reni, Carracci and Guercino.

Christina had also collected handicraft work, china, silver, coins, gems and, naturally, tapestries.[116] Many of these last had been purchased by her predecessors on the throne of Sweden for their palace in Stockholm; others Christina had acquired herself, including a set of woodland subjects commissioned from Delft.[117] Only a few of the tapestries have survived to our own day.

The library which Gabriel Naudé had created for the queen and which had already been her greatest pride in Stockholm, naturally accompanied her to Rome, transported via Antwerp on twelve Swedish warships. But the library was probably not ready in the Palazzo Riario before 1663,[118] when her first librarian, Lucas Holstenius, was succeeded by Giovanni Pietro Bellori. With its approximately 5,500 printed books at the time of the queen's death, this library could not perhaps rival Alexander VII's in size, but it contained a great many unusual manuscripts as well as an outstanding collection of Italian drawings.[119] The queen was always willing to place her books at the disposal of scholars, and the Benedictine church historian Jean Mabillon and the numismatist Ezekiel Spanheim were but two among the many who frequented the library. Spanheim also arranged her coin collection, which was one of the best then in existence.

Queen Christina's lively intellect, her ready wit and her knowledge of languages impressed everyone who came in contact with her. She took a keen interest in the natural sciences including astronomy and chemistry, although this did not prevent a parallel interest in astrology and alchemy. She even had a *destillarium* set up in her palace, where she hoped to be able to produce gold.[120]

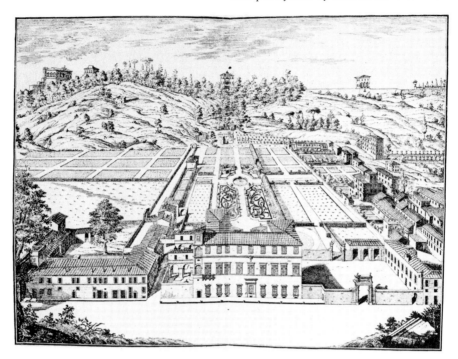

Palazzo Riario, Queen Christina's residence, engraving by G. B. Falda (GCS).

It was typical of Christina that at the same time she was also in touch with the famous astronomist Gian Domenico Cassini, who frequently visited Rome. He invited the queen to watch the two comets of 1665 through his telescope, and he dedicated his dissertation on the subject to her.[121] But despite this constant curiosity about the natural sciences, Christina's interest in these subjects remained somewhat superficial. In contrast her profound study of philosophy continued unabated during her years in Rome, as she pursued her personal search for the truth.

Already in January 1656 Queen Christina founded an academy. It did not survive very long, mainly perhaps because she was absent from Rome a great deal in the years immediately following, and it was anyway more in the nature of a literary circle. Among the questions discussed by the academy's 21 members at the Palazzo Farnese was "whether the day or the night is more propitious for poetic fury". Night was found to be the more favourable and its victory was celebrated in a ballet for the stars and the twelve hours of the night.[122]

When Christina was still reigning queen of Sweden she naturally had more opportunity for showing favour to scholars, even if direct contact with them was more restricted at that time. The same applied to her relations with artists. In Rome she was a passionate admirer of Gian Lorenzo Bernini, but she never commissioned any work from him as she did not feel she could afford the kind

Project for the "Chamber of the Muses" in Queen Christina's residence in Rome, drawing by anonymous artist. NMS, inv. no. *1045/1960*, fol. 10.

of fee he deserved. In his biography of his father, Domenico Bernini describes how the queen once visited Bernini in his studio and was received by the artist in the rough garb that he wore for work. Christina took this as the greatest compliment he could have paid her.[123]

Thus Queen Christina's patronage of the visual arts was somewhat limited. We shall return in the following chapter to the much greater impact which she had on the musical life of Rome.

Bernini and the Great Papal Commissions

When Fabio Chigi arrived in Rome in November 1651 to assume the office of secretary of state it was not long before he became acquainted with Gian Lorenzo Bernini. Bernini's son Domenico tells us that the mutual sympathy which was immediately obvious between the prelate and the artist gradually developed into a deep and lasting friendship.[124] There seems no reason to doubt this judgement. Domenico then relates—and a similar account appears in Baldinucci's *Vita del cavalier Bernini*—that by nightfall on the day of his election Chigi had already sent for Bernini to discuss the commissions which were to be entrusted to him.[125] Bernini was appointed *Architetto di Camera* and together with other *qualificati personaggi* would often attend on the pope at table, standing courteously with the others while Alexander alone was seated, until they could all withdraw to some other chamber for mutual discourse. The pope apparently showed the greatest appreciation for Bernini's conversational talents, and it is from Alexander's own Diary that we learn how Bernini would produce the plans and sketches which the pope wanted to examine and discuss during these after-dinner sessions.[126] Bernini became acquainted with many of those in the pope's entourage on these occasions, including Sforza Pallavicino who became his great admirer and, almost certainly, Virgilio Spada.

Already before his accession Alexander had begun to restore the memorial chapel of the Chigi family in S. Maria del Popolo. He now commissioned Bernini to execute the sculptural embellishment of the chapel and to decorate the church in its entirety. We shall return to this later when we consider Bernini's sculpture as a whole. But the work which roused Alexander VII's deepest interest, and which he regarded as the most important task facing him, was to complete the decoration of St. Peter's and to organise the space in front of the basilica. In his great personal committent to St. Peter's the pope was following in his predecessor's footsteps with the added incentive of his own profound knowledge and cultivated taste.

The colonnade around St. Peter's Square was by far the greatest building enterprise in Rome during Alexander VII's pontificate, and although it was not the first project to be executed it seems appropriate to start with it here.

The creation of a monumental open place in front of the Vatican basilica had long been desired.[127] At the time of Alexander VII's accession this still consisted of an irregular open area stretching north as far as the Leonine wall. The southern border was defined by a row of mean houses and the residence of the confessors of St. Peter's, the Palazzo dei Penitenzieri. To the east the space was bounded by buildings clustering quite unsymmetrically round the end of the streets cutting across the Borgo Leonino from Castel Sant'Angelo. In this area outside the basilica the faithful would gather in their crowds for the great Church festivals, to receive the blessing of the pope, *urbi et orbi*, from the benediction loggia above the central door of the church. It was also customary for the pope's coronation to take place in the open in front of the main entrance, and sometimes the pope would bless the crowds from a window in his private apartment high above the piazza, as he still does at the present time every Sunday at noon. On the day of *Corpus Christi* a solemn ceremony was held in front of the basilica, and since the middle of the sixteenth century the custom had been to fix a canvas covering on poles over the processional route.

It was recognised that a monumental piazza and the design of the surrounding architecture could provide an important corrective to the unfortunate proportions of the basilica's façade, which without the intended *campanili* now

Piazza S. Pietro with canopy arranged for the procession of *Corpus Christi*, painting by anonymous artist. Museo di Roma (Museum photo).

seemed too long for its height. It had also been suggested—even as long ago as the mid-fifteenth century—that premises could be provided for the various offices of the Curia and residences for its members in the buildings which could surround the piazza. Arcades should then run the length of these buildings round the whole square.

Under Innocent X, Carlo Rainaldi had submitted a proposal for a monumental piazza surrounded by buildings and arcades. Baldinucci claims to have seen four plans in the architect's studio for a piazza with four ground plans—a square, a hexagon, a circle and an oval—but it is not possible to determine how finished any of them were. Only one has been preserved in a contemporary drawing.[128] It is possible that this one, and possibly all the suggestions which Baldinucci saw, were actually produced later in opposition to Bernini's proposal.[129] In any case Rainaldi seems to have been unable to solve the problem of relating the streets from the Borgo Leonino with the piazza in a satisfactory manner, or relating the piazza itself to the existing buildings. Innocent X obviously lacked the energy and the interest to tackle the design of the piazza seriously.

But Alexander VII promptly addressed the problem. On 31 July 1656 he ordered a meeting of the congregation for the *Reverenda Fabbrica di San Pietro*,[130] as the planning of a piazza in front of the basilica came within its competence. It was decided that such a piazza should be built, and that Gian Lorenzo Bernini should be asked to submit his ideas.

One of the main factors restricting Bernini's freedom of action was the obelisk which Sixtus V had placed in front of the basilica. Naturally it was never suggested that this could be moved. At least to begin with, Bernini was also restricted by the main entrance to the vatican palace, which was to be retained and which had been located in the free-standing bell-tower from the time of Paul V. This tower, known as the Ferrabosco tower, was always rather old-fashioned, even when it was built, so its retention must have been something of a headache for Bernini. It was linked to the façade of the basilica by a low corridor wing, and even before Bernini various proposals had included a similar tower and wing on the south side, forming a square place in front of the basilica. This *piazza retta* was included in all Bernini's projects.

A month later Bernini had his first proposal ready to present to the congregation at its meeting on 19 August. At the same time he submitted an explanatory summary or *giustificazione*.[131] Cardinal Palotto, who was unable to attend in person, submitted a written statement on Bernini's plan, which he criticised on both liturgical and practical grounds: the piazza would be much too large, he claimed, and in view of the straitened finances of the Holy See it was inappropriate to embark on a vast building operation of this kind.[132] All we have to go on in trying to reconstruct this first proposal of Bernini's is the discussions held on the subject. It appears to have envisaged a near trapezoid piazza bounded by straight wings. The wing on the north side would run obliquely to the Ferrabosco tower, prolonging the corridor towards the façade, and would extend to the beginning of the Borgo Nuovo. A similar building was to be erected symmetrically on the southern side. A resolution was passed, including a comment that the pope wanted to launch this great building enterprise in order to provide work for the poor of Rome. We know that the subject was discussed among those in the confidence of the pope, and that his own preference was for a square piazza; in its resolution the congregation agreed with this solution.[133] Bernini was also commissioned to make a wooden model.

Before the model was finished, the pope ordered that part of the north side should actually be built in the shape of a temporary wooden construction, to give some idea on the site of what the finished design would look like.[134] It was important, for instance, to see whether the buildings blocked the view of the palace and the pope's window. According to Bernini's *giustificazione*, it was after inspecting this provisional erection that Alexander VII personally suggested an oval piazza, *"con giuditio più che humano risolse farlo in forma ovata... cosa che fece stupire l'istesso Architetto invecchiato in questa professione"*.[135] An oval piazza would make better use of the space; it would extend as far as the Leonine wall, and since the buildings would be much closer

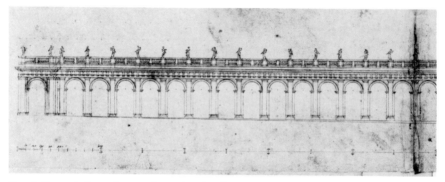

Bernini's workshop: the arcade project for the Piazza S. Pietro, presumably for the project with straight colonnade wings, detail of drawing, left half. BAV, *Chigi P VII 9*, fol. 35.

to the palace they would not block the view of the window. Many scholars believe that Bernini put the idea of an oval into the pope's head intentionally, claiming it as the pope's suggestion so as to pre-empt criticism of his project. In any case Alexander VII must have approved this fresh proposal from the start, thus demonstrating that he was open to new ideas.

The elevation of one of Bernini's first projects is shown on two drawings in the Vatican Library.[136] The wings were planned as double arcades, open on both sides, with arches between pilasters supporting a straight entablature crowned by a balustrade and statues. Such an arcade could only be constructed as a straight wing.

The model of this double arcade, commissioned in August 1656, must have been long in the making, as the congregation did not meet again until 17 March 1657. It was now that Bernini, in a new *giustificazione*, submitted his proposal for an oval piazza.[137] This must have come as a surprise to the congregation, but nevertheless it was approved, perhaps because it was presented as the pope's own idea.

This project roused a good deal of criticism both in the congregation and outside, and it was presumably as part of this opposition that Carlo Rainaldi submitted at least one of the counter-proposals mentioned above. A chalk drawing by Rainaldi in the Vatican library[138] shows a square piazza with blunted corners and loggia arcades all round. It was also probably at this point that a series of fifteen drawings was made, formerly in the Busiri-Vici collection and now in the Brandager collection, Faulkner Farm, Mass. These have sometimes been ascribed to Bernini, but Wittkower has argued convincingly against this supposition, and his view now seems to be generally accepted.[139] The real author of the drawings remains unknown. In some we see a piazza like a great multi-storey exedra in front of the basilica, symbolising arms opening to receive the visitor and recalling the anthropomorphic forms of mediaeval architecture.

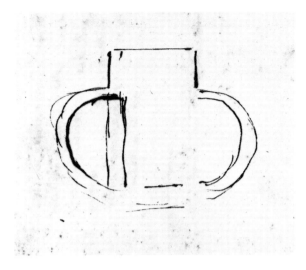

Bernini: drawing for the colonnades of St. Peter's showing straight colonnade on one side and two half circles. BAV, *Chigi H II 22*, fol. 155v.

Foundation medal for the colonnades of St. Peter's with double pilasters and straight *terzo braccio* BAV, *Medagliere.*

In his first proposal Bernini had not yet worked out the final form of his oval. It shows two semicircles on each side of a square space. The first rather tentative project for the colonnades suggests that Bernini may have been inspired by certain contemporary and variously fantastic pictures and reconstructions of antique buildings.[140] But although many scholars have discoursed upon this question, we cannot really be sure what models Bernini may have had.

From the oval evolved what is known as the *ovato tondo*, constructed according to a system of circles touching and interlocking with one another. This was a system which had been described earlier by Peruzzi as well as by Serlio and which was used in the ground plans of many oval churches during the Renaissance.[141] On an imaginary line running through the obelisk and

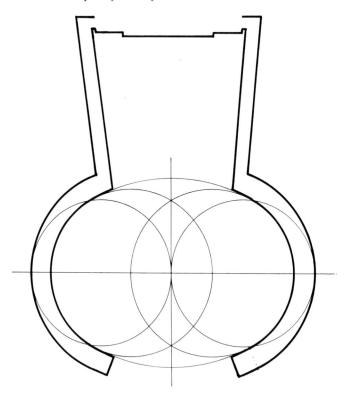

Geometrical system of Bernini's oval project for the Piazza di S. Pietro.

parallel to the façade of the basilica lie two circles intersecting at their centres. The point where the peripheries intersect is taken as the centre of a larger circle, which provides the "finishing arcs" that produce the oval based on the first two. On the same line running through the obelisk lie the centres of two circles touching one another at the point where the obelisk stands. At the centres of these circles the two fountains have been placed; the one on the north side was already there and only needed moving slightly. The greatest distance between the peripheries of these circles gives the width of the colonnade. We need not go into all the extremely complicated details of the geometrical system on which the plan of the piazza is based, but we can only admire Bernini's skill in adapting such a strict and complex system to the requirements of the site, to the main palace entrance, to the direction of the streets through the Borgo Leonino and the position of the palace in relation to the *piazza retta*,[142] while also considering the effect of all this on our perception of the façade of the church.

The foundations of the colonnades were laid by Alexander VII at a simple ceremony on 28 August 1657, and the medal struck to commemorate the event shows that the plans had been altered substantially since March.[143] The arcades and pilasters had been replaced by double columns supporting a flat entablature, and the double processional aisles had given way to four rows of double columns to create a three-aisled plan. Now for the first time the columns were freed from any dependence on walls or pilasters. Also the Ferrabosco tower had been abandoned, which means that the corridor towards the façade of St. Peter's had to be altered.[144] Presumably Bernini had managed to convince the pope that it would be impossible to keep the tower and yet to link the palace entrance to the Borgo Nuovo in any way that would be aesthetically acceptable. And it would certainly be cheaper to demolish the tower than to lay down a new street.

As was so often the case, further radical adjustments were made in the plans even after the foundations had been laid. Between 1657 and 1659 Bernini was kept busy with the exacting preparations and the technical difficulties of laying the foundations in the marshy terrain. It was during this preparatory stage that he definitely decided on single rather than double columns.[145] The final design was illustrated in an engraving by G. B. Bonacina, dated 1659, made in Bernini's studio and certainly under his direct supervision.[146] At the same time a large wooden model was made, probably including not the whole structure but only one exedra. This model has not survived.[147] It must have been extremely difficult to find the money for such a vast building project. And in fact the enormous cost was one reason for the congregation's original criticism of Bernini's project. However, in a report to the senate in 1660, the Venetian ambassador Angelo Correr says that the *Reverenda Fabbrica* was to bear the entire cost, and their revenues were in fact substantial. But it is also clear from Correr's report that the financial experts in the congregation, including Virgilio Spada, were worried: they estimated that the total cost would exceed the then colossal sum of one million scudi.[148] Thus it seems likely that the pope must have obtained additional funds elsewhere.

It was probably also during this last phase that the elevation of the colonnades received its final form. As we have already seen a determining factor in all solutions was the position of the obelisk. From this it followed that the imaginary line through the obelisk and parallel with the façade of St. Peter's must divide the exedras on either side into two exactly equal parts. At the eastern end the colonnade could not be allowed to extend so far as to block the view of the palace entrance from the Borgo Nuovo, which would also mean that the innermost section of the colonnade would actually screen the palace entrance. It was presumably this circumstance that provided a welcome excuse for demolishing the Ferrabosco tower. On the other hand it was impossible to give the palace entrance a monumental form without introducing too pronounced a break between the exedra and the straight arm towards the façade, which would have to meet at an oblique angle. The problem was solved by introducing in the angle at the point of transition rhomboid-shaped pillars which smoothly mediated the awkward junction—a solution that was both brilliant and unusual.[149] In the final version, however, the palace entrance is enhanced by an aedicule or projection formed by two columns which have been brought forward in front of the pillars. For the sake of symmetry the aedicule is repeated at the other end of the colonnade. Previously the palace entrance had been blocked by the Ferrabosco tower, but it could now be moved slightly forward and adapted to the colonnade architecture.

To the east the colonnade terminates in the same kind of square pillars as at the palace entrance, but in this case there is no need for the rhomboid form; here too the outermost columns are linked with the pillars by a short length of wall. This type of combination of column and pillar was quite new, appearing here for the first time in the history of architecture. The eastern end of the exedra is crowned by a triangular tympanum, which could not be repeated at the western end because of the junction with the corridor. This corridor was completed in 1659 with double pilasters, perhaps as a relic of the coupled-column proposal. In any case these double pilasters somewhat reduce the impression of length, and their rythm differed from that of the colonnades. The paired columns of the earlier proposal were retained only in the two porch-like aedicules in the middle of the exedras. Here too the columns have been placed in front of the pillars. The aedicules emphasise the longer axis of the oval and break the columnar rhythm of the exedras, which might otherwise have seemed monotonous.

The colonnades form three aisles; the middle passage, which is broader and covered by a barrel vault is well adapted to processions. In the outer aisles the columns support cross-beams forming a series of great coffers. This solution emphasises the tectonic aspect of the structure, recalling Michelangelo's porticoes for the Palazzo dei Conservatori.

Bernini: plan and elevation of the final project for the colonnades of St. Peters' engraving by Bonacina. BAV, *Chigi P VII 9*, fols 19v–20r.

Bernini: pilasters and entablature in the Piazza S. Pietro at the corner close to the *Portone di bronzo*, showing the oblique forms (Author's photo).

The Tuscan columns of the colonnades belong to the Doric order, and we should thus expect to see a Doric entablature complete with metopes and triglyphs such as Bernini in fact included in his first proposal. Later, however, he replaced this by an Ionic entablature with a frieze and dentils. Bernini was certainly aware that even during Classical Antiquity the rules were not always strictly applied—he had only to look at the Colosseum—and the Ionic entablature would give him an unbroken frieze running round the whole arcade like a ribbon, providing a counterforce to the vertical thrust of the columns. At first he had planned an attic above the entablature, but this was abandoned and replaced by a balustrade. With its many small vertical accents repeated rhythmically in the plinths and statues, the balustrade echoes the vertical statement of the columns and counteracts the horizontality of the entablature.

After the foundations were laid in August 1657, building began in March on the inner columnar ring of the northern colonnade; by 30 July 47 columns had already been raised.[150] Over the next few years work proceeded apace. Huge supplies of travertine were quarried from the plain below Tivoli and towed in barges along the Aniene and the Tiber for unloading at a special harbour for the use of the *Reverenda Fabbrica* close to the Ospedale Santo Spirito. The entire northern colonnade was complete by 1662, but when Alexander VII died in 1667 the southern exedra was still unfinished.[151] It was finished by 1671 under his successor Clement IX, who generously allowed Chigi's arms to embellish it.

At the same time work began on the 96 statues which were to crown the colonnades. They were all designed by Bernini, and he also worked out the iconographical programme to include the most famous saints and martyrs of the Church.[152] The statues were all made in his studio, most of them by Lazzaro Morelli working with eight other sculptors. At the time of Alexander VII's death, more than half the 96 statues above the main colonnades were

Bernini: Piazza S. Pietro; the colonnade in relation to the façade of the basilica, as seen from a point on the main axis of the oval (Author's photo).

Bernini: southern colonnade at Piazza S. Pietro, the middle aisle with barrel vault (CI).

Bernini: Piazza S. Pietro, the northern colonnade (Author's photo).

Bernini: Piazza S. Pietro,
eastern end of the
northern colonnade
(Author's photo).

finished, but the 44 statues which crown the pilasters of the corridors in pairs were not made until Clement XI's pontificate.

From the 1657 medal we can see that Bernini was already intending to close the piazza with a free-standing colonnade—the *terzo braccio*—between the two exedras.[153] The medal shows an arm with six pairs of double columns which reappears with only minor variations on the two later medals. In Bonacina's engraving of 1659, however, it has been given three columns on each side of an aedicule resembling those in the middle of the two exedras. The *terzo braccio* on the 1657 medal is straight, while the later version on Bonacina's engraving follows the curve of the oval. When the southern exedra was finished at the beginning of 1667, Bernini produced a new proposal in which the *terzo braccio* would have looked like a section of the colonnade surmounted by a clock-tower with three arches. This version of the arm is straight and set back a little to the east to form a small ante-piazza before the main oval piazza.[154] This suggestion was submitted to the congregation of the *Reverenda Fabbrica* in February 1667, but the congregation agreed with the pope, who wanted to postpone this question and give priority to the paving of the piazza and the design of its steps.[155] Alexander VII died in May and his successor abandoned the proposal on economic grounds. This idea was later revived in various versions, among others by Carlo Fontana in his *Tempio Vaticano* of 1694. Here, however, Bernini's last project for the *terzo braccio* has been set even further back and linked to the oval piazza by straight corridors, so that instead of Bernini's small forecourt there is an exact repetition of the *piazza retta* in front of the basilica. The result is a rigid and banal grandiosity which Bernini would never have countenanced.[156] According to another of Fontana's variants the whole *spina*, the buildings in the Borgo, was to be demolished as far as Castel Sant'Angelo—a suggestion which had already been made by Virgilio Spada as early as 1653.[157] As we know, the *spina* survived until 1937.

We have already mentioned the classical character of the colonnades, and the inclusion of certain anti-classical features such as the rhomboid pillars in the transition between the oval piazza and the *piazza retta*. The classical character is particularly marked in the façades terminating the two colonnades at the eastern end. The square endings are framed by slender pillars and the space between is broken only by two columns. Each façade is flanked by the just-visible columns of the aedicules facing the piazza and the corresponding aedicules facing away from it. The whole structure is crowned by a simple tympanum. These extremely straightforward and harmonious façades possess a serenity and an emphasis on clear unbroken forms that is Hellenic—one is almost tempted to say Attic—in character, recalling the Propylaea on the Athenian Acropolis. The classicism in Bernini's piazza architecture is all the more remarkable for being created at exactly the same time as the dynamic and visually conceived *Cathedra Petri*, to which we shall return below.

The well-balanced proportions between the height of the columns, the entablature, the balustrade and the statues is also worth noting. It is not the

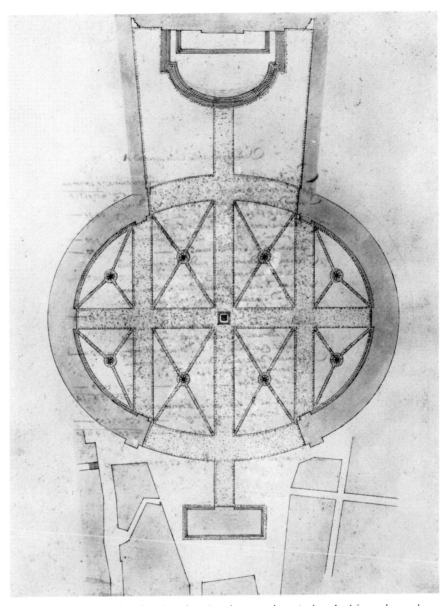

Bernini's workshop: plan drawing showing the *terzo braccio* detached from the oval, according to Bernini's final project. BAV, *Chigi P VII 9*, fol. 15r.

Bernini: Piazza S. Pietro with the *terzo braccio* curved between the two half-circles, engraving by G. B. Falda.

result of mathematical calculation as one might expect, and the observer seeks in vain for rational proportional relationships. Instead Bernini has carefully gauged the optical effect on the façade of the basilica. When the visitor stands on the main axis of the oval in one of the exedras, preferably perhaps in front of the palace entrance, looking towards the front of the church, he will find that its height coincides with the height of the colonnade. The attic of the façade appears as a continuation of the entablature and balustrade of the colonnade, and the statues on the façade of those round the sides of the oval. This is because the proportions between the height of the columns, the entablature, the balustrade and the statues in the oval piazza are the same as those between the pilasters and columns, the attic and the statues of the façade—something which cannot be pure coincidence. Bernini must surely have calculated the elevation of the colonnade in relation to the existing façade.[158] We know, too, that he was critical of this last; the façade without its *campanili* is too long for its height and Bernini had wanted to find some way of correcting this. The low corridors on each side of the *piazza retta* help by contrast to make the façade seem taller, as Bernini pointed out in his *giustificazione*,[159] and the fact that the corridors are not parallel but become further apart the nearer they come to the façade, seems to bring the front of the basilica closer; an observer in the oval piazza perceives the length of the façade as the same as the distance between the two corners where the colonnades and the corridors meet, i.e. the façade appears shorter than it really is.

The colonnades do not in fact define an enclosed space, since everywhere we can see between the columns into the area beyond; rather, they can be regarded as processional passageways from the basilica towards the Borgo or vice versa. Bernini himself has said that his colonnades are like the maternal arms of the Church, opening to receive those who approach the basilica over the tomb of the apostle.[160] But the visitor to the oval piazza nevertheless has the impression of being in an enclosed open place, an open-air room, a feeling which is certainly reinforced by the fact—rarely mentioned—that the piazza is slightly bowl-shaped. We should really think of it as an amphitheatre, and in seventeenth-century guidebooks and other notices it is referred to not as *piazza* but as *teatro* or *nuovo teatro*, the designation also used by Alexander VII in his Diary.[161] But it is of course a sacred theatre, which has always been very much in the nature of an extension into the open air of the basilica itself, a kind of great church under the heavens where crowds gather to pay homage to a new pope or to receive the papal blessing *urbi et orbi*, as well as a sacred place where the people can join the successor of St. Peter in the liturgy of the Eucharist.

⁜

The Scala Regia is a monumental stairway leading from the northern corridor behind the Portone di Bronzo up to the great ceremonial hall of the Vatican palace, the Sala Regia, and its history is inextricably linked to that of Bernini's colonnades. There had been an old staircase on this spot, used when the pope was carried in solemn procession on his *sedia gestatoria* to the basilica to officiate at the *cappella pontificia*, but it was too narrow, too steep and altogether inconvenient. The old corridor from the palace entrance in the Ferrabosco tower ran at right angles to the façade of the basilica, and from here it was possible to reach the Cortile di San Damaso, but there was no link between the corridor and the stairs.[162] Maderno had thought of linking them, but the technical difficulties were too great, largely due to the different level of the corridor and the lower section of the staircase. As we have seen, Bernini demolished the Ferrabosco tower and moved the Portone di Bronzo further to the east, letting the new corridor run obliquely to the façade of the basilica. Its course was determined partly by the last pair of columns in the colonnade and partly by the desirability of retaining a certain distance between the corridor and the façade itself. In the first projects for the corridor in 1659 the passage was still very narrow, and at first no link with the stairs was planned. Later the corridor was widened and at the same time the idea of linking it with the stairs and completely rebuilding these was born.

In planning the staircase Bernini was tied by the fact that it had to run along a terrace wall below the Vatican hill, and that the upper flight had to run along the south wall of the Cappella Sistina in order to reach the Sala Regia. The main axis of the lower flight had to be an extension of the main axis of the corridor, but the right-hand wall of the stairway was not parallel with such a line; because of the conditions we have just mentioned it had to converge with it towards the top.[163] Bernini thus had to move the left-hand wall outwards at the bottom of the stairs and let it also converge with the main axis towards the top. This involved considerable technical difficulties, since the lower flight of stairs passed beneath the Sala Regia, so that the floor and southern end wall of

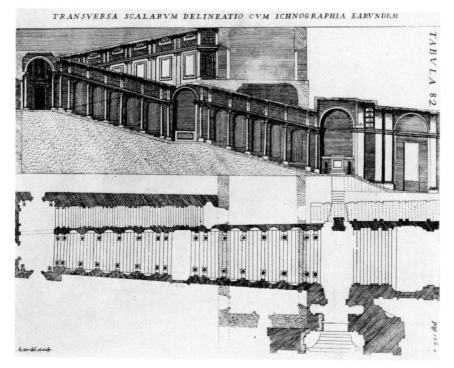

Bernini: the *Scala Regia*, plan and elevation, engraving (From Bonanni, *Numismata summorum pontificum* ..., 1715).

the great hall had to be supported by complicated wooden structures while work was in progress. The fact that the staircase passed under the Sala Regia also restricted its height. Added to which, the lower flight had to be made very long and narrow. Bernini alleviated this by placing columns a short way from the wall, supporting a longitudinal barrel vault.[164] This also counteracted the excessive narrowing effect of the converging walls. Bernini has reduced the height of the columns as the stairs close in, but he reduced them less than the loss of height in the stair well; also towards the top of the stairs he has placed them almost against the wall. Thus the stairs between the columns do not decrease in width nearly as much as the stair-well as a whole. To the spectator standing at the bottom of the stairs, all the columns seem to be the same size. To counteract the impression of overwhelming length even more, there is a landing half way up and a break in the barrel vault, where light comes in from a window at the side. Thus with great skill Bernini has exploited the extremely awkward space available,[165] making a virtue of necessity. In this task he was certainly helped by his knowledge and experience of the theatre. The technical and aesthetic problems were enormous, and Bernini personally regarded the Scala Regia as the most difficult task he had ever had to tackle.[166]

Bernini: *Scala Regia*, engraving by Alessandro Specchi (From Bonanni, *Numismata summorum pontificum . . .*, 1715).

We have no detailed information about the genesis of the stairs, but we know that they were started in the spring of 1663 and finished by 1666.[167] Their decoration was planned in detail by Bernini. Over the entrance arch there are two trumphet-blowing figures of *Fame* bearing Alexander VII's quartered arms crowned by the tiara and the papal keys. These were executed by Ercole Ferrata in 1664.[168] The staircase has an air of great festivity; it is no longer only a flight of steps leading from the palace to the basilica; it is the main ceremonial entrance to the papal palace, where the most eminent visitors mount to their official reception in the Sala Regia.

Bernini: *Constantine the
Great*, equestrian statue at
the foot of the Scala Regia
(Fototeca Unione).

The corridor meets the Scala Regia close to the spot were the northern
campanile would have stood, and at just that spot there is a doorway from the
entrance portico of the basilica. As the visitor leaves the portico and
approaches the Scala Regia he is faced by a wall which, when the door is open,
is visible from a long way away. For this site Bernini was commissioned to
make a statue of Constantine, the original founder of the basilica.

The commission actually dated back to 1654, when Innocent X had asked
Bernini to make a statue of the emperor which was to have been placed inside
the basilica on the spot where Queen Christina's monument was later built.[169]
A large block of marble had been acquired for this work, an equestrian statue
of Constantine which, as Wittkower demonstrates, would have filled exactly

into the niche concerned.[170] At the beginning of Chigi's pontificate the project was abandoned to be revived a couple of years later but now for a new position.

Work on the statue was in progress while the Scala Regia was being built. We know that Bernini was busy on it during 1662, and about that time both Queen Christina and the pope visited the artist in his studio and saw it there. It was probably not finished until 1668, however, and it was not unveiled until 1670.[171] The large payments made to Bernini personally suggest that he must have been essentially responsible for the execution of the sculpture.

Constantine is shown on horseback as we might imagine him before the battle of Ponte Milvio, when he saw a vision of the Flaming Cross and heard the famous words: "By this sign you will conquer." Bernini had studied ancient sources describing the appearance of the emperor,[172] who is seen here gazing up at the Cross, his face illuminated by light from the window behind it, so that the whole tableau has a visionary glow appropriate to the event it portrays. The posture of the rearing horse was used again by Bernini in his unfinished equestrian statue of Louis XIV, the *bozzetto* for which is in the Villa Borghese. The drapery behind the figure of the emperor reflects the drama of what is about to happen; the folds form powerful downward diagonals from left to right, parallel with the diagonals of the rider's body and the horse's front legs. But although the drapery thus emphasises the dynamic element in the tableau, it also represents something of a necessary compromise: the statue which had been intended originally for a much smaller niche inside the church would have been too small by itself here.[173] It is the dynamic and dramatic element that distinguishes this equestrian statue from the severe and static portraits of the Renaissance which were based on antique models, in particular the equestrian statue of Marcus Aurelius, although a similar approach can be found in the drawings of Leonardo da Vinci which Bernini may have seen.

At the beginning of Chigi's pontificate Bernini was commissioned to submit suggestions for a funerary monument for Alexander VII himself.[174] It had not yet been decided where this should be placed, but marble had been obtained and the pope began to discuss the plans with Bernini. However, the work on the monument was interrupted and not renewed until long after Alexander's death. Instead Bernini was to devote all his efforts to his many more important commissions, chiefly the colonnades round St. Peter's Square and the Scala Regia, as well as a major task inside the Basilica—the Cathedra Petri.

On 6 March 1656, before Bernini had been asked to make plans for the piazza, the congregation of the *Reverenda Fabbrica* decided that in accordance with the wishes of the pope the Cathedra Petri should be placed in the basilica's western apse behind the high altar. The apse ended in three great columnar niches, the one on the left containing Paul III's sepulchral monument and the one on the right Urban VIII's. The Cathedra Petri was to be placed between them and the commission was given to Bernini.[175]

A wealth of documentary material makes it possible for us to follow the

Del Cavalier Gio: Lorenzo Bernino

Bernini: project for the
Cathedra Petri, workshop
drawing. Royal Library,
Windsor Castle
(Copyright reserved.
Reproduced by gracious
permission of H.M.
Queen Elizabeth II).

history of the monument and the evolution of the plans from the first rough
sketches to the completion of the final version: the drawings and sketches have
been published by Brauer and Wittkower, and the accounts have been reproduced *in extenso* by Roberto Battaglia. But despite these documents and the
research which has been done, much remains uncertain.[176]

The Cathedra Petri, which had been in the basilica since the ninth century,
was a chair traditionally claimed to be the episcopal throne of St. Peter.
Scientific examinations at the end of the 1960s have shown that the throne in
question dates from the Carolingian age, and we now know that it was given to
Pope John VIII by Charles the Bald, perhaps when he was crowned emperor
in 875.[177] At first the chair must have served as the papal throne, which gave
rise to the special symbolical meaning attaching to it and to the false tradition
which claimed it as a relic from the time of St. Peter. As the episcopal throne of
St. Peter it came to be regarded as a symbol of the papal office, of the role of

Bernini: later project for
the *Cathedra Petri*,
workshop drawing (From
Brauer & Wittkower).

the Roman pontiff as teacher and guardian of the pure doctrine and the unity of the Church.[178] This conception stems from the symbolism of the empty throne in Classical Antiquity, invoking majesty and the presence of the ruler and sometimes shown with the Roman eagle above it. These ideas were inherited by the Early Christian Church, which often depicted the empty throne, generally in mosaic and often together with the dove of the Holy Spirit, symbolising the Pantocrator. Moreover the bishop's throne in Early Christian and mediaeval churches was often placed in the apse behind the high altar, where it came to symbolise the authority of the bishop and his role as shepherd of his flock. In the Vatican basilica the relic of St. Peter's episcopal throne was treated with the greatest veneration. Already during the Early Middle Ages it had been enclosed in a reliquary and placed above an altar dedicated to St. Peter. In the new basilica the Cathedra Petri was placed in the baptismal chapel, symbolising the subjection of the newly baptised to the

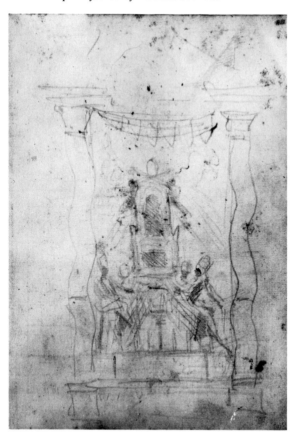

Bernini: autograph drawing
of the Cathedra Petri seen
between the columns of
the *baldacchino*. BAV, *Chigi
A I 19*, fol. 42v.

authority of the pope. This arrangement is known to us from a drawing by
Domenico Castelli in the Vatican Library.[179] The throne was preserved in a
wooden reliquary which can still be seen in the Museo Sacro of St. Peter's
which also possesses a copy of the actual cathedra. The reliquary was flanked
by two angels in adoration, and above it the Holy Dove hovered in a halo of
clouds. The whole structure was probably designed by Bernini, although none
of it was actually the work of his hand. It was finished by 1646.

When the pope now decided, only ten years later, to move the Cathedra
Petri and place it in the apse of the basilica, his idea was to give it a more
prominent position while also emphasising the association with the Early
Christian tradition of the episcopal throne in the apse. In Alexander's eyes the
cathedra was so important a symbol of the papal office that it called for a
worthier position in this church consecrated to the apostle and built over his
tomb.[180] We can think of many reasons why Alexander VII wished so urgently
to emphasise the authority of the papacy and its apostolic origins just at this
time, for never had the authority of the popes been so beset: it was denied by

Bernini: the *Cathedra Petri*. St. Peter's (Saskia Archive).

Bernini: *St. Augustine*,
detail of the *Cathedra Petri*.
St. Peter's (Anderson).

all the supporters of the Reformation—Lutherans, Calvinists and Anglicans
alike; it was contested by the Orthodox Churches and questioned by the
Jansenists. That the suggestion to move the cathedra was the pope's own is
expressly stated in the decree of 1656. We also know that Alexander took a
great interest in the subsequent plans, and we can be fairly sure that he was
behind the iconography of the monument.

Now that it had been decided to place the Cathedra Petri at the back of the
apse, the idea of providing the basilica with permanent fittings for the *cappella
pontificia*, with a papal throne in the apse and choir stools on either side as had
been suggested at the beginning of the seventeenth century, had to be abandoned. To this day the papal throne is placed beneath the Cathedra Petri for
the *cappella pontificia*, and choir stools of an extremely provisional kind are set
up for the cardinals and the canons of St. Peter's.

The congregation accepted Bernini's design for the new construction of the
cathedra on 17 March 1657, when they also approved his first plans for the
colonnades in the square.[181] Funds were allocated for the execution of the
monument, and 6,000 ducats were to be paid in three instalments—a sum

which was later increased to 8,000. Bernini personally was to receive 60 ducats a month for the colonnades, but it was felt that the cathedra would require a lot more work—Bernini was to make the wax models himself and to supervise the casting in bronze, the polishing, and the setting up of the sculptures—and for this he was to receive 200 ducats a month over a period of five years.

A drawing in the Royal Library at Windsor shows what must have been one of Bernini's very first suggestions.[182] Four bishops—it is not certain whether they are already the Fathers of the Church—are carrying on their shoulders a reliquary in the form of a chair. The composition is confined to the niche and flanked by the two columns, which it was intended from the start to replace by columns of red-and-white *cottanello* marble. Above the niche there hovers an archangel carrying the papal tiara in one hand and the keys in the other. Another very similar drawing was known only in reproduction until it turned up a few years ago on the London art market.[183] It shows a somewhat larger composition; the bishops protrude slightly out of the niche, and the throne is no longer carried by them—it is hovering. The archangel has been replaced by the Holy Dove in a radiant Glory and angels in adoration crown the columns.

A fairly small model was made, probably related to one of these sketches. Alexander noted in his Diary on 14 April 1658[184] that Bernini had shown him a clay model of the cathedra, two *palmi* high, and models of St. Augustine and St. Ambrose. Thus the iconographical scheme including the Church Fathers had been determined by this time. The accounts reveal that the Fleming Verpoorten, together with Ercole Ferrata and Antonio Raggi and Lazzaro Morelli already made full-scale models of the Church Fathers in 1658.[185] A beautiful *bozzetto* in stucco and clay which is in the Detroit Institute of Art, is thought to have been made at this point in the evolution of the monument.[186] The models were set up in the basilica on a wooden structure which was probably finished by April 1660.[187] This must have been what Andrea Sacchi saw on a visit to the basilica on Bernini's invitation. Pascoli mentions this visit in his biography of Bernini and reports Sacchi's criticism which provoked the artist's decision to increase the scale of the whole composition.[188]

Bernini must have worked on this larger-scale composition between 1660 and 1661, which meant that new models of the Church Fathers had to be made. From the accounts we can see that Lazzaro Morelli was mainly responsible for these, and from now on he becomes increasingly important as a kind of factotum, sometimes supervising the great studio where work on the monument was being conducted. The studio now employed about 35 artists, all specialists of various kinds. But already before it had been decided to enlarge the monument, the first agreement had been reached with Giovanni Artusi, who was to cast the sculptures in bronze.[189] In 1660 he cast six angels for the Glory above the throne. From this same time, when Bernini was struggling with the problem of the proportions of the monument and its appearance when viewed from the body of the basilica, we have a drawing by his hand of the cathedra seen from the nave and framed by the twisted columns of the *baldacchino*.[190] The window above the niche was probably already included as

Bernini: *Cathedra Petri*,
detail. St. Peter's (Anderson).

part of the composition in the 1660 model, and it was for the radiance round this that Artusi cast the first angels. The window with its direct light from behind must have caused a good deal of trouble, as Bernini could not use it to produce the kind of concealed light from above which he often used to create dramatic effects. In the final composition the window has been transformed into an oval aperture with the Holy Dove in stained glass. The Glory round the window has been enlarged to include not only the six angels already cast in bronze but also many other angels and *putti*, all in stucco and executed mainly by Ferrata, Raggi and Morelli.[191] The light from the window also assumes material form in bunches of gilded rays, resembling those in the niche of the *Ecstacy of St. Teresa*. Here the bundles of rays help to extend the composition, breaking out of the niche in front of the giant flanking pilasters which now provide a vast frame containing the whole mighty structure, instead of the single columns on each side of the niche. In fact the niche is now completely hidden, and of the columns we see only the capitals.

In the autumn of 1661 Artusi began to cast the Church Fathers. First he made St. Augustine.[192] Not since Antiquity had anyone cast such a large statue. They are all five metres high, and Artusi immediately ran into great practical problems. The first cast of St. Augustine was a failure, as the mould broke and the whole thing had to be redone. The second time the mould was buried in the

Bernini: *Cathedra Petri*,
detail of the angels in the
Glory. St. Peter's
(Saskia Archive).

ground to prevent it cracking. By the beginning of 1663 all four Fathers of the Church were ready, but the work on the cleaning and polishing and the carving of the decoration dragged on for some time. And the gilding had to wait until the statues were taken to the basilica and placed provisionally in position. They then had to be taken down again, and for a while the apse was transformed into a smoky, steaming workshop. The pope took the keenest interest in the progress of the work and on at least one occasion he visited the site in person to watch the gilding.[193]

The throne itself was the last part of the monument to receive its definitive form, between 1663 and 1665. Models of the angels flanking the throne were made and remade several times. Some of these are in the Museo Sacro of the basilica. The Austrian Giovanni Paolo Schor, who specialised on ornamentation, carved St. Ambrose's cope and the floral ornamentation of the seat of the throne with its acanthus leaves and stars, and he also painted the dove in the window.[194] But the reliefs on the throne were carved by Bernini himself, and are among the very few that we have from his hand.[195] On the back of the throne we see the *Pasce oves meas* (John 21:16–17), when Jesus appears to the apostles by the sea of Tiberias and entrusts his sheep—the Church—to Peter. The reliefs on the sides show the *Washing of the Feet* and the *Handing over of the Keys*, but they are barely visible to the visitor standing below.

The base of the cathedra is in black-and-white marble and red Sicilian jasper. This last was obtained from Trapani with the help of the Jesuits, who had contacts there and were able to arrange transport by sea.[196]

The final phase of the work took place while Bernini was in Paris in 1664, but his studio was now so well organised and had such efficient routines that the work could advance under the direction of Gian Lorenzo's brother Luigi Bernini, who often supervised the financial and practical affairs of the workshop, and Lazzaro Morelli. When Bernini returned to Rome the Glory was still not quite ready, and he promptly climbed the scaffolding and put the finishing touches to it himself. In January 1666 the cathedra was finished and unveiled on 17 January, the feast of the Cathedra Petri.[197] The evening before at the first Vespers the throne itself had been transferred to its new reliquary in solemn procession and in the presence of a great crowd of the faithful.

The visitor should if possible first see the Cathedra Petri from the far end of the nave, framed between the twisted columns of the *baldacchino*. Then as he approaches it he will experience the monument in all its true splendour. Its effect varies constantly depending on the light, which is never the same from morning to evening. Sometimes the strong morning light from the windows at the side seems to assume the material form of gilded rays flooding into the apse. Light and colour dominate our perception of this monument, which is almost as visual in its character as a wash drawing. The static nature of the first proposal has disappeared and now the whole tableau is alive with movement and an irresistible force. The Fathers of the Church and the throne are uniform in colour, predominantly dark and gilded bronze. We see these lower forms silhouetted against the gilded clouds which continue down beneath the throne. To some extent this lower part belongs to our temporal existence, while the rest belongs to the celestial world—the heavens are open. In the lower half the movement flows clearly from left to right, in a curving sweep from the shoulder and right arm of St. Ambrose and continuing into one of the volutes of the throne. The movement is reflected in the folds in his cope and even in St. Athanasius behind him. On the other side this flowing movement persists, partly in St. John Chrysostomos and through the volute to St. Augustine, to his arm and the folds of his mantle. There the movement ends. St. Augustine represents the most prominent and most serene of the four Fathers, and one is tempted to see this as a reproach to the Jansenists.[198] The throne hovers, unsupported, while the volutes and rounded curve of the seat and back introduce an upwards thrust that to some extent counteracts its weight, and above the light from the Holy Dove seems to flash like a burst of fire. At the centre all material form is dissolved, but as we move outwards the angels and *putti* become clearer and more substantial. At the centre all is stillness, while the movement increases in force as it flows outwards. The overall impression is of joy and triumph, a mood shared by the bronze *baldacchino* over the apostle's tomb. This is a dynamic composition, filled with overwhelming power. And because of its movement we feel drawn into a brief moment, frozen in time, reminding us perhaps of Bernini's theatrical sets or his short-lived festive decorations made of perishable materials and doomed to go up in smoke and flames and light in a dramatic display of fireworks. This is not a reliquary for the Cathedra Petri but a symbol of papal power, an apotheosis. Here Alexander VII and Gian Lorenzo Bernini wanted to show to the faithful, to heretics and to the heathen, a symbol of the apostolic institution of the papacy and the divine confirmation invested in the throne of St. Peter.

Bernini's Architecture—Three Churches and a Palace

Before discussing the three churches which Bernini designed during this pontificate, we must first look briefly at his contribution to the restoration of the Pantheon. The Pantheon, which the Romans often called *la Rotonda* but which was and still is officially the church of S. Maria ad Martyres, had been causing concern to both Paul V and Urban VIII. People were well aware of the Pantheon's significance as the best preserved of the antique monuments of Rome, and its dominating position in all mediaeval and later maps of Rome bears witness to its importance as an acknowledged centre in this overcrowded and rather jumbled district.[199]

During Alexander VII's reign quite extensive plans were made for the Pantheon under the supervision of a commission headed by Bernini.[200] Two columns of red granite were fetched from the Baths of Nero nearby and raised at the eastern end of the pronaos—Urban VIII had already replaced the actual corner column—and the architrave and capitals were embellished with Chigi's stars and oak-leaves. Bernini designed stuccoes for the coffers of the dome, also with Chigi's stars, but these were never made and the coffers remained covered by the same mousey-coloured plaster that we see today. Alexander VII wanted to cover over the open oculus through which the sun shines in, and to replace it by a stained glass window. Drawings made in Bernini's studio for this project have survived, but no window was made.[201] However, Bernini's ideas for incorporating the Pantheon into a planned urban setting, in which symmetrical streets on each side would make *la Rotunda* the central focus of an organised street network, are an important pointer to the way his mind was working with implications for the churches we shall be discussing below.

Every year in May Alexander VII would spend some time at his summer residence at Castel Gandolfo (one cannot help wondering why he didn't wait until later, to avoid the heat of Rome in summer), and he had enlarged and restored the palace built there by Urban VIII. This building has little architectural importance, and since Pius XI's radical restoration not much more than the façade remains of the seventeenth-century palace.

It fell to Bernini to provide plans for a new parish church in the piazza in front of the palace. When the foundations were laid in the spring of 1658 this church was dedicated to St. Nicholas, as we can see from a medal struck for the occasion.[202] Later, presumably during 1659, the church was rededicated to St. Thomas of Villanova, who had been canonised in November 1658. The foundation medal shows the church with a different façade, so once again as so often

Bernini: the church S. Tommaso da Villanova at Castel Gandolfo, engraving by
G. B. Falda.

elsewhere changes must have been made in the course of construction. The
pope took a keen personal interest in this church, which he always visited
when he was staying at Castel Gandolfo, and he discussed the plans with
Bernini at all stages. Bernini did not supervise the building himself, however,
entrusting it instead to his assistant Mattia de Rossi.

The interior ground plan is a Greek cross, but as sacristies were inserted
between the arms of the cross in the rear, the plan is really a hybrid, with a
Greek cross in front and an inscribed cruciform behind. Only the arm of the
cross on the entrance façade is free, but since this is the side that faces the
piazza the visitor standing in front of the church perceives it as a cruciform
building. Work proceeded rapidly. The dome was finished by 1659, and the
stuccoes inside during the following year.[203] There is a good deal about this
church that recalls the centralised churches of the Renaissance, particularly
Giuliano da Sangallo's Madonna delle Carceri in Prato. The ratios in width and
depth of the cross-arm is the same, 1:2, but the dome here is much higher and
entirely dominates the interior. The great difference, however, lies in the
powerful plasticity of the pilasters and cornices both outside and inside. From
outside it looks as though the cross-arms are attached to a central cubic block
which supports the dome, as the corners of the cube protrude between the
cross-arms. But in fact this is no central cubic block; the corners in question
are part of the pillars supporting the dome, and there is no equivalent interior
cubic space. The overall design is extremely lucid and logically defined.

The façade has two storeys with simple Tuscan pilasters below and pilaster-
strips above—these features, too, derive from the churches of the High
Renaissance. The plain entrance could have been borrowed direct from the late
fifteenth century, if it were not for the heavy pediment. Other details which

Bernini and Antonio Raggi: S. Tommaso da Villanova, Castel Gandolfo, interior of dome with stuccoes (Anderson).

distinguish the exterior from earlier models are the treatment of the corners and the projections in the entablature. On each side of the corner between the cross arms there are "pleated" pilasters, appearing to belong to the corner and contributing to the powerful assembly of verticals clustered there. And yet the projection in the entablature suggests that the pleated pilasters relate logically to the outermost pilaster on the side of the cross-arm. It is fascinating to see how the corner between the cross-arms with its massed verticals is repeated at the outer corner of the arm: the Prato church has double pilasters at the corners fulfilling more of a structural load-bearing function, whereas here the pilasters are part of an ornamental play of forms. There is even some ambiguity between the plastically conceived wall and the decoration which seems to have been draped over it like a beautiful veneer. Outside, the dome has a low

Bernini: the church S. Maria Assunta at Ariccia, engraving by G. B. Falda.

and quite unaccentuated drum, so that the ribs of the actual cupola seem to continue the vertical thrust of the façade pilasters, which culminates in the colonnettes of the lantern.

Inside, the dome has been given greater emphasis. It is supported on fluted pilasters which diverge from the Renaissance models by projecting vigorously from the four corners as though to underline their load-bearing function. Ornamentation is limited to stuccoes in the dome and pendentives, all the work of Antonio Raggi. The four evangelists occupy the pendentives, while episodes from the life of St. Thomas are shown in the oval medallions in the cupola. Here Raggi has repeated the decorations created by Schor in St. Peter's on the occasion of St. Thomas' canonisation.[204] The medallions are supported by *putti* sitting on the window pediments and carrying soft realistic garlands in striking contrast to the sober architectural forms. The ribs appear to cut across the coffers of the dome, a motif which we have seen in Pietro da Cortona's dome for Ss. Martina e Luca, but whether or not Cortona's decoration was finished before this church was begun is uncertain. The scheme may in any event have been known to Bernini. The coffers also continue behind the medallions, which thus appear to float in the air, carried only by the garlands.

The building materials are plain, as befits a parish church in the *castelli romani*. The interior is in white stucco and plaster—whether the present pale yellow and beige colour scheme is the original one is doubtful[205]—and the only touches of colour are provided by the three altar paintings. Pietro da Cortona's painting for the high altar is recessed into a concave retable designed by Bernini with double columns in *giallo antico*.[206]

In 1661, the same year that S. Tommaso di Villanova was finished, Agostino and Mario Chigi acquired the little township of Ariccia, which they purchased from the Savelli family. The old fort was rebuilt and made into a palace

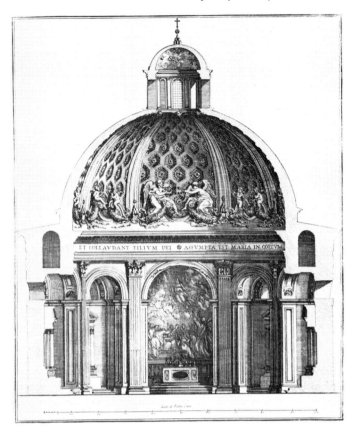

Bernini: S. Maria Assunta at Ariccia, section (From De Rossi, *Studio d'architettura civile*).

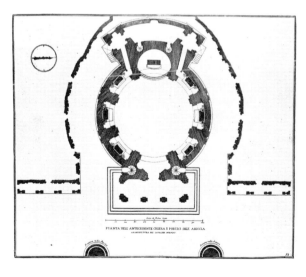

Bernini: S. Maria Assunta at Ariccia, plan (From Domenico De Rossi, *Studio d'architettura civile*, II).

without much alteration to the original architecture. This work was directed by Mattia de Rossi but probably under Bernini's supervision. Bernini was personally responsible for the plan of the church of S. Maria Assunta opposite the palace, which was completed within two years and consecrated in 1664.[207] These buildings, too—particularly the church—were of great personal concern to the pope. It was not difficult for him to visit Ariccia from Castel Gandolfo, and scattered notes in his Diary refer to frequent discussions between himself and Bernini about the plans.

The ground plan of the church is a circle, so that we have a kind of low cylinder crowned by a hemispherical dome. In front of this Bernini has placed an entrance portico with a triple arcade on pillars and a large tympanum. The church is flanked by low porticoes with flat entablatures on pillars, behind which there are wings forming a semicircle round the church, which thus becomes part of a systematised civic setting. The importance in this context of Bernini's plans for the Pantheon can be seen from drawings and preparatory studies which have survived.

This combination of a domed rotunda with an entrance portico at the front is also obviously inspired by the Pantheon, which Bernini would have been studying in detail at this time, and the same influence is also clearly noticeable in the interior. Here there are eight arched openings, the entrance arcade and the altar recess being slightly broader. The arcades are separated by majestic fluted Corinthian pilasters which together with the billowing rhythm of the arcades completely dominate the interior. Above them the entablature encircles the church in an unbroken ring directly supporting the hemispherical dome. The ribs of the dome cut across the coffers as they did in S. Tommaso, and are collected and bound together in a great ring round the base of the lantern.

In this church, too, plain materials have been used: outside, simple plaster with flat bands and inside stucco imitating marble and plaster; there is no multicoloured marble ornament. As at Castel Gandolfo a gently billowing and naturalistic festoon encircles the cupola above the cornice, with four angels and twelve *putti*. These are in stucco and were made by Paolo Naldini.[208] The church is dedicated to the Assumption of the Virgin, and the angels close to the chancel have prepared a crown for the Madonna, while the *putti* are strewing her way with flowers, all in accordance with the relevant accepted iconography. In the chancel apse a fresco illustrates the Virgin's miraculous ascension, leaving behind her the empty grave and the apostles in amaze. The painting is by Bernini's assistant Guillaume Courtois,[209] known as Borgognone, and it occupies the entire rear wall of the apse. Since the apse is partly screened by the giant pilasters, there is a strongly suggestive scenic effect; the visitor should become vividly aware of the mystery of the Assumption and the painted heavens resemble the real sky behind the church. The whole interior has been conceived in theatrical terms; here the faithful gather to witness the *sacra rappresentazione*, while the angels above prepare a joyful reception for the Queen of Heaven.

The most important and costly of the three churches which Bernini designed during this period is S. Andrea al Quirinale. This building was begun in 1658, the same year as the church in Castel Gandolfo, but it was not finished until very much later. Work on some of the stucco decoration even dragged on into the 1670s. Thanks to the *racconto* which the Jesuit fathers kept throughout, and which was recently discovered in their archives, we have detailed information about the progress of construction.[210]

The Jesuits had long since established their novitiate up on the Quirinal, far from the rush and bustle of the town. Under Innocent X the protector of the Order, Cardinal Francesco Adriano Ceva, had commissioned plans from Borromini to design a large and sumptuous church for the novitiate, but as the pope did not want a grand church so near the Quirinal garden, the project came to nothing. Alexander VII was more amenable however, and granted permission, but now Bernini was to produce the plans. Borromini was probably rejected because Prince Camillo Pamphili, who was offering to pay for much of the building, disliked him.[211]

The Jesuits wanted the church to have five altars and Bernini therefore hit upon the idea of a pentagon plan that looks like a direct loan from Serlio,[212] but he also submitted an alternative suggestion for an oval church parallel with the street lengthwise. It was the oval plan which gained acceptance. On 2 September the pope noted in his Diary that he had been shown the plan by Bernini and that he wanted the church moved slightly further back from the street, making it less visible from the Quirinal garden.

The foundations of the church were laid on 3 November, and already by November the following year the dome was complete, although its appearance was rather different from what we see today. It had undulating compartments between fairly high narrow windows, and there was neither oculus nor lantern. The alterations to the dome, which gave it the form it now has, were made between 1660 and 1672.[213] First an oculus was opened and a lantern built; the windows were then altered and reduced in scale, although the original height can still be seen on the outside of the drum. The compartments of the vault have been retained, but partly neutralised by the stucco decoration.

The oval plan of S. Andrea does not follow an *ovato tondo* system like the colonnades in front of St. Peter's or various Renaissance churches; instead it has been constructed according to a more complicated system, also based on Serlio.[214] But the greatest difference between this and earlier oval churches is that where they have chapel openings on their longitudinal axes, S. Andrea has pilasters; thus in this church there are chapels on each side of the point, marked by the pilasters, where the axis meets the periphery. As there is less emphasis on the longer axis, the visitor's sense of being enclosed by the room is all the stronger.

The entrance is covered by a barrel vault which juts up over the entablature, a theme derived from the Pantheon, and the visitor entering the church (today, unfortunately, passing through an ungainly wooden galilee) finds himself on the periphery of the oval, just at the point where the room reveals itself most

Bernini: S. Andrea al Quirinale, exterior (From G. B. Falda, *Il Nuovo teatro delle fabbriche*).

clearly, which was certainly Bernini's intention. The high-altar chapel is a shallow apse, separated from the oval space with scenic effect by paired columns with a segmental pediment, forming an aedicule and completely dominating the room. The light from a concealed window above also adds to the theatrical effect of this recess. On each side of the high-altar chapel and the entrance, the bays are slightly narrower than the four chapel openings. One of these lesser bays provides a passage to the sacristy and the others to smaller chapels, and they have flat architraves and *coretti*. Thus there is a rhythmical succession of motifs: two arcade arches, flat entablature, HIGH-ALTAR AEDICULE, flat entablature, two arcade arches—a rhythm that serves to emphasise the altar recess itself.

The interior embellishment of S. Andrea was paid entirely by Camillo Pamphili, whose ambition was to create a church *ricca e bella*.[215] To begin with the Jesuits were divided among themselves about the justification for accepting such a sumptuously decorated church, which many of them felt to be inappropriate to their Order's ideal of poverty. But the majority, including the general of the order at the time, Father Gian Paolo Oliva, decided that the rich adornment would be "ad majorem Dei gloriam" in accordance with the motto of the Jesuit Order, and since it was the gift of a wealthy patron it could not conflict with the virtues of poverty and simplicity which every Jesuit father still strictly observed in his own life.[216]

Thus, unlike the churches in Castel Gandolfo and Ariccia, S. Andrea is noted for its splendid multicoloured marble decoration. This was the work of Camillo Pamphili's *scarpellino*, Giovanni Maria Baratta, who had worked for the prince in S. Agnese. The total cost of the interior embellishment was almost three times as much as the cost of building the walls and dome, for which the Jesuits were responsible themselves. The floor is patterned in white marble and grey-blue *bardiglio*, and the chapel pilasters with their Corinthian capitals are

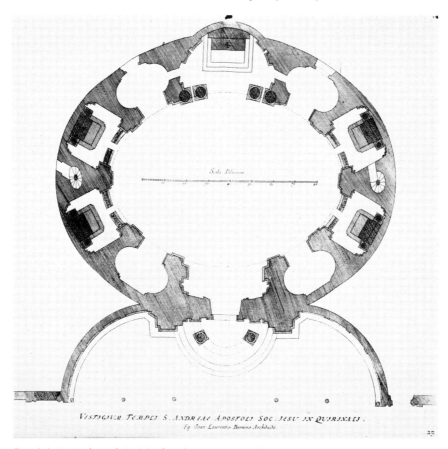

Vestigium Templi S. Andreae Apostoli Soc. Jesu in Quirinali.
Eq. Joan Laurentio Bernino Architetto.

Bernini: S. Andrea al Quirinale, plan (From Sandrart, *Insignium Romae templorum*).

of white Carrara marble. Flanking the high-altar apse are four great columns of red-and-white *cottanello*, and the same marble has been used for the arches to the chapels. The entablature is partly of white marble, while the cornice is stucco; the frieze and the spandrels over the chapel openings are of Sicilian jasper. In the dome the ribs cut across coffers of opulent stucco. A softly billowing naturalistic festoon, a plaything for groups of *putti*, encircles the dome, gently rising and falling round the windows. And above the windows there are male figures, fishermen like St. Andrew himself, made of stucco and reclining in semi-recumbent poses. The stucco ornamentation was executed by Antonio Raggi during the 1660s; Giovanni Rainaldi assisted him with some of the angels in the high-altar chapel, and Pietro Sassi was responsible for the coffers.[217]

In the interior warm colours—mainly shades of red—dominate the zone beneath the cornice, while white and gold provide the predominant theme in the dome. Thus there is a contrast between these two zones—evidence, as in the two previous churches, of the intimate relationship between architecture,

Bernini: S. Andrea al Quirinale, interior (CI).

ornamentation and iconography which Wittkower has analysed in so masterly a fashion.[218]

The painting over the high altar, Borgognone's *Martyrdom of St. Andrew*, seems to hover suspended in front of a blue mosaic background. Light floods the altarpiece from the concealed windows in the lantern of the apse. This represents the celestial light, which also assumes material form in gilded rays, and it is accompanied by *putti* and angels descending to gather up the soul of the apostle. Above the aedicule his soul can be seen in a white stucco sculpture, while the apostle himself gazes upwards, towards heaven and the Holy Dove in the lantern. We are intended to perceive the martyrdom of the apostle and his apotheosis as a divine drama, as we are drawn into a spectacle imbued with personal and inspired passion. All art was theatre to Bernini, in the sense that the feelings and emotions of the spectator were to be engaged. To produce this effect Bernini combines architecture, sculpture and painting into a single powerful whole.

Typical of Bernini's ornamentation is its playfulness, its obvious sense of

Bernini: S. Andrea al
Quirinale, interior toward
main altar (CI).

fun.[219] In S. Andrea, for instance, some of the cherubs are still fluttering
around in the lantern on their way to the empty places waiting for them in the
crowded circle of cherubs in the opening below, like a flock of small birds
alighting together on a convenient telephone wire.

The façade of S. Andrea is highly unconventional, and as Hibbard appositely
puts it, is "more of a monumental entrance or gateway than the traditional
mask before the west wall of a church".[220] Although the church itself is set
back from the street, its façade consisting of a single bay in the giant order and
a tympanum is linked to the alignment of the street by low curving walls on
each side. These concave walls conceal the convex form of the lower part of the
rotunda, and serve to emphasise the already great height of the façade. The
unfaced brick walls of the rotunda with its buttresses and windows is visible
above the low curving wings. The giant pilasters framing the entrance bay are
accompanied by corner pilasters broken at an obtuse angle, easing the transition between the façade and the curving church walls behind. At the same time
this arrangement gives us a cluster of verticals framing the façade, a corner
solution in typical Bernini style. The angular break is repeated in the entablature, which thus describes pointed folds silhouetted against the sky. The façade
pilasters frame a great lunette window, a single arch over the entrance; and
above the doorway a semicircular projecting roof is supported on two col-

Bernini: S. Andrea al
Quirinale, façade (CI).

umns—rather as though the lunette had swung out and been folded down. S.
Andrea's façade possesses an essential simplicity which creates a monumental
effect despite the modest scale.

In his treatment of the wall structure, with the pilasters like a decorative
veneer covering simple giant wall pillars, which in turn bend horizontally over
the lunette, Bernini has obviously been influenced by Michelangelo's modelling of the walls of buildings such as the Palazzo dei Conservatori and St.
Peter's.

Domenico Bernini tells how he once found his father at S. Andrea, looking
around with obvious delight.[221] Domenico asked him what he was doing there
all alone, and Gian Lorenzo answered that he often came to pray and to seek
comfort and relief from the burdens of everyday, as this was the only one of
his works in which he could find satisfaction. And we are still justified in
regarding S. Andrea al Quirinale as Bernini's most significant and consummate
architectural creation. But it is more than this: it is one of the finest products of
the Roman High Baroque. Indeed this church, which is so vibrant in its blend
of architecture and ornament, so richly joyful and life-enhancing in its riot of
colours and sumptuous range of marbles, stuccoes and gilding, is also one of
the most striking manifestations of the warm and optimistic religious spirit
which Alexander VII represented, in glaring contrast to the strict puritanism of
the Jansenists.

The palace which Flavio Chigi bought from Colonna in 1661 and then restored, had a long history.[222] In 1622 Cardinal Ludovisi had acquired it from the Colonna family, which was having financial problems at the time. Maderno was then commissioned by Ludovisi to alter and enlarge the palace but the work was never finished, and when Ludovisi became vice-chancellor a year later and moved into the Palazzo della Cancelleria, he sold the palace to Pierfrancesco Colonna. It is difficult to tell how much of Maderno's remodelling can be seen in the present palace, but the courtyard arcade with its arches on columns between pillars may be his, although otherwise the courtyard dates largely from Alexander VII's pontificate. We know that work started in 1664,[223] with Carlo Fontana acting for Bernini and directing the work, which involved pretty radical remodelling and enlargement. Gian Lorenzo Bernini probably issued general instructions, and we can assume that the façade is entirely his.

Since the original façade was relatively long, Bernini divided it into a slightly projecting central section with seven bays, flanked by shorter three-windowed wings. After the palace was sold to the Odescalchi family in 1746, the façade was extended even further; the central section was more than doubled in length, completely destroying the harmony of Bernini's composition.

Bernini returned here to a type of façade which had not been seen in Rome since the beginning of the sixteenth century, recalling Bramante's Palazzo Caprini, which no longer exists, and the Palazzo Caffarelli-Vidoni. All these Palaces have emphasised ground floors, but Bernini's has a plaster finish instead of rustication and windows instead of *botteghe*. Above the ground floor giant pilasters rise through the two upper storeys of the central projection. The wings are rusticated, although the blocks are smoothly cut, and have rustic quoins. At the junctions between the central projection and the wings, the great pilasters are met by "pleated" pilasters carrying over into the side sections. This gives us the cluster of stepped verticals so typical of Bernini's architecture, which we have already seen in the church at Castel Gandolfo. While the wings have fairly understated cornices, the central projection is crowned by a powerful cornice on brackets which in turn is topped by a balustrade that softens the sharp edge between wall and sky—a motif derived from Michelangelo's Palazzo dei Conservatori—and as in the Capitoline palace the balustrade is interrupted over every pilaster by a pedestal for a statue. But Bernini's cornice differs from those of the High Renaissance in that the brackets over the pilasters are closer to one another, so that their tremendous vertical thrust cuts right across the horizontal band of the cornice and would have culminated in the statues.

All the windows on the ground floor are *finestre inginocchiate*—literally, windows on their knees—with brackets under a flat pediment, apparently derived direct from the Palazzo Farnese. This last is also recalled in the windows of the *piano nobile*, with their small aedicules and alternating triangular and segmental pediments—a window type often used by Sangallo as well as by Michelangelo and Giacomo della Porta. Only the upper floor windows

Bernini: Palazzo Chigi, now Odescalchi, façade before 18th-century extension, engraving by G. B. Falda (From Ferrerio, *Palazzi di Roma*).

have more original surrounds. The archivolt of the main entrance is reminiscent of Mannerist architecture, while the balcony on its columns recalls Vignola. This dependence on Sangallo and Michelangelo, and the loan of details from sixteenth-century architecture, were typical of Bernini.[224] But there is no question of eclecticism, since Bernini has transformed all these forms and made them part of an entirely personal creation.

With the seven bays of its great central section, this façade already possessed a monumental majesty which was bound to impress. As designed by Bernini it was more lucid, more clearly defined, and the pilaster order made a greater impact by not being repeated *ad nauseam* along what has now become the excessively long façade. Among its many admirers was Nicodemus Tessin, who used it as his model for the façades of the Royal Palace in Stockholm.

In March 1664, the same year that Bernini began working on the façade of the Palazzo Chigi Odescalchi, he received an extremely flattering invitation from Louis XIV to submit designs for a new façade for the Louvre.[225] In April the following year, after submitting two alternative suggestions, he received word from Louis' minister, Colbert, and an invitation to come to Paris. It was difficult for Bernini to refuse, however involved he may have been with his papal commissions. The king was also hoping after the agreements in Pisa to be able to humiliate the pope further by robbing him of his most eminent architect and sculptor. Alexander felt bound to let Bernini go.[226] The artist was accorded a royal welcome at the French court, and was not slow to adopt the airs and graces of a *grand seigneur*. M. De Chantelou's famous diary[227] gives us a day-to-day account of Bernini's activities in Paris and Versailles and, what is even more valuable, of the discussion on art between the artist and his French colleagues and friends. During the summer of 1665 Bernini was working on a bust of the king, which is one of the finest portraits he ever made, while also producing a series of projects for the Louvre. But although French artists and architects may still have regarded Rome as the fount of all that was great in art, it was not easy to assimilate the Roman Baroque into the Parisian townscape, and none of Bernini's façade proposals were accepted. A couple of months later, by December 1665, he was back in Rome, where his large well-organised studio had kept things going in his absence: work had continued uninterrupted on the colonnades in St. Peter's Square, on the façade of the Palazzo Chigi, and on the Cathedra Petri.

Borromini, Pietro da Cortona and Carlo Rainaldi

Despite the setbacks he had suffered Borromini still stood at the height of his creative powers during the pontificate of Alexander VII. The dome and interior decorations of S. Ivo della Sapienza were finished, and the earlier decision to abandon the seven small columns of yellow marble which should have stood at the back of the chancel bay was now confirmed.[228] On 14 November 1660 the altar was consecrated by Cardinal Antonio Barberini, the

Borromini: the chapel of the Propaganda Fide, interior (CI).

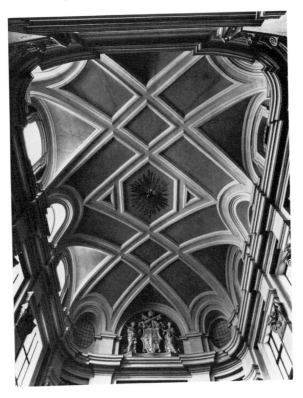

Borromini: the chapel of
the Propaganda Fide,
ceiling (CI).

church itself having been consecrated the day before. The following day the
pope said mass there, to mark the official opening of the university.

As architect for the great complex of the Propaganda Fide between the
Piazza di Spagna and S. Andrea delle Fratte, Borromini had succeeded Bernini
at a time when his rival's reputation was at its lowest ebb. In the autumn of
1646 the congregation in charge of organising church missionary activities had
appointed Borromini to the post at the command of Innocent X.[229] Borromini
retained Bernini's façade facing the piazza and the wing built by Gasparo
de'Vecchi for the missionary training college which was also housed there. The
cardinals in the congregation drew up a detailed building programme;
although the little oval church built by Bernini in the 1630s was to be kept, it
would in fact be superseded by a larger chapel in the south-western corner of
the site.[230] At first the work proceeded extremely slowly, not really speeding
up until Innocent X intervened in 1654. It was then decided to demolish
Bernini's oval church after all, and to locate Borromini's chapel on the same
spot.[231]

The building of the new chapel which was to be dedicated to the Three
Kings, did not begin until 1660. The façade on the street was more or less
finished by 1662, except for the attic which was added between 1665 and
1667.[232] The interior itself was ready by 1665, but the stucco decoration was

Borromini:
the chapel of the
Propaganda
Fide, façade
(CI).

not executed until after Borromini's death. Despite its modest dimensions the effect of this chapel is monumental, due to its giant pilasters. These are placed at fairly short intervals two by two, but not paired; two of the bays thus created are in the middle of the long walls, while the other four form the kind of corners that are so typical of Borromini. The narrow bays have openings with flat architraves topped by shallow niches for busts. The broader bays also have openings with flat architraves: the openings on the long walls lead to two chapels on each side, while one short-wall opening leads to the main altar and the other to the entrance. The chapel itself is rectangular with recesses opposite one another, a motif which Palladio also used. The giant pilasters carry no entablature, merely imposts and mouldings with a smooth continuation into the ribs of the flat vault. Here the ribs interweave to produce the same kind of pattern that Borromini had used in the Oratory and had also intended for the nave of the Lateran Basilica. Together these motifs combine to produce a remarkable coherent unity, clearly and firmly defined while also allowing for Borromini's usual rhythmical vitalisation of the walls.

Carlo Rainaldi, Francesco Borromini and others: S. Agnese at Piazza Navona (From G. B. Falda, *Il Nuovo teatro delle fabbriche*).

The façade on the Via di Propaganda is unusual in that it is not really a church façade and not really a palace. Nor is it possible to comprehend it as a whole from the front; it always has to be viewed at an angle, which perhaps explains why Borromini has created such a powerfully plastic or undulating effect with a concave bay in the middle of a long central projection. Giant pilasters are the dominating motif; they are very slightly concave at the junctions between the wings and the central projection as well as round the middle concave bay, and above them runs a sharply projecting cornice carried on brackets and giving rise to dark shadows. The windows are aedicular, concave and recessed into the wall, except for the central window which is convex in the middle of the receding bay. With their columns and pilasters, their lively and original pediments and modest but captivating leaf and flower decorations these windows provide a variety of interacting forms and effects of shadow and light that contrasts with the smooth undecorated walls of the ground floor and the wings.

It was just before work began on the chapel of the Propaganda Fide that Borromini was removed from his post as architect at the Oratory of the Philipines, despite the loyal backing of Virgilio Spada who was prior at the time. The project was completed by Camillo Arcucci, and largely spoilt by his mediocre talent.[233] At S. Agnese in the Piazza Navona Borromini had failed to gain acceptance for his ideas, and after Innocent X's death he clashed both with Prince Camillo Pamphili and with the other architects and craftsmen working there. Pamphili was incapable of understanding Borromini's originality, referring scornfully to his *"capricci inutili e modellature triangolari"*, his

Borromini: tomb of Pope
Sergius IV. Lateran
basilica (Oscar Savio).

unnecessary caprices and triangular ornaments. On 25 February 1657, after much intrigue, Borromini lost his post at S. Agnese as well.[234] He was replaced by a commission of undistinguished architects, among them Arcucci. Carlo Rainaldi tried not to oppose Borromini publicly, but when called upon he submitted a purely technical criticism of the state of the building. It then also fell to his lot to complete the dome with a lantern on a smaller scale than the one Borromini had planned, which was considered too heavy, and he used eight of the sixteen colonnettes which had already been made for Borromini's project. The *campanili* were then completed by Antonio del Grande and Giovanni Maria Baratta between 1663 and 1666.[235]

During the last few years of his life Borromini received further commissions from the Falconieri family. One of these was for the high altar in S. Giovanni dei Fiorentini, but here Borromini was restricted by the altar which Pietro da Cortona had started and left half-finished. Only in the funerary monuments

Borromini: tomb of
Cardinal Giussano.
Lateran basilica
(Oscar Savio).

on either side of the altar can we see signs of his originality, in the shallow
eliptical niches recessed in the slight concavity of the wall.[236]

Under Alexander VII the decoration of the Lateran Basilica was also
finished. The antique bronze doors which had once belonged to the *curia* of
the Roman Senate, brought from S. Adriano, and several funerary monuments
from the old basilica—most of them mediaeval—were placed along the aisle
walls. Here Borromini has also combined ancient fragments of mosaic and
marble colonnettes with new elements of his own to produce highly unconventional aedicular monuments, spaced along the aisles in rythmical relation to
the windows and pilasters.[237]

From 1653 until his death Borromini was also working on the church of S.
Andrea delle Fratte for the Marchese Paolo del Bufalo.[238] The project advanced
extremely slowly, and was still unfinished at Borromini's death. The dome
with its *campanile* on one side is intended as a *point de vue* for anyone
approaching the church along Via Capo le Case. This dome represents an
extreme expression of Borromini's strength and originality in the modelling of
architectural forms. The cylindrical inner structure of the dome is completely
hidden by the four buttresses; these are linked by concave compartments
separated by protruding window aedicules. But the dome never acquired the

Borromini: S. Andrea
delle Fratte, dome and
belltower (Anderson).

intended lantern, and with its unfaced brick walls it has the air of some ancient
monumental ruin.

Borromini's pathological melancholy increased with the years. He became
more and more isolated, full of doubts and uncertainties, avoiding all contact
with other people and burying himself in his work. His suspicious disposition
was giving way to pure persecution mania.[339] In the summer of 1667 he kept to
his bed with stomach trouble. One day he collected together all the drawings
which he had guarded so jealously throughout his working life, and burned
them to prevent them falling into the hands of his adversaries and rivals. A few
days later he suffered an acute nervous crisis, and after a mild dispute with his
servant his despair became so violent that he fell upon his sword. He survived
for a day, and after receiving absolution from his confessor died on 3 August
1667.

Pietro da Cortona: S. Maria della Pace and surrounding buildings (From G. B. Falda, *Il Nuovo teatro delle fabbriche*).

S. Maria della Pace, plan of church and square in front of façade (Detail of Nolli's map 1748).

At the beginning of Alexander VII's pontificate Pietro da Cortona was commissioned to create a new façade for the church of S. Maria della Pace, and to make a few minor alterations to the interior. The pope's particular interest in this church may have been due not only to his devotion to the Virgin, but also to the presence here of a Chigi chapel which the great Agostino had originally intended for his own memorial chapel. It has also been suggested that as the

Pietro da Cortona: S. Maria della Pace, façade (CI).

little fifteenth-century church was originally built in honour of Our Lady of Peace at the time of the peace between the Italian states in 1482, and since Alexander hoped at the beginning of his reign to act as a peaceful mediator between the great powers, he may have felt a special affection for the church on this account.[240]

At the beginning of 1656 Pietro da Cortona submitted a proposal for a new façade with a covered entrance portico resembling a semicircular columnar temple, to be placed in front of the old facade and providing a dramatic backdrop to the street setting. The street was not broad, and on a level with the façade it divided into two even narrower alleys. The pope was struck by the fact that a carriage could not drive right up to the church, and visitors always had to walk the last few steps. For this reason he wanted to enlarge the open space in front of the church and make a small piazza. He ordered that the property next to the façade be demolished, and provided funds for the purpose.[241] It was at this point that Pietro da Cortona submitted plans for extending the façade at the sides. Work proceeded so rapidly that the whole project was complete by 1657. Throughout the genesis and evolution of the plans Pietro da Cortona conferred with the pope and showed him his designs and models. Entries in the pope's Diary,[242] show that he followed the work with the keenest interest, and he composed the inscription of the façade himself—a message of peace.[243]

The main body of the church protrudes from an exedra into the little piazza in front of it, but the lower part of the exedra is entirely screened by buttresses and a wall on each side. We could describe this as a traditional triptych façade, except that the flanking sections are so deeply recessed. There are openings in the screening side walls next to the church itself, on the left for a side door into the building and on the right for an alley running along the wall of the neighbouring church of S. Maria dell'Anima. The outer bays of the walls consist of smooth panels between half columns. The dominating feature of the church façade is the semicircular portico which swells out into the piazza like half a small round temple. The architect seems to have been inspired by classical architecture and by Bramante and Peruzzi.[244] Here the columns are in pairs, reminding us that at just this time Bernini was planning his colonnades with their double columns round St. Peter's square, and as we have seen Bernini used a similar motif later in the façade of S. Andrea al Quirinale. Above this portico the façade of S. Maria della Pace is slightly convex, as though squeezed between the bordering pilasters, but just beyond the pilasters is a hint of concavity into which the convex section may appear to nestle. At the furthermost point on both sides, and in both storeys, there are also free-standing columns supporting an extended section of the entablature and framing the whole façade. The main entablature is supported in the middle, on each side of the window, by single columns recessed into the wall. These columns do not belong, as one might think at first, to the window aedicule, which is actually formed by pilasters carrying the segmental arch which breaks into the area of the triangular tympanum. This interlocking of two forms, this juggling with architectural features, and even a certain ambiguity—all are typical devices in Pietro da Cortona's work.

As in Cortona's façade for Ss. Martina e Luca, fillets start from the base of the window arches, threading their way behind pilasters and columns and re-emerging at the same level on the exedra—the effect is of ribbons binding together all the elements of this complex façade. The pilasters of the upper

Pietro da Cortona:
S. Maria della Pace,
detail of façade
(CI).

storey of the church itself reappear not only in the exedra but also in the façades of the buildings surrounding the piazza, whose appearance has been made to harmonise with the church.

With all these details the façade and the piazza together have much in common with contemporary theatre decorations—and this was certainly intentional. The pope refers to this piazza and the façade more than once as *Teatro* or *Portico e Teatro della Pace*.[245] The façade is not only a façade, nor is it simply three-dimensional in the manner of many Baroque façades; rather, a whole room has been created here, enclosing the visitor standing before the church. And there is an element of surprise in it all, for this architectural jewel has been set in the place where we would least expect to find it, in the midst of a jumble of narrow streets and dark alleys.

Soon after the church of S. Maria della Pace was finished, Pietro da Cortona created a new façade for S. Maria in Via Lata, a foundation dating back to the seventh century.[246] This façade is more sober and in some ways more classical than Cortona's usual style. The circumstances were also rather special, since it was difficult to do credit to the façade of the church on its site on the Corso.

The façade has two storeys with a very slightly projecting central section framed by pilasters in the lower storey and by half-columns in the upper. These carry over the entablature *en ressaut* so that there is no break in the vertical flow from ground level up to the triangular gable which crowns the main central compartment of the façade. This section is flanked by rather narrow bays, and the outermost pilasters are not carried over the entablature. The dominating feature of this façade—an unusual one—is the two-storey loggia with four columns on each floor. The central opening is slightly broader, and in the upper storey the entablature forms an arch jutting up into the triangular pediment above. This is a Serlian motif which, although it is unusual, does occur in Renaissance architecture. For instance, it was used by Leon Battista Alberti for the façade of S. Sebastiano in Mantua. In the case of S. Maria in Via Lata, Roman and Hellenistic models are often cited and it is widely believed that Pietro da Cortona may have been influenced by engravings of the ruins at Baalbek. Wittkower, who refers to these sources, also points out that Borromini used the Serlian motif and that Pietro da Cortona may have found his inspiration there.[247] However, as at Ss. Martina e Luca, there is also the influence of Tuscan architecture to be considered. The interior of the entrance portico for example, has certain elements which appear to derive from the sacristy of S. Spirito in Florence, built by Cronaca in 1489 and certainly known to Pietro da Cortona. A barrel vault is supported on two rows of columns, those of the street façade and free-standing columns in front of the inner wall of the portico. Pietro da Cortona has produced a characteristic

Pietro da Cortona: S. Maria in Via Lata, façade, engraving by G. Vasi, detail.

Pietro da Cortona: S. Maria in Via Lata, upper part of façade (Max Hutzel).

solution for the short apsidal ends of this portico, where the barrel vault appears to continue beyond the apses, which seem to be screening it from view. Whenever Pietro da Cortona introduces decorative details of this kind into his architecture or his painting, he shows delightful inventiveness and originality in the way he adapts and makes use of earlier prototypes.

Alexander VII harboured grandiose plans for remodelling the Chigi palace in Piazza Colonna and restoring the piazza in front of the family home. We shall return to this last project in another context. Pietro da Cortona submitted a design for the palace façade, which is known to us from a drawing in the Vatican Library. It is one of his many unrealised architectural projects.[248] The façade is conceived as a great exedra between flanking projections; in the exedra there is a splendid fountain with artificial rocks. Above this rusticated base, the *piano nobile* with its pilasters and columns and a dominating central arch provides a remarkably monumental and powerful palace façade.

Pietro da Cortona's last major architectural creation was the dome of S. Carlo al Corso.[249] This church, which was the national church of the Milanese and originally dedicated to St. Ambrose, had been begun in 1612 by Onorio Longhi and continued by Onorio's son Martino Longhi the Younger between 1619 and 1627. However, the crossing and the chancel tribune were not added until the 1660s, under the direction of a lesser-known architect, Tommaso Zanoli, and supervised by a commission which included both Borromini and Pietro da Cortona. The driving-force behind the project was Cardinal Luigi Omodei, who later designed the rather unsuccessful façade of the church himself. Pietro da Cortona was solely responsible for the plans for the dome, which was begun in 1668 and completed after his death the following year.

Pietro da Cortona: the
dome of S. Carlo al Corso
(Author's photo).

The treatment of the drum is both original and typical of Pietro da Cortona's fertile and imaginative style. The clustered pilasters are flanked by freestanding columns, and the wall behind these with its great windows rises behind the entablature, so that both columns and entablature are clearly defined by lines of shadow. Each set of columns and pilasters can be seen as forming a single unit, enlivened by the contrast of hard edges and soft curves; in the rhythmic flow round the drum the windows then provide the caesuras. But it is also possible to relate the columns to the architrave above the windows, in which case the clustered pilasters provide the breaks in the rhythm. Once again Cortona is typically ambiguous. A low attic above the drum has small horizontal oval windows surrounded by volutes and triangular fillets. Here, too, above the pilasters, there are small curved plinths or brackets, a motif that reappears in the architecture created by Cortona in his paintings. The vertical motifs of the drum and the attic are carried over *en ressaut* to continue in the ribs of the dome. The ribs are also clustered and culminate in the little bracket-like pilasters of the lantern—an old-fashioned feature with Mannerist roots. This coherent rhythm and the rich contrasts in the drum between light and shadow, between hard forms and soft, all combine to create a strikingly decorative effect. Apart from the superb plasticity of its forms, this dome seems also to be enhanced by the very air around it, as though an immaterial layer of *chiaroscuro* has draped itself over the material forms.

Girolamo Rainaldi, who as *Architetto del popolo romano* had worked on the buildings on the Capitol as well as on Pamphili's great palace in the Piazza Navona, died in 1655. He had combined Domenico Fontana's conservative style with impulses from North Italian architecture, but he lacked any ability to innovate. The façade of the Palazzo Pamphili is not at all satisfactory, and his proposal for S. Agnese was completely altered by his son Carlo. On Girolamo's death Carlo took over as *Architetto del popolo romano*, a post which brought him a certain amount of prestige. Together with his father he may have cherished a hope of working on the square of St. Peter's, but the new pope preferred the plans submitted by the slightly older but much more dynamic Bernini.

Nonetheless, Carlo Rainaldi is one of the great architects of the Roman Baroque, even if he falls short of the three giants, Borromini, Bernini and Cortona, and he developed a style of his own which Wittkower calls "a unique symbiosis of Mannerist and High Baroque stylistic features".[250] It was as the official architect to the city that he received two of his most important commissions during Chigi's pontificate, S. Maria in Campitelli and the churches in the Piazza del Popolo.

In the autumn of 1656 the Roman senate decided that the miraculous picture of the Virgin which was believed to have curbed the plague and reduced the number of its victims, should be provided with a more worthy setting. The picture was kept in the little church of S. Maria in Porticu. The three *conservatori* attended on the pope to ask for building permission and to apply for the requisite funds. Alexander's personal devotion to the Virgin was well known, and he showed an interest in the project from the start. However, when he visited the church of S. Maria in Porticu in January the following year, he declared that the site was unsuited to the kind of rebuilding envisaged. Instead it was decided that the picture should be transferred to S. Maria in Campitelli, which was to be altered and enlarged. The church had been founded in 1619 but had not been finished until 1648.[251] Carlo Rainaldi was commissioned to make plans for its rebuilding, and these were shown to the pope in the spring of 1658.

Judging from the drawings in the Vatican Library which are discussed by Wittkower, these first plans involved enlarging the existing church, which had a single aisle with two chapels on either side and a transept, by the addition of a domed sanctuary whose isolated columns would suggest a second transept with absidial terminations; and to this was to be added a rectangular choir.[252]

Presumably these plans did not satisfy the pope, who insisted that a completely new church should be built. The first plans which Rainaldi submitted for this project were probably ready in 1658, and are those now kept in the Archivio di Santa Maria in Campitelli.[253] They show an oval space and four openings with flat architraves: two are side chapels on the transverse axis of the

Carlo Rainaldi: project for S. Maria in Campitelli, drawing. Archivio del P. Gen. dei chierici regolari della Madre di Dio (BH).

oval, one is the entrance and one leads to the sanctuary. Between these are slightly smaller and lower openings leading to minor chapels and crowned by *coretti*. Round the entire oval and over all the chapel openings runs an unbroken architrave and a frieze, like a ribbon encircling the room. There is an echo here of S. Andrea al Quirinale, but without the tense drama of Bernini's church. Rainaldi's intended interior is more serene, more classical and, typically, more conservative. This church would have had a magnificent façade, including a two-storey loggia with two pairs of double columns carrying a flat entablature. The loggia is convex, but flanked on the ground floor by wall sections with pilasters placed obliquely to the central projection, in other words much the same interplay of concave and convex elements as we have seen in Pietro da Cortona's Ss. Martina e Luca. The two-storey loggia also recalls Cortona's façade for S. Maria in Via Lata.

The pope was anxious for building to begin, and on 23 January 1660 he allocated a first sum of 15,000 scudi.[254] But there were still delays as Rainaldi's project proved too expensive; he had himself estimated the cost at 83,000 scudi, which meant that the pope's 15,000 was not going to go very far.[255] Some saving was therefore necessary, and by the time foundations were laid in 1662, the plans had been simplified. A medal struck at the time[256] shows that the two-storey loggia has been closed in, although the façade is again convex and flanked by two powerful wings. And behind this still majestic façade we

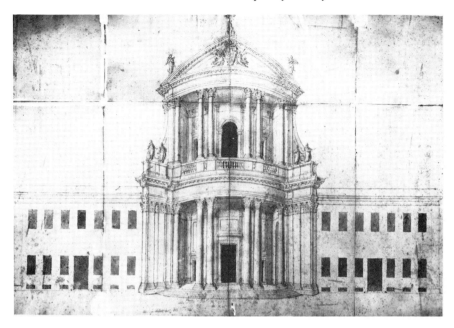

Carlo Rainaldi: façade project for S. Maria in Campitelli, drawing. Archivio del P. Gen. dei chierici regolari della Madre di Dio (BH).

can see a large dominating dome. It is impossible to tell whether this was to be round or oval. A new medal was struck a few months later;[257] the convex façade has now become flat, which also means that the oval interior is rectangular. The domed space at the rear has been retained, however, with its wide concave niche for the miraculous picture.

The following year, 1663, building began on the choir and the façade, which were both finished four years later, shortly after Alexander VII's death. The rest of the church was built between 1673 and 1675, but its decoration was not complete until the 1690s.[258]

The interior of S. Maria in Campitelli as executed is thus rectangular and wholly dominated by its great Corinthian columns. As in the original oval project there are large chapels on each side half way along the nave, broad and high enough to suggest a transept. These mid-way chapels are flanked by smaller chapel recesses with lower openings and balconies above. The large chapels have two free-standing Corinthian columns on each of their side walls, which break through the crowning entablature *en ressaut*; they form a short bay with a door and a balcony above. Exactly the same bay is repeated at the junction between the nave and the domed sanctuary, and yet again in front of the apse. A coherent rhythm thus unites the whole interior. These pairs of columns cut into our view of the domed space, like protruding sets on a theatre stage, accentuating the church's interior depth. The use of columns, as Witt-

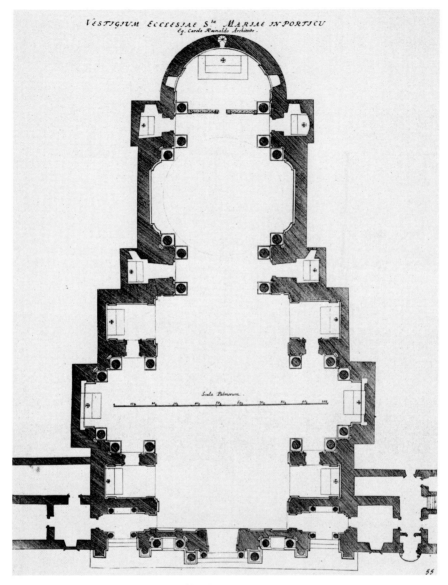

Carlo Rainaldi: S. Maria in Campitelli, plan (From Sandrart, *Insignium Romae templorum prospectus*).

kower has pointed out, is a North Italian feature; another is the type of plan that involves a conflict between the main and transverse axes, an example of which can be seen in S. Salvatore in Bologna but which has here been subordinated to a grandiose spatial design in the true Roman spirit.[259] The dome itself is something of an anti-climax; it is low with a very low drum and oval windows, and the visitor standing in the central space is led to expect a transept to the domed area and is surprised to find none. The idea was that this domed

Carlo Rainaldi: S. Maria in Campitelli, interior (SBAAL).

space should be regarded as a sanctuary for the miraculous picture. This minute little icon is framed in a magnificent decorative setting, a tabernacle directly inspired by Bernini's bronze *baldacchino* in St. Peter's. It was made by Melchiorre Caffà and Ercole Ferrata, from a design by Giovanni Antonio de Rossi in 1667, while Schor added the picture frame the following year.

The façade of S. Maria in Campitelli shows certain affinities with the façade of Ss. Vincenzo ed Anastasio ten years earlier. However, Rainaldi has elaborated the aedicule motif more consistently. This also stems from Northern Italy, where it can be seen in Girolamo Rainaldi's façade for S. Lucia in Bologna and in even earlier examples in Milan. Carlo Rainaldi adapts this motif to Roman ideas by emphasising the plasticity of the columns, and adding powerful pediments and other strongly accentuated projections. As Wittkower has pointed out, the façade of S. Maria in Campitelli strikes us as a revival of

Carlo Rainaldi: S. Maria in
Campitelli, façade (CI).

the Roman bath scheme.[260] The modest entrance aedicule is set in a much larger
aedicule with free-standing Corinthian columns; this second aedicule rises to
the height of the whole ground floor, and its triangular pediment juts up into
the second storey. The aedicular columns are repeated in the three-quarter
columns flanking the central section of the façade, and they also reappear in the
upper floor. Where the ground-floor columns break through the entablature
en ressaut, the upwards thrust is taken up and continued by the pedestals of the
upper columns, creating a series of strongly accentuated verticals through the
whole façade. In the upper floor the window aedicule with its freestanding
composite columns and broken segmental arch is also set in a larger aedicule,
whose own segmental pediment intrudes into the great crowning pediment of
the façade, thus repeating the motifs introduced in the lower storey. There is a
sharp break in the main pediment above the flanking columns and the central
aedicule, so that it appears in spiky silhouette against the sky. Both floors are
crowned by a flat architrave carried on columns close to but independent of

Carlo Maderno and Carlo Rainaldi: S. Andrea della Valle, façade (Alinari).

the wall, which thus continues behind these and under the projecting architrave in a way that is reminiscent of Ss. Vincenzo ed Anastasio: Rainaldi's façade, too, is extremely plastic and appears to consist of several layers—a layer of columns and a layer of solid smooth walls which we can glimpse behind them. An unusual feature of S. Maria in Campitelli is that the outer flanking bays of the lower storey are connected to the palaces on either side and represent a kind of transitional element, part church and part palace.

While work on S. Maria in Campitelli continued, Carlo Rainaldi also completed the façade of S. Andrea della Valle. Here, however, his hands were tied by the start Maderno had already made in 1624. Rainaldi's chief contribution was to increase the emphasis on verticality by introducing breaks in the pediment as at S. Maria in Campitelli.[261] The façade has therefore lost much of the serenity that Maderno intended. The volutes at either side of the upper storey have been abandoned, again to accentuate the vertical movement more powerfully. However, the façade does not quite correspond to Rainaldi's

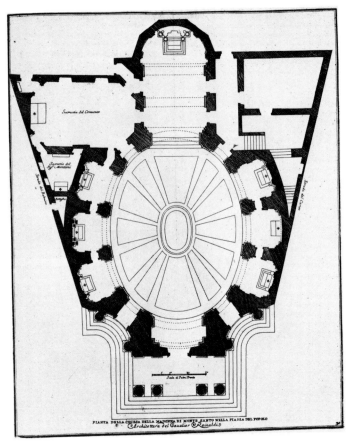

Carlo Rainaldi: S. Maria di Monte Santo, plan (From De Rossi, *Studio d'architettura civile*, III, 1721).

intentions either; it is more severe, more restrained in the use of decorative and sculptural details, probably because of the influence of Carlo Fontana who was Rainaldi's assistant between 1661 and 1662.[262] Despite the many hands which helped to make it, this church façade—a Late Baroque modification of a High Baroque continuation of an Early Baroque conception—is one of the most imposing and majestic in Rome.

The twin churches in the Piazza del Popolo, S. Maria di Monte Santo and S. Maria dei Miracoli were also begun during Alexander VII's pontificate.[263] The idea dated back to 1658, when the Carmelites were given permission to build a church on the corner site between the Corso and Via del Babuino. This triggered plans for a more comprehensive project to include two symmetrical churches, which may well have stemmed from Alexander VII, in view of his particular interest in the urban development of Rome. We shall return to this aspect of the affair in the following section.

Carlo Rainaldi was commissioned to plan the two churches in January 1658.

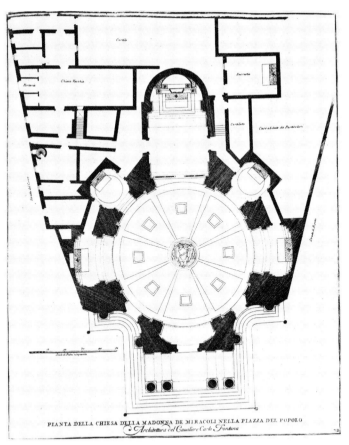

PIANTA DELLA CHIESA DELLA MADONNA DE MIRACOLI NELLA PIAZZA DEL POPOLO
Architettura del Cavaliere Carlo Fontana

Carlo Rainaldi: S. Maria dei Miracoli, plan (From De Rossi, *Studio d'architettura civile*, III, 1721).

In his first proposal, however, he had obviously not yet found a way of exploiting the situation. He has given the churches simple, flat façades with paired pilasters, and has completely ignored the importance of their domes as part of the overall view. Nor has he solved the problem of the obtuse angles between the streets and the piazza.[264]

Initially the right-hand church was ownerless, but the pope decided that it should be assigned to the Franciscan tertiaries and be given the name S. Maria dei Miracoli. In 1661 Rainaldi produced a fresh proposal with half-columns instead of pilasters. In December the same year the foundations of S. Maria dei Miracoli were laid by Cardinal Girolamo Gastaldi, while the left-hand church, which was actually the first to be planned, was started later, on 15 July 1662.[265] A foundation medal was struck, showing that Rainaldi had now arrived at the idea of a classical temple pediment carried on free-standing columns and outlined against a fairly high attic. The domes of both churches were circular. The street corners now had a concave form so that the buildings could be more

Carlo Rainaldi: S. Maria dei Miracoli with attic as first planned (From F. De Rossi, *Ritratto di Roma moderna*, 1689).

easily adapted to the irregular sites. But the nature of the site also caused Rainaldi to redesign the Carmelite church and give it an oval plan.[267] S. Maria dei Miracoli, on the other hand, could retain its circular plan but with the emphasis on the transverse axis. The scale of the porch was adjusted so that the columns from the upper storey of Bernini's *campanile* for St. Peter's could be used. Although Rainaldi was responsible for the new oval plan for the left-hand church, Carlo Fontana was now working as his assistant and is certain to have made an active contribution to the plan. For instance the dome over the oval space ran into great difficulties, both constructionally and even aesthetically, as it differed from the dome of the other church. Carlo Fontana solved the problem by broadening the drum of the dome at the sides by swelling the walls just there. However, work on both the churches ceased for lack of funds, and when Alexander VII died in May 1667 only the Carmelite church had risen to the level of the entablature.

Piazza del Popolo with its two churches as actually built, detail of engraving (From J. Blaeu, *Nouveau Théâtre d'Italie, IV, 1704*).

Work recommenced in 1673 when Cardinal Gastaldi provided quite a large sum of money for the two churches, and two years later Prince Giovanni Battista Pamphili made a donation to the church of the Franciscan tertiaries. Rainaldi continued as architect of S. Maria di Monte Santo, but under the supervision of Gian Lorenzo Bernini. Bernini, whose contributions for the period 1674–1675 are documented,[268] introduced one important alteration: the rather heavy attic was abolished and replaced by a balustrade; the classical pediment thus stood out more emphatically. The church was finished for the Holy Year of 1675. The same year work recommenced on S. Maria dei Miracoli, and here Rainaldi remained in charge with Fontana acting as his assistant. This second church was completed four years later.

Several lesser known architects working in Rome at this time are worthy of mention, in particular Antonio del Grande, a Roman born.[269] Del Grande was given only one major public commission, for Innocent X's Carceri Nuovi on Via Giulia, but was kept fully occupied with private commissions for the Pamphili and Colonna families. Camillo Pamphili and the princess of Rossano had a wing added to their palace on the Corso, facing on to the open place in front of the Collegio Romano. Antonio del Grande, working here between 1659 and 1661, provided the new wing with an unimaginative and conservative façade inspired by Girolamo Rainaldi's Palazzo Pamphili in the Piazza

Piazza Colonna with Palazzo Chigi, engraving (From G. B. Falda, *Il Nuovo teatro delle fabbriche*).

Navona. But he designed a very impressive vestibule with a monumental staircase which is one of the most imposing in Rome, appearing just when such grand palace stairs were beginning to be fashionable in the Eternal City.

In 1654 Cardinal Girolamo Colonna, a learned and art-loving prelate much respected for his personal integrity, commissioned Antonio del Grande to add a gallery wing to the old Colonna palace.[270] This too was a novelty in Roman palace architecture, and an unusual feature in the gallery is its termination at each end in a square space behind columns. The roof of the gallery is said to have been finished in 1665, but its decoration dragged on for several decades. When the cardinal died in 1669 the palace passed to Lorenzo Onofrio Colonna, who housed his picture collection there.

The Aldobrandini family's second palace on the Corso near the column of Marcus Aurelius had been bought by the Chigi family in 1659. This was very skilfully restored and enlarged by Felice della Greca. The architect retained the façade on the Corso as the main front, behind which he placed the entrance and the staircase.[271] The façade on the Piazza Colonna was almost entirely rebuilt; at the same time the hovels between the palace and the column were demolished. The work was completed between 1665 and 1666. There are no real innovations in this façade; rather, it is a successor to the traditional palace façade as developed in the later half of the sixteenth century by Giacomo della Porta.

Alexander VII and Urban Planning in Rome

Alexander VII's lively interest in architecture was matched by his general concern for the embellishment and development of the city as a whole. The Genoese agent in Rome, Ferdinando Raggi, mentions in one of his memoranda that the pope kept a wooden model of Rome in his study, which included every smallest detail.[272] Naturally this model has not survived, nor is it mentioned in any other source. One wonders how Raggi could know anything about the contents of the pope's study, for even if he had been received in audience it would certainly not have been there. Alexander's own Diary provides more reliable evidence of his interest in Rome.[273] Apart from the many references to works of art and artists of which we have already quoted a number, the Diary includes frequent mention of streets, piazzas, fountains, palaces and churches, usually without any comment but certainly because the pope intended to talk about them to an architect—often Bernini—or to some city authority such as the *maestri di strada*, or because he had already been discussing them in connection with various projects. We see for instance that one of his first acts as pope was to revive the *Congregazione delle strade* and to arrange for it to meet more frequently; also that he was concerned about the fountains and anxious to see that they worked properly. Nor was he unaware of the aesthetic value of these fountains, and at the end of his reign he was planning to move some of them. The fountain in the Piazza Colonna was to have been moved to SS. Apostoli, for example, and the one on the Quirinal to Piazza S. Marco. Alexander also saw that the streets were kept clean and accessible; he gave orders for the paving or repair of streets where carriages used to get stuck, and there is frequent mention of the removal of rubbish that was hampering the traffic. In 1662 he ordered the demolition of the Arco di Portogallo,[274] a Late Antique arch over the Corso near Via della Vite, which was obstructing free passage along the street. The pope regarded commerce and trade as inappropriate to the grander piazzas; he renewed Innocent X's prohibition of commerce in the Piazza Navona, the flower-sellers had to leave the Pantheon portico, and the traders in the piazza in front of the Pantheon were later removed to Piazza in Pietra nearby.

In one perhaps rather surprising entry in the Diary for September 1656 the pope mentions that trees are to be planted along Rome's streets (unfortunately he doesn't say which) and specifies that they were to be elms. Falda's map of Rome dated 1676 shows that the street from S. Maria Maggiore to S. Croce in Gerusalemme and the one which no longer exists from S. Eusebio to S. Bibiana, are lined with low and obviously recently planted trees, clearly from Alexander VII's pontificate. The same map and other early pictorial views also show an alley in the Forum area, the Campo Vaccino, with several rows of trees to give shade during the heat of the Roman summer.

According to a draft proposal which is still in the Vatican Library and which, although undated and unsigned, is certainly from Alexander VII's pontificate,[275] about 5,500 trees were to be planted along the streets in the deserted areas inside the Aurelian wall and along some of the old thoroughfares from the city gates out into the Campagna. Obviously the intention was to systematise these unpopulated districts and, without actually building there, to connect them by way of their alleys with the old built-up areas. It would be interesting to find out how the tree-planting plan arose. It seems clear that it

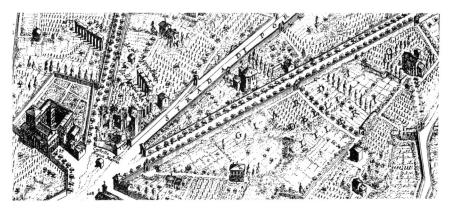

Detail of Falda's map of Rome 1676, showing street from S. Maria Maggiore to S. Croce in Gerusalemme lined with trees planted during the reign of Alexander VII. The church to the left is S. Eusebio and the open space in front is part of the present Piazza Vittorio Emanuele.

was Alexander VII's suggestion, but we do not know where he got it from.[276] Was it in fact a completely new idea? Or did it come from the beginning of the century, from Paul V and his plans for Trastevere? Maybe the explanation lies in the fact that Rome had more—and bigger—parks and more magnificent gardens than any other contemporary European town, and tree-lined alleys had been a predominant feature of these parks even since the Renaissance. We need only recall Sixtus V's Villa Montalto which is criss-crossed by tree-bordered walks (see Vol. 1, p. 13).

Thus the Diary provides evidence of Alexander VII's lively and almost pedantic interest in a great many details connected with his city. But we should perhaps beware of giving him too much credit on this account: by a lucky chance his Diary happens to have survived, but other popes may well have kept an equally watchful eye on the upkeep and development of Rome, without leaving any diary notes behind. The examples of Paul V and Urban VIII come readily to mind.

The most important impulse behind this pope's—and indeed his pre-decessors'—civic plans for Rome was nonetheless the city's position as the foremost place of pilgrimage in the West and the capital of Catholic Christendom. We know from other sources that Alexander VII commissioned the open places in front of S. Carlo ai Catinari, the Chiesa Nuova, and S. Maria in Trastevere.[277] We have also noted how he ordered an open place to be made in front of S. Maria della Pace, so that the church could be reached by carriage.

We have already discussed the particular interest that was devoted to the Pantheon and we know that Bernini was to produce suggestions for regulating the streets in the surrounding area.[278] As early as 1657 it was decided that the buildings actually joined to the Pantheon should be demolished, but there was opposition from the owners of the property and nothing was done until 1662.

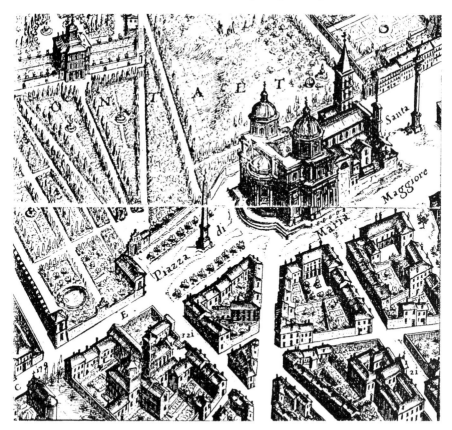

Detail of Falda's map of Rome 1676, showing trees planted on either side of the obelisk in front of the apse of S. Maria Maggiore.

Bernini's plans for streets radiating from the piazza on both sides of the Pantheon could not be realised, however, presumably because they would have cost too much.

St. Peter's Square must be regarded as Alexander VII's greatest and most significant contribution to the embellishment of Rome, and we have seen how the design of the piazza was related not only to the basilica and the palace, but also to the Borgo Nuovo and the surrounding houses.

Another major piece of town planning was the development of the Piazza del Popolo and its twin churches. It was not until these churches were actually being planned, that the idea of exploiting them in a civic context to provide a ceremonial entrance into Rome was born. What was then rather a narrow piazza inside the city gate was the first sight of Rome to greet the visitor, and most visitors arrived this way along the Via Flaminia. Now, after Alexander VII's vision was realised, a vista of great beauty opened up before the traveller's eyes. Few cities, it was widely claimed, could boast such a splendid approach, with the two colonnades forming a kind of propylaeum from which

Bernini: *Daniel*, marble. Chigi chapel in
S. Maria del Popolo (CI).

three streets radiated out to carry the visitor into the heart of the city.

Pietro da Cortona's proposal for a monumental façade for the Palazzo Chigi represented one element in a grand planning project. Alexander VII dreamt of creating a piazza here to rival Piazza Navona and provide a new centre for the city of Rome. Palazzo Ludovisi was to be purchased, and the piazza in front of it combined with Piazza Colonna to form one great rectangular square.[279] Trajan's column was to be moved here as a twin to the column of Marcus Aurelius, and the Acqua Vergine should be extended to terminate here in two fountains. It was typical that Chigi envisaged antique monuments as the central focus of the square, rather than a fountain as in the Piazza Navona. However, this whole project had to be abandoned on economic grounds.

At the very end of Chigi's pontificate plans were being launched for building a triumphal arch or gateway next to the Quirinal Palace as a counterpart to the Porta Pia, and to set up the statues of Castor and Pollux on either side of it. A drawing of this gate has survived from Bernini's studio, and there is a note in the pope's Diary "i dioscuri metterli di quà e di là alla porta". But Alexander died the following year and the project was forgotten.[280]

Finally a project in which Bernini was involved should be briefly mentioned here: plans to provide the slope leading up to SS. Trinità dei Monti with a

Bernini: *Habakkuk*, marble. Chigi
chapel in S. Maria del Popolo (CI).

system of stairways, ramps and terraces.[281] Bernini completed a model which
can be dated from 1660 approximately. This has disappeared, but some drawings of it have survived. The project was the result of a French initiative.
Mazarin was involved, working through the Abbé Benedetti, his agent in
Rome, and a donation from a Frenchman was also part of the picture. The idea
was to glorify Louis XIV, here in front of the French king's own church, and
an equestrian statue of the monarch was to dominate the scene from the middle
terrace. But it was quite impossible to implement such a scheme during Chigi's
reign: the very thought of a statue of Louis XIV in the centre of Rome was
detestable to Alexander VII, and without his gracious approval no building
permit could be granted. The project was therefore postponed, and this great
stairway leading up to Trinità dei Monti—mistakenly known as the Spanish
steps but designed by Francesco De Sanctis and paid for by the French—was
not built until 1724–25.

Sculpture during Chigi's Pontificate

Bernini was kept so busy by the great public enterprises for Alexander VII,
that he had little time to spare for private patrons. While still a cardinal, Chigi

Antonio Raggi: *The Death of St. Cecilia*, marble relief. S. Agnese (Alinari).

had commissioned some work for his family's chapel in S. Maria del Popolo which Raphael had originally built and decorated for Agostino Chigi.[282] Immediately after his accession he began to expand this project, turning his attention to the rest of the church as well.[283] Raphael's pupil Lorenzetti had executed two prophets, *Jonah* and *Elijah*, and Alexander now wanted sculptures for the two remaining niches. Within a year of becoming pope he had commissioned Bernini for the task. The pope consulted Lucas Holstenius on the iconography, and Holstenius promptly suggested *Daniel* and *Habakkuk*.[284] Daniel in particular was a favourite subject in Early Christian art, symbolising steadfast faith and trust in the resurrection, and therefore especially fitting in a memorial chapel. Many scholars have affirmed that this harking back to Early Christian themes in the seventeenth century was perfectly intentional.

Some preparatory sketches for the *Daniel* in Leipzig show how Bernini drew on his studies of the *Laocoon* group, in particular the figure of the father—one of many examples of the inspiration he derived from antique

Melchiorre Caffà: *The Ecstasy of St. Catherine*, marble relief. S. Caterina a Monte Magnanapoli (Max Hutzel).

models for his sculptures.[285] The *Daniel* was executed between 1655 and 1657. No drawings for the *Habakkuk* have survived, but the resemblance between the angel who is about to lift the prophet by a lock of hair to carry him to Daniel, and the angel in the *Ecstacy of St. Teresa*, is very marked. The *Habakkuk* was placed in the chapel in 1661. The two earlier statues were moved so that Bernini's prophets could stand diagonally opposite one another, thus creating a space spanning the whole chapel and connecting the two figures involved in the event.

In the autumn of 1655 the church was embellished with a marble cornice which curls its way round the whole interior, following the arcade and providing precarious support for the female saints and martyrs draped around it. This adornment, which sadly destroys the simple fifteenth-century character of the church, was the work of several of Bernini's pupils, among them Ercole Ferrata and Antonio Raggi. The façade of the church was also altered by the addition of two great volutes.

During the 1660s the interior of S. Agnese in the Piazza Navona was decorated for Prince Pamphili.[286] Ercole Ferrata executed the *St. Agnes on the Pyre* in the right-hand chapel. This is a free-standing statue in a simulated perspective setting, resembling in many ways Duquesnoy's classicism of the 1630s, except that it is much more dramatic. Like Bernini, Ferrata has chosen to portray a moment of climax: quelled by the power of prayer the flames are dying down and leaving the saint unharmed. Ferrata's other work in the church is a relief of the Martyrdom of St. Emerentiana in the large niche to the right of the high altar. The artist was working on the model for this *Martyrdom* for several years during the 1660s, but its execution in marble was delayed until almost the end of the century, when Leonardo Reti finished it.[287] The result is a text-book example of the classical rules of composition, concentrating on a few figures in well-defined groups, and it shows that despite his close association with Bernini—who greatly admired the younger man and gave him a number of important jobs—Ferrata nevertheless tends by choice towards the classicism of Algardi.

Antonio Raggi, like Ferrata a native of the Como region which had produced several generations of sculptors, was 14 years Ferrata's junior and artistically much more dependent on Bernini. For a great many years he was the master's closest colleague and right-hand man. When, very young, he first arrived in Rome he had worked in Algardi's studio but was later engaged by Bernini for the decoration of the nave of St. Peter's in 1647. He did his best work in stucco, but has also left several pieces in marble. One of his most characteristic and original works is the marble relief, the *Death of St. Cecilia* on the left of the high altar in S. Agnese, on which he was working between 1660 and 1666.[288] The commission had first been given to a lesser known colleague of Bernini's, Giuseppe Peroni, but when he fell ill in 1660 Raggi took over the execution of the project, and we can probably assume that the composition is also his. The relief swarms with figures, which in contradiction to the classical requirements of clarity and simplicity are massed together in complicated groupings. Those in the foreground are almost three-dimensional and some even break out of the frame, while the background figures are in low relief. This is also Algardi's device for creating depth in carved relief. But Raggi's figures are elongated, slender and soft, quite unlike Algardi's firmly modelled forms; and here there is a nervous, restless air about the fluttering draperies. Thus the overall effect of Raggi's relief differs sharply from that of Ferrata's on the other side of the altar.

The Maltese sculptor Melchiorre Caffà was commissioned in 1660 to design another altar relief for S. Agnese, a *St. Eustache*. However, when the artist died at the end of the 1660s, this work was completed by Ercole Ferrata.[289] Caffà had arrived in Rome as a very young man and been trained by Ferrata, but he was naturally also greatly influenced by Bernini. His most characteristic work is the *Ecstacy of St. Catherine* in S. Caterina a Monte Magnanapoli.[290] At a superficial glance and particularly in photographs this relief over the high altar may seem to resemble Bernini's *Ecstacy of St. Teresa*, but in fact there are

Bernini's workshop: the
Elephant and Obelisk in
front of S. Maria sopra
Minerva (SBAAL).

important differences. Bernini worked consistently in three dimensions, while
Caffà depicts his saint in relief—a relief that somehow fails to "lift" from its
background of alabaster and multicoloured marble which is meant to signify
clouds. Caffà shows great skill in his treatment of the marble and his group of
figures is undeniably elegant, but there is also a softness here that borders on
the sentimental. However, this last seems to be characteristic of several sculptors of Caffà's generation and should not therefore be regarded as especially
typical of his work. The greatest difference between the *St. Catherine* and
Bernini's *St. Teresa*, however, is the absence of drama. Caffà has avoided
Bernini's method of heightening the dramatic effect with the help of light, and

his relief is placed straightforwardly in a large concave altar retable. There is admittedly a lantern above the altar, symbolising the open sky from which angels are descending, just as in the *St. Teresa*, but the dramatic potential has not been fully exploited, perhaps because the lantern is too high to belong to the composition in any meaningful way and it cannot create the effects of light which Bernini would have rejoiced in.

The last major monument of any importance to be produced during Alexander's reign was the *Elephant and Obelisk* in front of S. Maria sopra Minerva.[291] When this work was unveiled in the summer of 1667, the pope had been dead for about a month. The obelisk belonged to the Dominicans, who had discovered it when digging in the garden of their monastery.[292] Immediately on his return from Paris Bernini was commissioned to design a monument for it; it is not certain who took the initiative, the pope or the Dominicans themselves. In any case the pope was interested in the scheme, and he consulted Athanasius Kircher to learn more about the obelisk and the hieroglyphs inscribed on it. Father Kircher reported that the obelisk "was consecrated by the Egyptians to the highest genius, whom they called World Spirit or World Soul, and they held that its seat was fixed in the Sun",[293] and in 1666, even before the monument was finished, he published his *Obelisci Aegyptiaci... interpretatio* in which he discusses the interpretation of the hieroglyphs on this monolith. A couple of Bernini's drawings for the monument have been preserved, and the design can thus be ascribed to his hand. Execution, on the other hand, was left entirely to Ercole Ferrata.

The pope was involved in the composition of the inscriptions on the socle, which clearly bear witness to the allegorical importance of the monument. This subject has been examined in detail by Heckscher, who shows that because of its association with the Egyptian cult of the sun, the obelisk was regarded by contemporary scholars as a symbol of Divine Wisdom.[294] The play on words in the Latin inscriptions also tells us that the elephant is no longer a "docile and noble giant among beasts" but for Bernini and his contemporaries it is "a pictorial reminder of the highest qualities of the human mind". The whole dedication becomes a subtle eulogy of Alexander VII, who despite his bodily weakness was spiritually strong, and whose mind bore the burden of Wisdom as the elephant bears the weight of the obelisk on its back.

Painting during Chigi's Pontificate

In the field of monumental painting Chigi's pontificate was not a very active time and major public commissions were comparatively few. Pietro da Cortona now dominated the scene and enjoyed the highest repute among the painters. Work on the cartoons for the aisle mosaics in St. Peter's occupied him for the greater part of this period.[295] At the time these were regarded as one of his most important commissions, although today it is often forgotten that they are his work. He was also completing the frescoes in the Chiesa Nuova and supervising the work on Alexander VII's gallery at the Quirinal Palace.

Pier Francesco
Mola: *Joseph
making himself
known to his
Brethren*, fresco.
Quirinal Palace
(BH).

Within a year of becoming pope, Alexander VII had turned his attention to
the Quirinal Palace, where he lived not only during the summer but for most
of the year. Since Paul V, his predecessors had done little that was of any
importance to the palace. Urban VIII had preferred to live in the oldest part of
the building, which had been built during Gregory XIII's pontificate. Some
frescoes which Agostino Tassi and Andrea Sacchi had executed have since been
lost. Alexander decided straight away to decorate the long gallery in the wing
along the courtyard which Domenico Fontana had built fifty years before.
Unfortunately this gallery was divided into three rooms during the Na-
poleonic era, but most of the frescoes have survived.

This commission was an important one, and it was natural that it should go
to Pietro da Cortona.[296] However, Cortona was content merely to direct the
work of others here. He did not execute a single painting himself, employing
instead a team of no less than sixteen variously well-known painters to work
under him—some of them representing quite different artistic currents from
his own. Carlo Maratti and Pier Francesco Mola were given the most important assignments: they were responsible for the two frescoes on the end walls.
Gian Francesco Grimaldi, Paul Schor, Borgognone, Ciro Ferri and others
worked in the smaller compartments on the long walls, and several landscapes
were executed by Gaspard Dughet with figures by Baldi and Lauri. However
impartial Pietro da Cortona may have tried to be in selecting artists for this
job, many were bitter at being passed over and his choice caused considerable
controversy in artistic circles, as we can see from the criticism expressed by
Passeri in his artists' biographies.[297]

Carlo Maratti: the
Nativity, fresco.
Quirinal Palace
(SBAAL).

Pier Francesco Mola was probably given an important role here, since the pope had seen some of his earlier production and was delighted by his style of painting. Alexander became a great admirer of Mola's work and later commissioned his own portrait from the artist. Mola's great fresco in the Quirinal Palace, completed in 1657, depicts *Joseph making himself known to his Brethren.*[298] There is a lucidity in this composition that recalls the classicism of Domenichino and Sacchi, but Mola works with greater plasticity and a livelier tempo in recounting the story and, above all, with a tendency towards Bolognese *chiaroscuro* apparently inspired by Guercino. His rich palette includes both ochre and green together with blue and red, but without allowing any single tone to dominate, and it is just this even treatment of colour that bears witness to Mola's North Italian heritage and the influence of Guercino. As so often in Domenichino the action takes place in the foreground, but a view opens up behind between architectural wings with a cloudy sky and the massed leaves of great trees. The romantic atmosphere pervading this picture is another sign of Mola's North Italian and particularly Venetian inspiration.

Maratti's *Nativity* on the opposite end wall was regarded as the most outstanding painting in the gallery. Maratti had already shown what he could make of this subject in S. Giuseppe dei Falegnami, where he had worked with sharp contrasts between light and shade. In the St. Joseph chapel in S. Isidoro, painted between 1653 and 1654, he had achieved artistic maturity although the influence of his master, Sacchi, was still clearly visible particularly in *The*

Flight into Egypt. But, as Bellori has pointed out, we are also reminded in this chapel of Guido Reni, and the painting in the dome clearly shows the influence of Lanfranco. We could even speak of Maratti's "momento lanfranchiano".[299]

That Maratti was given such an important commission in the Quirinal in preference to other artists of greater repute may have been because he had found favour with Pietro da Cortona or, more probably, because Gian Lorenzo Bernini had recommended him to Alexander VII.[300] His *Nativity* in the gallery shows that he has absorbed impulses from Lanfranco into his own personal style, combining Lanfranco's treatment of light with Pietro da Cortona's more dynamic and exuberant manner, at the same time freeing himself from Sacchi's classicism. Briganti speaks of "meditazione, sia pur in chiave barocca su testi da Raffaello a Correggio..."[301] and declares the result to be one of the greatest paintings produced in Rome during this period.

During the 1650s and 1660s Pietro da Cortona also completed the internal decoration of the Chiesa Nuova. *The Assumption of the Virgin* in the apse which is linked both stylistically and in its composition to the fresco in the dome and, like this last, has affinities with Lanfranco's dome in S. Andrea della Valle, was begun in 1655, the same year which saw the completion of the Pamphili gallery. In 1659 scaffolding was erected under the pendentives of the dome for the paintings of the four prophets, *Isaiah*, *Jeremiah*, *Ezekiel* and *Daniel*, which were finished the following year.[302]

The plans for the decoration of the nave were probably already complete, but the work was not carried out until a few years later. Pietro da Cortona made detailed drawings for the stuccoes there and in the short barrel vaults in the choir and transept. These were executed by Ercole Ferrata and Cosimo Fancelli, who were associated with Pietro da Cortona's studio. Work began in 1662 and was finished in 1665.[303] The main theme consists of alternating equilateral and elongated hexagonal coffers in gilded stucco with large white acanthus flowers, and cherubs in white marble-imitation stucco. But unlike Ss. Martina e Luca the transverse arches do not cut across the coffers here; instead they provide a clear framework within which the coffers are arranged. Thus although the ornamentation here is opulent, it is also more strictly and architecturally structured than any of Pietro da Cortona's previous work. The nave has five bays and the middle three are covered by a single great *quadro riportato*. Here the coffers are allowed to continue behind the picture, which thus appears to be air-borne, supported only by four gilded stucco angels.

Pietro da Cortona began to paint this picture himself in January 1664.[304] It depicts the Virgin, prompted by St. Philip Neri, miraculously averting an accident during the building of the church—a return to the theme of the miraculous icon for which Rubens had created his altar paintings sixty years earlier. The painting does not demand to be perceived as a hole in the ceiling, complete with the kind of simulated perspective effects which Pietro da Cortona had previously created; instead it is like an easel painting with its own perspective. This approach to ceiling painting had been developed by artists in Venice from Tintoretto to Veronese, whose works Pietro had seen on his visit

Pietro da Cortona: *The Miracle of the Virgin*, ceiling fresco and stuccoes in the nave of Chiesa Nuova (Max Hutzel).

Nicolas Poussin: *Diogenes*. Musée du Louvre, Paris (Villani & Figli).

to the Republic. But this painting also shows the great difference between Pietro's secular decorative work created to glorify a princely patron or the family of a papal nephew, and his ecclesiastical art addressed to the congregation of the faithful and ranging itself in a tradition stemming from Domenichino and Lanfranco.

Despite their overwhelming splendour the overall effect of the decorations in the Chiesa Nuova—the richly plastic stuccoes in the vault with their clear composition and balanced harmony of white and gold combined with the opulent colours of the frescoes—is one of joy and warmth, a *Magnificat* in honour of the Virgin which can perhaps be compared with the music of Carissimi—spiritual, despite its highly poetical style. Thus this church, built at the end of the sixteenth century and intended by St. Philip to remain simple and white, was transformed by Pietro da Cortona's decorations and later even more by the eighteenth-century addition of oval-framed paintings over the chapel openings and ornate organ galleries, into one of the most sumptuous interiors of the Roman Baroque.

The frescoes which Prince Camillo Pamphili commissioned for his palace at Valmontone about forty kilometres east of Rome, must also be counted as Roman works. Between 1657 and 1661 Pier Francesco Mola, Giambattista Tassi known as *il Cortonese*, Gaspard Dughet, Borgognone, Francesco Cozza and Mattia Preti were all working there.[305] For several years Mola was the

Nicolas Poussin: *The Autumn*, Musée du Louvre, Paris (Villani & Figli).

painter most favoured by the prince, and he was given the best commissions at Valmontone. Later, however, Mola quarrelled with Camillo Pamphili about his fee, although he had been treated in all other ways with the greatest consideration and had become a member of the prince's *famiglia*. He refused to go on with the frescoes in the Stanza dell'Aria, and after fruitless negotiations Camillo Pamphili lost patience and destroyed everything that Mola had done.[306] Instead, during 1661, Mattia Preti worked at the palace while stopping off briefly in the region of Rome on his way from Naples and before settling in Malta for good. All the frescoes in the Valmontone palace were destroyed or badly damaged during the Second World War, and too little now remains of these once important works to give us any real idea of their value. Preti's badly damaged ceiling frescoe, a personification of *Air*, was one of his very best works as well as being one of the first examples of the new style in painting which was to dominate in Italy after 1650.[307] Francesco Cozza, formerly a pupil of Domenichino's, adopted this style in his personification of *Fire*, also badly damaged. These paintings lack the firm and almost architectural structure of the older compositions. The whole ceiling is crowded with figures of more or less equal power and lacking the solid individual treatment they receive in the earlier ceiling paintings. They also appear to have been disposed at random, some of them being cut short by the cornice or the frame, and there seems to be no common focus to give coherence to the composition as a whole.

Claude Lorrain: *The Father of Psyche Sacrificing at the Milesian Temple of Apollo.* The National Trust; Anglesey Abbey (CI).

Nicolas Poussin died while Bernini was in France, having been active up to the very last. In the figure compositions of his later years he has carried even further the serene monumentality of the paintings made in the 1650s, and the stillness of the figures is now often even more marked, introducing an almost motionless quality into his compositions.[308] In his late landscapes he goes beyond the moods which he had worked with previously, so that in the *Diogenese* in the Louvre, for instance, the sinister atmosphere which we so often found in his earlier paintings has disappeared. It is full of light. Our gaze moves gently towards the background along a winding path leading to a calm idyllic lake, where happy people are bathing. In the light background behind the tree-tops we glimpse, perhaps to our surprise, the great Nicchione of the Vatican Belvedere courtyard. The mood of this picture is of course associated with its subject: Diogenes was so poor that he owned only a drinking bowl; and then one day he met a young man drinking from his cupped hands, whereupon Diogenes happily threw away his bowl. The anecdotal and almost joky element in this story provides the artist with no grounds for introducing anything sinister.[309]

Similarly in the *Four Seasons*, painted for the Duke of Richelieu between 1660 and 1664, he illustrates nature in her different aspects at the different times of year. At the summer harvest the air is filled with gentle warmth, while in autumn dark clouds pile up in the sky, and so on. Blunt has called these four

Salvator Rosa: *Figures Crossing a Bridge in a Rocky Landscape.* The National Trust; Ickworth (CI).

pictures "the supreme examples of pantheistic landscape painting".[310] When Poussin died, he had formed no personal school in Rome: almost all his paintings had been made for French patrons, and although he had innumerable admirers and many friends in Italy, he had few followers there. His severe classical ideals had been little understood by contemporary Roman artists and connoisseurs, although at the time of his death the star of the Roman classicists was in the ascendant.

The increasingly heroic grandeur of Claude Lorrain's landscapes reached its most monumental expression in the paintings made between 1652 and 1663 on mythological or biblical subjects: the *Landscape with the Adoration of the Golden Calf* of 1653 was the first in this series,[311] while one of the last was the *Landscape with the Father of Psyche Sacrificing at the Milesian Temple of Apollo*, painted in 1663 for Angelo Albertoni,[312] whose son was later to marry into the Altieri family of Clement X. This painting is generally referred to as the "Altieri Claude" and is now in a private British collection. There is a striking contrast between the buildings on the left and a group of great trees seen against the sky on the right. The foreground is in shadow and here the aspect is solemn, almost melancholy; towards the background, however, this mood begins to dissolve and, in the view over the river lapped in a soft misty light, it approaches the sublime. Claude painted for several Roman patrons, and many of his works could therefore be seen by other painters in the Roman collections. For this reason Claude had a greater impact on the Roman art world than his contemporary Nicolas Poussin.

Among the many painters who followed Pietro da Cortona's footsteps we

Salvator Rosa: *Soldiers by Treas.* By kind permission of the Viscount Scarsdale; Kedleston Hall (CI).

find not only his own faithful pupil Ciro Ferri, born in 1643 one year after the completion of the Barberini ceiling, but also the slightly older Francesco Romanelli (died 1662) and Giacinto Gimignani (1611–1681), although the latter is perhaps closer to Sassoferrato. In this group we must reckon Guillaume Courtois, known as *il Borgognone*, who often worked for Bernini and who executed the fresco in the apse of the Ariccia church. And, lastly, there was young Filippo Gherardi, but as he was active during the following pontificates he belongs more properly to the Late Baroque. Romanelli was associated especially with the Barberini family, whom he followed into exile. In France he produced several works of some importance to French Baroque artists, for instance Le Sueur.

One of the strangest painters of this period is Salvator Rosa.[313] This artist was born in Naples and grew up there, so his artistic origins were in the Neapolitan school. However, he left home for good in 1639, when he was only 24 years old, and after spending almost ten years in Florence he settled in Rome in 1650, remaining there until his death in 1673. He is well known and admired for his fantastic landscapes, often painted in dark colours with ravines and fearful cliffs, wild crags, violent stormladen skies, vast waterfalls, overgrown ruins and lurking brigands. These romantic elements were part of his Neapolitan heritage. But regardless of whether the subject is a hermit's life, a mythological event or a violent scene of battle, the landscape always has an intrinsic value of its own. In some ways Salvator Rosa heralded the romanticism of the eighteenth century, which regarded him as the equal but also the antithesis of Claude Lorrain. Rosa leads us into a world of fear, uncertainty,

Salvator Rosa:
Self-Portrait. Palazzo
Saracini Chigi, Siena
(Alinari).

and sometimes melancholy, while with Claude we enter an Elysian, Arcadian landscape in which all is tranquillity and light. The publication of his etchings—a first edition appeared in 1656—showing bandits in terrifying and fantastic landscapes, has helped to spread Salvator Rosa's fame outside Italy.

And yet a closer examination of Rosa's work, suggests that particulary as a young man the artist was profoundly influenced by Claude Lorrain.[314] To mention but one example, his *Landscape with Erminia* in the Estense Gallery in Modena, is composed like one of Claude's landscapes with clustered groups of trees in the wings and a broad, distant view. Later, however, Rosa seems to have felt the influence of Netherlandish painters such as Pieter van Laer, Swanevelt, and even Bril. During the 1650s he drew closer to Claude again, but after about 1660 there is no longer any real affinity between them. By this time Rosa's landscapes have become increasingly abstract and melodramatic, in some ways showing a greater resemblance to Gaspard Dughet.

Salvator Rosa saw himself as a painter in the classical Roman style, and there are of course some elements in the structure of his landscapes that are reminiscent of the earlier masters, but his Neapolitan training is too strong and the mood of his paintings reveals a creative mind that is completely different from that of Nicolas Poussin—the artist with whom he liked to compare himself. What we know of his personality only confirms the difference. Already in Florence he had become the central figure in a circle of artists, and was active not only in painting but also in composing music and acting; he also wrote satires mercilessly castigating contemporary society.[315] A satire against Bernini at the carnival of 1639 made the artist Rosa's enemy for life. Later he was not averse to satirising both the pope and the Chigi family, sometimes subtly and sometimes pretty crudely. This kind of criticism, more or less open, was not unusual in writing, but Salvator Rosa is one of the few to have carried it over into the visual arts. Perhaps Rosa was something of an early romantic in his view of genius; at any rate he was in no doubt at all about his own gifts.

Around the middle of the seventeenth century there were several concurrent trends in Roman painting, and it is not always easy to draw clear boundaries between them.[316] Alexander VII's gallery in the Quirinal Palace, where the most varied styles appear side by side, provides a representative sample of most of the currents. There were also several artists working on minor commissions, executing frescoes in the lesser palaces or altar paintings in various churches. And finally there were the *bamboccianti*; of this group, Cerquozzi died in 1660 and Codazzi in 1672. Many of these painters were foreigners, particularly Dutchmen, who formed a frequently rather riotous Bohemian coterie in the district around Via della Croce and Via Margutta, where many of the "fiamminghi" had their lodgings. These foreign artists and many Italian masters of second rank, painted not for prelates or princes, not for churches or palaces, but for ordinary Roman burghers who were just beginning to buy works of art for the adornment of their homes. These buyers wanted paintings of cabinet format, generally on canvas, and subjects included landscapes and still-life, flower motifs and devotional pictures. Thus not all collectors or connoisseurs belonged to the recently wealthy families of the papal nephews; many came from the intelligentsia, for example Cassiano dal Pozzo and Francesco Angeloni, and many others for the first time from the middle classes. To satisfy the needs of these consumers a flourishing art market had developed, which meant that artists who failed to acquire an ecclesiastical or noble patron could still get some return for their labours.

Although the *bamboccianti* were constantly criticised by the proponents of classicism, there were more classical features in much of their work than their contemporaries may have realised. Codazzi, for example, built up his landscape compositions on the same lines as those masters of the classical landscape, Claude and Dughet, although his landscapes were then often peopled by figures painted by Miel and Cerquozzi. In fact it was more often the *bamboccianti's* choice of subjects against which the classical camp railed so fiercely.

At the same time, other artists like Pietro Testa (died 1650) and Salvator Rosa, who represented what Wittkower has called a crypto-romantic movement, also found themselves overshadowed by the classical current as represented by Claude and Maratti. During the 1660s this group became increasingly dominant, receiving what almost amounted to a badge of official approval when in 1664 Bellori, current *principe* of the Academy of St. Luke, held a discourse—subsequently published under the title *Idea* as a preface to his book of artists' biographies in 1672—in which he set forth the definitive programme of the classical school.

The confirmed co-existence in Rome of so many apparently competing trends was partly due to the more varied pattern of patronage. And in the end even some of the artistocratic art lovers, the cardinals and princes as well as the intelligentsia, began to buy the works of the Bohemians so despised by the classical purists, and *bambocciate* were actually being added to the great collections. A single example of this can suffice, but it would be easy to find many more: Mario Nuzzi was very popular in Rome as a painter of flower pieces—hence his nickname Mario de' Fiori;[317] the small figures which he sometimes included were painted by others—his *Seasons* is a case in point, with figures painted by Carlo Maratti. This painting was bought by Chigi and is now in the palace in Ariccia.

Alexander VII Departs this Life

Throughout his pontificate Alexander VII was plagued by the kidney trouble that had afflicted him for most of his life. During the summer of 1666 his condition deteriorated, and it was only by summoning all his strength that he managed to carry on. In the autumn he improved a little, and it was then that he dispatched a letter to all the Catholic princes appealing for help against the Turks; on 3 February 1667 he granted a subsidy of 100,000 scudi to the Venetians, and ordered the papal galleys to prepare to go to their support in the spring. When the duke of Chaulnes arrived in Rome to assume office as the new French Ambassador, the pope received him from his sick bed.[318] In March Alexander held two consistories although he was still confined to his bed and despite the objections of his physicians. On Easter Sunday, 10 April, he had himself carried to the balcony of the Quirinal Palace to bestow the blessing *urbi et orbi*, but the strain caused a serious relapse.[319] On 15 April he delivered a moving speech of farewell to 36 cardinals who had gathered round his bed. His mind was still perfectly clear and in his discourse he looked back over the years of his pontificate: he affirmed that he had always been guided by the best of intentions; he was satisfied with his work on the liturgy, on church building in Rome and the general embellishment of the city, as well as with the support he had given to the Catholic princes in their struggle against the enemies of Christendom. Finally he begged the cardinals to forgive him for his faults and frailties. This exertion left him weaker than ever. On 19 May he received extreme unction, and on 22 May he died peacefully, 69 years old.

Many historians have judged Alexander VII rather harshly. We have already seen that he failed to realise on the political front the high hopes aroused at his accession. But the many political setbacks depended on circumstances beyond his control, mainly of course on the persistent enmity of Mazarin and later of Louis XIV. Anti-papal propaganda in France and the hostility of the Jansenists also fanned the flames of the unfair criticism levelled at this pope and his pontificate. Constant suffering certainly accounted for his failure to rule as firmly as people had expected. His initial severity towards his relatives and his later volte-face when he brought them to Rome and helped them on their way to fortune, left an unpleasant aftertaste. In the world of church affairs Alexander VII made an important contribution, which included his stand against Jansenism, his organisation of missionary activities, and his various statements on questions of moral theology. And in the world of art and culture his achievements easily match those of Urban VIII.

But Alexander VII was never popular in Rome. He was not a pope to appeal to the crowds. A pope who composes Latin inscriptions, who builds churches and palaces but does not manage to reduce taxes or improve food supplies, who spends most of his time with poets and scholars—such a man will never become the darling of the Roman populace. His effective measures against the plague were soon forgotten, and the ordinary people never forgave him for helping his relatives on their way to riches. However personally virtuous and pious he may have been, the Romans would not be wooed. Looking back from a distance it is easier for us to set the negative aspects of his reign in relation to the positive. Perhaps, too, we can discern in his kind of piety something that corresponds more nearly than that of any previous pope to the attitudes of our own times. Perhaps Alexander VII was the first pope to represent a modern brand of Catholicism.

Coat of arms of Clement IX, Clement X, and Innocent XI (From Filippo Juvarra, *Raccolta di targhe*, 1732).

CHAPTER III

Clement IX, Clement X and Innocent XI (1667–1689)

The Conclave of 1667

With the death of Alexander VII, Bernini lost one of his greatest patrons; an epoch in the artistic and cultural life of Rome was drawing to a close. During the ten years or so that remained of Bernini's working life much was to change in the cultural climate of the city. As we shall see, the reasons for this were many and various. Alexander's immediate successor, Giulio Rospigliosi, occupied the thróne of St. Peter for a mere two years, which meant that his pontificate made no great personal impact and can be described as a kind of extension and conclusion of Chigi's reign. The next two popes, Clement X and Innocent XI, had little in the way of artistic or scholarly interests, and the number of major official commissions available to artists steadily declined. There were also changes in those levels of society which evoke and determine the manifestations of culture. Consequently, for Bernini the period between the death of Alexander VII in 1667 and his own death 13 years later was something of a period apart.

During the conclave of 1667 the cardinal commanding the largest number of votes, no less than 24, was naturally the dead pope's nephew, Flavio Chigi. Against this Antonio Barberini could muster only 16 of Urban VIII's cardinals, while between the two parties the *squadrone volante* accounted for a mere 10.[1] Chigi, who was otherwise quite uninterested and even indolent when it came to Church politics, behaved with surprising energy and diplomatic skill during this and the succeeding conclaves. Nevertheless he failed to achieve a sufficient majority for his candidate, Cardinal d'Elce. Instead the *squadrone volante* headed by Azzolino won the day, with the election of Giulio Rospigliosi. Cardinal Rospigliosi was widely esteemed and, what was more important, was the only candidate who managed to remain on good terms with both the Spanish and the French kings. At first Chigi was strong in his personal opposition to the very idea of Rospigliosi as pope, and the candidate himself expressed an earnest desire "to leave the conclave still a respected cardinal". But Azzolino and his supporters proceeded with great caution, indomitable energy, and a good portion of diplomatic cunning. In the end Chigi gave way, and after three weeks of negotiations Giulio Rospigliosi was elected pope on 20 July by a large majority. Queen Christina had long been a personal friend of the new pontiff's and she received the news of his election in Hamburg where she had stopped on her way back from a visit to Sweden. There she arranged a great feast in celebration, to the scandalised consternation of the good Protestant burghers of that town.

Clement IX and his Pontificate

The new pope took the name of Clement IX and the motto *Clementia*. One of the medals struck during his pontificate carries the inscription ALIIS NON SIBI CLEMENS, "Clement to others, not to himself". Giulio Rospigliosi was widely recognised as a conscientious and judicious man of considerable diplomatic experience; with his kindly nature, his generosity and his unpretentious conduct he had already won the affection of the Roman people.[2] Carlo Maratti and Giovanni Battista Gaulli have both left portraits of this pope in which the physiognomy is remarkably similar: the pope is shown to be thin, frail and of pale complexion, just as the Venetian ambassador Grimani described him, "*gracile di corpo e di complessione delicata*".[3] Although the pope forbade any discussion of his health at his court, it was general knowledge that he suffered from hernia and had worrying attacks of dizziness; it was recognised that he could not be expected to enjoy a long reign.

Thus the *squadrone volante* had achieved Rospigliosi's election and Decio Azzolino was rewarded with the post of secretary of state. The advent of a new pope had always previously meant changes in all the major offices, but Clement IX decided to keep most of the men who had worked for his predecessor. It is perhaps interesting to note that Clement IX's entourage included two future popes, namely his *maestro di camera* Emilio Altieri, who was to be his successor, and the *datarius* Pietro Ottoboni from Venice, an experienced lawyer who was to succeed as Alexander VIII in 1689.[4]

Rospigliosi had always disapproved of nepotism, and this was in fact one reason for his adoption by the *squadrone volante*. But once he became pope he found it difficult to withstand the pleas of his relatives in Pistoia. He sent for them already in the summer of 1667, but on the express condition that they stayed in Rome only so long as he remained pope. Clement's brother Camillo Rospigliosi was made *Gonfaloniere di Santa Romana Chiesa*, while two of his numerous sons—Tommaso and Giambattista—became commander of Castel Sant'Angelo and commander of the papal guard respectively. Another nephew, 38-year-old Jacopo Rospigliosi, who had been appointed nuncio in Brussels, was called home and given his cardinal's hat. Although this made him a cardinal-nephew, he remained subordinate to Azzolino. His younger brother Vincenzo became commander of the papal galleys. Thus although the customary sinecures and lucrative titles were distributed more or less as expected, Clement did not follow his predecessors' example when it came to financial benefits: he granted his nephews no incomes besides the fees attaching to their posts, and he firmly refused to let them have money from the *Camera apostolica* or from any other Church funds.[5] His brother Camillo later became a wealthy man, but only because he inherited the pope's private fortune.[6] All

Carlo Maratti: portrait of Pope Clement IX. Pinacoteca Vaticana (Museum photo).

the members of the Rospigliosi family lived remarkably modest lives in terms of their own times, proving to be discreet and reserved. Later, however, Giambattista Rospigliosi founded what was to become one of the foremost Roman families, having married the heiress of the extremely wealthy Genoese Pallavicino family—an alliance to which Clement only reluctantly agreed.

Otherwise generosity was perhaps Clement IX's most obvious virtue. The Venetian ambassador wrote rather maliciously of the countless papal lackeys to be met with in the streets of Rome, delivering baskets of fruit or flowers to the many recipients of the friendship of the pope, for Clement loved both giving and receiving gifts.[7] His charity was liberal, and he was particularly generous to the hospitals which he frequently visited in person. He also resumed the old tradition of providing food for the poor each day from the papal kitchen, often serving it himself. On Maundy Thursday 1668, 400 poor pilgrims were cared for in this way. On Holy Saturday he heard confessions in St. Peter's for three and a half hours.[8]

Clement IX also won the hearts of the Romans by abolishing the hated tax on flour on the day before Christmas Eve 1667, although this meant that the *Camera apostolica* lost a substantial source of revenue. Fortunately harvests had been good two years running, and it was therefore possible to reduce the price of bread. Clement also appointed a commission of cardinals to investigate the system of tax collecting in the papal states, and to see what could be done to lighten the burden on the people.[9] Many of the restrictions on the food trade introduced by his immediate predecessors were abolished, and commerce in grain and vegetables became free again within the papal states.[10]

Despite these measures the economy of the papal states was still obviously in the doldrums. In his 1671 report the Venetian envoy Antonio Grimani described the situation as almost hopeless: the tax collectors were unable to collect the requisite tributes from the various provinces; agriculture everywhere and particularly in the countryside round Rome was at a standstill, partly because grain was being imported by the authorities in great quantities and at such low prices that it seemed hardly worthwhile cultivating the land.[11]

During his brief pontificate Clement IX managed to make several major contributions in the field of ecclesiastical administration. Alexander VII had failed to enforce his decrees against the French Jansenists, and four bishops who had obstinately refused to subscribe to his formula were to have been subjected to judicial proceedings. Clement, who had been in personal contact with the Jansenists when he held the nunciature in the Spanish Netherlands, showed great patience and diplomatic skill. The proceedings were dropped and after lengthy negotiations the pope succeeded instead in persuading the four bishops to sign. A period of relative calm on the theological front then followed, and this "Clementine Peace" went a long way towards reducing the tension particularly in France. Even the Sorbonne, traditionally a very hotbed of anti-Roman opinion, found cause to praise Clement IX.[12]

Clement IX's good sense is clearly evident in several important measures, mostly of a purely administrative kind, which he introduced in connection with Church missionary activities. For instance missionaries were forbidden to participate in any kind of trade; in this way Clement succeeded in remedying the frequent anomalies that had arisen particularly in Asia and South Africa.[13]

Even in the political sphere, where his predecessor had suffered such bitter setbacks, the skill and wisdom of the new pope bore fruit. In Crete war had been raging for 22 years, and the Turks had gained possession of the whole island apart from Candia, which had been struggling gallantly to resist capture.[14] To prepare the way for joint Christian action against the Turks, Clement offered to mediate between France and Spain and actually succeeded in bringing about peace negotiations in Aachen, with the result that Louis XIV was satisfied at least temporarily with a few minor gains. Once peace was assured, Clement concentrated on seeking humanitarian and military help for the Christians of Crete. Large subsidies were paid, an international hospital was planned in Candia, and the papal galleys were made ready under the command of Vincenzo Rospigliosi. The pope also received the promise of help from Spain, from the emperor, and from the Catholic German princes; only the Protestants refused him any support. Louis XIV, on the other hand, was so anxious not to jeopardise his good relations with the Sublime Porte that his soldiers fought under the papal banner. The combined papal and Venetian navies reached Crete in the summer of 1668, disembarked their troops, and returned with substantial reinforcements the following year in June. But Candia's situation was hopeless and its defence exhausted; in the end the Venetians had to open negotiations. On 6 September 1669 Candia capitulated on honourable terms. This tragic news reached Rome in the middle of October, when the pope was already seriously ill,[15] Clement's grief over this defeat weakened his health even more and about a month later brought him to his grave.

Spectacle and Drama during Rospigliosi's Pontificate

No economic crisis or papal austerity could quench the enthusiasm of the Romans for all kinds of festivities and spectacles. Again, there is plentiful material waiting to be tapped in the shape of drawings, accounts and contemporary descriptions, and perhaps most important of all the many records still in private archives.

Clement IX's *possesso* on 3 July 1667 was held with the customary pomp.[16] On the Capitol the buildings were hung with gold-threaded damask, while wine flowed from the fountains below the ramp and the city officials distributed generous quantities of bread to the poor. The arch of Septimius Severus was embellished with a special temporary inscription, and at the entrance to

Float at the carnival 1668 with personifications of the seven planets, drawing by P. P. Sevin. NMS, *THC 3622.*

Queen Christina received by Clement IX at a banquet, drawing by P. P. Sevin.
Kungliga Biblioteket, Stockholm.

the Orti Farnesiani, through which the cavalcade always passed, Carlo
Rainaldi erected a triumphal arch in stucco and wood with gilded columns and
allegorical figures in plaster. He had prepared the whole structure in under
four days. Again, at Clement X's *possesso*, the Romans enjoyed the customary
spectacles, and this time Rainaldi built a triumphal arch on the Capitol itself, as
various contemporary engravings show. But the arch which he erected at the
Orti Farnesiani was even more original than on the previous occasion, with
oblique flanking sections and columns resembling one of his own church
façades, and a multitude of allegorical figures. It was greatly admired.[17]

The short pontificate of the humane and learned Pope Clement IX was a
golden age for art, music and drama. The carnivals of 1668 and the following
years were celebrated with festivities on a scale undreamt-of under the austere
rule of Alexander VII. But Clement IX imposed one very typical restriction on
the carnival celebrations: it had long been customary to make Jews run races
against one another along the Corso to a chorus of jeering and invective; this
barbaric custom, whereby the Jews often found themselves almost literally
running the gauntlet, was forbidden by Clement IX in 1668.[18]

When the new pope assumed office, Queen Christina was still in Germany
and thus missed the carnival of 1668. In her absence Colonna's and the pope's
nephews took the leading roles. Magnificent cavalcades paraded along the
Corso, with floats and allegorical spectacles arousing the enthusiastic admiration of all. The Rospigliosi family's float was drawn by 12 horses and lit by an
array of torches representing Vesuvius spitting flames. To the delight of the

populace the crater emitted not ash and lava but a stream of confectionery. Lorenzo Onofrio Colonna's float carried personifications of the planets enthroned in the clouds. These roles were played by members of Roman high society. Another float, constructed for the Marquis Giovanni Giorgio Costa-guti, consisted of a huge confectionery stand with sweetmeats ranged on shelves one above the other, and confectioners threw baskets of sweets and candies to the crowds.[19]

A performance of the opera *La comica del cielo* with music by Abbatini was given in the Rospigliosi family's Palazzo Fiano on the Corso. The pope himself was responsible for the libretto, which told the story of a saint. It was inspired by Spanish drama, particularly by the work of Calderon de la Barca which Rospigliosi had seen as nuncio in Madrid. His drama was strictly moral, always concluding with the triumph of the Faith; it was also usually rather dull and repetitive but relieved by striking sets, designed in this case by Gian Lorenzo Bernini. The improvised theatre was crowded, and the audience was kept happy during the intervals by generous supplies of confectionery.[20]

In May 1668 peace was celebrated between France and Spain. This peace had been achieved as a result of the pope's mediation, and the French ambassador, the duc de Chaulnes, now organised a grand firework display in the Piazza Farnese. The design was Bernini's, and it consisted of a globe hovering above a ring of flames. On the globe three figures sat enthroned, personifying Papal Government, War, and Peace. War was laying down his weapons and Peace her palms before Papal Government, which was thus portrayed as saving the world from threatening dangers.[21]

In November Queen Christina returned to Rome, and Clement IX arranged an appropriate reception for her as a token of his friendship. On 9 December, three weeks after her return, she was invited to dine in public with the pope. The ceremonial followed closely the forms that had been created for the queen's earlier dinner at Alexander VII's table in 1665. The pope entered

Giovan Paolo Schor: *trionfi*, representing scenes from the Passion of Christ at a banquet given by Clement IX, drawing by P. P. Sevin. NMS, *THC 3609.*

Fireworks in the Piazza Farnese, celebrating the peace between France and Spain in 1668, presumably designed by Bernini, drawing by P. P. Sevin. NMS, *THC 3624.*

Carlo Rainaldi: triumphal arch for the *possesso* of Clement X in 1670, engraving by G. B. Falda.

Carnival float 1669 with Maria Mancini as Circe, drawing by P. P. Sevin.
NMS, *THC 3625.*

Queen Christina's balcony at the carnival 1669, engraving by G. B. Falda (GCS).

Filippo Acciaioli: stage set, probably for *L'Empio punito* 1669, drawing by P. P. Sevin. NMS, *THC 3635*.

immediately after the queen. When he had seated himself, his majordomo stepped forward to hand him his table-napkin, but the queen took the napkin and passed it to the pope herself. Christina's table was slightly lower than the pope's, and was only partly under the papal canopy. A number of prelates and others of elevated rank were permitted to watch the ceremony, but papal etiquette forbade the presence of any other ladies besides the queen. However, the ladies of the Rospigliosi family were allowed a glimpse of all this magnificence by peeping through gaps in the hangings that covered the walls—a comical detail that is clearly shown in a drawing by Sevin. The tables were decorated with the usual *trionfi*, sculptures in sugar representing the arms of the Rospigliosi and Vasa families as well as allegories and biblical subjects. Throughout the meal solemn music was played.[22]

At the beginning of the new year and through Azzolino's good offices, the pope granted Christina an annual pension of 12,000 scudi, which in view of the queen's continual financial difficulties must have been extremely welcome.[23]

The carnival of 1669 was one of the most splendid Rome had ever witnessed. The pope had decreed that horses only should race along the Corso; in other words he did not allow the customary competitions between boys or between old men.[24] Queen Christina had reassumed her role as the leading light at all the festivities, and had erected a splendid stand at the corner of the Piazza San Marco and the Corso from which she could watch the races. The stand had actually been made for the carnival of 1666, and had been dismantled and stored in a warehouse ever since. It was built in two storeys and covered the corner façades of the palace. Above the queen's box there was an enormous royal crown, and a large *baldacchino* had been erected over the whole structure.[25] The queen was on good terms with Maria Mancini, but she wisely recognised her own inability to compete with the other woman's youth and

Susterman: portrait of
Cardinal Leopoldo de'
Medici, engraving by
Clouet (BAV).

beauty and instead emphasised her royal dignity, watching the carnival processions from her box with 24 cardinals in attendance. Maria Mancini appeared
first as Armida with a retinue of 24 nobles in Turkish attire, while the Romans
joked about which of the two ladies could boast the more splendid following.
Later Maria reappeared as Circe, enthroned on a float above cages of tigers,
lions, deer, bears and apes.[26]

From this time onwards Queen Christina dominated Rome's theatrical
world. During the carnival of 1669 she rented the present Palazzo Giraud
Torlonia in the Borgo Leonino. The palace possessed a theatre at which Italian
comedies were performed every Friday and Spanish every Sunday, but only
during carnival. Here, for instance, Filippo Acciaioli put on his comedy
L'empio punito in the presence of 26 cardinals. To the delight of the audience
Acciaioli excelled in the art of stage scenery, and his comedy required no less
than ten different sets.[27] The queen also engaged the famous Tiberio Fiorilli,
who was later to occupy a predominant position in the theatrical life of Paris
under Louis XIV. Together with her intimate friend, the French comte
d'Alibert, she was forging plans to establish a permanent theatre in the Tor di
Nona and had even engaged Carlo Fontana for the purpose, but things did not
work out quite as the queen had hoped. The princess of Rossano, still eagerly
partaking in the fashionable pleasures, also put on comedies at her palace on
the Corso. On one occasion she had 12 cardinals in attendance for a single
performance.[28]

Cultural Life and Art

Clement IX devoted much time and interest to the promotion of humanist scholarship. He gave financial support to Allacci, who was Greek born and who had become the foremost connoisseur of Greek language and literature in the west. A versatile man, he turned his mind to everything from Classical culture and archeology and Byzantine history to the ecumenical issues of the day. He also showed an interest in the history and culture of the Etruscans, and was in fact one of the first scholars to do so.[29]

Giovanni Bona and Michelangelo Ricci were commissioned by the pope to found an academy of ecclesiastical history, but as the pope died the following year these plans unfortunately came to nothing. Bona was active in the dispute with the Jansenists, although he disapproved of the excessive lengths to which some anti-Jansenists were willing to go. But the history of the Church was not Ricci's sole interest; he was also one of the greatest mathematicians of his time. A pupil of the famous Evangelista Torricelli, he enjoyed extensive international contacts. In 1681 he was raised to the cardinalate.

At his first consistory in December 1667, Clement IX granted the red hat to Leopoldo dei Medici, one of the most gifted of the cardinals produced by the Medici family. Together with his brother Grand Duke Ferdinand II he had founded the Florentine Accademia del Cimento, devoted mainly to physical experiments, and he was also behind the first publication of Galileo's collected works in 1656. He owned a notable art collection which included antique sculptures and paintings of the highest quality, as well as coins, gems, manuscripts and drawings—the last of which provide the essential basis of the Uffizi's great collections of drawings.[30] The Uffizi's unusual collection of portraits of artists was also started by Leopoldo dei Medici.

✽

Bernini was a personal friend of Pope Clement IX. Their friendship probably dated from the time when Bernini designed the scenery for Rospigliosi's opera *S. Alessio*, which had been performed at the Barberini theatre.

The colonnades round St. Peter's square were almost complete and all the columns in place when Clement IX ascended the papal throne. Work had continued during the conclave, and now all that remained to finish was the corridor on the southern side. The statues which were to crown the colonnade were being made in Bernini's studio, and it was estimated that about two months work would be needed for each one.[31] In February, just before the death of Alexander VII, Bernini had submitted his proposal for terminating the piazza with the *terzo braccio* or "third arm". However, it was thought that such a project would be far too costly, and Clement IX felt bound to abandon it.[32] This may seem a little surprising in view of the fact that a few years later he launched a project together with Bernini for the rebuilding of the choir of S. Maria Maggiore, which was expected to cost at least as much.

Bernini: *Self-portrait*, drawing. Royal Library, Windsor Castle (Copyright reserved. Reproduced by gracious permission of H.M. Queen Elizabeth II).

Immediately after becoming pope, Clement IX gave Bernini another important commission: the decoration of the Ponte Sant'Angelo.[33] Over this bridge people crossed the Tiber to approach St. Peter's from the centre of town, and its adornment was obviously felt to be a matter of some urgency. This was the route taken not only by simple pilgrims but also by ambassadors and princes arriving for a ceremonial audience in the Vatican; here, too, the cavalcade crossed the river at every pope's *possesso*.

Bernini was now commissioned to produce a set of marble angels bearing the Instruments of the Passion. In November 1667 the pope put 10,000 scudi

The Castel Sant'Angelo with fireworks, showing Bernini's angels on the bridge and the new parapet with iron grille, detail of engraving by M. G. Rossi 1692 (GCS).

aside for the work on the bridge.[34] First of all Bernini had the old parapet replaced by wrought-iron grilles alternating with pedestals on which the angels would stand. The grille was also extended a little way along the river-banks at the southern end of the bridge. The idea was that the water should be visible from the piazza and from the bridge, and Domenico Bernini tells us that in discussing this project his father also described the role of water in his fountain designs, explaining its importance as an intrinsic part of the whole—indeed, it was the water which brought such monuments to life.

The idea of decorating the Ponte Sant'Angelo with angels was connected with the bridge's own name and its links with the Castel Sant'Angelo. Both names commemorate the miraculous appearance here of an angel replacing his sword in its sheath, as a sign to Pope Gregory the Great of the end of a terrible plague which had been ravaging the city. Moreover, angels were frequently portrayed in the religious art of the Counter-Reformation, and several churches such as the Gesù had chapels specially dedicated to the guardian angels. Angels carrying the Instruments of the Passion—regarded as *Arma Cristi* or *Vexilla et Signa Triumphi*—were also a reminder of our salvation through Christ's Passion and His death. Angels with the Instruments of the Passion thus appeared frequently as symbols of the Eucharist.[35] Clement IX's personal piety probably also favoured the choice of this theme. It is perhaps significant that the reverse of one of his medals—the one inscribed ALIIS NON SIBI CLEMENS—shows a pelican, the bird which was traditionally believed to have torn blood from its own breast to feed its young and which

Bernini: *Angel with the
Crown of Thorns.*
S. Andrea delle Fratte
(Anderson).

was therefore regarded as a symbol of Christ. And so ten angels with the
Instruments of the Passion were to prompt reflection and repentence in the
hearts and minds of those who crossed the bridge on their way to St. Peter's in
the same way as the Stations of the Cross. Meditation on the sufferings of
Christ was becoming an increasingly important part of spiritual acts of piety in
the Catholic Church, and on this bridge it would be possible to meditate upon
Christ and share His suffering, from His scourging up to the time when the
lance was plunged into His side after His death.[36]

The chronology of the sculptures has been much debated, but scholars now
agree that they must all have been finished by 1669.[37] Bernini himself made
only two of the statues, namely the *Angel Carrying the Superscription* and the
Angel Carrying the Crown of Thorns. We know that the pope visited the
artist's studio in the summer of 1668, but the sculptures were not then ready. It
was probably on a subsequent visit that the pope saw them finished and

Bernini's workshop: *Angel with the Crown of Thorns*, replica. Ponte Sant'Angelo (Author's photo).

declared them too beautiful to be exposed to wind and weather on the bridge. He commissioned two copies to replace them. These were executed by Bernini's assistants and placed on the bridge, while the originals remained in the artist's studio until 1729, when his grandson gave them to the church of S. Andrea delle Fratte where they can still be seen. The other angels were executed by Bernini's assistants Antonio Raggi, Lazzaro Morelli, Paolo Naldini, Cosimo Fancelli, Giulio Cartari, Ercole Ferrata, Antonio Giorgetti and Domenico Guidi. Probably, however, Bernini was far more involved in the making of the statues than is often believed. He provided sketches for them all, and he considered the impact they would make from the shifting viewpoints of a spectator crossing the bridge.[38]

The angels are very similar to those which Bernini had made earlier for the bronze *baldacchino* and the *Cathedra Petri*. They have the same grace that verges on the tender, and the facial expressions at least of the two statues executed by Bernini himself are full of pathos. Hair and garments lift as though blown by a sharp gust of wind, revealing the shapely and almost feminine limbs as far as the thighs. In Bernini's view an angel must obviously be portrayed with a body of perfect beauty, from which follows the predominating softness and gracefulness which is almost sensual in its effect. But the pathos and the fluttering draperies are also intended to rouse in the spectator the emotions that accompany meditation on the sufferings of Christ. Modern

Bernini's workshop: *Angel with the Superscription*, replica, Ponte Sant'Angelo (Author's photo).

spectators may well see something paradoxical in the contrast between the mysterious piety which Bernini has depicted and the sensual softness of the physical forms.[39] We may find it difficult to free ourselves from associations that come readily to the twentieth-century mind, and to look instead at these sculptures as pure form; but if we succeed, we cannot but admire the elegant linear rhythm of arms, drapery and wings, together with the clearly plastic rhythm generated by the relationship between the drapery and the bodies beneath. Bernini's own *Angel Carrying the Crown of Thorns* emerges as one of the finest sculptures ever produced by the Roman Baroque.

The other eight sculptures on the bridge, made during 1669, do not achieve the same consummate artistry, as Bernini's assistants were given a free hand to work on the master's designs. Thus there are obvious stylistic differences in the treatment of the drapery, and even in the proportions between head, trunk and limbs. Despite Bernini's sketches, which impose only limited restrictions, each angel can be said to be typical of the particular artist executing it.[40] But the

CVIVS·PRINCIPATVS
SVPER·HVMERVM·EIVS

Ercole Ferrata: *Angel Carrying the Cross.* Ponte Sant'Angelo (Author's photo).

overall impression is magnificent; the ten angels endow this unique bridge with a matchless air of festivity, subtly combined with the solemnity that its location requires.

✻

During this pontificate Bernini was entrusted with another important commission, namely the new chancel façade of S. Maria Maggiore, which he was unable to complete before the pope died. The basilica's old-fashioned mediaeval chancel apse clashed with the two domed chapels which flanked it. Already during Paul V's reign Flaminio Ponzio had hoped to provide a more

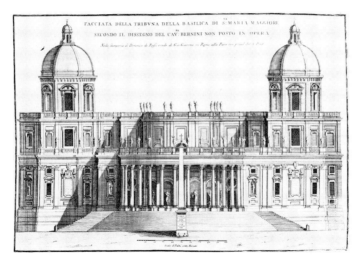

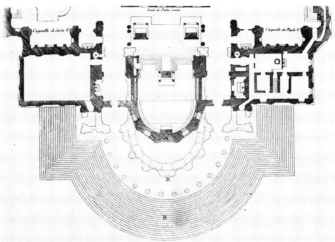

Bernini: project for the new apse of S. Maria Maggiore, elevation and plan, engravings (From Domenico De Rossi, *Studio d'architettura civile*, III, 1721).

pleasing design for this part of the basilica, but his proposals were never used.[41] Bernini first planned a completely new and larger choir, with a crowning dome, a colonnade round the apse, and a great external staircase.[42] The façade would have recalled one half of a round, domed antique temple, and was certainly intended as an effective focus for Sixtus V's great thoroughfare, the Strada Felice, where S. Maria Maggiore is visible all the way from the Pincio. Clement IX planned to put Alexander VII's sepulchral monument in the new choir as well as his own, which he envisaged as a simple slab. Alexander, as we have seen, had commissioned Bernini to create his funerary monument, but how far the plans had proceeded when the pope died is not known. In any case nothing further was done about it during the reign of Rospigliosi.

Clement IX allocated 150,000 scudi for the new building. His relatives protested at this: they did not expect the frail elderly pope to live much longer and were not prepared to shoulder heavy costs after his death. The decision to demolish the old apse was also greeted with protests, as it would have meant destroying Torriti's mosaics. Nor did the furore die down when the pope promised to move the mosaics into the new apse. The choir itself was to be decorated by Maratti. As it was immediately obvious that the cost of the rebuilding threatened to exceed all expectations, Clement appointed a commission to investigate possible reductions. Bernini's first plan for a fully domed funerary chapel was replaced by a plan with a simplified dome and finally by a straightforward extension of the existing apse. He ordered a large wooden model. The foundations of the new choir were laid on 21 September 1669, and it was hoped to have it finished for the Holy year of 1675.[43] When Clement IX died in December 1669, work had barely begun and the future of the whole undertaking was in doubt.

Death of Clement IX and Election of his Successor

It was generally felt in Rome that the news of the fall of Candia drove Clement IX into his grave. Previously, and despite his illness, he had seemed to be in good heart. In fact he was using all his strength to create a defensive alliance against the Turks and to stop them advancing further into Europe, even appointing a congregation of cardinals for the purpose. However, it was once again Louis XIV's pro-Turkish attitude that stood in the way of any hopes of coordinated European action.[44] Disregarding the state of his health Clement visited the seven principal churches of Rome during the autumn, but the effort put too great a strain on him and his condition deteriorated. On 29 November he held a last consistory from his bed; eight prominent and worthy men including the aging *maestro di camera* Emilio Altieri and the ascetic and saintly Giovanni Bona, were elevated to the cardinalate. The pope's strength then declined rapidly; on 2 December he received extreme unction, and on 9 December he died.

Clement IX's body was carried by torchlight in solemn procession from the Quirinal Palace to the Vatican. A great crowd had gathered along the route to pay their last respects, and many people wept.[45] The Romans genuinely mourned this pope who had been so gentle and good; it is no exaggeration to say that few before him had been so loved.

The subsequent conclave is especially interesting to Church historians, because of the unusual wealth of information available to us, in particular the frequent letters passing between Cardinal Azzolino and Queen Christina.[46] The queen kept the cardinal informed about events in Rome and acted as his intermediary with the ambassadors of the Great Powers. So keen was her interest that she sometimes wrote as many as three letters a day. Further, all the voting lists from this conclave and several ambassadorial reports have also been preserved.[47]

For once there were no vacancies in the College of Cardinals, and when the conclave began 56 of its 70 members were present; others arrived later, bringing the numbers up to 67. There were a good many more *papabili* than usual, and of these the previous nuncio in Poland, Pietro Vidoni, was generally the favourite. He was known as a capable and energetic man; he was the *squadrone volante's* preferred candidate as well as being Queen Christina's choice. The party line-up was the same as last time, with Flavio Chigi and Francesco Barberini leading their own groups and Azzolino heading the *squadrone volante*.

The conclave opened on 20 December 1669, and during the unusually harsh winter weather the cardinals suffered severely from the cold in the chilly rooms at their disposal; when the *tramontana* blew, they were further plagued by the smoke from the temporary stoves which had been installed. At first Chigi was prepared to go to almost any lengths to get d'Elce elected after his failure to do so at the previous conclave, but his candidate was vetoed by the French ambassador on Louis XIV's behalf. There then followed a period of total uncertainty which lasted for a full two months, during which fruitless negotiations and votes succeeded one another daily. Throughout these weeks the *squadrone volante* and Queen Christina worked hard to bring about Vidoni's election. People knew that he was Louis XIV's favoured candidate for the papal throne, and this naturally meant that the Spanish cardinals and their supporters opposed him and let it be understood that the Spanish queen-regent was against him. Instead, with Chigi's help, they tried to launch Benedetto Odescalchi, but this attempt was also foiled by Louis XIV's opposition. By the time the Spanish regent announced that she was not prepared to veto any candidate, it was too late; Chigi had switched loyalties and attached himself to the pro-French party. In the end Grimani, the Venetian ambassador, managed to persuade the Spanish and French ambassadors to agree to accept a candidate from among Clement IX's cardinals, although Chigi insisted that Vidoni be excluded. He and Francesco Barberini then agreed together to promote Emilio Altieri. Azzolino and the *squadrone volante* were taken completely by surprise and had no time to launch a counter-attack. At the last minute, however, a new obstacle appeared: Altieri begged repeatedly and in tears to be spared election. He was too old, he declared, and utterly unworthy to bear such a great responsibility. His electors refused to consider his protests and more or less forced him to accompany them to the Sistine Chapel for the last decisive vote on the afternoon of 29 April. Another hour passed before Altieri finally agreed to accept the tiara. Out of affection for his predecessor he then took the name Clement X, although it was not customary for two successive popes to bear the same name.

This remarkably lengthy conclave provoked much adverse comment and many bitter complaints. There is no doubt that interference from secular quarters greatly complicated the issue and probably few conclaves in modern

CLEMENS   DECIMVS
PONT.   MAX.

François Collignon:
portrait of Clement X,
engraving (CGS).

times have been so affected by unwarrantable pressures from outside. The Spanish ambassador declared that Altieri's election marked a victory for Spain, a claim which was just as false as the French ambassador's boast that Louis XIV was behind his election. In fact the real victor was Flavio Chigi, and he had every reason to look forward to a position of considerable influence when his friend and relative Cardinal Paluzzo Paluzzi became the *cardinal padrone* of the new pope.[48] The conclave was a defeat for Azzolino and the *squadrone volante*, but it was to Azzolino's credit that he had tried to follow an election policy independent of the Great Powers and geared only to the interests of the Church, thus paving the way for the non-political papal elections of the future.[49]

Clement X and his Reign

Emilio Altieri had already enjoyed a long career, first as a lawyer in the Curia and later as nuncio in Poland; in 1627 he had been made bishop of Camerino and had proved to be a good administrator and spiritual leader. He won Urban VIII's confidence and was made governor of the Marches. Innocent X sent him

Giovanni Battista Gaulli:
portrait of Cardinal
Paluzzo Altieri, engraving
by Clouet (BAV).

as nuncio to Naples, where he remained during the critical period of
Masaniello's rebellion. After falling into disfavour with Innocent he retired to
Camerino, but was recalled to the Curia by Alexander VII. He was made a
cardinal only when his predecessor lay on his deathbed. Without having
undergone the customary ceremonies of *"chiusura e l'apertura della bocca"*,
without even having received his cardinal's hat in a public consistory, and
without being granted a titular church, he attended the conclave and emerged
as the new pope.

Clement X was fairly short and rather corpulent, but he bore himself with
natural dignity. He was held in general affection for his kindly, generous ways,
and everyone recognised the goodness of his heart. He was also humble and
sincere. When the Venetian ambassador Grimani wrote that "his disposition is
like that of an angel", he was only expressing the general opinion. As pope he
continued to live extremely simply; he was a man of regular habits, although
these were not the habits of ordinary people: he rose two or three hours before
sunrise in summer and winter alike; he dressed without help and then said
mass, sometimes giving audience as early as 5 o'clock in the morning. In the
evening he took his main meal immediately after sundown and retired at once
for the night.[50]

Clement let it be known from the start that he would show great caution in
his use of Church funds; he regarded himself as a simple financial administrator, and was wont to say that he would one day have to render account to

Our Lord. After Clement IX's often rather imprudent spending, this was something new.

In view of his advanced age the pope recognised the importance of finding a capable man to assist him, and his choice fell on Cardinal Paluzzo Paluzzi degli Albertoni. The cardinal's nephew Gaspare Paluzzi was married to the pope's niece Laura Caterina Altieri, sole heiress of the family. The name Altieri was conferred on both the cardinal and his nephew. Gaspare became the general-captain of the Church and commander of Castel Sant'Angelo, and his father Angelo, a hero of the Cretan war, was made commander of the papal galleys. Gaspare thus became head of the Altieri family, inheriting the palace which the pope's father had built near the church of the Gesù. Plans to extend the palace were immediately put in train.

At the age of 47 Cardinal Paluzzo Altieri, now officially *cardinal padrone*, was an experienced and clever man destined to become the real power in the Curia with unlimited influence over the pope. It was generally known that the aged and often over-kindly Clement would sometimes forgetfully promise the same mark of favour to several different people, and the cardinal felt compelled to keep a careful check on those received in audience by the pope. Clement X was extremely unwilling at first to allow his relatives any opportunity to acquire great wealth, but Cardinal Altieri's position gave him the chance to grow rich more or less automatically, and in any case the pope became less restrictive as he grew older.[51]

The finances of the papal states were far from healthy, and however much Clement wanted to reduce taxes, he was unable to do so. The treasury was hard pressed as a result of his predecessor's open-handedness and the costly aid he had granted to the Christians of Crete. In 1671 Grimani wrote that the Papal States were in a singularly poor way and their revenues were small. In the Campagna the area under cultivation was continually shrinking, and poverty began to spread to the formerly wealthy provinces of the Marches and Romagna.[52]

However, Clement X did what he could to boost agriculture, and in Rome he tried to encourage the weaving industry. Despite all the difficulties there was some slight recovery from the depression which had reached its lowest level around the middle of the seventeenth century. Above all the new pope was keen to help the poor and those who had fallen into debt. With this in mind he promulgated a number of sensible measures which bear witness to his concern for those in need.[53] He cared for the spiritual and physical well-being of the labourers in the Campagna, and spent large sums of money on hospitals, colleges, monastries and charity. By 1672 it was estimated that he had already spent 125 thousand scudi on alms.[54]

In the field of foreign policy the Turkish threat was still the most urgent problem, and like his predecessor Clement hoped to unite the Christians in a common stand. An attack on Poland was feared, and since from Poland the Turks would probably be able to threaten Sweden's Baltic possessions, Swedish co-operation was also sought—Sweden being at that time at the height of her power. For this reason Clement X wrote to Charles XI in October 1672 with the co-operation and support of Queen Christina. Charles XI answered courteously but evasively, declaring quite definitely that no such collaboration was possible as there could never be any question of direct negotiations with a pope.[55] On 15 December Clement had a solemn Te Deum sung in St. Peter's in thanksgiving for John Sobieski's victory over the Turks, and his relief was great the following year when Sobieski was elected king of Poland.

Throughout his pontificate Clement X was in conflict with Louis XIV, whose ecclesiastical policy not only went directly against the interests of the Holy See but also contradicted earlier agreements. A major source of conflict concerned the French king's right, established at the council of Lyons in 1274, to appropriate the revenues of certain French bishoprics during vacancies. Louis XIV now extended this right, without consulting the pope, to apply to all the bishroprics in France. The pope's protests were ignord, while Cardinal Altieri angered the French by instituting countermeasures in Rome, some of them without the pope's sanction. Among other things he restricted the ambassadors' right of asylum which they had now extended to include large areas round their residences. He also compelled diplomats, against all custom and tradition, to pay import duties. The situation became really serious when the cardinal refused the ambassadors of the Great Powers a common audience with the pope, at which they had hoped to put forward their complaints.[56] Once he even refused Queen Christina an audience, which hurt her deeply. She declared that while she might forget the insult, she intended to inform the pope personally of what had happened the very next day. And this she did. Paluzzi lost face, but the queen's courage caused great satisfaction to the many opponents of the cardinal.[57] The Romans as a whole disapproved of the cardinal's powerful position, and witty tongues declared that while the pope retained his power to bless and sanctify, *benedire et sanctificiare*, the cardinal had assumed the power to *reger et gubernare*, to rule and govern.

On one famous occasion when the French ambassador d'Estrées was being received in private audience by the pope, he submitted his king's and even his own personal demands in such an arrogant tone that the pope became angry and rang the bell for his chamberlain to bring the audience to an end. When the ambassador refused to retire the pope started to rise, only to find himself being pushed back into his chair by his importunate visitor. Now truly incensed Clement X shouted that d'Estrées was excommunicated for using violence against the head of the Church.[58]

In May 1672 Louis XIV attacked Holland. Although the pope appreciated the help which the king promised to give the Catholics in Holland, he was worried that the war would jeopardise his own action against the Turks. In the subsequent war between France and Spain, Clement X made desperate efforts to secure a peace, but with meagre results.

Up to now Clement X's health had been reasonably good, but in the summer of 1676 he developed dropsy and a fever which left the doctors at a loss. Despite his illness he was still holding audiences in the middle of July, but towards the end of the month his condition deteriorated. On 22 July all the cardinals currently in Rome were summoned to his bedside. Queen Christina also arrived to take leave of the dying man. With great devotion the pope received the sacraments and died the same afternoon at the age of eighty-six.

The Election of Innocent XI

This time the cardinals had to enter conclave at the very height of summer.[59] As before the French and Spanish parties were almost equally strong, which meant that despite having only seven electors the *squadrone volante* was able to play a decisive role. In view of Louis XIV's hostility towards cardinal Altieri, nobody connected with the cardinal had any chance of being elected. Cardinals Alderano Cibo and Benedetto Odescalchi were regarded as the most *papabili* of the candidates. The two men were good friends. Odescalchi was known for his strict piety, his solicitude for the poor, his hostility to nepotism, and his interest in reform, but Louis XIV had always previously impeded his election. On several occasions d'Estrées had intervened with astonishing arrogance, admonishing the cardinals through the door to the conclave. Chigi and Rospigliosi were working for the election of Odescalchi, and they now had d'Estrées on their side. On 22 August the French ambassador had written to Louis XIV, artfully suggesting that Odescalchi's election would represent a defeat for Altieri. The king's answer arrived on 13 September, and in it he agreed to accept the election of Odescalchi, provided that his own royal prerogatives should be respected in France. On 21 September Odescalchi was elected, accepting only after the cardinals promised to agree to fourteen articles of reform. These, which came to constitute his pontifical programme, were concerned mainly with the congregations of the Holy Office and Propaganda, general moral reform in Rome, the appointment of worthy bishops and priests, a reduction in clerical luxury, savings in the administration and reforms in the legal system. Odescalchi assumed the name of Innocent XI in memory of Innocent X, the pope who had originally made him a cardinal.[60]

Benedetto Odescalchi was born in Como in 1611, son of a prosperous family of merchants. As a young man he embarked on the study of law, but contact with the Capuchins persuaded him towards a career in the Church. His rise in the Curia was rapid. Urban VIII sent him to the Marches to collect taxes for the Castro War, a task which he handled with notable leniency. Later he became papal governor of Macerato, where he so distinguished himself that in 1645 Innocent X raised him to the cardinalate. Evil tongues insinuated that bribes to Donna Olimpia had helped the young man to advance, but everything we know of his unwavering integrity contradicts such a likelihood. Cardinal Odescalchi lived quietly, devoting himself indefatigably to works of charity. He helped personally to alleviate hardship in times of plague and during the inundation of the Tiber. As pope he intended to live a life of even greater simplicity. The ceremonies of court life were to be reduced to a minimum; his own conduct was extremely modest and he allowed only the

Domenico Guidi: portrait bust of Pope Innocent XI, marble. Unknown location (Courtesy Heim Gallery, London).

smallest sums to be spent on his table. At his *possesso* he renounced all display and specifically forbade the erection of triumphal arches. He found the homage paid to his person hard to bear, and he showed himself as rarely as possible in public. The gout and kidney stones from which he suffered also constrained him to a quiet life, and he never set foot in the gardens of the Vatican or the Quirinal.[61]

Innocent XI's appearance matched his ascetic nature. He was tall and thin with a great hooked nose, prominent cheekbones and a scant pointed beard. He was never anything but grave and solemn, his voice sombre. He was exceedingly conscientious and pondered long before making up his mind, but once he had taken a decision he stuck to it resolutely. As a recluse his experience in the political field had been rather meagre, and his retiring habits had brought him very little knowledge of the ways of men. Furthermore, there were serious gaps in his theological training.

To the surprise of his Roman subjects Innocent XI refrained with great determination from favouring his own relations. On the day he was elected pope he sent for his nephew Livio Odescalchi, whose guardian he had been and for whom he felt great affection. He told his nephew not to expect any favours; Livio was not given apartments in the Vatican, and was permitted to visit the pope only occasionally to recite the rosary with him. The pope provided some support to other needy relatives but always from his own pocket.

Alderano Cibo, whom Innocent held dear as a friend, was made secretary of state, but without being granted the status of *cardinal padrone*, and the position of the secretary of state in the Curia has remained on these terms ever since. Innocent's confessor Ludovico Marracci and his chaplain Bonaventura da Recanati ranked high in the pope's entourage, where several Oratorians were also prominent. In fact the papal court as a whole revealed a more spiritual character than it had done under any of the immediately preceding popes. Antonio Pignatelli became *maestro di camera* and was raised to the cardinalate in 1681.

An Austere Pontificate

It was during this pontificate that the first steps were taken towards the final abolition of papal nepotism. Father Oliva, general of the Jesuit Order, wrote a *memoriale* in 1676 to the secretary of state, Cibo, in which he declared that while nepotism was to be expected at the court of a secular prince it was not appropriate to Christ's vicar and head of His Church on earth. To quote Oliva: *"non ingrassare, col Patrimonio del Crocefisso, i più prossimi"*.[62] It took a man of Innocent XI's spiritual force to breach the custom of centuries. This pope was the first to refrain absolutely from seeking the support of his closest kin, never allowing his family to enrich themselves in any way at the Church's expense. By the spring of 1677 Innocent had already prepared a bull which would put an end to nepotism once and for all, and a draft was sent to the members of the Sacred College for their comments.[63] Azzolino did not believe the time was right for such a measure. Rospigliosi and Altieri were in favour of it, while Chigi and Barberini upheld the traditional view that the evil lay not in nepotism as such but in its abuse. As a result of the opposition Innocent refrained from promulgating the bull. First under Antonio Pignatelli who became Pope Innocent XII was nepotism finally forbidden in the bull *Romanum decet pontificem* of 22 June 1692.

The members of the Sacred College came to realise that in Innocent XI they had acquired a strict master who disapproved of all worldly ways. Cardinals Ludovisi and Francesco Maidalchini were sternly exhorted to conduct themselves in a manner befitting their rank. Ludovisi was forbidden to consort with women, after rumours of his frivolous life had reached the ears of the pope. Innocent was extremely chary of creating new cardinals, and there were no promotions to the cardinalate until 1681. Sixteen men then received the red hat, all Italians and all worthy recipients with the possible exception of Benedetto Pamphili, son of the princess of Rossano. By this act the pope wished to show his gratitude to Innocent X, but it also meant deviating uncharacteristically from his normal austerity in the granting of favours.

When Innocent XI ascended the papal throne the financial situation was so bad that national bankruptcy threatened. During the preceding year expenditure had exceeded income by no less than 173,976 scudi, and the national debt was estimated at over 50 million.[64] Before the pontificate was many days old, a systematic economy campaign was launched. The customary outlay on the coronation and *possesso* was severely reduced, and the gifts customarily distributed on these occasions were renounced. Two posts, that of general of the church and commander of Castel Sant'Angelo, which were usually granted to papal nephews, were allowed to lapse. Alderano Cibo was given the post of legate to Avignon, but without any emolument. Several positions in the Curia, which had long been pure sinecures, were abolished, and those who held two or more positions had to make do with the income from one only. Even Queen Christina felt the force of the papal cutbacks when the annual pension granted by her friend Clement IX was cancelled. The papal nuncios were informed that the revenues from vacant sees were to be used to help to finance the struggle against the Turks, and in almost all countries a tithe was set on church income.[65]

As a result of all these measures an immediate saving of 100,000 scudi was made. By the time some *monti* were reduced from four to three per cent the pope had balanced the budget, and not much more than a year later the *Camera Apostolica* could report a surplus for the first time since the days of Sixtus V. Innocent XI was particularly anxious to alleviate the lot of the poor, for which reason he put a stop to the profitable lending activities of the Roman Jews, as he considered the interest they demanded to be unreasonably high.[66]

Innocent XI took firm action against certain private persons who had accumulated their own stores of grain, which they would sell at high prices when times were hard. The Falconieri family were amongst those whose supplies were confiscated. This affair caused a great sensation, as so many people were implicated. Innocent then arranged that the papal corn chamber should buy a certain amount of grain every month from Holland and elsewhere. The bakers of Rome were obliged to buy exclusively from this store, and to produce loaves of a standard weight. As a result the Romans were at last able to enjoy good bread, after long complaining that their loaves were almost uneatable.[67]

In other respects Innocent's trade policy was more liberal, to the great benefit of agriculture.[68] Italy's economic crisis had reached its lowest point during the previous decade and a certain upturn, albeit a modest one, could now be expected.[69] But the crisis was still a real one: as at the beginning of the century, several of the old feudal families were disposing of their lands and possessions, sometimes with consequences that Innocent XI could certainly not have envisaged. Thus in 1696, several years after Innocent's death, Livio Odescalchi bought the Orsini castle at Bracciano which had been that ancient family's proudest possession since the fifteenth century.

Innocent XI's austerity and profound piety left its mark on the spiritual life of Rome. He impressed upon the clergy the importance of preaching the gospel and teaching the fundamental tenets of the Christian Faith to the young. Priests were to submit themselves to spiritual exercises twice a year, and in 1677 it was decreed that all the sick in the hospitals of Rome should receive a visit from their spiritual directors.[70] The pope also prescribed that the mass be celebrated with suitable reverence without interruption from talk or conversation among the congregation. It is revealing that this prohibition had to be repeated twice.[71] There was certainly something of the severity of the Counter-Reformation in all this, but now combined with a new depth; we are left with the impression of a spiritual maturity which had not perhaps been so marked a hundred years earlier.[72]

Innocent XI kept a very strict eye on the morals of the Roman people. Women were urged to avoid luxury in dress. The fashionable French décolletage introduced into Rome by Maria Mancini was forbidden by Innocent XI, to the great indignation of his flock. However, when he found that the prohibition was being flouted, he decreed that only public prostitutes could appear in decolleté and priests were forbidden to give communion to those not respectably dressed.

During the first carnival of the new pontificate the pope unwillingly allowed two operas to be performed at a small theatre, but he reinforced the old rule against women performing on stage. The theatre which Queen Christina had started at Tor di Nona was closed down and used as a storehouse for grain. The pope could not prevent theatrical performances in private palaces, but no tickets were to be sold to the general public.

Innocent was extremely reluctant to allow the usual carnival processions. In 1684, and again in 1688 and the following years, the carnival was forbidden altogether in view of the prevailing hard times. Naturally the pope's severity aroused a good deal of protest and there was no shortage of satirical comment, all of which left Innocent quite unmoved.

Throughout his pontificate Innocent XI was in conflict with Louis XIV regarding the right of *régale* and the appointment of bishops.[73] When the king revoked the Edict of Nantes granting freedom of religion to the Huguenots, the pope at first approved. However, when he saw the consequences of the king's action, he let it be known that the conversion of the Huguenots by force did not please him at all. He also wisely counselled James II not to reintroduce Catholicism into England; if the king had followed the pope's advice, he might never have been supplanted by William of Orange.

In Rome Innocent intended to have his own way, and to the fury of the ambassadors he abolished their right of asylum, or extended franchise round the ambassadorial residences. When the French ambassador occupied the Palazzo Farnese with a show of arms he was excommunicated; the French church in Rome, S. Luigi dei Francesi, was put under interdict.[74] First under Innocent XI's successor, Alexander VIII, did any reconciliation with France become possible, mainly because Louis could not afford to acquire more enemies. In the end Innocent XII achieved a settlement, and the French bishoprics which had been vacant for so long were once again filled.

Arnold van Westerhout: *L'Abiura del Molinos*, in the church of S. Maria sopra Minerva, engraving. ING:GS, *FC 14438.*

Queen Christina came into conflict with Innocent XI from the start.[75] In the first place the immunity which she had originally enjoyed within her own palace was abolished, and she therefore supported the French ambassador in his protests; secondly, the loss of her pension meant a substantial financial loss; finally, and not least vexing, her theatrical activities were impeded. Strangely the queen showed no great understanding for the spiritual austerity of this pope, and his uncompromising restrictions on certain aspects of cultural life were alien to her. First towards the end of Christina's life, when she had herself achieved greater spiritual depth, were the two reconciled. A month before her death the queen wrote a most touching letter to the pope, begging his forgiveness. Deeply moved, Innocent XI sent her his absolution and gave her his blessing.

Quietism

On the religious front Innocent XI's pontificate saw the conclusion of the long controversy over the form of piety in the Catholic Church generally known as Quietism.[76] This movement had greatly influenced the spiritual life of the Church during the last few decades, not only in Italy but also in France, and many people regarded it as the most dangerous heretical sect to have appeared in the Catholic Church for centuries. It had started in reaction to the severity inherent in the Counter-Reformation and to the systematised spiritual exer-

A. Clouet: portrait of
Pope Innocent XI,
engraving (BAV).

cises which the Jesuits in particular had promoted. Instead of the regular
discursive contemplation of certain tenets of the Faith, or the Last Judgement,
or events in the life of Jesus, Quietism advocated passive, silent submission. It
was not a question of seeking God by way of meditation; it was rather that in
response to the state of perfect inaction God would grant the soul the ability to
recognise and love Him. Man alone availed nothing, according to Quietist
teaching; instead he should place himself without reservation in the hands of
God, without recourse to any effort of the intellect or the will. In theological
circles the risks associated with this attitude were soon recognised: once a
believer has submitted himself passively to God, he effaces himself and sinks
into acquiescence—and this, many confessors pointed out, was in fact a
manifestation of laxity and lack of spiritual discipline.

The most renowned leader of the Quietists was the Spanish priest Miguel de
Molinos, who worked in Rome from 1663 until he was summoned before the
Inquisition 22 years later. His *Spiritual Guide*, published in 1675, aroused
considerable interest and opposition, and ran through three Spanish and seven
Italian editions. Molinos had arrived at certain paradoxical conclusions: the
soul should submit itself wholly to God and become as dead; any activity was
harmful, disturbing the state of grace; we should pray without words, simply
trusting in the presence of God; and it is not necessary to reflect upon the three
virtues of faith, hope and charity. Nor need we ask ourselves whether we are
truly following God's path, as every kind of thought is an evil element in the

spiritual life, even a reflection upon our own actions. He who submits his will wholly to God need not actively strain for the attainment of Christian perfection, nor strive against temptation by reaching out for the opposite virtues.[77]

Molinos became one of the most popular confessors in Rome. Nuns, priests and members of the religious orders sought him out, and he had many followers even among the higher clergy. His ideas as expressed in the *Spiritual Guide* appeared fairly harmless. Cardinals such as Azzolino and Aldorano Cibo were among his admirers, and even Innocent XI, who as a cardinal had become acquainted with the Spaniard, was favourably disposed towards him. With Queen Christina he was frequently to be found; the two held daily discussions, sometimes lasting for several hours at a stretch.[78]

Certain disquieting consequences of Molinos' teaching soon became apparent. Many people were obviously coming to despise oral prayer, and in some circles traditional acts and pious customs—associated perhaps with the Holy Water or the Rosary—were rejected or fell into disuse. People regarded themselves as being without sin and made no attempt to resist temptation, ascribing their evil thoughts and deeds to the devil. But Molinos still found support at the highest levels. The Jesuit Gottardo Bellhuomo, who had written a thesis on prayer in opposition to Molinos' teaching, saw his own work placed on the Index. A similar thesis by Paolo Segneri met the same fate in 1681. Also, independently of the Jesuits, an enquiry was made among the confessors in Rome about the results of the new methods of prayer. At last, however, it reached the ears of the Inquisition that in his eagerness to show the insignificance of people's personal actions, Molinos himself was guilty of immorality; further, he declared that a man can be overpowered by the devil and commit crimes against morality, but as these are not subject to his collaboration or his will, they cannot be regarded as sins.

As a result of these accusations Molinos was arrested by the papal police in the summer of 1685. The pope had been reluctant to countenance such a step, but in the end he was forced to consent. When Molinos' house was searched, no less than 20,000 letters were found, of which 200 were from Queen Christina; they were all destroyed out of consideration for those concerned.[79]

Even within the Inquisition itself Molinos had his supporters; Cardinal Azzolino was one. And Innocent XI, whose own theological training had not been very extensive, was uncertain in his own mind about the possible consequences of the Quietist doctrine. The influence of Molinos' ideas on Queen Christina's spiritual life emerges clearly from her notes in the margin of the proceedings reports, and from her own maxims. She was particularly attracted by his scorn for the outer forms of piety, which she always regarded as evidence of bigotry.

After two years of investigations and hearings the Inquisition condemned Molinos' quietist teachings, as derived from his letters and summarised under 68 headings. The final stage of the trial was solemnly staged in S. Maria sopra Minerva; Molinos renounced his errors and was condemned to life imprisonment. The Romans flocked to the scene and were disappointed to be denied the sight of a heretic at the stake. For the rest of his life Molinos was confined to a monastery, merely being required to say a specified number of prayers each day.[80]

Science and Culture under Altieri and Odescalchi

With her intelligence, her learned interests, and naturally her royal prestige, Queen Christina was still playing a leading part on the Roman cultural stage. Once she had abandoned her role in the political sphere, the world of learning and art became her true kingdom. Although Rome had long enjoyed the presence of innumerable scholarly and learned persons and the art of conversation had flourished there, this woman quickly came to occupy a prominent position in the essentially clerical city. She was of course endowed with cultivated taste, and although very selective in admitting people to her circle, her library enabled her to help many scholars, among them both historians and natural scientists.

The new academy which Queen Christina founded in 1674, the *Accademia Reale*, was more serious in intent than its predecessor established in 1656. The academicians—eleven savants to start with—were concerned with a great variety of topics, but their most passionate interest was in philosophy and morality.[81] One of the aims of the academy was to cultivate the Italian language, which was used in all their discussions. The members included the mathematician Vitale Giordani, a pioneer of geometry, the lawyer Giambattista de Luca, and Pietro Bellori. The secretary, at least at first, was Francesco Camelli, who was in charge of Christina's collections of medals and coins. Giovanni Alfonso Borelli, another academician, wrote a work entitled *De motu animalium*, which was of fundamental importance to the science of zoology and which was published with the help of financial support from the queen. This same Borelli was one of the first men to climb Etna, on the occasion of the eruption of 1669, and in 1675 he lectured to the *Accademia Reale* on the subject of the volcano. Christina also provided Borelli with a pension.[82]

The queen herself never made formal speeches at her academy, but she used to engage the members in the kind of learned discussion at which she excelled. She was famous for her witty and intelligent conversation, and for her mastery of the satirical and often crushing retort.

The academician who was to prove most important to the world of art was Giovanni Pietro Bellori, whose artists' biographies, *Vite dei pittori, scultori ed architetti*, were published in Rome in 1672. Queen Christina had probably become acquainted with Bellori soon after her arrival in Rome, but she first employed him at her court as librarian and archivist during the 1680s. By this time Bellori was an old man, with a long career in the world of scholarship behind him.[83] In his youth he had been trained by Francesco Angeloni, the greatest contemporary connoisseur of Antiquity and intimate friend of Domenichino and Monsignor Agucchi, both of whom Bellori must have

Wolfgang Heimbach:
portrait of Queen
Christina. English private
collection (NMS).

known. Indeed, this contact determined his view of art for the rest of his life. Over the years he acquired a remarkable knowledge and understanding of everything connected with Antiquity and art. In 1670 Clement X made him *antiquario di Roma*, to superintend the city's ancient monuments under the *camerlengo*, the now aging Cardinal Antonio Barberini.

In writing the *Vite* Bellori was not interested in producing a chronicle or complete history of art as Vasari or Baglione had done. Instead he picked out the artists who seemed to him, in light of his classicist stance, to be the most significant, and wrote their biographies. It is not surprising to find that he was helped in this enterprise by his friend Nicolas Poussin.[84] Bellori's method was interesting, including as it did a detailed description of the attitudes, gestures, facial expressions, colours and drawing in every individual work of art.

The *Vite* is provided with an introduction, *L'Idea della pittura*, which had been delivered as a lecture to the Accademia di S. Luca. Here Bellori developed his most important theses. The artist, he declares, creates his own idea of perfect beauty by studying objects and figures in nature, selecting the best of these and combining them in his ideal conceptual world. The ideal which the artist creates in this way surpasses nature, which is never perfect in itself, and provides the basis for his work of art. Bellori condemns naturalism, as represented by Caravaggio and his successors, although he includes these artists in the *Vite* as an example of their school. The grounds for his condemnation is their uncritical imitation of nature as she is, without the ennobling influence of the ideal. He also condemns Mannerism and the Baroque, the last of which he calls *fantasie fantastiche*. For Bellori the perfect relationship betwen art and nature is to be found in Antiquity—that is to say, Antiquity as he knew it in the art of the Augustan Age. And the supreme example, surpassing even Antiquity itself, is of course the art of Raphael, although Carracci, Domenichino and Nicolas Poussin are also to be admired. He recommends the study of these artists not as models for imitation but as guides to perfect beauty. Obviously this view of art was based entirely on the style that had been prevailing in Rome since the beginning of the century and which was represented by just such names as Agucchi and Domenichino. But Bellori's *Vite* served to spread and reinforce the ideas embodied in the style, and his work acquired the status of a canon which determined attitudes to art throughout most of the eighteenth century and even to some extent into the nineteenth.

Bellori's influence was greatly enhanced by his close friendship with Nicolas Poussin, and the contacts which this gave him with the *Académie de France* in Rome, founded in 1666. All the influential French artists were associated with this academy at some period or periods during their careers.

Bellori could not bring himself to an appreciation of Bernini's art, which he found too remote from his own chosen models of classical idealism. As a result of Bellori's enormous prestige, this negative attitude was to colour the general view of Bernini right up to the beginning of our own century.

✻

Camillo de'Massimi had long been one of the most distinguished patrons in Rome. Clement X had made him *Maestro di Camera* and raised him to the cardinalate.[85] He was closely associated with the Altieri family, who consulted him on all questions of taste in the course of decorating their great new palace. After Poussin's death Massimi gave much of his patronage to Carlo Maratti, having his portrait painted by the artist and arranging for him to receive several other important commissions. He was also a keen admirer of Claude, who painted some of his last great landscapes for Massimi, among them *A Coast View with Perseus and the Origin of Coral*, now in the Earl of Leicester's collection at Holkham Hall. Spurred by his theoretical interests, Massimi was also the inspiration behind the reorganisation of the *Accademia degli Umoristi*, one of Rome's more famous academies. He was a passionate collector of Antique art, and was remarkably knowledgeable on archeological questions. He continued to commission copies of Antique works, particularly interesting examples being copies of the illustrations from a Late Antique manuscript of Virgil in the Vatican Library. This *Virgilio del cardinale Massimo* was much admired in the eighteenth century.

The various international colleges, or centres for theological studies, were also an important feature of the world of scholarship in Rome. The contacts established between the *Collegio Germanico* and the Catholic states in Germany, for example, had important implications. However, it was still the *Collegio Romano*, where Jesuit students learned to follow a serious and Chris-

Carlo Maratti: portrait of
Giovanni Pietro Bellori.
Private collection, Rome
(Arte Fotografica).

tian way of life, which had the greatest impact on the spiritual life as such. The
college gave doctoral degrees not only in theology and philosophy but also in
canon law, thus competing with the University of Rome, the Sapienza. Most of
the priests in Rome were educated at the *Seminario romano*, where both
Gregory XV and Clement IX had studied in their youth. Clement VIII had
founded the *Collegio Clementino* for young nobles, both Roman and foreign,
who wished to study theology.

Festivities and Music

During Clement X's pontificate the carnival was held each year with great
splendour, and operas were an important part of the festivities. Shortly before
the death of Clement IX, Queen Christina had decided to establish what was
to become Rome's first public theatre. Suitable premises were available at the
Tor di Nona, which had long been in use as a prison until Innocent X built the
new prison on Via Giulia. Carlo Fontana decorated the theatre entirely in
wood.[86] The auditorium was not large, roughly 14 metres wide and 16 metres
long, but it was furnished with several rows of boxes. The stage was 8 metres
wide, and since the building was not large enough to house a stage of that
depth, an extension was built at the back, hanging over the bank of the Tiber
like a great balcony. It was a matter of no little technical difficulty to make this
construction safe. The theatre was finished by 1670, but no performances were

Carlo Maratti: portrait of
Cardinal Camillo dei
Massimi, engraving by A.
Clouet (BAV).

held during that year's carnival on account of the conclave, and the opening
had to wait until the following year.

Queen Christina then sought Clement X's permission to arrange public
performances in the new theatre, but her approach was undiplomatic and
permission was granted not to her assistant and theatre director, Jacques
d'Alibert, but to Filippo Acciaioli. Later a compromise was reached, and the
two men worked together. The theatre opened with Nicolò Minato's opera
Scipione Africano to music by Francesco Cavalli.[87] It was preceded by a
homage to Clement X and Queen Christina composed by Alessandro
Stradella. Later the same year *Il Novello Giasone* was performed there. This
opera was also by Cavalli but dedicated to Maria Mancini-Colonna. In 1673
the magnificent opera *Eliogabalo* was performed, with eighteen changes of
scene and three ballets; as well as Pasquini's *Amor per vendetta*. The next year
Caligola was produced, with stage sets by Acciaioli. We know that he excelled
in creating the spectacular effects so beloved of the Roman audiences, but we
have no detailed information about the appearance of this scenery.[88] At all
these performances the female roles were played by women, a custom which
had been forbidden since the days of Sixtus V but which revived under the
tolerant Clement IX. Restrictions were re-imposed by Innocent XI, who also
forbade singers belonging to church choirs to appear on the theatre stage.

The following year, 1675, was Holy Year and there were consequently no
operas, and by the next year there was a new pope. Innocent XI immediately
prohibited public theatrical performances, which he considered immoral, and
operas and plays could thus only be staged in private palaces. The theatre at the

Filippo Acciaioli: stage set, probably for the Tor di Nona theatre 1671, drawing by
P. P. Sevin. NMS, *THC 3629.*

Tor di Nona was closed, and did not re-open for sixteen years, by which time
Queen Christina had been dead for some years. The theatre was then completely rebuilt by Carlo Fontana, at the expense of d'Alibert. The auditorium
was designed to run parallel with the street, making it much more spacious; the
stage was also larger than before. The auditorium now looked as most theatres
have done ever since, with its horse-shoe shape and boxes in six tiers one above
the other.[89] The Tor di Nona was thus the ancestor of our most common type
of theatre auditorium.

Queen Christina was passionately interested in music. In this field it was
possible for her to provide considerable patronage,[90] as it was naturally much
less costly to put on an opera or give a concert than to commission a sculpture
or build a palace. In fact the queen did more for music than for the theatre
during her sojourn in Rome. According to the rules every meeting of the
Accademia Reale had to commence with a *sinfonia* and every speech must
conclude with a *cantata.* For this purpose Christina selected many of the best
composers and musicians of her times, and took every opportunity to listen to
music or arrange concerts at her palace. Among those whom she engaged was
Bernardo Pasquini, who dedicated his opera *L'amor per vendetta* to the queen
in 1673. Arcangelo Corelli dedicated his first important work to her in 1681,
after which he directed all concerts of any importance in Rome. Above all,
however, Alessandro Scarlatti enjoyed Christina's favour, ever since his first
work, the opera *Gli equivoci nel sembiante*, had impressed her at the theatre in

Concert in a Roman
church, drawing by P. P.
Sevin. NMS, *THC 3628*.

the *Collegio Clementino* in 1679. The following year she appointed the still
very youthful composer as her director of music. Scarlatti's second opera,
L'Honestà negli amori was performed in 1680 at Bernini's private theatre.[91]
These were the years when Scarlatti composed the *Miserere*, the oratorio *Agar
et Ismaele esiliati*, and the opera *Il Pompeo* which was produced in 1683 at the
Colonna theatre. The following year Scarlatti left Rome to settle in Naples.

At the Palazzo Riario, Queen Christina associated continually with singers
and musicians. Loreto Vittori gave her music lessons, Marazzoli was her
chamber virtuoso, the composer Pasquini her harpsichordist and organist,
while Antonio Masini composed chamber music for her. She also engaged
several famous singers, among them Angela Maddalena Voglio, known as
Georgina, and various *castrati* such as the Melani brothers whom she had met
in Stockholm. One of the greatest events to take place at the Palazzo Riario
was a special *Accademia per musica*, held in 1687 to celebrate the enthronement
of James II of England and the visit of his ambassador, Lord Castlemain. The
music was composed by Pasquini to a libretto by Alessandro Guidi and
Cardinal Albani, later pope Clement XI. The choir had 100 singers, accompanied by 150 string instruments under the direction of Arcangelo Corelli.[92]

Everything that we know of Queen Christina's taste in this field suggests

Anonymous artist:
portrait of Cardinal
Benedetto Pamphili,
engraving (BAV).

that not only did she expect music to enhance her dignity with pomp and ceremony; she also seems to have been genuinely musical. Carl-Allan Moberg has suggested that in order to understand and appreciate Gesualdo's "speculative compositions" with their contrast between sensual eroticism and a melancholy longing for death, Christina must have been extremely gifted musically, "and her taste in music must have been fastidious ...". But towards the end of her life she seems to have become extremely attached to chamber music. "The fragile chamber music quality of an ensemble of solo singers and an intimate music of the affections ... of the waning High Renaissance were more in tune with her heart."[93]

One of the great musical patrons of this period was Benedetto Pamphili, son of Camillo and the princess of Rossano, and after Queen Christina's death he took over her role.[94] As early as 1672, when he was only nineteen years old, he put on the opera *Erminia* with a libretto which he had written himself. An opera performed at his villa at the Porta Pia in 1677 was attended by Queen Christina and many other ladies, much to the annoyance of Innocent XI, who objected to women visiting the theatre.[95] And what enraged the pope even more was Pamphili's audacity in allowing singers from the papal chapel to perform on stage—in, of all things, female roles! The young man was severely taken to task, although this did not stop him being made a grand master of the Maltese Order the following year. Not surprisingly, however, he had to wait for his cardinal's hat until 1681.[96]

Giov. Antonio De Rossi, the Palazzo Altieri, engraving by G. Vasi.

As grand master Pamphili renovated and decorated the Order's villa on the Aventine, which became his favourite residence. Detailed accounts show that he was interested in the minutest details, from the villa's famous trellised pear and orange trees and the rare blooms which he himself acquired, to the bowling-alley and *la neviera*.[97] During the 1680s Scarlatti composed for him and Corelli was his musical director. Innumerable operas and concerts were later held at his home, as the two succeeding popes—Alexander VIII and Innocent XII—were more tolerant. When Georg Friederich Händel visited Rome in 1707 he was Pamphili's guest.

Architecture under Two Popes

During the pontificate of Alexander VII Bernini had dominated the architectural scene, and the artist was still at the height of his fame under Clement IX. When the pope died in December 1669, work on the new choir for the church of S. Maria Maggiore had barely begun. At the beginning of the following pontificate travertine was still being acquired, and a large wooden model was apparently in progress.[98] But then the project fell victim to Clement X's savings campaign. To the relief of the Roman populace the pope decided to leave the old apse alone, and the mosaics which had already been removed were replaced. The wooden model is now lost, and Bernini's project is known to us only from contemporary engravings.

Nonetheless it was felt that the simple mediaeval brick apse looked inappropriate between the two more recent domed chapels, and Clement X commissioned Carlo Rainaldi to design a façade, on much less costly lines than the

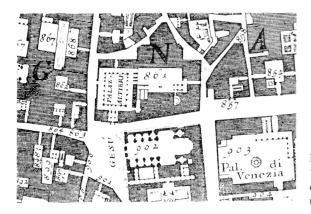

Detail of Nolli's map 1748, showing the location of the Palazzo Altieri close to Il Gesù.

one proposed by Bernini.[99] Rainaldi's façade, which was completed already in 1673, is in fact a simplified version of Bernini's model. It was similarly based on the façade of Domenico Fontana's old Cappella Sistina, and its pilasters were made to continue round the travertine-clad apse. As in Bernini's proposal a high attic above the apse links the two chapels together, but it seems much heavier without the colonnade which in Bernini's design would have provided the dominating theme. Rainaldi has also adopted the great stairway introduced by Bernini, and this is the only motif which succeeds in holding the façade together. Otherwise the effect is one of fragmentation, mainly because Rainaldi has broken up the flanking sections with narrow projections on both sides. It should also be remembered that the stairway was not originally as imposing as it is today; the street level in front of the apse was lowered during the nineteenth century and the staircase extended by about ten extra steps.[100] Rainaldi's chancel façade is hardly a masterpiece, and Bernini was deeply disappointed that his own project for the choir was never realised.

Despite the prevailing papal frugality Clement X's nephews soon set about extending their old family palace. The Altieri had lived on the same site for several generations and Clement himself had been born there. His brother Giambattista Altieri, who was already a cardinal when Emilio was still a mere *monsignore* in the service of the Curia, had added to the old palace and given it a façade facing on to the Piazza del Gesù. The architect had been Giovanni Antonio De Rossi.[101] This somewhat conservative palace with its great central projection and windows recalling the style of the sixteenth century had been big enough for the cardinal; but the family of a papal nephew now required something on quite a different scale to reflect its new status.

Carlo Fontana was appointed to design the new extensions and he submitted a proposal for an imposing, homogeneous and symmetrical building. The old façade was to be reduced to a slightly projecting wing and the main entrance located in the centre of a great palace block surrounding a large rectangular courtyard.[102] This proposal was impractical; it took no account of the Gesù, and the main entrance would have to have been squashed in awkwardly behind

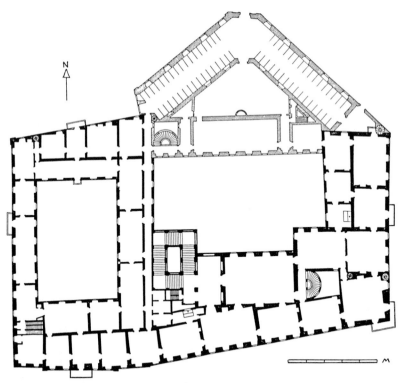

Giov. Antonio De Rossi: The Palazzo Altieri, plan of the piano nobile (After A. Schiavo, *Il Palazzo Altieri*).

this church. Another design, possibly a variation on the first one and submitted by Fontana himself, was copied by Tessin on a visit to Rome in 1673 when he worked for a while in Fontana's studio. The drawing is now in the National Museum in Stockholm, and it shows that Fontana made certain adjustments, adopting traditional Roman solutions and retaining the old palace courtyard alongside a new larger one.[103]

For reasons of which we know nothing Fontana's proposal was turned down and the commission went to Giovanni Antonio De Rossi, who was thus engaged to enlarge the palace he had built twenty years before. It is not known exactly when work started, but the purchase of adjoining property began in 1671 and continued until 1674.[104] The Altieri were eager to finish building as soon as possible and wasted no time. The pope was an old man, and they feared that funds would dry up when he died and the whole enterprise would come to nought. They were also afraid that his successor might listen to the vociferous protests of the Jesuits, who were extremely alarmed at the sight of this enormous palace rising up next door and more or less threatening to suffocate their church. And so during 1672 work proceeded apace, even by torchlight at night.[105] The building appears to have been virtually finished by

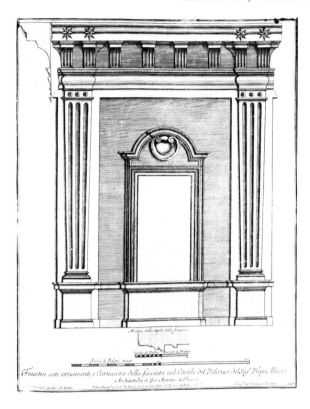

Giov. Antonio De Rossi: window in the courtyard of the Palazzo Altieri, engraving (From Domenico De Rossi, Studio d'architettura civile).

1676 while Clement X was still alive; but although the pope frequently visited the Gesù it is claimed that he never set foot in the palace. Perhaps he did not want to fan the complaints of nepotism that were already widespread among the people of Rome.

De Rossi showed great skill in adapting the palace to a site whose location and extent afforded a good many problems. He kept the archaic façade on the piazza more or less as it was. He also used the same type of window design as he had done twenty years before, but above the central window he now added the Altieri stars and a crowning papal tiara.[106]

Along the Via del Plebiscito, parallel with the side of the Gesù church, a long wing was added, also with three storeys. But unlike the rooms in the old palace with their flat ceilings, the rooms in the *piano nobile* here were vaulted, which meant that the new third storey was very much higher and its crowning cornice a good deal taller than the old façade. The effect of this is not disturbing, however, since the new wing is partly concealed by the church and the old façade still functions as the main palace frontage. The corner nearest the Palazzo Venezia, where the new wing terminates, has been monumentalised with rustication in all storeys and balconies on two storeys on the corner

Carlo Fontana:
S. Marcello al Corso,
façade (CI).

itself—a detail which has no parallel in any other part of the palace and which was a novelty in Rome.

Fontana had envisaged two courtyards located symmetrically within the palace block. De Rossi located his *cortili* next to one another, however, without any thought of symmetry. Perhaps there is some connection between this solution and the design in the Tessin drawing in Stockholm, which may have been an alternative stemming from Fontana himself. However, nothing is known of any contact between the two architects. Behind the old façade there is an arcaded *cortile d'onore*; from one side, where the portico is open in both directions, the visitor passes immediately into the second larger courtyard. The first courtyard has a noble and dignified air, with pilasters in the *piano nobile*, window pediments decorated with the Altieri star, and fluted pilasters in the upper storey. There is something almost Neo-Classical about these pilasters, and about the several rather stiff brackets under the cornice. At the back of the courtyard the upper storey is recessed to allow for a terrace above the *piano nobile*—an idea based on traditional sixteenth-century models. In contrast the larger courtyard is more domesticated, and it is here that we find the stables and coachhouses. Here too the decoration is modest with pilaster strips creating a slight touch of plasticity. The great palace stairway is reached from

Carlo Fontana: Cappella Cibo, interior. S. Maria del Popolo (CI).

the portico in the first courtyard, as is usual in older palaces, but it has been given a very much more monumental design. To make more room for the stairs, the staircase itself juts out into one corner of the second courtyard, and a similar projection has been introduced into the south-eastern corner as well for the sake of symmetry. In older Roman palaces stairs seldom represent a monumental element. It is difficult to recall, for example, the appearance of the stairs in the Palazzo Farnese or the Lateran Palace. But, in the Palazzo Altieri, De Rossi has built one of the most magnificent palace stairways in Rome.

The Altieri palace aroused considerable interest in its time, not on account of its size—it was criticised too for its lack of symmetry—but because of its interior design and its costly embellishment. An important name in this last connection is that of Carlo Maratti, and we shall return to this artist and his contribution later. It is possible that De Rossi supervised the decoration inside the palace. We know that he left designs for stucco-work here, some of which were copied by Tessin.[107] But the chief adviser to the Altieri family on matters of taste was Camillo de'Massimi, who thus came to play much the same role in the life of the new papal family as Guido Bentivolio had once played in the days of the Barberini.[108]

While their palace was being built, the Altieri family chapel in S. Maria sopra

Minerva was also being decorated. Designs had been prepared by Camillo de'Massimi. The chapel is covered by a barrel vault, with the family's heraldic stars in the coffers. The walls are divided into bays by black-and-white marble pilasters, and are decorated with unusual encrustations in rectangles and roundels of green and yellow marble, probably inspired by the kind of Antique Roman encrustations that can be seen in the Pantheon nearby. There is in fact a strangely Neo-Classical air about this chapel almost a century before its time, reflecting of course the profound feeling for Antiquity that guided Camillo de'Massimi's personal taste. The altar painting is by Carlo Maratti, depicting the presentation to the Queen of Heaven of the saints canonised by Clement X: Gaetano da Thiene, Francisco de Borja, Rosa de Lima, Pius V and Juan de la Cruz. Clement X visited the chapel when it was completed in August 1672, but the painting was not delivered until four years later.[109]

Bernini's proposal for S. Maria Maggiore's chancel façade was his last major architectural undertaking. He received no more assignments of this kind from subsequent popes, nor any major projects from private individuals. This was probably due to the economic crisis, but the master also lacked the enormous energy that he had commanded in his younger days. Bernini retained his prestige as the favourite of kings and popes, but in the field of architecture he was no longer an influential figure. Among the leading architects in Rome he was replaced during the 1670s and 1680s by Giovanni Antonio De Rossi and Carlo Fontana.

As pupil and assistant to Bernini, Fontana enjoyed no real fame until after the master's death in 1680. One of his first mature works, which we may also consider to have been his greatest, is the façade of S. Marcello al Corso, built between 1682 and 1683.[110] Here we see how the free and imaginative style of the Baroque has been tamed to produce a restrained unequivocal and almost cold Classicism; despite elements such as the concave curvature and the engaged and free-standing columns, every detail is lucidly proclaimed: part is added to part, and unlike Maderno's façade for S. Susanna every wall projection corresponds exactly to the diameter of the columns; further, every column is backed by a pilaster in the wall—a motif borrowed with almost pedantic exactitude from Antique models.

The same clear departmentalisation and lucid composition appears in the chapel which Fontana built between 1682 and 1684 for Cardinal Alderano Cibo in S. Maria del Popolo. Consecrated in 1687,[111] the chapel is planned as a Greek cross with very short arms covered by narrow barrel vaults. The vaults are supported on pairs of columns in Sicilian *diaspro*, and each column is backed by a pilaster of black-and-white marble. The crossing is covered by a dome without any drum. In plan and elevation this little chapel is a typical example of what is usually called Baroque Classicism, the foremost representative of which was in fact Carlo Fontana. But the use of polychrome marble, preferably in the warm dark colours of *bianconero antico*, the reddish brown Sicilian *diaspro*, *verde antico*, and the warm cream of alabaster, was also generally typical of the late seventeenth century in Rome.

Bernini's workshop:
the tomb of
Rodrigo Lopez de
Silva and his wife
Beatrix. S. Isidoro
(Anderson).

Sculpture

In the field of sculpture Bernini still reigned supreme, and in his old age he created several remarkable works. Two funerary chapels were built during the 1660s and 1670s, due directly or indirectly to his hand. The De Silva family chapel in S. Isidoro was founded by Roderigo Lopez De Silva and his wife Beatrix; according to an inscription on the wall it was consecrated in 1663 and had been built by Bernini.[112] In fact Bernini cannot have done more than produce designs for the sculptures, which according to Wittkower were probably made by Giulio Cartari and Paolo Naldini. In this chapel Bernini developed the theme introduced in the Cornaro chapel, where busts of the deceased flank the altar like spectators, and the scenic effect and theatrical illusion draw the beholder into the chapel to partake in the drama. The De Silva chapel is on a much smaller scale, so that Bernini was not able to repeat exactly the same effect, but he nevertheless achieves a similar kind of tangibility and engages the attention of the spectator in the same compulsive way. The accompanying virtues—*Mercy* and *Truth* on one side, *Justice* and *Peace* on the

Bernini: portrait of
Gabriele Fonseca, marble
S. Lorenzo
in Lucina (CI).

other—are so overwhelmingly large that the beholder feels dwarfed by their presence. The deceased are portrayed in marble-framed reliefs supported by the allegorical figures. The medallions above were added in the eighteenth century.

A few years later the Fonseca family commissioned designs from Bernini for a chapel in S. Lorenzo in Lucina. Gabriele Fonseca was a Portuguese who had been court physician to Innocent X. He died in 1668 but his bust may not have been finished until the early 1670s.[113] The chapel has four niches for portrait busts, but only that of Gabriele Fonseca is executed entirely by Bernini. The others were made much later. The altar painting of the *Annunciation*, a copy of a work by Guido Reni, is carried by jubilant angels in high relief who appear to have flown down from the shallow dome of the chapel. Fonseca is inclining slightly forward out of his niche, looking towards the altar; there is no doubt that he is represented as participating in the mass with reverent devotion. He is holding one hand to his breast and clutching a rosary in the other; his mantle falls in deep dramatic folds. Bernini has come a long way since he made the funerary bust of Mantoya in 1623 almost forty years before. Both busts are equally true to nature, both are recognisable portraits of their subjects. In the case of Mantoya we know that the physical resemblance was found to be remarkable; the Fonseca bust, on the other hand, expresses a deeper insight that captures the subject and portrays him in the grip of profound emotion—a combination of impassioned love and reverence to which Bernini may have been inspired by the *Spiritual Exercises* of St. Ignatius and which the saint has called *amor reverencial.*[114] This depth of feeling is characteristic of all Bernini's late works. The connection between the portrait and the altar painting is much more intimate here than in the De Silva or the Cornaro chapels. Here the beholder is engaged not so much by illusions and scenic effects, as by the sharp intensity of Fonseca's emotional mood.

At the beginning of Clement X's pontificate Cardinal Paluzzo Altieri commissioned Bernini to make a sculpture portraying the Blessed Lodovica Albertoni. The cardinal actually belonged to the old Roman Albertoni family, and perhaps as a gesture of courtesy towards his cardinal, the pope had sanctioned the cult of Lodovica in 1671. The sculpture can be dated with reasonable certainty to the years 1671–1674.[115]

The old Cappella Albertoni in S. Francesco a Ripa in Trastevere was provided with a recess behind the altar for the sculpture. The niche opening is high and not very wide, its walls narrowing behind the portrait as though to thrust it forward on a stage, but without any illusory perspective effects. The chapel itself is dark, lit only by the white light falling on the sculpture from a concealed window at the side of the recess.

The idea of placing the relics of a martyr in the altar of a church was an ancient tradition dating back to Early Christian times. Since Stefano Maderno had placed a recumbent *St. Cecilia* in the church of S. Cecilia in Trastevere around 1600, saintly images under the altar of churches had become customary. Bernini placed his *Lodovica Albertoni* above the altar, however, letting her depict one stage in a dramatic event. The *Blessed Lodovica* is dying of a fever. Her head falls heavily back, her eyes are half-closed, her mouth open, her hands clutching at her breasts, her passionate expression resembling Fonseca's. The fall of her dress forms shadowy cavities, the drapery gathered in dramatically undulating folds over her body but framing her face with pliant curves. This soft and feminine gentleness is somehow enhanced by the naturalistic couch with its little lace pillow. There is something far removed here from the depiction of the ecstacy of Bernini's earlier *St. Teresa*, an experience occurring beyond the limits of our wordly perceptions, elevating and separating the saint from the beholder. Here we see instead a dying woman filled with religious passion, like some illustration to the *Ars moriendi*, an edifying book that was much in fashion at the time.[116]

From the dying woman's couch a coverlet of warm-coloured marble cascades down towards the altar, creating a kind of link between the *Blessed Lodovica* and the spectators in the chapel. Above the sculpture, in a magnificent gilt frame also designed by Bernini, there is a painting of the *Virgin and Child with St. Anne*, a work of Giovanni Battista Gaulli, who often collaborated with Bernini at this period. Cherubs or winged infant heads fly down towards us, partly cutting across the frame of the picture, with the same kind

Bernini: the
Cappella Altieri
with *Beata Lodovica
Albertoni.*
S. Francesco a Ripa
(Fototeca Unione).

of playful illusory effect as in S. Andrea al Quirinale. The contrast between the
dark chapel and the light altar recess reinforced the beholder's sense of witnes-
sing an almost painfully realistic portrayal of the dying woman. The light
emphasises the whiteness of the marble which assumes a deathly pale sheen.
And yet the light does not play the same iconographic role here as in the
Ecstacy of St. Teresa, nor is there any real link between the dying woman and
the altar painting: we cannot be sure whether the picture shows us something
which she can also see with the inner eye of the visionary.

To continue the comparison with the Cornaro chapel, everything here is
much simpler. The rich polychrome marble surroundings have been abandoned, perhaps on grounds of frugality. Presumably Bernini has made a virtue
of necessity, emphasising the sculpture itself and concentrating all attention to
the figure, which perhaps arouses in us a more intimate experience of the

Bernini: *Beata Lodovica Albertoni*, detail. S. Francesco a Ripa (Alinari).

Blessed Lodovica in her last moments on earth than we received of *St. Teresa* in her state of ecstacy.

While Bernini and his assistants were working on the *Blessed Lodovica Albertoni*, the master himself was also supervising the work on Alexander VII's tomb.[117] He had originally received this commission from Pope Alexander in person, but work did not begin during Clement IX's pontificate, probably because the pope wanted to place the monument in the new choir to be built in S. Maria Maggiore. When this project was abandoned under Clement X, Bernini was able to return to the task and Flavio Chigi acquired a new location for the tomb, not now in S. Maria Maggiore but in St. Peter's above the door to one of Michelangelo's spiral stairs. Such a position above a door could have proved awkward, but Bernini succeeded in exploiting it, letting the door itself symbolise the grave, perhaps as the gateway to the kingdom of death.

A clay and wooden model of the whole tomb was commissioned in December 1671, and this was ready in August the following year. Work continued until 1678, when the body of Alexander VII, which had been laid in a temporary resting place, was transferred with all due ceremony to the new tomb.[118]

The pope is depicted kneeling in prayer, probably in accordance with Alexander's own wishes. We know that the idea of death was constantly in his

Bernini and his
workshop: the
tomb of Alexander
VII. St. Peter's
(Fototeca Unione).

thoughts. This monument marks a striking contrast to the triumphant ruler in
the tomb of Urban VIII which Bernini had made about thirty years earlier. On
each side and below the kneeling pope are four virtues, *Caritas, Prudentia,
Justitita*, and *Veritas*. The great shroud of Sicilian *diaspro* over a travertine core
spreads out below the papal statue in massive folds partly covering the door.
One fold is held up by *Death*, a skeleton with an hour-glass. Even the
prominence given to *Death* certainly agreed with Alexander VII's instructions.
Veritas, portrayed here as a graceful woman, is not a virtue in the usual sense
but something for which man should strive, something which he should
practise. Truth, we are told, is also to be revealed by time. In this case *Truth*
probably refers to the humiliations suffered by Alexander VII in his efforts to
unite the Christians in the struggle against the Turks. *Death* not only represents the power which brings earthly life to a sudden end; it is also the power
which reveals *Truth*.[119]

The tomb of Alexander VII was Bernini's last great sculpture. From the
accounts which have survived it appears to have been the result of a farreaching
and systematically organised subdivision of labour, to a much greater extent
than any of Bernini's earlier works.[120] When this monument was made Bernini
was an old man, needing more assistance for an undertaking of such a size. But

Bernini: Tabernacle
for the Holy
Sacrament.
St. Peter's (CI).

he had obviously not lost his ability to direct and supervise large and complex projects. He gave instructions for making the model, and may have put some of the finishing touches to it himself. Of the sculptures, probably only the pope's head was entirely his own work, the rest of the figure being the work of two members of his studio. Several of the other figures are the result of collaborative efforts, mainly involving Giulio Cartari, Bernini's favourite pupil at the time, as well as his son Paolo Bernini who was beginning to work as a sculptor. The documents also show that four stages can be distinguished in the execution of the figures. First the marble blocks were prepared by a stonemason; the figure was then chiselled by a sculptor of good repute, while a younger or less experienced artist was responsible for details and smoothing the surfaces. Lastly, the final polishing was accomplished by a specially trained craftsman.[121] When the monument was unveiled in 1678, Pope Innocent XI protested against the portrayal of *Veritas* as a naked woman, although this accorded with iconographical tradition. And so a special drapery had to be made in bronze, and painted to resemble stone.

It is a mark of Bernini's astonishing creative power and talent for organisation that while Alexander VII's tomb was in the making, he conceived and realised another major monument in St. Peter's, namely the altar and tabernacle for the Cappella del SS. Sacramento, which was executed between 1673 and 1674.[122] The idea of creating a tabernacle for the Sacrament worthy of St. Peter's dated back to Urban VIII, and Alexander VII had shown equal interest. The commission was an important one, not only because of the greatness and dignity of the basilica itself, but also because of the scale of the monument. Something more than an ordinary altar tabernacle was required to house the consecrated host which pilgrims and other worshippers came here to adore.

In the end it was Clement X who gave the commission to Bernini. It is not known for certain when the artist began to work on the surviving designs, and it is possible that they were based on ideas which had been submitted earlier. A beautiful drawing in the Leningrad Hermitage shows the tabernacle as a small, round, domed temple, hovering above the altar and surrounded by four kneeling angels carrying candlesticks; the angels are either lightly supporting or perhaps gesturing towards the tabernacle, much as the Church Fathers surround the *Cathedra Petri*.[123] In another drawing there are three or even four angels on each side. Finally the angels were reduced to two and freed from direct contact with the tabernacle; in the final version they are expressing their adoration and wonder at Christ's presence in the Sacrament. Bernini appears to have made the models for these angels himself, and for the small apostle statues encircling the temple, one above each column, and for the Risen Christ which crowns the dome.[124] The angels and statuettes were then cast in bronze by Lucenti, chiselled by Carlo Mattei, and then gilded. The tabernacle stands behind the altar on a tall base of *portasanta* marble. The dome of the little tempietto is obviously inspired by the dome of St. Peter's and is richly decorated with lapis-lazuli; the columns are of gilded bronze. The whole monument is imbued with the veneration and solemnity due to the tabernacle of the Holy of Holies in the greatest temple of Christendom.

✻

The strict Classicism of Carlo Fontana in the Cappella Cibo represents one of the movements within the High roman Baroque, but there were others. In Bernini's wake we also find the church of Gesù e Maria on the Corso close by, with its painted and sculptural decoration. We have no definite information about the early building history of this church. It was consecrated in 1675, but building had been in progress for a long time before that, and the sculptural ornamentation was not finished until much later.[125] The choir and high altar were executed by Carlo Rainaldi between 1678 and 1680, and are among his best works. The tombs and their sculptures were being planned by Rainaldi during 1684. All this decoration was financed by Giorgio Bolognetti, who was bishop of Rieti. Four tombs were built for the bishop and his family, all of which appear to have been finished by 1690.[126] The arrangement is unusual in that each of the four monuments is designed together with two confessionals between the pilasters which flank the side chapels. This creates a kind of platform on which the busts of the deceased are placed, either in pairs deep in conversation with one another, or singly looking towards the high altar. The bishop himself kneels on the left side, as was customary for the founder of a church. Opposite him we see Francesco Maria Bolognetti, a Maltese Knight, stepping forward on his platform and gesticulating in impassioned prayer. Carlo Rainaldi was probably responsible for the overall design, but the work was executed by Michel Maille (generally known in Rome as Michele Maglia), Francesco Aprile and Francesco Cavallini.[127] The first two were pupils of Ercole Ferrata, while Cavallini's master was Cosimo Fancelli, a close associate of Pietro da Cortona. Aprile died in 1685, before these sculptures were finished, but Maille lived until 1700.

Carlo Rainaldi: the church of Gesù e Maria, view of interior toward main altar (Max Hutzel).

To modern eyes the sculptures in Gesù e Maria might appear rather worldly, with the eager gesticulations of the gentlemen deep in their discourse and the knight poised apparently in mid-leap, but this was not at all the intention. To their contemporaries it would seem natural that their prayers and their piety,

Francesco Aprile: tomb
sculpture of the Bolognetti
family. Gesù e Maria
(Anderson).

Carlo Rainaldi: the church of Gesù e Maria, interior (Max Hutzel).

Michele Maglia: the tomb of Francesco Maria Bolognetti. Gesù e Maria (Anderson).

their love and religious passion should be expressed in striking gestures and attitudes, and throughout the seventeenth century artists had been concerned to find the attitudes appropriate to every level of feeling. And in the present case the whole church—and not just a single chapel like the Cornaro chapel or the Cappella Raimondi—is included in the decoration. The aim is to draw the visitor into the drama that confronts him in the *Coronation of the Virgin*, a large painting by Giacinto Brandi framed by Rainaldi's magnificent multi-coloured marble surround. The drama, the participation in what is happening on the altar, the figures turning towards the choir and commenting on what they see—all this goes back to the model Bernini created with the groups of ancestors in the Cornaro and Raimondi chapels.

Painting

Since the death of Pietro da Cortona in 1669, the painter enjoying the greatest prestige in Rome was Carlo Maratti. At the same time this artist was the standard-bearer of the classical camp, whose chief representatives had previously been Sacchi and Poussin, although like Poussin himself Maratti did not often work on the great decorative commissions. It should not be forgotten, however, that the leading figure on the Roman artistic scene as a whole was still indubitably Gian Lorenzo Bernini, and the way in which the master's influence extended even into the field of painting will become apparent in the following pages.

The older tradition represented by Domenichino was continued by Domenichino's own pupil Francesco Cozza, who was finishing the great ceiling in the Libreria Pamphili at about the time that Bernini began to work on Alexander VII's tomb. After the middle of the century a new style had emerged in Roman painting.[128] Previously, the Baroque style had built on the Renaissance approach to pictorial space, building it up as a logical whole according to the laws of perspective; every figure possesses its own individual plastic value but is generally subordinated to some character of central importance. The actions which these figures perform are lucidly and unequivocally depicted. Now, instead, a swarm of figures can fill a whole ceiling. No single actor seems to predominate and none are subjected to any rules of perspective. The first example of the new style was Mattia Preti's frescoed ceiling in the Palazzo Pamphili in Valmontone, which dated from 1661. As these frescoes were largely destroyed during the Second World War, Francesco Cozza's ceiling in the Libreria Pamphili has come to occupy a central position in the history of Roman Baroque painting.

The Libreria Pamphili is located in a house built by Don Camillo Pamphili in the Piazza Navona on the right as you face the church of S. Agnese. With its Serlian window it echoes the gallery window on the Palazzo Pamphili, creating a symmetrical balance on each side of the church. Apart from the library the building also provided residential quarters for the clergy attached to the church, and the premiss of the *Collegio Innocenziano*. The Pamphili library had been inherited from the home of Innocent X, and included many works on philosophy, history, theology, and above all law. Camillo Pamphili's collection of musical scores and the library belonging to Cinzio and Pietro Aldobrandini, which the princess of Rossano had inherited, had now also been added. The library remained in private hands and had no connection with the college.

Don Camillo saw the finished building before he died in 1666, and had already drawn up a contract for the ceiling frescoes in the large library with Francesco Cozza, who had worked for him previously in Valmontone. Payments for the frescoes are documented between 1667 and 1673, but most of the work was apparently completed by 1670. It is even thought that Don Camillo may have approved the sketches before his death.[129]

The fundamental break with the earlier tradition of ceiling painting is the lack of any illusionistic architecture in Cozza's library fresco; the whole ceiling is covered with human figures, birds, heraldic emblems and clouds. The beholder should feel as though he were gazing upwards into an open sky teeming with allegorical figures; there is no very coherent structure, the figures appear to be grouped at random, and they all have more or less the same plastic value. The firm, plastic figure drawing and the warm, full colours balanced to produce definite tonal effects, all bear witness to the influence of Domenichino on his pupil.

The iconography of the ceiling is difficult to fathom, consisting as it does of rather obscure allegories all jumbled together without any obvious system,

Francesco Cozza: ceiling
fresco in the Libreria
Pamphili. Collegio
Innocenziano (ICCDcop).

and, as it would seem, without a dominant *concetto.* Waterhouse describes the
ceiling as "something like decorative nonsense".[130] In the middle of the fresco
we see a brightly lit half-naked female figure with a book under one foot and
holding the Lamb of God. She represents that Theological and Philosophical
Wisdom for which the Pamphili pope was supposedly famed. Four large
isolated figures symbolise the arts that benefitted especially from Pamphili
patronage: *Music, Poetry* which was particularly dear to the heart of the
princess of Rossano, *Architecture* and *Sculpture.* The cosmic aspect is emphasised by allegories of the four elements. Even some of the Olympian gods are
included: *Venus* sitting in her chariot drawn by peacocks and greatly resembling the princess of Rossano, *Flora* with her hands full of flowers and perhaps
alluding to Don Camillo's horticultural interests, and of course *Fortuna* with
her wheel, to whose favour the Pamphili family owed its elevation and status.

Francesco Cozza: allegory
of *Music* and other figures,
detail of ceiling fresco in
the Libreria Pamphili.
Collegio Innocenziano
(ICCDcop).

Putti are grouped round these figures, some carrying papal attributes such as
the tiara and keys, others bearing the stars and lilies of the Aldobrandini and
Pamphili families. There are also horses prancing securely on whisps of cloud
and figures meandering in space as though on *terra firma*. We are gazing at an
unreal dream-like world, an apotheosis of the Pamphili family.

*

At about this time one painter frequently worked in close collaboration with
Bernini and became a protégé of the master. His name was Giovanni Battista
Gaulli from Genova, popularly known as Baciccio.[131] He arrived in Rome in
1657 at the age of eighteen, and apart from a few short visits elsewhere stayed
there until his death in 1709. On Bernini's advice he had been appointed in
1666 to paint the pendentives in S. Agnese in the Piazza Navona with allegorical virtues. The paintings were commissioned by the Pamphili family, more
specifically by the princess of Rossano, but surviving documents show that
Gaulli had already been employed by Don Camillo and the contract was
probably drawn up just before the latter's death. Two years passed before
work began, and the paintings were unveiled on the feast of St. Agnes, 21
January 1672.[132]
    Each of the four pendentives contains from three to five main figures,
apparently disposed somewhat randomly but in fact forming part of a well-

balanced composition, which has been skilfully adapted to the trapezoid space available. The colours are unusually light and clear, the figures appearing in silhouette against a luminous sky. In fact light plays an important part in these frescoes. It models the forms and brings brilliance and life to the colours. The play of light and shade and the clear contours typical of Gaulli sometimes recall the reflections of sunlight on ripples of water. These are compositions of great charm, radiating that almost profane *joie de vivre* so typical even of religious subjects in seventeenth-century Rome. In the treatment of light and the choice of palette it is easy to see the influence of Correggio's paintings in Parma, and on Bernini's advice the young Gaulli had in fact gone to see this artist's works before embarking on his own frescoes.

The *Virtues* have been joined by several other allegorical figures, three in each field, forming a *concetto*, almost a story; each virtue has its corresponding "anti-virtue", an evil quality or vice. Thus *Justice* triumphs together with *Peace* and *Truth* over *Injustice. Wisdom* is joined by *Hope* and *Providence* to confound blind *Ignorance. Chastity* is crowned by *Temperance* and conquers *Lust.* Finally, together with *Charity* and *Faith, Fortitude* triumphs over *Paganism.*[133]

The pendentives were understandably a great success, and before they were finished Gaulli had already been given one of the most important commissions in Rome at that time, namely to make paintings for the dome and vault of the Gesù. Giovanni de' Vecchi's manneristic paintings in the dome were considered unworthy of their location, and although it had been assumed that the decoration of the choir would be paid for by the Farnese family, since the great cardinal had chosen it as his final resting-place, no painting had in fact yet been done. The Jesuits should have seen to the decoration of the vault over the nave, but this too had been neglected. And after paying for the Castro War, the Farnese dukes of Parma had no particular interest in financing the decoration of a church in Rome.

There is no doubt that at this time the Jesuits were particularly anxious to emphasise their power and importance, as Molinos and his supporters were so obviously and successfully competing with them, winning supporters among the aristocracy as well as in the highest ranks of the clergy. In 1661 Father Gian Paolo Oliva had become superior general of the Society of Jesus, a position which he retained until his death twenty years later. He was familiar with conditions in Rome, and was personally acquainted with a number of artists, among them Bernini.

Several names had been suggested for the work in the Gesù, including Lanfranco's pupil Giacinto Brandi and Pietro da Cortona's pupil Ciro Ferri, as well as Carlo Maratti who appeared best placed to be given the commission.

But now Father Oliva turned to Bernini for advice. He recommended Gaulli, giving his personal guarantee that the young artist would be fully capable of succeeding. Oliva then put forward Gaulli's name with the rest, and Bernini's nominee was accepted. On 21 August 1672 a contract was signed,[134] whereby Gaulli was to bear the cost of gilding the dome and the vault, while

Giovanni Battista Gaulli: *Triumph of Chastity*, spandrel fresco in S. Agnese (Alinari).

the Jesuits were to pay for scaffolding, plaster, carpentry and masonry work.[135] This subdivision of the costs between artists and patrons was customary and had centuries of tradition behind it.

The paintings of the Holy Trinity and saints of the Jesuit Order in the dome were ready by Christmas Eve 1674 as stipulated in the contract. These dome frescoes, the *Vision of Heaven*, are so badly damaged that it is difficult to make out any of the details.[136] Gaulli has obviously been influenced by earlier domical frescoes. As we know, he had seen Correggio's dome in Parma, while Lanfranco's paintings in S. Andrea della Valle and Pietro da Cortona's in the Chiesa Nuova were close at hand in Rome. His overall composition stems largely from these last. In places the layers of stucco cut across the surrounds of the small round windows, so that the clouds on which the saints are seated appear to be floating downwards into the body of the church itself.

The pendentives were unveiled two years after the dome was completed. Queen Christina visited the church to admire them.[137] The iconography of the pendentives is unusual. A common solution was to place one of the four Evangelists or the cardinal virtues in each pendentive. Here, instead, *The Four Evangelists* fill one pendentive, *The Four Doctors of the Latin Church* occupy the second, *Lawgivers and Leaders of Israel* the third, and the *Prophets of Israel* the fourth.[138] The figures thus appear in groups as they did in S. Agnese. However, the space here is more restricted, terminating at the base in an acute angle, which cramps the figures even further. This may be why they reveal a plasticity far beyond that of the S. Agnese paintings, strongly recalling Domenichino's pendentives in S. Andrea della Valle. Again Gaulli has allowed the thick layers of stucco to cut across the cornice framing the pendentives. This idea was already in evidence in Domenichino's work, but Gaulli has gone much further in striving for illusionistic effects. Again his figures appear to hover in the room, independent of the actual frame of the pendentive. The most attractive of these paintings is the *Lawgivers and Leaders of Israel*, which is dominated by the great patriarchal figure of Moses with the tables of the Decalogue. Below him is the powerful figure of a man writing in a book, either Aaron or the first Historiographer. The massive curved back, naked to the waist, thrusts out of the pictorial space, tense as a bow and strikingly illusionistic.

In 1677, the year after the pendentives were finished, Gaulli began on the great vault and *The Triumph of the Name of Jesus*,[139] a subject of crucial importance to the Jesuits: the Gesù is dedicated to the name of Jesus, and the special emblem of the Society of Jesus is the monogram, IHS, the first three letters of Jesus as written in Greek. The tradition of the adoration of the name of the Godhead was an ancient one, of which many examples appear in the Old Testament. Among the Jews the name of God was imbued with a special sanctity and great power, and the early fathers bear witness to the reverence paid to the name of Jesus in the Christian Church. Here, in the vault of the Gesù, the radiant monogram surrounded by countless hosts of angels, sheds a blinding light over the heavens. The whole scene strongly resembles the *apparati* which used to accompany the Forty Hours Devotion.[140] As they approach the name the angels are absorbed into the divine light, dissolved in it, while those further from the source are increasingly clear in form and movement. In a semi-circle below the heavenly host there are saints worshipping the name; on the left we see the Three Kings, the first gentiles to adore the Holy Child in His crib, and portrayed here as the leaders of a group of secular potentates. There is also a group of holy women, and on the right we can distinguish priests, cardinals and popes. At the furthest end, towards the crossing, the damned are overthrown, blinded by the divine light radiating from the name of Jesus. They include several identifiable vices such as Greed, Vanity and Heresy.

Giovanni Battista Gaulli:
*The Leaders and Lawgivers
of Israel*, fresco. Il Gesù,
spandrels under dome
(Max Hutzel).

Gaulli first envisaged his composition in a rectangular frame with semicircular ends, like a great *quadro riportato* placed over the gilt arches and coffers of the vault. The same idea had been used by Pietro da Cortona fifteen years before in the Chiesa Nuova. On this occasion, however, such a composition was not considered to be grand enough. Pascoli tells us that when Father Oliva expressed his dissatisfaction, Bernini intervened and suggested extending the composition and letting it break out of its frame.[141] Further, to create the illusion of a host of the blessed that really hovers between the vault and the church below, and of vices hurling dramatically downwards into the space beneath them, he suggested that the gilt decoration on the vault should be partly painted over in black, as though the clouds and the falling figures were casting their shadows there. Thus the beholder sees banks of clouds that appear to hang in the air inside the church, while angels swarm round the name of Jesus that appears to be high up above the ceiling itself. The saints seem to be below the level of the vault, and the evil spirits to be genuinely tumbling down. The original frame which is apparently being carried by the stucco angels can still be seen, but it now seems to form the opening in the vault through which the figures float or tumble down and through which we gaze up towards the sky.

White stucco statues have been placed under the ceiling, above the great cornice and in the window openings. Iconographically they belong to the ceiling, participating in the adoration of the name of Jesus. They are said to

Giovanni Battista Gaulli: *Adoration of the Name of Jesus.* Il Gesù, ceiling of nave
(Rigamonti).

have been designed by Gaulli, but they were executed by Antonio Raggi, Michel Maille and others.[142] As we have seen, the details of the painting become more fully realised as they leave the dazzling source of light, and on the very periphery they are transformed into full three-dimensional sculptures. This was probably also inspired by Bernini, who loved combining painting and sculpture in a single work of art.

Some mannerist painters, such as Giulio Romano in the Palazzo del Te in Mantua, had already broken through the picture plane both inwards and upwards, and something of the same illusion appears in Pietro da Cortona's great Barberini ceiling, but never before had this illusionistic effect had such force and power as in the vault of the Gesù. This magnificent ceiling transforms the rather severe sixteenth-century architecture of the church, to create one of the most splendid interiors of the Roman Baroque. When the vault was unveiled on New Year's Eve 1679, people came to gaze at it in droves.[143] Some, particularly the learned advocates of Classicism, were critical; but there was no doubt at all about the appreciation of the general public. And Queen Christina herself joined the ranks of Gaulli's admirers after viewing the finished ceiling at the beginning of January 1680.[144]

Now only the semidome of the apse remained to be decorated. Father Oliva wrote to the duke of Parma, the present head of the Farnese family. This family had originally built the Gesù and they had special rights (and could therefore perhaps be persuaded of certain obligations) over the choir of the church. Father Oliva praised the work which Gaulli had already done, and finally succeeded in obtaining the money necessary for finishing the work. The subject chosen was the *Adoration of the Lamb* as described in the book of the Apocalypse (5:8–12). The painting was finished in 1683.[145]

The relative roles of Gaulli, Father Oliva and Bernini are not known to us in detail. Bernini's suggestions in connection with the composition are not to be found in any surviving documents, but are vouched for by Pascoli and other contemporary witnesses and have been accepted more or less unanimously by all art historians. As for Oliva's role, we can be virtually certain that he decided on the iconographical programme. Above all, he procured the money, and we also know that he followed and supervised the work from beginning to end. Pascoli tells us that Father Oliva visited the church daily to see how work was progressing, bringing with him small gifts of sweetmeats, cakes, vegetables or sometimes even poultry.[146] Oliva was both tactful and patient in his dealings with the temperamental and hypersensitive Gaulli. Pascoli writes that Father Oliva promised the artist, in writing, compensation for having painted more than the original contract had stipulated. Unfortunately Oliva died before the apse fresco was finished and the Jesuits were unwilling to pay anything over the contracted sum. Gaulli then proceeded to tear up the guarantee he had been given, and, if it had not been for Bernini's intervention, would have refused to finish his painting.[147] This was probably the last service which Bernini was able to do for his friend and protégé Gaulli before his own death shortly afterwards.

Giovanni Battista Gaulli: *Adoration of the Lamb of God.* Il Gesù, apse (Alinari).

Gaulli also enjoyed a substantial reputation as a portrait painter. According to Pascoli he painted all the cardinals and popes since Alexander VII. Very few of his portraits have survived and there is still some research to be done regarding his activity in this field.[148] The few portraits known to us, for example those of Clement IX and Cardinal Leopoldo de'Medici, demonstrate a keen insight and an ability to capture the character of his subjects. The pope is portrayed just as we would imagine this humane, good, but extremely frail man to have been. The portrait of the learned cardinal is almost astonishingly personal; Gaulli had certainly not idealised him, emphasising his family traits —the long nose, the thick lips and the prominent jaw (Illustration, p. 265).

Bernini was greatly impressed by Gaulli's talent, and arranged that several other important commissions came his way. Thus while he was still working at the Gesù, Gaulli was commissioned to make two altar paintings for S. Andrea al Quirinale, one of which we shall return to in a later context. Another major painting was made as part of the decorative scheme in the Altieri chapel with Bernini's *Blessed Lodovica Albertoni*, namely the *Virgin and Child with St. Anne*.[149] The Virgin is gently handing the Christ Child to St. Anne, while small joyful *putti* are strewing flowers over them; it is an idyllic and intimate family group. The figures are sitting under a tree which partly screens the sky; and in the background we catch a glimpse of the landscape behind, which seems inspired by Annibale Carracci's ideal landscapes. With its warm colouring dominated by shining jewel-like reds and blues, the picture provides a foil for

Giovanni Battista
Gaulli: *Virgin and
Child with St.
Anne*, painting over
the tomb of Beata
Lodovica Albertoni.
S. Francesco a Ripa
(Alinari).

the white marble of Bernini's sculpture. Very similar is a painting of *Christ and
the Woman of Samaria* in the Galleria Spada, although this time there is greater
emphasis on the landscape, which sets the mood of the whole picture. In some
ways Gaulli's painting reflected the spirit of Bernini's sculpture: with his
fluttering draperies, his rippling shadow-filled folds, his billowing outlines,
and not least his effects of light, Gaulli approaches very close to Bernini's late
style. This can be seen clearly in the Cappella Albertoni, where we find the two
artists creating the same intense and emotional mood.

Carlo Maratti, who had missed the hoped-for commission to paint the vault
of the Gesù, was engaged instead to execute an altar painting for the same
church. In the right-hand cross-arm a magnificent new altar had been built in
1672 by Pietro da Cortona's nephew Luca Berettini for the relics of St. Francis
Xavier. It had been financed by a wealthy and influential monsignore, Gian-
francesco Negroni, who had purchased for himself the office of president of
the papal *annona*. Later, because of the position he had acquired, Innocent XI

raised him to the cardinalate. Immediately before Pietro da Cortona's death in 1669, Negroni had asked the artist to produce some designs for the altar.[150] The painting, which was probably executed between 1674 and 1679, portrays St. Francis in India. The dying man lies stretched out on the ground, while those around him gesture towards him: a wealthy Portuguese merchant on the left who looked after the sick and lonely missionary, and a soldier on the right who shows him to one of the natives. Angels are descending from a luminous sky, strewing flowers over the body of the saint. The composition is magnificent in conception, with a drama which cannot fail to grip the beholder. The saint's face is lit by the strong heavenly light, his eyes are closed, he could almost be sleeping peacefully; there is no sign of pain. It is only those standing round him—with whom the beholder identifies—who perceive death as a separation. But St. Francis himself experiences death and eternity solely as an internalised vision.

It is interesting to compare this painting with Gaulli's version of the same subject, painted for the Jesuits' novitiate in S. Andrea al Quirinale and dated 1676.[151] The scene has been reduced to include only the dying man and the angels descending from heaven. St. Francis is lying on the ground, his face brightly lit from above, his gaze directed towards the open sky which is the source of the light. But here the heavens are very close; St. Francis is aware of the angels hovering immediately above his head. The sky and the earth merge; there is no longer any distance between the saint and the heavens; he is already among the angels. In neither version is there any perception of death as something tragic; it is not the last breath of the old life but the beginning of a new one. Maratti has produced a great historical painting, and Gaulli a painting full of mysticism: the miracle has become the main theme.[152]

While Maratti was painting the *Death of St. Francis Xavier*, he was also working on another important commission, namely the ceiling in the principal hall of the Palazzo Altieri. Like the great hall in the Palazzo Farnese this was not a banqueting hall but an audience chamber which symbolised the family's rank and declared its status. On ceremonial occasions lackeys dressed in the family livery would wait to attend on the distinguished guests, and the room was therefore known as the *Sala dei staffieri*. As was the custom among the foremost noble families in Rome, the chamber was hung with the Altieri family arms under a *baldacchino* of red cloth over a construction closely resembling an altar.[153]

Carlo Maratti was chosen to paint this ceiling on the advice of Camillo de' Massimi, and the artist in turn consulted Bellori on the iconography.[154] Surviving documents show that the painting was executed between 1674 and 1677.[155]

Maratti organised his painting in the white cavetto vault as a great *quadro riportato*, with a carved gilt frame enclosed in a border painted in *chiaroscuro* to resemble stucco. The painting is an *Allegory of Clemency*, alluding of course to the name of the pope. At the base of the composition are the four seasons, represented by *putti* carrying appropriate attributes: flowers for spring, fruits for summer and so on. Above these is Justice bearing a book of law and the

Giovanni Battista Gaulli:
*Death of St. Francis
Xavier.* S. Andrea al
Quirinale (BH).

fasces, Wisdom in a helmet carrying spear and shield, and Abundance with the horn of plenty. On the right we see Prince Gaspare Altieri in armour with his badge of office as *Gonfoloniere di Santa Romana Chiesa*—a parasol-like canopy in the yellow and purple colours of Rome and with the crossed keys of the papacy. Above these the chief figure of *Clementia* is enthroned, with the ruler's staff to symbolise good government and an olive branch held out protectively over a globe. A *putto* holds up a tablet inscribed with the words CUSTOS CLEMENTIA MUNDI: guardian of clemency throughout the world. Another *putto* carries an oar, alluding to the government of the Church.

The *concetto* underlying the composition is that papal clemency, tolerant and merciful, embraces the whole world, and this cosmic dimension is further emphasised by the presence of the *Four Seasons.* Clemency is aided by Wisdom and Justice and the Altieri family represented here by Prince Gaspare; the result of their rule is Abundance and Prosperity. This is a flattering allegory of the supremacy of the ruler, a theme which from now on was to become increasingly common at many European courts.

Carlo Maratti: *Death of
St. Francis Xavier.* Il Gesù
(Anderson).

The picture is strictly contained within its frame according to the classical
rules of composition. There is no question of the kind of illusion that Gaulli
and Bernini were creating in the Gesù at this time, in order to enhance the
splendour of their composition. But this also means that Maratti's figures have
to compete for space, and the overall effect is rather overwhelming, almost
violent. This impression is reinforced by the somewhat glaring colours which
include sharply contrasting blues, purples, and a golden yellow. Two *bozzetti*
still in the Palazzo Altieri are rather different from the final version,[156] at least in

Carlo Maratti: *Clementia mundi*, ceiling fresco in the Gran Salone of Palazzo Altieri (BH).

Giacinto Brandi: *The Fall of the Angels*, ceiling fresco in the nave of S. Carlo al Corso (SBAAL).

Giacomo Bichi: portrait of
Lorenzo Onofrio Colonna,
engraving by F. Spierre.
ING:GS, *69131.*

their colouring, which probably corresponds more closely to Maratti's intentions. The colours in the fresco itself may have suffered from the artist's lack of
experience in the technique of this kind of painting.

In his *Vita di Carlo Maratti Pittore* Bellori tells us that when the painting in
the centre of the ceiling was complete, the artist realised that the rest of the
vault looked too bare, so before removing the scaffolding he began to plan
further frescoes for the short ends and the spandrels between the windows,
which would have contained allegories continuing the iconographical programme suggested by Bellori.[157] None of this was ever realised, but it is
possible to reconstruct Maratti's intentions from a number of drawings which
have been preserved in various collections. *Religion* and *Faith* would have
embellished one end wall, and *Evangelical Truth* and *Wisdom* the other—all as
befitting a papal palace. The spandrels on one long wall would have contained
Sacred and Christian Rome, Peace, and *Virtue Crowned by Honour.* At first
Time was also included, but as there were only three spaces this idea had to be
abandoned. The *Four Parts of the World* would have been on the opposite side,
and for the same reason two of these would have shared one spandrel.[158]

Roughly contemporary with the Altieri vault is the ceiling painted by
Giacinto Brandi in S. Carlo al Corso, which is dated 1674. The composition is
somewhat similar to Maratti's ceiling in the Palazzo Altieri, but it has fewer
figures. Like Pietro da Cortona in the Chiesa Nuova, Brandi has painted his

Antonio Del Grande: the Gallery in Palazzo Colonna, interior (Anderson).

picture as a great *quadro riportato*. The stucco-work surrounding the painting is also rather similar, and in fact the artist—Cosimo Fancelli—had also worked previously in the Chiesa Nuova. Even Brandi's light colours seem to have found inspiration in Pietro da Cortona's late style.

✶

In 1672 the marriage between Lorenzo Onofrio Colonna and Maria Mancini finally broke down, and in the aftermath of this somewhat turbulent experience Colonna virtually retired from Roman society and public life to spend more time on his collection of art.[159] When his uncle Cardinal Girolamo Colonna died in 1666, Lorenzo Onofrio had inherited the great gallery built and recently finished by Antonio del Grande, and he now devoted himself to enlarging the collections which the gallery housed. He ordered and purchased paintings from all the principal artists in Rome, from the *bamboccianti* and Salvator Rosa to Claude and Gaspard Dughet. He was particularly interested in mythological subjects and fables, and above all in landscape painting. Dughet did no less than twelve landscapes for him, which are still in the gallery together with the works ordered from Francesco Grimaldi. Claude was commissioned to do eight landscapes between 1663 and 1680,[160] but these are now dispersed. Thus, after the king of Spain, Colonna was Claude's most important

Gaspard Dughet:
landscape fresco in
Palazzo Colonna (MV).

patron. In the old part of the palace, in a room serving as a summer residence, Dughet was commissioned to make a series of landscape frescoes.[161] These form a coherent landscape divided by illusionistic colonnettes and pilasters, with views over brooks and ravines and waterfalls and distant blue mountains, all in lyrical and idyllic mood.

Between 1675 and 1678 Colonna had the ceiling of the great gallery painted by Giovanni Coli and Filippo Gherardi from Lucca.[162] Both artists were pupils of Pietro da Cortona, and after a few years in Venice had been sent for by Cortona in 1669 to execute paintings in S. Maria in Campitelli in Rome. Unfortunately they arrived the day after Cortona had died, and the commission fell through. Coli and Gherardi were intimate friends; they lived and worked together, and their lives as well as their styles are inseparable.

The subject of the Colonna ceiling has been taken from the family's history and consists of scenes from the life of Marc Antonio Colonna. It is understandable that Lorenzo Onofrio should interest himself in the past glories of his family. Like so many of the noble Roman families, his own had fallen into debt and been forced to sell most of its land and estates. It must have pleased Lorenzo Onofrio to recall the victory of his ancestor Marc Antonio, when as commander of the papal galleys he had defeated the Turks in the battle of Lepanto in 1571.

Giovanni Paolo Schor, Giovanni Coli & Filippo Gherardi: ceiling frescoes in the Gallery of Palazzo Colonna (BH).

Giovanni Coli & Filippo Gherardi: *The Battle of Lepanto*, ceiling fresco in the Gallery of Palazzo Colonna (ICCDcop).

Antonio Gherardi:
Presentation of the Virgin,
ceiling painting in S. Maria
in Trivio (SBAAL).

The ceiling in the Colonna Gallery consists of a *quadratura* which had already been painted by Giovanni Paolo Schor,[163] and Coli and Gherardi now had to paint figures in this architectural framework and the great *quadri riportati* in the centre of the ceiling. The main painting in the middle depicts *The Battle of Lepanto*, in which a confused mass of ships, masts, weapons and soldiers appear against a luminous sky. All the *quadri riportati* are surrounded by illusionistic stucco frames, and between them we catch glimpses of the open sky. Below, the cornice round the gallery provides a kind of imaginary terrace, where groups of people are painted to resemble living participants. They include Turks in garbs of shimmering cloth, soldiers in shining armour, canon, parts of ships, arms, and mighty Turkish standards—the trophies of the victors—painted as magnificent fluttering patches of colourful silk. The illusionistic architecture is combined with the ceiling, neither breaking nor enlarging it. This approach to ceiling composition closely resembles the work of the artists' former master Pietro da Cortona in the Pamphili Gallery and in the battle scenes of the Palazzo Pitti. But Coli's and Gherardi's style, with its brilliant Venice-inspired palette, is nevertheless un-Roman. The final impres-

Domenico Maria Canuti & Enrico Haffner: ceiling fresco with the *Apotheosis of St. Dominic.* Ss. Domenico e Sisto (Max Hutzel).

sion is one of festivity and triumph; the whole ceiling is an *allegro con brio.*

Even more Venetian in style and colouring than these ceiling frescoes are those painted around 1670 by Antonio Gherardi in S. Maria in Trivio.[164] This artist is not to be confused with Filippo; the two Gherardis were not related. Antonio's frescoes consist of 18 ceiling panels in the brilliant colours and compositions typical of Venetian painting.

In quite a different style is the *Apotheosis of St. Dominic* in Ss. Domenico e Sisto, painted by Domenico Maria Canuti and Enrico Haffner between 1674 and 1675.[165] Canuti was born in Bologna in 1620 and was a pupil of Guido Reni. Here we have an example of genuine *quadratura* painting, for which

Giacinto Brandi: ceiling fresco with the *Apotheosis of St. Silvester with the Virgin Mary and other Saints.* S. Silvestro in Capite (Thomas Poensgen).

Filippo Gherardi: *Triumph of the Name of Mary*, ceiling fresco in S. Pantaleo (Thomas Poensgen).

Canuti's assistant Haffner was responsible. The illusionistic architecture recalls the *quadratura* tradition dating back to Giovanni and Cherubino Alberti, but has now been developed to much greater lengths. Balconies and balustrades overlap with one another in ascending layers. Two arches span the room and above the windows, and the beholder seems to be gazing up at the open sky far above the vault of the little church, a sky lit by the golden radiance of a myriad angels disappearing upwards into regions infinitely high. The effect is almost dizzying. This way of treating the entire vault as a single whole was un-Roman; it was alien to the style of Pietro da Cortona and closer to the methods of Genoese painting.[166]

Domenico Maria Canuti also painted the ceiling in a large room in the Palazzo Altieri with an *Apotheosis of Aeneas*.[167] Here, too, a luminous open sky is populated by heroes and gods above a balustrade, while great broken pediments, crowns and the Altieri stars are depicted in a *quadratura* that seems to lift the ceiling from the real architectural space.

One of the ceilings that most consistently exemplifies this style was painted by Giacinto Brandi for S. Silvestro in Capite, depicting the *Glory of St. Silvester*.[168] There is no illusionist architecture here. The whole vault is full of angels and saints, all illuminated by the divine radiance. No figure dominates; the spectator has to discover the main actors for himself. The ceiling was executed between 1681 and 1682, and is perhaps the purest example of the new style in ceiling painting that developed in Rome after the middle of the century.

In the little church of S. Pantaleo between 1687 and 1690, after Coli's death, Filippo Gherardi executed a ceiling fresco depicting the *Triumph of the Name of the Virgin*, which is more closely related to the composition produced by Bernini and Gaulli for the Gesù. Here Gherardi allows his figures to break out of the frame round a *quadro riportato* and to cover the whole vault down to the tops of the windows.[169]

All these ceilings were precursors of the climax reached in Andrea Pozzo's great painting in S. Ignazio, which was executed between 1691 and 1694, a good ten years after Bernini's death.[170] The illustionistic architecture which sets the stage for the whole ceiling comes right down into the window area. Columns and arches reach up into the heavens above the vault like an irresistible force towering above us and losing themselves in the bright sky. The entire structure is strictly architectural, and here we can identify a close connection with the *apparati* for the Forty Hours Devotion. Andrea Pozzo was a lay brother of the Jesuit Order, and he had designed and made an enormous construction for just such an occasion in the Gesù in 1685.[171] In S. Ignazio Pozzo has brought the entire church into his conception, so that the perspective effect appears only when the spectator stands on a particular spot on the floor. Even the dome, and the slightly later architectural décor in the vault of the chancel apse then become part of this incredibly skilful illusionistic scene. The iconographical theme is the glorification of the Jesuit Order, and it goes much further than Gaulli's paintings in the Gesù. Here we see the triumph of

Andrea Pozzo:
Quarantore decoration
in Il Gesù 1685 (From
A. Pozzo, *Prospettiva de'*
pittori et architetti,
1693–1700).

the missionary activities of the Order in the four continents of the world. After the defeat of the Quietist movement, the Order was at the peak of its power and influence. But this painting too falls outside Roman art traditions. Andrea Pozzo came from northern Italy, as can be seen from his light and varied palette and the touches of brilliant colour, among which gold and blue are more important than they are in works belonging to the Roman tradition.

Bernini in Old Age

Domenico Bernini tells us in his biography of his father that every Friday for 40 years Bernini would attend a service known as *la divozione della buona morte*, "the devotion of the good death", in the church of the Gesù.[172] A brotherhood had been created in 1648 especially to promote just this type of

Andrea Pozzo: ceiling fresco in S. Ignazio (Anderson).

Giovanni Battista Gaulli:
portrait of Gian Lorenzo
Bernini. Galleria Nazionale
d'Arte Antica (ICCD).

devotion, which was typical of the nature of Jesuit piety with its emphasis on accustoming the faithful to the idea of death. Spiritual exercises of this kind were intended as a kind of training for the deathbed, helping people to accept their end in a manner fitting to true Christian believers. These ideas had been presented in 1620, in a short book by St. Robert Bellarmino, *De arte bene moriendi*, which was itself based on various sixteenth-century manuals devoted to the preparation for death. The original model for all these works was the fifteenth-century *Ars moriendi*. Originating in the Netherlands, this book became widely known in Italy and the rest of Europe.[173]

Under the influence of this special form of piety Bernini's last work, the *Sangue di Cristo*, came into being. This was originally a drawing, which Bernini had engraved by François Spierre in 1670.[174] We see from slightly below the Crucified Christ suspended above an ocean of blood which pours from His five wounds—the precious blood which purges the faithful of their sins. A host of angels surrounds the figure of Christ, whilst His sacrifice is offered up by His mother to the Heavenly Father above the Cross. The picture is probably inspired by a painting which used to be placed in front of the high altar in the Gesù during the special Friday devotions, and which also depicted the Crucified Christ and the interceding Virgin. The purifying power of the blood of Christ was an old and still potent theme, frequently occurring in the writings of St. Maria Maddalena de' Pazzi, who was canonised by Clement X and whose words are actually quoted on Bernini's engraving.

Bernini's *Sanque di Cristo* also served as the frontispiece to a little book published in 1670 by the artist's nephew, the Oratorian Father Francesco Marchese. This priest, who was later to attend Bernini's deathbed, was an active opponent of Molinos and Quietism, and had frequently discussed with Bernini the subject of death and the manner of preparing for it.[175] The full title of Marchese's book summarises much of the ideology we have been discussing: *Unica speranza del peccatore che consiste nel sangue del N.S. Giesù Cristo*, or "The only hope for the sinner lies in the blood of Our Lord Jesus Christ".[175]

Bernini's late works bear witness to a new deeper dimension in his spiritual life. As a young man this energetic artist with his unique gifts and creative powers could perhaps have been described as an average Christian, at least in terms of his own times. As the years passed his perspective changed and he ultimately achieved a remarkable level of religious sensibility and insight.[177] Naturally many people's ideas altered as they grew older, then as today, but it would be a mistake to dismiss Bernini's attitude as no more than an expression of old age. It was probably inspired in part by the mood of the times; it seems to embody a type of piety which had not been so prominent at the beginning of the seventeenth century as it was towards the end. The severe Counter-Reformation puritanism that flourished in many quarters in the years immediately after the Council of Trent had gradually weakened its hold: we have only to compare Sixtus V with Urban VIII or St. Charles Borromeo with the two Barberini cardinals. But towards the end of the seventeenth century a new and somewhat different form of piety emerged, more profound and possessing greater intensity. Pope Innocent XI was a prominent representative of this type of piety, at least as serious and puritanical as Sixtus V a hundred years earlier but possessing also a deeper dimension in the conduct of his life. On his death in 1689 he was revered by the people as a saint. The process of his beatification began in 1714 but was not concluded until 1956.

The year before his death Bernini made his last sculpture, a *Bust of the Saviour* or *Salvator Mundi*, showing Christ raising his right hand in blessing. Bernini offered this sculpture to Queen Christina, but as she felt unable to pay the artist appropriately the queen refused to accept it. When Bernini died in 1680 it turned out that he had bequeathed the bust to Christina, who placed it in her bedroom. She prized the sculpture highly, wishing to keep it always near her, and when she breathed her last nine years after Bernini's death, the bust was before her eyes. Nicodemus Tessin saw the sculpture in Queen Christina's home during his second visit to Rome, and has described its position there.[178] Under the bust was a base of Sicilian *diaspro* supported by two gilded wooden angels; the angels in turn knelt on a tall socle, also of gilded wood. The whole construction was 198 cm high.[179] The sculpture stems from an old fifteenth-century Italian tradition of saints represented in half-figure intended as devotional images for the home. Verrocchio, for example, made many portraits of this kind.

In her will the queen left the bust to Pope Innocent XI, with whom she was

Bernini: *Sanguis Christi*, engraving by F. Spierre. ING:GS, *FC 69108.*

reconciled on her deathbed. After the pope's death the bust was owned by Livio Odescalchi. In 1713 it was still listed in an inventory of the works in the Palazzo Odescalchi, but it then disappeared without trace until Lavin recently found that a marble bust of Christ in the Chrysler Museum in Norfolk, Virginia, is almost certainly identical with this vanished work.[180] Several drawings, which before Lavin's discovery were our only source of information about the appearance of Bernini's last work, also tally with the Norfolk bust. Drawings and bust alike demonstrate the deeply emotional content, what we could almost call the softness, that pervades the works of Bernini's old age. But it would be misleading to see any Quietist influence in the *Salvator Mundi*. So far as we know Bernini had no contact with this movement. Rather, he was associated with the Jesuits, its most passionate opponents. Domenico Bernini tells us that his father attended mass every morning, and after finishing work in the evening he would visit the church of the Gesù to pray.[181] The idealisation and the emotional dimension in the *Salvator Mundi* can probably be regarded instead as a further development of the "ideal" seventeenth-century school, as represented by Andrea Sacchi and his associates, all of whom were active long before Molinos began to spread his ideas in Rome.

Queen Christina's genuine appreciation of Bernini's art is confirmed by her words in a letter to Angelo Morosini: "I have such a high opinion of the said Bernini that I gladly take every opportunity to do him a good turn, for he has proved himself the greatest and most outstanding man in his craft who ever lived".[182] Domenico Bernini also claims that when Christina heard the size of Bernini's fortune, estimated at 400,000 scudi on his death, she declared: "I would be ashamed if he had served me and had left so little."[183]

According to Domenico Bernini, Queen Christina was numbered among Bernini's friends. This was certainly so, although it is perhaps difficult to establish the degree of intimacy that prevailed. But there are certainly no grounds for denying the friendship altogether, as some scholars have done, dismissing Domenico's claim as an idle boast intended to enhance his father's reputation. Domenico also tells us that on his deathbed Gian Lorenzo "urgently implored Cardinal Azzolini to supplicate Her Majesty the Queen to make an act of love to God on his behalf. He thought... that that great lady had a special language which God understood, while God used a language with her that she alone could understand" (translated by Irving Lavin). Christina's answer is characteristic of the religious nature of the ageing Queen. She replied that she would do everything within her power to be heard by Our Lord, on condition that Bernini also promised to pray for her, so that God would grant her the grace of His perfect love, "and so that one day we may all be together with the joy of love, and enjoy God forever".[184] Queen Christina appears by this time to have achieved a deeper personal piety, with perhaps an authentic element of mysticism in it.[185] Several quotations from her letters, her notes and her maxims bear witness to this, and it is known that she profoundly admired St. Catherine of Genoa as well as Molinos, with whom she spent some time every day. Bernini had also developed a deeper spiritual quality in his own life, and despite the rather different forms which their piety assumed, he recognised that the Queen had sustained an important spiritual experience and acquired religious insights not given to all. For this reason Domenico Bernini's account is extremely interesting, since it helps us to appreciate Bernini's relations with the spiritual movements of his times and to understand something of his attitude in face of death.

Epilogue

After the death of Clement IX, Bernini received few if any major public commissions, partly no doubt on account of his great age. In the year that Clement X was elected pope Bernini was seventy-two years old. Although he was still as energetic as he always had been, age must have been beginning to take its toll, and at the time of his own death ten years later under Innocent XI he was of course a very old man, particularly in terms of his own times. When Bernini died his studio was disbanded; the last commission which it undertook under Bernini's supervision was Alexander VII's funerary monument during the 1670s. Thus several of Bernini's pupils were now left to their own devices, without the firm hand of the master for guidance or his artistic genius for inspiration. They had to make their own way in Rome as best they could, and the times were far from favourable.

But the absence of major commissions during the last ten years of Bernini's life depended on several other factors apart from the age of the artist. Even a talented painter such as Carlo Maratti found it difficult to make any real impact. His reputation could certainly be compared with that previously enjoyed by Bernini or Pietro da Cortona, but he received few official commissions and worked mainly for private patrons producing smaller-scale work. It is also significant that even when a man as gifted and wealthy as Camillo de' Massimi became a cardinal, he had no palace built and no ceilings painted. His most important contribution to the life of the arts was to act as a kind of aesthetic consultant to the Altieri family.

The economic decline in the Papal States, which was connected with a similar decline throughout Italy at this time, bore much of the blame for the new situation. The popes were forced to exercise extreme frugality. Innocent XI in particular adopted a severely restrictive economic policy, and with his serious and somewhat puritanical disposition he was in any case out of sympathy with the joy and warmth that pervaded the art of masters such as Pietro da Cortona, Bernini, and their pupils. With few exceptions the Roman nobility of the seventeenth century was insolvent, playing a very small part in promoting or supporting cultural life. No new wealthy families connected with the popes rose to prominence. Rospigliosi's nephews were never given the opportunity to enrich themselves at the expense of the Church, nor was Altieri more generous, while under Innocent XI papal nepotism more or less disappeared. The time was long past when learned and art-loving prelates could settle in Rome with time on their hands and enough money to indulge their cultural interests. And lastly, very few members of the Roman middle class had either the cultural background or the economic means to provide support for the arts. In other words patronage, as it had flourished during the age of the

Borghese, the Ludovisi and the Barberini, was now definitely a thing of the past.

Thus in the latter part of the seventeenth century there was no group of patrons in Rome possessing that combination of wealth, intellect and taste which had previously provided such fertile soil for the flowering of the Roman Baroque. Scholarly interests were now directed towards science, literature and music rather than building and the visual arts, which partly explains why the role of the patron was being taken over by the art critic.[186] Thus Bellori wielded more influence on artistic developments than even many of the greatest artists in the earlier period. And Bellori heralded the definitive triumph of the Classical line; Carlo Maratti and his pupils now reigned supreme with hardly any competition from the opposing camp.[187]

While the authority of the pope was being increasingly ignored in the political sphere, Rome was also gradually losing its leading role in cultural life. Other artistic centres, some of them already well established, were now tending to supersede Rome. There was Naples, enlivened by the Spanish influence of Jusepe de Ribera, and boasting such artists as Francesco Solimena and Luca Giordano, who also worked elsewhere. Genoa had Bernardo Strozzi, who also worked in Venice for a time, while in Venice itself Tiepolo was at the height of his fame, and Daniele Crespi was active in Milan and Lombardy. Nor should we forget architects such as Longhena in Venice and Guarino Guarini and Juvarra in Piedmont. It was perhaps typical of this period that Domenico Fetti, although a Roman born, worked as court painter in Mantua and Turin.

When France under Louis XIV established itself as the leading European power around the middle of the seventeenth century, the shift in focus was accompanied by a revolution on the cultural front. Even Richelieu and Mazarin, the latter an Italian himself, still accepted the cultural dominance of Rome, and Louis began by doing the same, regarding it as quite natural to send for Bernini to Paris. But in a way Bernini's French sojourn marked the end of Roman hegemony, since it was the opponents of Bernini's Louvre project who won the day. The time was not far distant when the whole of Europe would look to Paris as the fount of all that was best in art and culture.

Rome was to enjoy a late flowering during the first half of the eighteenth century, however, under popes such as Clement XI (1700–1721), Benedict XIII (1724–1730), Clement XII (1730–1740) and Benedict XIV (1740–1758), the greatest pope of the eighteenth century. It was during the first half of the eighteenth century that many monuments were built which are still a striking and memorable part of the urban landscape of Rome: the Piazza S. Ignazio and the so-called "Spanish steps" at SS. Trinità dei Monti, which were actually built as a French project with French money, the façades of the Lateran Basilica and S. Maria Maggiore, and the famous Fontana di Trevi.

It was also during the eighteenth century that Rome became, perhaps more than ever before, the city which attracted lovers of classical Antiquity and others interested in scholarship and the arts. This was the age that inspired a Venetian like Piranesi to produce his romantic *vedute* of the great monuments of ancient and present-day Rome, or enabled a German archeologist like Winckelmann to become *antiquario di Roma*; it was the age that drew so many famous travellers to the Eternal City, among them literary figures such as Goethe, royal personages such as King Gustav III of Sweden, architects like Robert Adam who imported classical architecture to the British Isles, or simply keen critics and observers like Charles de Brosses. These and many others came to Rome not to see contemporary art, nor as before to seek commissions and embark on a career, but to study the ancient monuments of the city, and perhaps above all the antique sculptures which were to be found there in far greater numbers than anywhere else. The popes themselves did much to promote the newly awakened interest in the Antique: Innocent XI prohibited the export of antique works of art, and Clement XI launched the idea of a new museum in the Vatican which was later realised under Pius X and Clement XIV, for whom the museum was named the Museo Pio-Clementino. Thus, during the eighteenth century, Rome made a special place for itself as a new kind of international centre belonging equally to the whole of Europe.

* * *

ABBREVIATIONS

In the notes:

Brauer & Wittkower
  H. Brauer & R. Wittkower, *Die Zeichnungen des Gianlorenzo Bernini*, ("Römische Forschungen der Bibliotheca Hertziana", IX–X), Berlin 1931.

Diary of Alexander VII
  R. Krautheimer & R. B. S. Jones, "The Diary of Alexander VII: Notes on art, artists and buildings", *Römisches Jahrbuch für Kunstgeschichte*, XV (1975), 199–233.

Kauffmann, *Bernini*
  H. Kauffmann, *Giovanni Lorenzo Bernini: Die figürlichen Kompositionen*, Berlin 1970.

Pastor
  L. Von Pastor, *Geschichte der Päpste seit dem Ausgang des Mittelalters*, Freiburg im Br. 1929.

Relazioni ambasciatori veneti
  Le relazioni della corte di Roma... dagli ambasciatori veneti, ed. N. Barozzi & G. Berchet, 2 vols, Venezia 1877–79.

In the captions:

BAV
  Biblioteca Apostolica Vaticana
BH
  Bibliotheca Hertziana
CI
  Courtauld Institute, London
GCS
  Gabinetto Comunale delle Stampe
ICCD
  Istituto Centrale del Catalogo e della Documentazione
ICCDcop
  Copied after original photograph from ICCD
ING:GS
  Istituto Nazionale per la Grafica: Gabinetto delle Stampe
NMS
  Nationalmuseum, Stockholm
MV
  Musei Vaticani
SBAAL
  Soprintendenza ai Beni Ambientali ed Architettonici del Lazio

NOTES

CHAPTER I

[1] For the boyhood and political career of Giulio Mazzarino see V. Cousin, *La jeunesse de Mazarin*, Paris 1865.

[2] It has long been a matter of controversy not only among novelists but also among scholars as to whether there was a love affair between Mazarin and the dowager queen. Some scholars, such as Pastor, dismiss the question as mere slander, while others believe

that the two were linked in a secret marriage; since Mazarin had not even taken minor orders it would have been possible for him, in theory, to contract a marriage in secret. However, no proof whatsoever has ever been found that Mazarin married the queen. Many scholars, although not all, nonetheless believe that the correspondence between the two shows that they were in fact lovers. U. Silvagni, *Il cardinale Mazzarino; con ricerche nove e documenti inediti*, Torino 1928, 268, 315 and *passim*.

[3] Pastor, XIV:1, 15ff.

[4] Taddeo Barberini's *memoriale* in P. Pecchiai, *I Barberini*, ("Archivi d' Italia", 5), Roma 1959, 178.

[5] For the conclave of 1644 see Pastor, XIV:1, 15–22.

[6] H. Coville, *Étude sur Mazarin et ses démêlés avec le pape Innocent X*, ("Bibliothèque de l'école des hautes études. Sciences historiques et philologiques", 210), Paris 1914, 20.

[7] I. Ciampi, *Innocenzo X Pamfili e la sua corte*, Imola 1878, 14 note 3. The coat of arms of Pope Innocent X is represented in some alternatives. According to D. L. Galbreath (*Papal Heraldry*, 2nd ed., London 1972, 98) the best reading is, in the jargon of heraldry, "Gules, a dove silver holding an olive-branch vert, and a chief azure charged with three fleurs-de-lis gold divided by two pallets retraits in base gules".

[8] Pamphili had been created cardinal *in petto* already in 1627: his creation was published the following year, and in 1630 the hat was bestowed on him. For Pamphili's family background and ecclesiastical career, see Pastor, XIV:1, 23f., documents 23, note 1.

[9] For Innocent X's character and personality see Pastor, XIV:1, 27, note 2 with documents and sources. In their *relatione* to the senate, the four Venetian ambassadors, who brought the congratulations of the *Serenissima Repubblica* to the newly elected pope, mention the pope's modesty and patience, "...la sua modestia, la pazienza, la integrità, la virtù, la mira di non disgustar alcuno". *Relazioni ambasciatori veneti*, II, 50. However, Giovanni Giustiniani later wrote, "Parla per ordinario poco e rare volte di materia di lettere, diffondendosi per lo più in discorsi economici; il temperamento tira al melanconico, e se talvolta burla e trascorre in qualche facezia non vi ha molta grazia, onde se crede che in ciò contrafaccia la sua naturale disposizione". *Ibid.*, 92.

[10] For Donna Olimpia Maidalchini see Ciampi, *op. cit.*, 10–19; Pastor, XIV:1, 28f. One Venetian ambassador Contarini, describes her in the following words, "...è Dama d'ingegno e spirito virile, e solo si fa conoscere donna per la superbia et avaritia...", *Relazioni ambasciatori veneti*, II, 69. Modern biography: D. Chiomenti Vassalli, *Donna Olimpia Maidalchini o del nepotismo nel Seicento*, ("Storia e documenti", 31), Milano 1979.

[11] Pastor, XIV:1, 30. Cf. Alvise Contarini's report of 1648 in *Relazioni ambasciatori veneti*, II, 71.

[12] Pastor XIV:1, 31; *Relazioni ambasciatori veneti*, II, 71.

[13] Pastor, XIV:1, 32.

[14] For the influence that Donna Olimpia had over the pope see Pastor, XIV:1, 32 and documents 33, note 1. Cf. *Relazioni ambasciatori veneti*, II, 102 and *passim*; Ciomenti Vassalli, op. cit., 79 and *passim*.

[15] Pastor, XIV:1, 33. The Venetian ambassador Giustiniani's judgement is striking: Maidalchini was "...giovine ottuso... che veruno scienza non poteva nè voleva apprendere per la poco capace natura: brutto di corpo, di forme, di faccia malcreato, inurbano...", *Relazioni ambasciatori veneti*, II, 126. In spite of this, it was later reported that he was of a friendly character, and he was much loved by the poor for his generosity.

[16] For the Barberini inquest see Pastor, XIV:1, 42ff.; Pecchiai, *op. cit.*, 182–189.

[17] Coville, *op. cit.*, 25f., 70.

[18] *Ibid.*, 9–107 and *passim*. Cf. I. Malgeri, *Relazioni del Cardinale Giulio Mazarini con gli Stati d'Italia dal 1642 al 1648 secondo documenti inediti dell'Archivio Vaticano*, Roma 1929, 27f.

[19] G. Demaria, "La guerra di Castro e la spedizione de' presidii", R. deputazione sovra gli studi di Storia Patria; *Miscellanea di Storia Patria*, Serie 3, IV (1898), 247f. Cf. Coville, *op. cit.* 118ff. Malgeri, *op. cit.*, 44–57.

[20] Coville, *op. cit.*, 124ff. Cf. G. Gigli, *Diario romano*, ed. Riciotti, Roma 1958, 282.

[21] Gigli, *Diario*, 304. In his memoirs, Fontenay-Mareuil gives a detailed account of his negotiations with the pope, but his manuscript ends before the official reception in the Quirinal. *Mémoires de Messire Du Val Marquis de Fontenay-Mareuil*, ed. L. J. N. Monmerquè, 2 vols, Paris 1826, *passim*.

[22] Pastor, XIV:1, 57; Coville, *op. cit.*, 148.

[23] For relations with Venice and papal aid during the war against the Turks see Pastor, XIV:1, 257–267.

[24] On the insurrection of Masaniello and the pope's standpoint see Pastor, XIV:1, 62ff., and E. Visco, *La politica della S. Sede nella rivoluzione di Masaniello. Da documenti dell'Archivio Vaticano*, Napoli 1923. According to Cafaro, the insurrection was inspired by the political ideas of Tommaso Campanella (1568–1639), who produced in his *Civitas solis* (1602) an utopian design for a kind of theocratic republic under the protection of the Church. V. Cafaro, *Mase Carrese e la rivoluzione di Masaniello*, Pozzuoli 1951.

[25] Visco, *op. cit.*, 12.

[26] On the peace negotiations before 1644 see K. Repgen's comprehensive work, *Die Römische Kurie und die Westfälische Friede. Idee und Wirklichkeit des Papsttums im 16. und 17. Jahrhundert*, ("Bibliothek des Deutschen Historischen Instituts in Rom", XXIV–XXV), Tübingen 1962–65. For Innocent X and the Treaty of Westfalia, see Pastor, XIV:1, 73–101. All the material from Chigi's *nunziatura* at the peace negotiations in V. Kybal & G. Incisa della Rocchetta, *La nunziatura di Fabio Chigi(1640–1651)*, I:1–2, ("Miscellanea della R. Deputazione Romana di Storia Patria", XIV–XV), Roma 1943–1946. Cf. P. Sforza-Pallavicino, *Della vita di Alessandro VII*, Prato 1839, 130ff.

[27] Pastor, XIV:1, 99, note 5.

[28] For Innocent X's action against the Farnese see G. Carabelli, *Dei Farnesi e del ducato di Castro e Ronciglione...*, Firenze 1865, 165–175. Cf. Demaria, *op. cit.*, 249ff.; Pastor, XIV:1, 270f.

[29] The memoirs of Cardinal de Retz were published in several editions during the 18th century. Modern editions of his works, J. F. P. de Gondi, cardinal de Retz, *Oeuvres du cardinal de Retz*, nouv. éd., ed. A. Feillet, 10 vols, Paris 1870–1896. Cf. L. Batiffol, *Le cardinal de Retz: ambitions et aventures d'un homme d'ésprit au XVIIᵉ siècle*, Paris 1927.

[30] More than 34000 Irish soldiers left Ireland after the defeat. Over the following years many thousands—men, women and children—were deported to Barbados. Indeed, Cromwell had planned to move the whole population of Ireland to make room for the English, but soon found that this was not possible. For the war in Ireland, see S. R. Gardiner, *History of the Commonwealth and Protectorate 1649–1660*, 3 vols, London & New York 1894–1903. A more recent study is T. L. Coonan, *The Irish Catholic Confederacy and the Puritan Revolution*, Dublin 1954.

[31] For Cardinal Astalli-Pamphili, his personality and career see *Dizionario biografico degli italiani*, IV, 453f.

[32] Pastor, XIV:1, 34; cf. Chiomenti Vassalli, *op. cit.*, 166f.

[33] *Relazioni ambasciatori veneti*, II, 103.

[34] P. Sforza Pallavicino, *op. cit.*, I, 158f.

[35] For Chigi's personality see *ibid.*, 116, and *Dizionario biografico degli italiani*, II, 214.

[36] Sforza Pallavicino, *op. cit.*, 170.

[37] Ciampi, *op. cit.*, 154–163. Cf. Gigli, *Diario*, 401–403.

[38] Chiomenti Vassalli, *op. cit.*, 195.

[39] Ciampi, *op. cit.*, 168; Chiomenti Vassalli, *op. cit.*, 222.

[40] Sforza Pallavicino, *op. cit.*, 206f.

[41] Pastor, XIV:1, 134f.

[42] T. M. Alfani, *Istoria degli Anni Santi...*, Napoli 1725, 457f. Grain was imported and a maximum price stipulated.

[43] Pastor, XIV:1, 136f. For the celebrations during Holy Year 1650 see A. Santarelli, *Trattato del Givbileo dell'Anno Santo e degl'altri Givbilei*, Roma 1650. On the indulgencies see B. Poschmann, *Das Ablass im Licht der Bussgeschichte*, Bonn 1948.

[44] Pastor, XIV:1, 139.

[45] For Catholic missionary activities in China see Pastor, XIV:1, 149ff.

[46] Pastor, XIV:1, 151f. The question of the Chinese rites came to the fore again under Benedict XIV (1740–1758), who enforced his predecessors' decrees, causing insuperable problems for the missionaries in China. Finally, in 1939, the *Propaganda Fide* reversed previous decisions authorising "acts of veneration of the ancestors provided they held no religious significance", a decision which came two hundred years too late.

[47] Pastor, XIV:1, 160.

[48] Extensive study in Pastor, XIV:1, 161–256. Documents in L. Ceyssens, *La fin de la première période du jansenisme: sources des années 1654–1660*, ("Bibliothèque de l'Institut historique belge de Rome", XII–XIII), Bruxelles & Rome 1936–1965.

[49] Sforza Pallavicino, *op. cit.*, 179–186.

[50] Pastor, XIV:1, 206 and 249f.

[51] For the administration of the States of the Church at the time of Innocent X see Pastor, XIV:1, 267–270.

[52] A. Coppi, *Discorso sulle finanze dello Stato Pontificio dal sec. XVI al principio del XIX*, Roma 1855, 16. M. Petrocchi, *Roma nel Seicento*, (Istituto di Studi Romani: "Storia di Roma", XIV), Bologna 1970, 78.

[53] In 1646, export of olive oil from Rome was forbidden. Petrocchi, *op. cit.*, 43, 53. During the whole century a strict control of prices was maintained on meat in order to prevent speculation. At this time by far the largest quantity of meat consumed was mutton; pork and various products of pork, were imported from Norcia, and in Italy, those who deal with these products, are called *norcini* to this day. *Ibidem*, 44.

[54] Gigli, *Diario*, 308.

[55] Pastor, XIV:1, 269 and note 2.

[56] Petrocchi, *op. cit.*, 35, 78.

[57] Gigli, *Diario*, 400 and *passim*.

[58] *Relazioni ambasciatori veneti*, II, 74f.

[59] For the sociological aspects of Rome in the 17th century see Petrocchi, *op. cit.*, 55–90; literature quoted by this author, listed 172–183.

[60] C. di Bildt, "Christina di Svezia e Paolo Giordano II", *Archivio d. Società Romana di Storia Patria*, XXIX (1906), 5–32.

[61] F. Haskell, *Patrons and Painters*, Oxford 1963, 114–119.

[62] F. Cancellieri, *Storia dei solenni possessi dei pontefici*, Roma 1804, 207–256; list of literary sources for the *possesso* of Innocent X. One description is by a Swede from Norrköping, Laurentius Banck, *Roma triumphans seu Actus Inaugurationis & Coronationis Innocentii Decimi... brevis Descriptio*, Franekere 1645. John Evelyn's description in *The Diary of John Evelyn*, ed. De Beer, II, 279–281.

[63] Gigli, *Diario*, 262.

[64] Evelyn, *Diary*, II, 279ff.

[65] Detailed description in Cancellieri, *op. cit.*, 219; also H. M. Freiherr von Erffa, "Die Ehrenpforten für den Possess der Päpste im 17. und 18. Jahrhundert", in *Festschrift für Harald Keller*, Darmstadt 1963, 344.

[66] Gigli, *Diario*, 263.

[67] Cancellieri, *op. cit.*, 215, 250; von Erffa, *op. cit.*, 346.

[68] Evelyn, *Diary*, II, 282.

[69] Cancellieri, *op. cit.*, 253; Evelyn, *Diary*, II, 282. For the *macchina* in Piazza Navona

see M. Fagiolo Dell'Arco & S. Carandini, *L'effimero barocco: Strutture della festa nella Roma del '600*, I, 134 ff., ("Biblioteca di storia dell'arte", 10), Roma 1977.
[70] Evelyn, *Diary*, II, 282.
[71] *Ibidem.*
[72] Gigli, *Diario*, 280, 304.
[73] *Ibid.*, 312.
[74] F. Clementi, *Il carnevale romano nelle cronache contemporanee dalle origini al secolo XVII*, I, Città di Castello 1939, 495.
[75] *Ibid.*, 497.
[76] Gigli, *Diario*, 332.
[77] Clementi, *op. cit.*, 498.
[78] A. Ademollo, *I teatri di Roma nel secolo decimosettimo*, Roma 1888, 42, 45.
[79] Clementi, *op. cit.*, 508.
[80] Gigli, *Diario*, 383.
[81] Clementi, *op. cit.*, 518.
[82] *Ibid.*, 520. The libretto, an adaptation of Calderón de la Barca's *No siempre lo peor es cierto*, evidences the influence of Spanish drama in Italy at this time. P. Bjurström, *Den romerska barockens·scenografi*, ("Svenska Humanistiska Förbundet", 88), Lund 1977, 55.
[83] Ademollo, *op. cit.*, 65.
[84] Gigli, *Diario*, 431.
[85] At the carnival 1647. *Ibid.*, 296.
[86] *Ibid.*, 430.
[87] *Ibid.*, 356 f.
[88] H. Siebenhüner, *Das Kapitol in Rom*, ("Italienische Forschungen", herausgegeben von Kunsthistorischen Institut in Florenz, Dritte Folge, I), München 1954, 96, 116. Cf. F. Fasolo, *L'opera di Hieronimo e Carlo Rainaldi*, Roma s.a., 142 f.
[89] Gigli, *Diario*, 443, 453.
[90] H. Millan, "An early seventeenth century drawing of the Piazza San Pietro", *The Art Quarterly*, XXV (1962), 229. Millan also summarises earlier discussions of the bell-towers. The most extensive study is D. Frey, "Berninis Entwürfe für die Glockentürme von St. Peter in Rom", *Jahrbuch d. Kunsthistorischen Sammlungen in Wien*, N.F., XII (1938), 203–226.
[91] F. Ehrle, "Dalle carte e dai disegni di Virgilio Spada", *Atti della Pontificia Accademia Romana di Archeologia*, Serie III, *Memorie*, II (1928), 21–28 and "Appendix", 77 ff., with Spada's *relatione*.
[92] S. Fraschetti, *Il Bernini: la sua vita, la sua opera, il suo tempo*, Milano 1900, 165 f. Ehrle, *op. cit.*, 23 and note 105. Cf. Brauer & Wittkower, *Die Zeichnungen des Gian Lorenzo Bernini*, ("Römische Forschungen der Bibliotheca Hertziana", IX), Berlin 1931, 38 ff. Martino Longhi's memoriale is reproduced by J. L. Varriano, *The Roman Ecclesiastical Architecture of Martino Longhi the Younger*, (Diss., University of Michigan, 1970; typescript copy in microfilm-xerography, Ann-Arbor, Michigan, 1974), "Appendix" V, 181–184.
[93] Documents quoted by Fraschetti, *op. cit.*, 166, note 6, and 167, note 1.
[94] D. Frey, *op. cit.*, 224. Two drawings from Bernini's studio in the Vatican Library (*Vat. lat.*, 13442, fols 3 and 4) are reproduced by Brauer & Wittkower, *op. cit.*, Tafel 156, 157. Borromini's projects, E. Hempel, *Francesco Borromini*, Wien 1924, 92, and Taf. 52.
[95] Brauer & Wittkower, *op. cit.*, 43 f.; Wittkower, *Bernini*, 215 f.
[96] R. Enggass, "New attributions in St. Peter's: The spandrel figures in the nave", *Art Bulletin*, LX (1978), 96–108.
[97] According to Gigli, *Diario*, 342, the floor was finished in October 1649. Cf. Fraschetti, *op. cit.*, 213.
[98] Pastor, XIV:1, 280.

[99] *Relazioni ambasciatori veneti*, II, 75 f.

[100] For the best survey of the Lateran Basilica before Borromini, based on recent research and the archeological findings, see R. Krautheimer, S. Corbett & A. K. Frazer, *Corpus Basilicarum Christianarum Romae*, V, (Pontif. Istituto di Archeologia cristiana: "Monumenti di antichità cristiana", Serie II, II), Città del Vaticano 1977, 1–85 and *passim.* Much valuable information is drawn from a contemporary description by C. Rasponi, *De Basilica et Patriarchio Lateranensi*, Roma 1657.

[101] Some of these frescoes are shown on a drawing from Borromini's studio in Berlin (Staatl. Museen, Kunstbibliothek, *Hdz 4467*), first published by K. Cassirer, "Zu Borrominis Umbau der Lateransbasilika", *Jahrbuch der Preuszischen Kunstsammlungen*, XLII (1921), 62, Abb. 8.

[102] The brick pillars are also shown in the Berlin drawing mentioned in the previous note, and on Borromini's plan of the old basilica in the Albertina, Vienna (*IT AZ 374*). In Borromini's day only four of the old columns were still left, two on the south side close to the main entrance, and the first and fourth columns on the north side. Cf. *Corpus basilicarum*, V, 23, 49, and fig. 57.

[103] *Corpus basilicarum*, V, 22.

[104] E. Hempel, *Francesco Borromini*, Wien 1924, 97. Hempel's work, although much research has been done since it was published, is still of basic importance. For Virgilio Spada and his background see above, vol. I, chapter III, 302. It has often been pointed out that Spada's presence was indispensable to the handling of Borromini, who was known to be a hypochondriac. To what extent Spada—as an *architetto dilettante*—also influenced Borromini's plans is not known. It may be safe to say that he certainly acted as an intermediary between the pope and the architect.

[105] H. Egger, "Francesco Borrominis Umbau von S. Giovanni in Laterano", in *Beiträge zur Kunstgeschichte Franz Wickhoff gewidmet*, Wien 1903, 154 f.

[106] These drawings are reproduced in *Corpus basilicarum*, V, figs 57–69.

[107] Biblioteca Apostolica Vaticana, codices. *Vat. lat. 11257* and *Vat. lat. 11258*; a transverse section in Albertina, Vienna, *IT AZ 383*. The drawings are reproduced in P. Portoghesi, *Borromini: Architettura come linguaggio*, Milano 1967, plates LVII–LXIV. For a discussion of the drawings, see *Corpus basilicarum*, 52 and A. Blunt, *Borromini*, London 1979, 137 f.

[108] Blunt, *op. cit.*, 137.

[109] Stockholm, Nationalmuseum, *Cronstedt 8091*. First identified and published by P. Portoghesi, *Borromini nella cultura europea*, Roma 1964, Tav. 256.

[110] Biblioteca Apostolica Vaticana, *Vat. lat. 11257*, c. 258; reproduced in *Corpus basilicarum*, Fig. 59.

[111] *Corpus basilicarum*, 49 and Fig. 57; Plate I. Cf. Egger, op. cit., 156.

[112] *Corpus basilicarum*, 23, 49, 60; Figs 57, 68, 69.

[113] H. Thelen, "Zur barocken Umgestaltung des Langhauses der Lateran-Basilika", *Kunstchronik*, VII (1954), 264 f. See reconstruction of vaulted room in Portoghesi, *Borromini*, 1967, 159.

[114] Complete quotation from Bianchi Lombardi in Portoghesi, *Borromini*, 1967, 160. Cf. K. Cassirer, (*supra*, note 101), 56.

[115] The Albertina plan *374* shows Borromini's new arches in the west wall of the transept from where they would continue round the main apse. Cf. *Corpus basilicarum*, 51, and Fig. 57.

[116] *Corpus basilicarum*, 22, 56 f.

[117] Hempel, *op. cit.*, 98. Gigli (*Diario*, ed. , Ricciotti, 327) mentions that the basilica was all covered by Oct. 1648, and that in Oct. 1649 it was finished (*Diario*, 343).

[118] *Relazioni ambasciatori veneti*, II, 76. "Per la perfezione di questo edificio mostra particolar premura Sua Beatit., mandando a sollecitarlo ogni giorno e conducendovisi lui stesso frequentemente a vederlo, con haverli assignato 70 m. scudi, che vengono di Spagna per la Bolla della Cruciata. Vi applica medesimamente alcune grosse condanne e

compositione pecuniarie dovute al fisico (sic)." Cf. Pastor, XIV:1.

[119] Hempel, *op. cit.*, 95. Cf. *Corpus basilicarum*, 19.

[120] Cassirer, *op. cit.*, 55, 57, Cf. M. Dvořák, "Francesco Borromini als Restaurator", *Kunstgeschichtliches Jahrbuch der K. K. Zentral-Kommission*, I (1907), *Beiblatt*, 89–98. Dvořák believes that it was Borromini's own intention to preserve as much as possible of the old basilica.

[121] Contemporary statement by the procurator of the Trinitarians, Juan de Bonaventura who knew Borromini well, quoted by Portoghesi, *Borromini*, 1967, 158f.

[122] M. Fagiolo, "Borromini in Laterano. 'Il Nuovo Tempio' per il Concilio universale", *L'Arte*, N. S., IV (1971), 10, and notes 17f.

[123] Rasponi, *op. cit.*, 85.

[124] *Ibidem*, 85: "... ovatae formae spatia ... quibus in spatijs relicta est intacta Constantinianorum parietum antiqua facies, vetustatis memoria, et posteritatis erga ipsum pietate, ac Religione venerabilis..."

[125] *Corpus basilicarum*, 19; Fagiolo, *op. cit.*, 6 and note 14.

[126] Fagiolo bases his comments on Rasponi's interpretation, but points out that in fact not all scholars are of the same opinion, *op. cit.*, note 14.

[127] Fagiolo, *op. cit.*, 6ff. G. Prado & G. B. Villalpando, *In Ezechielem explanationes*, Roma 1596; also by the same authors, *De Postrema Ezechielis prophetae visione... explanationum pars secunda*, Roma 1604. For further literature on the subject see Fagiolo, *op. cit.*, note 29. Fascinating though these ideas are, Fagiolo's arguments do not seem conclusive to the present author.

[128] In their main outlines Fagiolo's ideas about the iconography of the basilica have been accepted by Blunt, *Borromini*, London 1979, 144f.

[129] The problems regarding the building history of the Palazzo Carpegna, the plans and the chronology, have been solved by Manfredo Tafuri in his article, "Borromini in Palazzo Carpegna. Documenti inediti e ipotesi critiche", *Quaderni dell'Istituto di Storia dell'Architettura*, Serie XIV, fasc. 79 A 84 (1967), 85–107.

[130] The plan drawings in the Graphische Sammlung Albertina in Vienna are, for the smaller project, *1024, 1025, 1033, 1039*; for the larger project with rectangular courtyard, *1010, 1012, 1014a, 1015, 1017*. Cf. Tafuri, *op. cit.*, figs 11–17; 20 and 23–28.

[131] The plans with oval courtyard, in the Albertina, are *1019 a–b*.

[132] Paolo Marconi argues, against Tafuri, that some of Borromini's more grandiose projects for the palace could be dated after 1643. P. Marconi, "Storia e architettura del palazzo. L'intervento di Borromini. Il restauro", in *Accademia Nazionale di S. Luca*, Roma 1974, 44.

[133] According to Battisti the symbolism of this stucco festoon may be the *Ospitalità* and the *Buona Fortuna*. E. Battisti, "Il simbolismo in Borromini", in *Studi sul Borromini*, (Atti del Convegno promosso dall'Accademia Nazionale di San Luca), Roma 1967, I, 242.

[134] Blunt, *Borromini*, 167f.

[135] Hempel, *op. cit.*, 51f.

[136] E. Battisti, in a very detailed article ("Il simbolismo in Borromini", in *Studi sul Borromini*, I, 231–281), shows Borromini's predeliction for the kind of enigmatic emblems that his contemporaries loved. Blunt (*Borromini*, 172) also shows that some of the emblems in the Palazzo Falconieri ceilings are taken from two emblem books much read in the seventeenth century, P. Valeriano, *Hieroglyphica*, Basel 1556, and Junius Hadrianus, *Emblemata...*, Antwerpiae 1585.

[137] Accounts referring to the construction of the Villa Doria-Pamphili were published by Oscar Pollak, "Alessandro Algardi (1602–1654) als Architekt", *Zeitschrift für Geschichte der Architektur*, IV (1910/11), 69ff.

[138] Biblioteca Apostolica Vaticana, *Vat. lat., 11257*.

[139] P. Portoghesi, "Intorno a una irrealizzata immagine Borrominiano", *Quaderni dell'Istituto di Storia dell'Architettura*, N. 6 (1954), 12–28. Later, and more detailed

study in Portoghesi, *Borromini nella cultura europea*, Roma 1964, 221–265. Cf. A. Nava Cellini, "Il Borromini, l'Algardi e il Grimaldi per la Villa Pamphilj", *Paragone*, N. S., Arte, XIV (1963), N° 159, 67 ff.

[140] *Francesco Borromini: Mostra di disegni e di documenti vaticani*, (catalogue), ed. H. Thelen, Biblioteca Apostolica Vaticana 1967, 10 f. Cf. M. Heimbürger, "Alessandro Algardi architetto?", *Analecta Romana Instituti Danici*, VI (1971), 197–224.

[141] The following description quoted from Portoghesi, *Borromini nella cultura europea*, 224 ff.

[142] Portoghesi has pointed out that the prototype may have been certain villas planned by Peruzzi and Serlio (*Borromini nella cultura europea*, fig. 177 f.). Borromini also seems to have studied Vincenzo Scamozzi's treatise, *Idea dell'architettura universale*, (*ibid.*, 230, note 9).

[143] *Ibid.*, 231.

[144] A. Nava Cellini, "L'Algardi restauratore a Villa Pamphilj", *Paragone*, N. S., Arte, XIV (1963), N° 161, 25–37.

[145] G. Masson, *Italian Gardens*, London 1961, 155 f.

[146] Bellori, *Vite*, ed. E. Borea, 408.

[147] Passeri, *Vite*, ed. J. Hess, 200.

[148] Heimbürger, *op. cit.*, 198 f.

[149] Pollak, *op. cit.*, (*supra*, note 137), 51 f., 57.

[150] Heimbürger, *op. cit.*, 199.

[151] Pollak, *op. cit.*, 69–76.

[152] R. Preimesberger, "Pontifex Romanus Aeneam praesignatus. Die Galleria Pamphilj und ihre Fresken", *Römisches Jahrbuch für Kunstgeschichte*, XVI (1976), 224.

[153] *Ibidem*. Cf. important contribution to Girolamo and Carlo Rainaldi by F. Fasolo, *L'opera di Hieronimo e Carlo Rainaldi*, Roma s.a., 119, 122, 125 ff. Also G. Eimer, *La Fabbrica di S. Agnese in Navona*, I, ("Acta Universitatis Stockholmiensis", 17), Stockholm 1970, 34 ff. For the purchase of property see Garms, *op. cit.*, 49.

[154] Biblioteca Apostolica Vaticana, *Vat. lat.*, *11258*, fols 150 ff. The spada papers were discussed by Dagobert Frey, "Beiträge zur Geschichte der römischen Barockarchitektur", *Wiener Jahrbuch für Kunstgeschichte*, N. E., III (1924), 69 f.

[155] Biblioteca Apostolica Vaticana, *Vat. lat. 11258*, fols 150 f.: "Congregazione per la fabrica della Casa Pamphilia... da tenersi ogni giovedì la mattina nel med^{mo} Palazzo in Piazza Navona con l'intervento di Girolamo Rainaldi e franc° Borromini Architetti m° Lodovico capomastro et uno de familiari della S^{ra} Olimpia alla presenza mia..." In the margin there are remarks such as "Il Papa consentì al pensiero del Borromini" or "Il Papa risolse che...", "Il Papa disse...", etc.

[156] The drawings related to the Palazzo Pamphili in the Vatican Library are in *Vat. lat. 11258*; cf., *Francesco Borromini*, Mostra, (*supra*, note 138), Nos 6 ff.; the drawings are reproduced in Portoghesi, *Borromini: Architettura come linguaggio*, (*supra*, note 107), Tav. XCV–XCVII.

[157] Francesco Borromini, No 13, *Vat. lat. 11258*, fol. 172.

[158] Preimesberger, *op. cit.*, 237 and Fig. 10 f.

[159] The drawings for the façade are *Vat. lat. 11258*, fols 177, 176, 180 (in this order); cf., *Francesco Borromini*, Nos 14–16.

[160] F. Fasolo believes that Girolamo Rainaldi's first project can be dated as early as 1645–47 (*op. cit.*, 130), but to the present writer his arguments seem to be inconclusive. Cf. G. Eimer, *op. cit.*, 54. Eimer suggests (*op. cit.*, 41) that a theatrical performance of the life of St. Agnes modelled by the Pamphili in 1650 may have given them the idea of building a new church. However, this seems unlikely, since the opera in question was not performed in the palace at Piazza Navona but in the Pamphili palace on the Corso.

[161] K. Noehles, "L'architetto Giovanni Battista Mola e la sua guida romana del 1663", *Arte lombarda*, XI (1966), 196.

[162] Eimer, *op. cit.*, 63 f.

[163] *Ibid.*, 65 f., 76 f.

[164] The main fundamental study of the building history of S. Agnese, which is extremely well documented, is G. Eimer, *La Fabbrica di S. Agnese*, (*supra*, note 153). Rainaldi's earlier plans in particular are discussed by F. Fasolo, *op. cit.*, 130–146. Cf. K. Noehles, review of Fasolo's work in *Zeitschrift für Kunstgeschichte*, XXV (1962), 166–177. An important phase of the building activity is discussed by F. Trevisani, "La fabbrica di S. Agnese in Navona: estate 1653", *Storia dell'Arte*, XXIII (1975), 61–72; note 1 contains a useful bibliography. See also R. Preimesberger, "Das dritte Papstgrabmal Berninis", *Römisches Jahrbuch für Kunstgeschichte*, XVII (1978), 159–181.

[165] Eimer, *op. cit.*, 90 f.

[166] Biblioteca Corsiniana, Rome, *Cod. Cors. 168*, fol. 291. Cf. Eimer, *op. cit.*, 101 f., and Tafel LIX. On the attribution of the Corsini drawing to Carlo Rainaldi see Noehles in *Zeitschrift f. Kunstgeschichte*, XXV (1962), 171–174.

[167] Eimer, *op. cit.*, 113.

[168] The two Rainaldi façades are shown in a drawing in the Raccolta Bertarelli, Castello Sforzesco in Milan, *Cod. Martinelli IV*, fol. 22 (reproduced by Eimer, *op. cit.*, Taf. LXI); for the attribution of this drawing to Carlo Rainaldi see Eimer, *op. cit.*, 145. Rainaldi's façade is also shown in a drawing in the Vatican Library, Codex *Chig., P. VII, 9*, fol. 85; reproduced by Eimer, *op. cit.*, Tafel LXIII and LXV.

[169] Eimer, *op. cit.*, 156, 159 f.

[170] Preimesberger, *op. cit.*, (*supra*, note 152), 159.

[171] Trevisani, *op. cit.*, 64.

[172] Eimer, *op. cit.*, 279 ff., 283 f.

[173] For Borromini's suggested changes and what was actually carried out see Eimer, *op. cit.*, 298 ff., 310 ff.

[174] Noehles in *Zeitschrift für Kunstgeschichte*, XXV (1962), 173.

[175] Eimer, *op. cit.*, 313 and Tafel LXXXVIII.

[176] The drawings in the Albertina are N[os] *IT AZ 51, 55, 59*; they are reproduced in Eimer, *op. cit.*, I, Tafs XCVII, C–CI. For the medal and Borromini's drawing, *ibid.*, Tafel LXXXIV.

[177] Eimer's reconstruction *op. cit.*, 307; discussion of the influence of Hadrian's Villa, *ibid.*, 308.

[178] Eimer, *op. cit.*, 365 ff.

[179] *Ibid.*, 330 ff.

[180] *Ibid.*, 335 f., 376 f.

[181] On further influence of this type of façade outside Italy see Eimer, *op. cit.*, 552.

[182] F. Borsi, *Bernini architetto*, Milano 1980, 315. See also, by the same author, "Il palazzo di Montecitorio dal Bernini al Fontana", in *Il Palazzo Montecitorio*, Roma 1967, 3 ff., and fig. 13 in which is reproduced a painting by Matthia de Rossi, assistant to Bernini on this building project, showing the façade as originally planned. Borsi suggests, on what grounds is not quite clear, that it was Innocent X who wanted his nephew to have this palace built and that the idea, and perhaps also the plans, date from 1650, the year which most authors quote for this project. However, from the documents quoted by Borsi in *Bernini architetto*, 315, it is clear that construction did not start until spring 1653.

[183] Borsi (in *Il Palazzo Montecitorio*, 29 ff.) makes a detailed analysis of this *bugnato roccioso* and discusses its origins.

[184] Because of his Spanish connections—he was a personal friend of King Filip IV—Niccolò Ludovisi was involved in the fall of Cardinal Astalli Pamphilj in 1654. He died ten years later as Spanish viceroy of Sardinia.

[185] Biographical notes in *I Longhi: una famiglia di architetti tra Manierismo e Barocco*, ed. L. Patetta, Milano 1980, 6 ff.

[186] None of the official church documents relating to the building of the façade survive, but the dates 1646–1650 are quite certain as demonstrated by J. L. Varriano, *op. cit.*,

(*supra*, note 92), 37 f. The old church is shown on the map of Rome 1625 by Maggi-Maupin-Losi; the interior, apse and choir, were remodelled in the 1760s. Regarding economic difficulties in finishing the façade see Haskell, *Patrons*, 183, note 3. Cf. *I Longhi*, 113–118.

[187] Varriano (*op. cit.*, 41) refers to Rudolf Wittkower's analysis as being the most penetrating that has been made, (*Art and Architecture*, 1958, 187). Cf. H. Sedlmayr, "Fünf römische Fassaden", in *Epochen und Werke. Gesammelte Aufsätze z. Kunstgeschichte*, II, Wien & München 1960, 57–63.

[188] Varriano, *op. cit.*, 44.

[189] Varriano stresses the importance of the corner columns, which, in his view, makes the façade three-dimensional; it was the first time that columns were used to achieve movement round a corner. However, Varriano may not have noticed that the three dimensions are already implicit in earlier façades, for instance Soria's façade for S. Maria della Vittoria which has a whole bay complete with pilasters turned at an angle of ninety degrees to the street on the left. It is true, however, that the use of a column to achieve this three-dimensionality had a special scenic effect and was a theme that became popular in several Roman church façades, most important perhaps in Pietro da Cortona's façade for S. Maria della Pace. Hans Sedlmayr has also mentioned the three-dimensionality of the façade of Ss. Vincenzo ed Anastasio (*op. cit.*, 57–63), when speaking of its two layers, "...eine Anordnung aller Formen der Fassade in zwei Schichte. In die vordere sind alle plastischen Werte gezogen, die rückwertige ist Folie in einem ähnlichen Sinne wie die Wand hinter hellenistischen Säulenvorhängen".

[190] N. Whitman, "Roman tradition and the aedicular façade", *Journal of the Society of Architectural Historians*, XXIX (1970), 108–123.

[191] Wittkower (*Art and Architecture*, 183, 187) denies the link between this façade and Rainaldi's façade to S. Maria in Campitelli, but see Varriano, *op. cit.*, 46 f., and the discussion in Whitman's article, *op. cit.*, 118.

[192] Bernini, Domenico, *Vita del Cavalier Gio. Lorenzo Bernino*, Roma 1713, 80 f.; Wittkower, *Bernini*, Cat. No 49.

[193] For the dates of *Truth Unveiled by Time* see Brauer & Wittkower, 37.

[194] The iconography of *Truth Unveiled* is extensively discussed by H. Kauffmann, "Veritas", in *Giovanni Lorenzo Bernini: Die figürlichen Kompositionen*, Berlin 1970, 194–221. The allegory of *Truth Unveiled by Time* goes back to Classical Antiquity and to the Bible. It seems to have been Erasmus who took it up and made it one of the favourite themes of the Renaissance. F. Saxl, "Veritas filia Temporis", in *Philosophy and History: essays presented to Ernst Cassirer*, 2nd ed., New York & London, 1963, 200. Cf. M. Laurain-Portemer, "Mazarin et le Bernin à propos du Temps qui découvre la vérité", *Gazette des Beaux-Arts*, LXXIV (1969), 185–200. Cf. M. Winner, "Berninis Verità: Bausteine zur Vorgeschichte einer Invenzione", *Munuscula discipulorum. Kunsthistorische Studien Hans Kauffmann zum 70. Geburtstag 1966*, Berlin 1968, 393–413.

[195] Brauer & Wittkower, Taf. 20.

[196] Wittkower, *Bernini*, 33.

[197] S. Fraschetti, *Il Bernini: La sua vita, la sua opera, il suo tempo*, Milano 1900, 112 and 113 note 1. Mazarin in fact sent to Bernini a "brevet d'architect du Roy". Laurain-Portemer, *op. cit.*, 185 and note 54.

[198] Paolo Giordano Orsini's letter to Mazarin and Mazarin's answer are reproduced by Laurain-Portemer, *op. cit.*, notes 49, 50. On Bernini's reluctance to leave Rome see *ibid.*, 192 and note 8. Mazarin's agent in Rome, abbé Benedetti, refers in a letter to Mazarin 6 August 1660 to Bernini's situation under Innocent X and the reasons for his staying in Rome; this letter is quoted by M. Laurain-Portemer, "Mazarin, Benedetti et l'escalier de la Trinité des monts", *Gazette des Beaux-Arts*, LXXII (1968), 278 and note 56.

[199] Wittkower, *Bernini*, Cat. No 43, figs 54, 55.

[200] *Ibid.*, Cat. No 44.

[201] Documents in I. Lavin, *Gianlorenzo Bernini: Unity in the Visual Arts*, New York & London 1980, 191. In his testament, dated 1638, Francesco Raimondi required that his brother Marcello and his mother were to obtain a chapel in S. Pietro in Montorio and that they were to spend 4000 ducats within three years of his death. Francesco died in 1638, but only in the following year did the authorities permit the concession of the chapel, and the act of concession was drawn up in February 1640. This last year seems, therefore, more certain as a *terminus post quem* for Bernini's design. For the dates of the altar reliefs and the tomb sculptures see Wittkower, *Bernini*, 214, and A. Nava Cellini, "Ritratti di Andrea Bolgi", *Paragone*, N. S., *Arte*, XIII (1962), N. 147, 33.

[202] G. B. Passeri, *Vita de' pittori, scultori ed architetti che hanno lavorato in Roma*, ed. J. Hess, Leipzig & Wien 193 f., 334.

[203] Discussed by Lavin, *Unity in the Visual Arts*, 28 ff.

[204] Wittkower, *Bernini*, Cat. No 48 and "Addenda", p. 276. The two most recent important studies on the Cappella Cornaro are in H. Kauffmann, *Giovanni Lorenzo Bernini*, (*supra*, note 194), 136–169, and in I. Lavin, *Bernini*, (*supra*, note 201), 77–145 and 196–210, Cf. Salerno's bibliography in E. Lavagnino, G. R. Ansaldi & L. Salerno, *Altari barocchi in Roma*, Roma 1959, 86.

[205] Domenico Bernini, *Vita*, (*supra*, note 192), 83.

[206] It used to be thought that work on the chapel started soon after Corner had come to Rome in 1644 and that Francesco Travani's medal of 1647, showing the chapel, celebrated the completion of its architecture (Brauer & Wittkower, 37). However, according to Lavin's documentation, the cardinal was not given the right to the chapel until 1647 (*op. cit.*, 198 and 206 ff.) The medal, therefore, only celebrates the initiation of works.

[207] Kauffmann (*Bernini*, 166) has shown that the use of portrait busts of the deceased facing each other on the side walls of a funerary chapel comes from Venice. Cf. Lavin, *Bernini*, 92.

[208] Lavin gives a complete list of the marbles used in the chapel, *op. cit.*, 202 and fig. 292.

[209] Wittkower (*Bernini*, Cat. No 48) questions the authenticity of Federigo Corner's portrait: the incised pupils and irises of the eyes, he points out, are too mechanical for Bernini himself. This bony thin face is almost a caricature and very different from Bernini's other contemporary portrait busts which are generally more idealised. Cf. the portrait bust of *Duke Francesco I d'Este*, Museo Estense, Modena, dated 1650–51 Wittkower, *Bernini*, Cat. No 54, Pl. 84. On the possibility of identifying the portraits in the chapel see Kauffmann, *Bernini*, 163 f., but cf. Lavin, *Bernini*, 200.

[210] A. Blunt, "Gianlorenzo Bernini: illusionism and mysticism", *Art History*, I (1978), 75 f. Cf. Kauffmann, *Bernini*, 166, and Lavin, *Bernini*, 92 ff., and figs 207 f.

[211] Kauffmann, *Bernini*, 166.

[212] Blunt, *op. cit.*, 75 and note 46. Lavin, however, in his discussion of the arrangement of the donors' portraits in this chapel (*Bernini*, 93, note 6) states, contrary to Blunt, that theatre boxes did in fact exist already at the beginning of the 17th century in Venice, although no early illustrations of them have been preserved. To the present author the simulated architectural perspective behind the portraits makes it clear that Bernini cannot have been intending to show the donors sitting in theatre boxes.

[213] Lavin's interpretation of the portraits of the deceased as participating in the Mass on the altar (Lavin, *Bernini*, 101 f.) is not convincing. In fact, not one of the deceased is actually looking down at the altar. The Eucharist, Lavin points out, had a central place in St. Teresa's devotional life, and her raptures often (but not always!) took place after Holy Communion. Certainly the Eucharist—here also stressed by the relief on the altar front (not incidently, by Bernini's hand; see Lavin, *Bernini*, 125)—was an essential theme in any funerary chapel according to post-Tridentine tradition, and does not necessarily have to be linked to the devotion of St. Teresa. Thus the Eucharist is, for

example, also a central theme in the Cappella Aldobrandini in S. Maria sopra Minerva, with Barocci's painting of the *Last Supper* (cf. *supra*, vol. I, 98).

[214] Bernini presumably read St. Teresa's description of her mystical experiences in the *Libro de su vida* of which an Italian translation had been published in Rome already in 1599 by Giovanni Francesco Bordini. Lavin points out (*Bernini*, 78f.) that a *Compendium* on the life of St. Teresa, compiled by Alfonso Manzanedo de Quiñones, who had been *promotore* in the process of canonisation, was published in 1647; Lavin believes that Bernini knew this author personally. See also recent study, S. Warma, "Ecstasy and Vision: two concepts connected with Bernini's *Teresa*", *Art Bulletin*, LXVI (1984), 508–511.

[215] Quoted from E. A. Peers, trans. and ed., *Saint Teresa of Jesus; The Complete Works*, London & New York 1963, I, 192f.

[216] For the angel and his arrow as the Messenger of Divine love, *il celeste cupido*, the literary sources of this theme and the influence from platonic-neoplatonic thought see Kauffmann, *Bernini*, 156.

[217] Earlier representations of the ecstasy of St. Francis of Assisi had established an iconographical theme that had also been used by Bernini in the Cappella Raimondi, and this theme was apparently used by Bernini *mutatis mutandis* for his *St. Teresa*, as can also been seen from the preparatory drawings. H. Kauffmann, "Der Werdegang des Theresagruppe von Giovanni Lorenzo Bernini", in *Essays in the History of Art presented to Rudolf Wittkower*, London 1967, 223. For the drawings see Brauer & Wittkower, figs 23b–25a.

[218] Particularly in chapter XX of the *Libro de su vida* St. Teresa describes her ecstasies and raptures; a particularly famous passage is para 3 of this chapter: "In these raptures the soul seems no longer to animate the body, and thus the natural heat of the body is felt to be very sensibly diminished: it gradually becomes colder, though conscious of the greatest sweetness and delight. No means of resistance is possible, whereas in union, where we are on our own ground, such a means exists: resistance may be painful and violent but it can almost always be effected. But with rapture, as a rule, there is no such possibility: often it comes like a strong swift impulse, before your thought can forewarn you of it or you can do anything to help yourself; you see and feel this cloud, or this powerful eagle, rising and bearing you up with it on its wings." Quoted from Peer's translation (*supra*, note 215).

[219] Kauffmann, *Bernini*, 158.

[220] Kauffmann points out (*op. cit.*, 161) that St. Teresa's features must not be interpreted as expressing sensuality; thus her open mouth, according to the symbolism of the time, shows that she is in direct contact with God. J.-B. Saint-Jure S. J. (1588–1657) writes: "J'ai ouvert la bouche de mon âme et j'ai attiré mon air spirituel, qui est Notre-Seigneur; ... Ouvre ta bouche, et beaucoup, et avec de grande désirs, et je la remplirai." H. Brémond, *Histoire littéraire du sentiment religieux en France depuis la fin des guerres de religion jusqu'à nos jours*, III, Paris 1925, 274. Also Lavin (*Bernini*, 112) remarks that St. Teresa's features suggest a purely internal experience.

[221] J. Pope-Hennessy, *Italian High Renaissance and Baroque Sculpture*, text vol., London 1963, 110.

[222] *Libro de su vida*, Chapter 27, paras 1, 4; chapt. 28, para. 4.

[223] L. de Grandmaison, "La religion personnelle: L'élan mystique", *Études*, L, vol. 135 (1913), 327. Cf. Brémond, *op. cit.*, II, Paris 1925, 588.

[224] Ecstasy has been thoroughly studied in the field of psycophysiology and psychiatry as a symptom of certain mental diseases. See fundamental study by P. Janet, *De l'angoisse à l'extase*, 2 vols, Paris 1926–28. On ecstasy in the history of catholic mysticism see comprehensive article in *Dictionnaire de spiritualité ascétique et mystique...*, IV, Paris 1961 (several authors). In the paragraph "Psychologie et faits occasionnels", Henri Gratton discusses the transverberation of St. Teresa as the best known example of what he calls *extase supranormale*. The following long quotation

(2178f.) may summarise and clarify the problems involved: "Cette extase a souvent été interprétée come une crise hysterique et cataleptique. Le symbolisme et les expressions corporelles révéleraient la volupté sexuelle ou l'auto-érotisme inavoué de la sainte. Certains auteurs, d'orientation psychoanalytique, y ont vu l'equivalent ou le déguisement hystérique de l'orgasme, ou la satisfaction sublimée d'une pulsion sexuelle, ou, enfin, la manifestation d'une regression vers la fusion préobjectale originelle. Dans un sens opposé, on a revendiqué la valeur uniquement sacrée et mystique de cette extase. Le langage symbolique, évoquant l'amour humain, ne serait qu'allégorique, purement littéraire et traditionnel.—A notre avis, la transverbération de sainte Thérèse, ainsie que d'autres extases mystiques, présentent un double phénomène psychologique important. D'un coté, le moi investit son énergie propre au niveau de certaines de ses fonctions en une intensité telle qu'il laisse ses autres fonctions spécifiques (d'adaptation, de contrôle et d'intégration) en un déficit énergétique plus ou moins accusé. D'un autre coté, il y a sublimation, entendue comme processus psychologique selon lequel le moi capte et s'associe inconsciemment certaines énergies instinctuelles au bénéfice de ses propres activité, objets ou buts. Cette sublimation explique la présence des manifestations à coloration instinctivo-affective de la transverberation. Elle contribue, d'autre part, à un accroissement de l'énergie psychique et à la ferveur des sentiments."

[225] Blunt, *op. cit.*, (*supra*, note 210), 77f. For the Jesuits see J. de Guibert, *La spiritualité de la Compagnie de Jésus: esquisse historique*, ("Bibliotheca Instituti Historici S.I.", IV), Roma 1953, and, for the *Esercizî spirituali*, particularly 98–127 and 525–541.

[226] C. di Bildt, "Cristina di Svezia e Paolo Giordano II duca di Bracciano", *Archivio della Società Romana di Storia Patria*, XXIX (1906), 29; the letter is dated 26 July 1652.

[227] Domenico Bernini, *Vita*, 83.

[228] Important studies, with documents, of the *Four Rivers Fountain* have been made by S. Fraschetti, *Bernini*, (*supra*, note 92), 179–201; Brauer & Wittkower, 47–50; R. Wittkower, *Bernini*, 1955 and 3 rd ed., 1981, Cat. No 50; H. Kauffmann, "Romgedanken in der Kunst Berninis", *Jahrbuch 1953 der Max-Planck-Gesellschaft*, Göttingen 1954, 55–80; H. Kauffmann, *Gian Lorenzo Bernini*, (*supra*, note 194), 174–193; R. Preimesberger, "Obeliscus Pamphilus: Beiträge zur Vorgeschichte und Ikonographie des Vierströmebrunnens auf Piazza Navona", *Münchner Jahrbuch der bildenden Kunst*, XXV (1974), 77–162; N. Huse, *Gianlorenzo Berninis Vierströmebrunnen*, (Inaugural-Dissertation 1966), München 1967—summarised in abbreviated form in "La fontaine des fleuves du Bernin", *Revue de l'Art*, VII (1970), 7–17.

[229] C. D'Onofrio, *Le Fontane di Roma*, Roma 1957, 65f.; the original state of this fountain is shown in fig. 51.

[230] Document first reproduced in Fraschetti, *Bernini*, 179, note 2. Cf. Preimesberger, "Obeliscus...", 91.

[231] Hempel, *Borromini*, 93f., Taf. 51. Cf. D'Onofrio, *Le fontane*, 203, and fig. 175.

[232] Domenico Bernini, *Vita*, (*supra*, note 192), 86f.

[233] Fraschetti, *Bernini*, 180, note 2.

[234] The most important dates regarding the fountain were already published by Fraschetti, *Bernini*, 180ff., and Brauer & Wittkower, 47ff. Cf. Preimesberger, "Obeliscus...", 114, and notes 259ff.

[235] Gigli, *Diario*, (*supra*, note 20), 323.

[236] *Ibidem*.

[237] *Ibidem*.

[238] Preimesberger, "Obeliscus...", 115. The unfinished fountain was standing in the middle of the Piazza Navona during the festivities of Holy Year 1650 and is shown on Barrière's engraving, (see illustration, p. 28).

[239] For the Giocondi *bozzetto* see E. Sestieri, *La fontana dei Quattro Fiumi e il suo bozzetto*, Roma 1970. The Bologna bozzetto was first published in S. Zamboni, *Da Roma a Pinelli*, Bologna 1968, 11–25, and Tav. 1, and by the same author in "Gian Lorenzo Bernini: un modello per la 'Fontana dei Quattro Fiumi' ritrovato", *Rapporto*

della Soprintendenza alle gallerie di Bologna, VII (1971), 31–43.

[240] For the drawings relating to the fountain see Brauer & Wittkower, 47ff., and figs 25b, 26–28.

[241] Wittkower, *Bernini*, 30.

[242] The most detailed discussions of the iconography of the fountain are to be found in the studies cited above, note 228. See also G. Pochat, "Ueber Berninis Concetto zum Vierströmebrunnen auf Piazza Navona", *Konsthistorisk Tidskrift*, XXXV (1966), 72–79.

[243] On Athanasius Kircher see E. Iversen, *The Myths of Egypt and its Hieroglyphs in European Tradition*, Copenhagen 1961; Preimesberger, "Obelischus...", 135; C. Reilly, *Athanasius Kircher S. J.: Master of a Hundred Arts*. 1602–1680, ("Studia Kircheriana", Schriftenreihe d. Internat. Athanasius Kircher Forschungsgesellschaft, I), Wiesbaden & Rom 1974; V. Rivosecchi, *Esotismo in Roma barocca: Studi sul Kircher*, Roma, 1982. See also following chapter, note 66.

[244] Preimesberger, "Obeliscus...", 136.

[245] *Ibid.*, 140. Cf. N. Huse, *op. cit.*, note 36 with quotation from Lualdi.

[246] *Ibid.*, 138.

[247] Kircher's inscription reads as follows, "Innocentius X. cum anno instaurandae iustitiae sacro / ex uno virginis Aquae fonte / quattuor effudit fluvios, / antiqui Paradisi, / hoc est, iustitiae specimen exhibet, / et seculum renovat."—quoted from Preimesberger, "Obeliscus...", 142.

[248] Kauffmann, *Bernini*, 189f.

[249] Preimesberger, "Obeliscus...", 142.

[250] "Giace il simulacro di questo fiume, quasi prostrato, sopra di scabrosi macigni, per poter meglio vagheggiare la dorata Colomba: ch'egli in alto di ammiratione riverisce, assisa sopra del sasso pensile."—from Lualdi, *Istoria ecclesiastica*, II, Roma 1651, quoted from N. Huse, *op. cit.*, note 36.

[251] Cf. Preimesberger, "Obeliscus...", 146.

[252] According to N. Huse the fountain represents the realm of Nature such as this is exposed in contemporary philosophy with which Bernini was familiar, "...le Bernin a représenté débordants de vie, dans la fontaine des Fleuves, les trois règnes de la nature, le minéral, le végétal et l'animal." *Revue de l'art*, (*supra*, note 228), 14. However, to the present author Huse's interpretation seems inconclusive.

[253] Fraschetti, *Bernini*, 191. Somewhat different figures in Wittkower, *Bernini*, 219, but probably based on documents not quoted by Fraschetti.

[254] Accounts in Fraschetti, *Bernini*, 181ff., and Wittkower, *Bernini*, 219.

[255] Gigli, *Diario*, 386.

[256] L. G. Cozzi, "Piazza Navona: feste e spettacoli", in *Piazza Navona Isola dei Pamphili*, Roma 1970, 61.

[257] Domenico Bernini, *Vita*, 92. More about contemporary praise and criticism of the fountain in Fraschetti, *Bernini*, 198ff.

[258] Domenico Bernini, *Vita*, 109.

[259] One such *macchina* was displayed in the Piazza Navona at the *possesso* of Innocent X; see above, p. 25. See also M. Fagiolo dell'Arco, "Quarantore, fochi d'allegrezza, catafalchi...", *Ricerche di storia dell'arte*, I–II (1976), 42f., and figs 15–17. Fagiolo dell'Arco also points out that some of the iconographic themes of the *Four Rivers Fountain* were already present in this *macchina*, which was conceived by Bernini, *op. cit.*, 49.

[260] Cozzi, *op. cit.*, 78–86; the first *allagamento* that has been recorded took place on June 23rd 1652, *ibid.*, 78.

[261] Wittkower, *Bernini*, 226; Cat. No 55.

[262] *Ibid.*, Cat. No 51. Wittkower lists six portrait busts of Innocent X, but only two of these can be attributed to Bernini himself.

[263] *Ibid.*, Cat. No 54.

[264] For the organisation of Bernini's studio and his assistants see *ibidem*, 34.

[265] A monograph on Alessandro Algardi is being prepared at present by Jennifer Montagu.

[266] Regarding Algardi's portraits see Wittkower, *Art and Architecture*, 355 (note 18); cf. N. Heimbürger-Ravalli, *Alessandro Algardi scultore*, Roma 1973, with list of five portrait busts of Innocent X, Cat. No 36 ff.

[267] Documents in O. Pollak, *Die Kunsttätigkeit unter Urban VIII.*, II, Wien 1931, 281–292. For the dates of the tomb see also Bellori, *Vite*, ed. E. Borea, 406, notes 2 f. Cf. H. F. Senie, "The Tomb of Leo XI by Alessandro Algardi", *Art Bulletin*, LX (1978), 90 ff.

[268] Wittkower, *Bernini*, 198. Senie points out the striking resemblance between Algardi's composition of the tomb and Annibale Carracci's *Madonna and Child with Saints John and Catherine* of 1593, now in the Pinacoteca of Bologna (*op. cit.*, 94 and fig. 5). See also Bellori's detailed description of the tomb in his *Vite* (ed. Borea, 410), in which he states, "... e tutte le figure sono animate nella proprietá de gli affetti loro".

[269] For the discussion of the iconography of Leo XI:s tomb see Senie, *op. cit.*, 90 f.

[270] Wittkower (*Art and Architecture*, 356) points out that Ferrata and Peroni, who according to Passeri assisted Algardi, did not join his studio until after 1647, when the tomb was virtually finished. Passeri, *Vite*, ed. Hess, 208 f.

[271] Heimbürger-Ravalli, *op. cit.*, Cat. No 51.

[272] J. Montagu, "Alessandro Algardi's Altar of S. Nicola da Tolentino, and some related models", *Burlington Magazine*, XCII (1970), 282–291.

[273] For the painters of the so-called *bambocciate* see G. Briganti, L. Trezzani & L. Laureati, *The Bamboccianti. The Painters of Everyday Life in Seventeenth Century Rome*, Roma 1983, (translation from the Italian ed., *I Bamboccianti*, Roma 1983).

[274] *Ibid.*, 133 ff.

[275] *Ibid.*, 141, 146, 151 ff., figs 5.25–27.

[276] This painting has previously been variously attributed to Dirk Helmbreker or Jan Miel. Briganti's attribution to Cerquozzi is now generally accepted. *The Bamboccianti*, 150, note 36.

[277] *Ibid.*, 91–131.

[278] *Ibid.*, 250–257.

[279] C. C. Malvasia, *Felsina pittrice: vita dei pittori bolognesi*, ed. 1841, II, 179 ff.

[280] Passeri, *Vite*, ed. Hess, 331.

[281] J. Bousquet, "Les relations de Poussin avec le milieu romain", in *Nicolas Poussin*, ouvrage publié sous la direction de André Chastel, (Centre National de la Recherche Scientifique: "Colloques Internationaux. Sciences Humaines"), Paris 1960, 1–18; and S. S. Rinehart, "Poussin et la famille Dal Pozzo", *Ibidem*, 19–30. K. Badt, *Die Kunst des Nicolas Poussin*. Köln 1969, 93–104.

[282] J. Bialostocki, "Poussin et le Traité de la Peinture de Léonard", in *Nicolas Poussin*, 133–140.

[283] A. Blunt, *Nicolas Poussin*, (The A. W. Mellon Lectures in the Fine Arts, 1958), Text vol., London & New York 1967, 167 ff.

[284] *Ibid.*, Cat. Nos 74 and 76.

[285] *Ibid.*, Cat. No 87. Cf. *L'Ideale classico del seicento in Italia e la pittura del paesaggio*, (Città di Bologna: "V Mostra Biennale d'arte antica"), catalogo, Bologna 1962, 191 f.

[286] Blunt, *Poussin*, Cat. No 174 and Text vol., 165, 294. Cf. *L'Ideale classico*, 198 f., and Cat. Nos 75, 76.

[287] Blunt, *Poussin*, Cat. No 170; cf. *L'ideale classico*, 207 f., and Cat. No 81.

[288] M. Roethlisberger, *Claude Lorrain: The Paintings*, I, New York 1979, 31 ff.

[289] *Ibid.*, 8 f.

[290] M. Kitson, *Claude Lorrain: Liber veritatis*, London 1978. The *Liber veritatis* which previously belonged to the Duke of Devonshire's collection, is now in the British Museum.

[291] *L'ideale classico*, 236. Some of the best known of Claude's seaport landscapes are *Seaport with the Embarkation of the Queen of Sheba*, from 1648, now in the London National Gallery, *Lib. ver.*, No 114, and *Seaport with Ulysses Returning Chryseis to her Father*, in the Louvre, *Lib. ver.*, No 80.

[292] I. G. Kennedy, "Claude and architecture", *Journal of the Warburg and Courtauld Institutes*, XXXV (1972), 260–283.

[293] *Lib. ver.*, Nos 113 and 119.

[294] On the discussion of these two replicas, why they were painted and who ordered them, see Roethlisberger, *op. cit.*, 279 ff. It seems that the London picture, together with *Embarkation of the Queen of Sheba*, (*Lib. ver.*, No 114), were first ordered by Camillo Pamphili while he was still a cardinal, and when he fell into disfavour after renouncing the cardinalate, it was acquired by the duke of Bouillon.

[295] That it was time for a revaluation of Gaspard Dughet was made clear at the exhibition in Bologna 1962, *L'ideale classico*, 256 ff.

[296] For these frescoes and for the discussion of Dughet's style its evaluation and various problems regarding chronology see M. R. Waddingham's excellent article, "The Dughet problem", *Paragone*, N. S., Arte, XIV (1963), N° 161, 37–54. Cf. S. J. Bandes, "Gaspard Dughet and San Martino ai Monti", *Storia dell'Arte*, XXVI (1976), 45–60.

[297] An exhibition of Dughet's work was held in London 1980. *Gaspard Dughet called Gaspard Poussin 1615–1676: A French Landscape Painter in Seventeenth Century Rome and His Influence on British Art.* Exhibition 1980 (catalogue), London 1980.

[298] For the frescoes in the Palazzo Pitti see M. J. Campbell, *Pietro da Cortona at the Pitti Palace: A Study of the Planetary Rooms and Related Projects*, ("Princeton Monographs in Art and Archeology", 41), Princeton 1977, 6–62. Cf. G. Briganti, *Pietro da Cortona*, 215 f., 221 f.

[299] Campbell, *op. cit.*, 63–164; Briganti, *op. cit.*, 225, 235 ff.

[300] On the influence in France of Pietro da Cortona's decorative style see Campbell, *op. cit.*, 171 ff. Cf. M. Laurain-Portemer, "Le palais Mazarin à Paris et l'offensive baroque de 1645–1650: d'après Romanelli, P. de Cortone et Grimaldi", *Gazette des Beaux-Arts*, VIᵉ per., LXXXI (1973), 151–168.

[301] See above, vol. I, 343.

[302] A. Sutherland Harris, *Andrea Sacchi: Complete Edition of the Paintings with a Critical Catalogue*, Oxford 1977, Cat. No 75.

[303] For Sassoferrato's style see F. Macé de Lepinay, "Archaïsme et purisme au XVIIᵉ siècle: les tableaux de Sassoferrato à S. Pietro de Pérouse", *Revue de l'art*, XXX (1976), 38–56; and F. Russel, "Sassoferrato and his sources: a study of seicento allegiance", *Burlington Magazine*, CXIX (1977), 694–700.

[304] For Mattia Preti, the formation of his style and the frescoes in S. Andrea della Valle, see S Mitidieri, "Mattia Preti detto il cavalier calabrese", *L'Arte*, XVI (1913), 428–442; also M. Marini, "Mattia Preti magnum picturae decus", *Ricerche di storia dell'arte*, I–II (1976), 103–128.

[305] Briganti (*op. cit.*, 103) speaks of "una sorta di veronesismo".

[306] On 17th November 1647 Pietro da Cortona wrote from Rome in a letter to Cardinal Francesco Barberini: "... sto cominciando a fare i cartoni della Cupola si ancho della tribuna della Ciesa (sic) nova". O. Pollak, "Italienische Künstlerbriefe aus der Barockzeit", *Jahrbuch der Königl. Preusz. Kunstsammlungen, Beiheft* 2, XXXIV (1913), 13. Cf. Campbell, *op. cit.*, 206, note 99.

[307] The artist was paid 4000 scudi for the works on the frescoes in the dome. Documents in O. Pollak, "Neue Regesten zum Leben und Schaffen des römischen Malers und Architekten Pietro da Cortona", *Kunstchronik*, N. F., XXIII (1911/12), 564.

[308] R. Preimesberger, "Pontifex romanus per Aeneam praesignatus", *Römisches Jahrbuch f. Kunstgeschichte*, XVI (1976), 245.

[309] Briganti, *op. cit.*, 251. The artist was paid 3000 scudi, Preimesberger, *op. cit.*, 247.

[310] The iconography has been the subject of a very extensive study by Preimesberger, *op. cit.*

[311] Preimesberger, *op. cit.*, 281.

[312] *Ibid.*, 254 ff.

[313] Paolo Giordano Orsini wrote in a letter to Queen Christina in Sweden on 26th July 1652, that Pietro da Cortona was then painting the history of Aeneas and still had to finish the choir in the Chiesa Nuova, but that the mosaics in St. Peter's kept him busy and that it would take him many years to finish them. C. di Bildt, "Christina di Svezia e Paolo Giordano II", *Archivio d. Società Romana di Storia Patria*, XXIX (1906), 29. Cf. Briganti, *Pietro da Cortona*, 252 f. For Pietro da Cortona's mosaics in the vestibule of the Chapel of the Sacrament in St. Peter's see F. DiFederico, *The Mosaics of Saint Peter's: Decorating the New Basilica*, University Park & London, 1983, 61.

[314] J. Genty, *Pier Francesco Mola pittore*, Lugano 1979, Tav. 101.

[315] Regarding the conditions in Rome during the last days of this pontificate see Gigli, *Diario*, 448 ff., and Pastor, XIV:1, 276.

[316] Gigli, *Diario*, 455.

CHAPTER II

[1] For the following, see C. M. Cipolla, "The decline of Italy", *Economic History Review*, 2nd Series, V (1952), 178–185.

[2] *Ibid.*, 178 f.

[3] *Ibid.*, 185 f.

[4] For the conclave of 1655 see *Conclavi de'Pontefici Romani*, II, Colonia 1691, 499–607; S. Pallavicino, *Della vita di Alessandro VII, Libri cinque*. Opera inedita..., 2 vols, Prato 1839–40, II, 223–263; Pastor, XIV:1, 303–309; extensive account also in A. Eisler, *Das Veto der Katholischen Staaten bei der Papstwahl seit dem Ende des 16. Jahrhunderts*, Wien 1907, 103–139.

[5] *Conclavi...*, II, 533. Text in Eisler, *op. cit.*, 304; for the date 13 February, Pastor, XIV:1, 307 and note 4.

[6] Gigli, *Diario romano*, ed. Ricciotti, Roma 1958, 464.

[7] For the *possesso* of Alexander VII see Gigli, *Diario*, 465, 467; F. G. Cancellieri, *Storia de' solenni possessi de' sommi pontefici...*, Roma 1802.

[8] For the youth of Fabio Chigi and his upbringing see article "Alessandro VII" in *Dizionario biografico degli italiani*, II, 205 ff. by M. Rosa. Fabio Chigi was born in Siena on 13 February 1599. He studied at the university of Siena and among his teachers was the famous humanist and linguist Celso Cittadini; for four years he also studied theology at the same university and took a doctor's degree in theology in 1626. Chigi arrived in Rome in 1629 and was soon after made *referendario della Segnatura di grazia e giustizia*. After a couple of years he was sent as vice-legate to Ferrara where he became a friend of the legate, Cardinal Giulio Sacchetti. In 1634 he was sent as the pope's representative to Malta and was ordained priest and consecrated bishop of Nardò in Puglia, where, however, he never set foot. In June 1639 he was sent to Cologne as papal nuncio. Cf. Pastor, XIV:1, 311.

[9] For Alexander VII:s personality and appearance see Pallavicino, *op. cit.*, I, 267 ff. Also *Relazioni degli ambasciatori veneti*, II, 169, 171, 243. See also the comprehensive and well-balanced article, signed P. Richard, in *Dictionnaire d'histoire et de géographie ecclésiastiques*, II, Paris 1914, cols 229–244.

[10] For the piety of Alexander VII, see F. Callaey, "La physionomie spirituelle de Fabio Chigi (Alexandre VII) d'après sa correspondance avec le p. Charles d'Arenberg fr. mineur capucin", in *Miscellanea Giovanni Mercati*, V, (Biblioteca Apostolica Vaticana: "Studi e testi", 125), Città del Vaticano 1946, 451–476. Cf. G. Incisa della Rocchetta, "Gli appunti autobiografici d'Alessandro VII nell'archivio Chigi", in *Mélanges Eugène Tisserant*, VI, (Bibl. Apost. Vaticana: "Studi e testi", 236), Città del Vaticano 1964, 439–457. See also the Venetian ambassador Sagredo's report in *Relazioni ambasciatori veneti*, II, 243, 253.

[11] *Introduction à la vie dévote* was first published in 1609; it was later translated into many European languages, including Swedish (Stockholm 1888); an Italian translation by P. Antoniotti S. J. was published in 1621, but Fabio Chigi was familiar with French. Another important work by St. François de Sales is *Traité de l'amour de Dieu*, Lyon 1616. Cf. H. Bremond, *Histoire litteraire du sentiment religieux en France*, I, Paris 1916, 68 ff.

[12] *La bonne philosophie et l'art de salut. Ov. Institution de vivre parfaitement comprise en trois preceptes*, par N. S. P. le pape Alexandre VII. Et traduit de latin en françois par F. Martial, Paris 1658.

[13] G. Incisa della Rocchetta, *op. cit.*, 448; cf. Pallavicino, *Vita di Alessandro VII*, I, 36.

[14] Callaey, *op. cit.*

[15] Pastor, XIV:1, 314.

[16] Cardinal Pallavicino is sometimes referred to as Pietro Sforza Pallavicino. This is a mistake, however, originating in the title page of his life of Alexander VII, where the author is called P. Sforza Pallavicino, but P. here means *padre*, or *pater*. His christian name is in fact Sforza, which was his mother's family name: as a christian name it is unusual. His most famous work is the history of the Council of Trent, *Istoria del concilio di Trento . . .*, 2 vols, Roma 1656–57, which was written to counter Paolo Sarpi's history of the same council (*supra*, vol. I, chapter II, note 18).

[17] Regarding Giovanni Bona, created cardinal by Clement IX in 1669, and his writings and his influence on the spiritual life of the 17th century, see article by L. Ceyssens, in *Dizionario biografico degli italiani*, XI, 442–445, with bibliography.

[18] Regarding the pope's relatives, see Pallavicino, *Vita di Alessandro VII*, I, 281–292.

[19] *Ibid.*, II, 18. Pastor, XIV:1, 317 f. and note 4, and document in "Anhang", *ibid.*, 1174. The cardinals' pronouncements are to be found in *Cod. Ottob. 1061*, manuscript in the Vatican Library.

[20] Pallavicino, *Vita di Alessandro VII*, II, 21.

[21] *Relazioni ambasciatori veneti*, II, 266; cf. Pallavicino, *op. cit.*, I, 283.

[22] Pastor, XIV:1, 319. According to Pallavicino (*op. cit.*, II, 230) it was Flavio who bought the village of Farnese, paying partly with his own money and partly with the help of the pope; he then gave Farnese to his cousin.

[23] *Relazioni ambasciatori veneti*, II, 265. For Flavio Chigi see also article in *Dizionario biografico degli italiani*, XXIV, 747 ff.

[24] *Relazioni ambasciatori veneti, loc. cit.*

[25] The Genoese agent Ferdinando Raggi, quoted by A. Neri, *Costumanze e sollazzi: aneddoti romani nel pontificato di Alessandro VII*, Genova 1883.

[26] *Dizionario biografico degli italiani*, XXIV, 743.

[27] F. Corridore, *La popolazione dello stato romano (1656–1901)*, Roma 1906, 14. For the population of the City of Rome see J. Beloch, *Bevölkerungsgeschichte Italiens*, II, Berlin & Leipzig 1940, 13.

[28] For the following see Angelo Correr's report in *Relazioni ambasciatori veneti*, II, 217 ff., 247.

[29] A. Coppi, *Discorso sulle finanze dello stato pontificio dal secolo XVI al principio del XIX*, Roma 1855, 16.

[30] *Relazioni ambasciatori veneti*, II, 218. However, in 1661 Sagredo estimates the public debt at 39 millions, *ibid.*, 246.

[31] Gigli, *Diario*, 464, 469, 471.

[32] Pallavicino, *Vita di Alessandro VII*, I, 314 f. Cf. Gigli, *Diario, passim.*

[33] A. Fanfani, *Storia del lavoro in Italia dalla fine del secolo XV agli inizi del XVIII*, Milano 1943, 339.

[34] M. Petrocchi, *Roma nel seicento*, (Istituto di Studi Romani: "Storia di Roma", XIV), Bologna 1970, 35 f., 44.

[35] *Relazioni ambasciatori veneti*, II, 247.

[36] Pastor, XIV:1, 322.

[37] For Sacchetti's promemoria see M. Zucchini, "Una scrittura del cardinale Giulio Sacchetti a papa Alessandro VII per rimettere in piedi l'arte dell'agricoltura", *Economia e Storia*, IV (1957).

[38] Petrocchi, *op. cit.*, 58ff.

[39] For the plague of 1656 see Pastor, XIV:1, 324f.

[40] Beloch estimates that in Naples alone 160 000 people died of the plague, *Bevölkerungsgeschichte Italiens*, I, Berlin & Leipzig, 1937, 180.

[41] Beloch, *Bevölkerungsgeschichte Italiens*, II, Berlin 1940, 13.

[42] For the Oriental policy of Alexander VII see Pastor, XIV:1, 361ff. More recent research in M. Petrocchi, *La politica della Santa Sede di fronte all'invasione ottomana (1444–1718)*, Napoli 1955, with bibliography; see also bibliographical notes in Petrocchi, *Roma nel seicento*, 170f. Cf. I. Rainer, *Rom und der Türkenkrieg 1663–64*, Modena 1964.

[43] Rainer, *op. cit.*, 10f., and *passim*.

[44] On the relations between King Louis XIV and the pope at this time see Ch. Gérin, *Louis XIV et le Saint-Siège*, I, Paris 1894, 283–346.

[45] *Ibid.*, 284.

[46] Pastor, XIV:1, 368.

[47] For the following see detailed account in Pastor, XIV:1, 369–377; and Gérin, *op. cit.*, 283ff. Of various contemporary reports mention can be made of *Relatione di tutto ciò che passò tra il pontefice Alessandro VII e la Maestà del re christianissimo nell'anno 1662 il 20. Agosto per l'insulto fatto da' papalini al duca di Crechi regio ambasciatore*, [s.n.t.].

[48] On these negociations and the peace of Pisa see Gérin, *op. cit.*, I, 419–482.

[49] For the reforms in the papal curia see Pastor, XIV:1, 390ff.

[50] *Ibid.*, 392.

[51] Petrocchi, *Roma nel seicento*, 97ff. Cf. Pastor, XIV:1, 390f.

[52] For the following see Petrocchi, *op. cit.*, 98.

[53] For St. Carlo da Sezze see excellent article by J. Heerinckx, "Charles de Sezze", in *Dictionnaire de Spiritualité ascétique et mystique*, II, Paris 1953, cols 701–703.

[54] *Trattato delle tre vie della meditatione e stati della santa contemplatione*, Roma 1654.

[55] Se article "Jansénisme" in *Dictionnaire de théologie catholique*, VIII:1, Paris 1923, cols 318–529. The Jansenist controversy during Alexander VII is also treated in great detail in Pastor, XIV:1, 423–493. For the sources see L. Ceyssens, *La fin de la première période du jansénisme: Sources des années 1654–1660*, I–II, ("Bibliothèque de l'Institut historique belge de Rome", XII–XIII, 1963–1965).

[56] For Chigi's correspondence see *La correspondance antijanséniste de Fabio Chigi nonce à Cologne plus tard Alexandre VII*, ed. A. Legrand & L. Ceyssens, ("Bibliothèque de l'Institut historique belge de Rome", VIII, 1957).

[57] The fundamental principle of the moral system of Probabilism is that "A doubtful law does not bind" (Lex dubia non obligat). In this case it is also applied do divine law. The advocates of this system require that any person who is in doubt about a particular line of conduct should genuinely seek certainty. They emphasise that the "opinion of liberty" must be obviously probable, and here probabilism differs from laxism, in that the person in doubt may follow the opinion of liberty if there is a solid reason in favour of this opinion, even though the opinion of one law may seem more probable. Probabilism as a theory was first developed in Spain at the end of the 16th century by the Dominican B. de Medina. It was later taken up by moral theologians among the Jesuits. The most famous of these was Francisco Suàrez (1548–1617). See article "Probabilisme" in *Dictionnaire de théologie catholique*, XIII, Paris 1935, cols 418–619. On Alexander VII and probabilism there is a detailed account in Pastor, XIV:1, 477–488. For the following see also I. von Döllinger & Fr. H. Reusch, *Geschichte der Moralstreitigkeiten in der römisch-katholischen Kirche seit dem sechzehnten Jahrhundert mit Beiträgen zur Geschichte und Charakteristik des Jesuitenordens*, 2 vols, Nördlingen 1889.

[58] Pastor, XIV:1, 487.

[59] See article "Chinois rites" in *Dictionnaire de théologie catholique*, II:2, Paris 1910, cols 2369ff., and in *Dictionnaire d'historie et de géographie ecclésiastique*, XII, Paris 1953, cols 731ff.

[60] On the controversy about the immaculate conception of the Virgin see article "Immaculée conception" in *Dictionnaire de théologie catholique*, VII, Paris 1921–22, cols 845–1218; and for Alexander VII particularly col. 1174. For reasons of health Alexander had already been granted dispensation from the Breviary when still only a priest, and instead he recited the *Officium parvum Beatae Mariae Virginis*. G. Incisa della Rocchetta, "Gli appunti autobiografici d'Alessandro VII nell'archivio Chigi", in *Mélanges Eugène Tisserant*, VI, (Bibl. Apost, Vaticana: "Studi e Testi", 236), Città del Vaticano 1964, 445.

[61] F. Ughelli, *Italia sacra sive de episcopis Italiae et insularum adiacentium...* tomus nonus, Romae 1662. There are also later editions, one of which was printed in Venice 1717–1722.

[62] For Giovanni Bona and his spiritual teaching see article by J.-M. Canivez in *Dictionnaire de spiritualité ascétique et mystique*, I, Paris 1937, cols 1762–1766. Cf. L. Ceyssens, "Le cardinal Jean Bonna et le jansénisme...", *Benedittina*, X (1956), 79–120 and 267–328; also article by the same author in *Dizionario biografico degli italiani*, XI, 442–445. Bona's complete works were published under the title *Johannis S. R. E. cardinalis Bona, opera omnia tribus tomis comprensa*, Parisiis 1677–78; and later editions Antverpiae 1694 and 1739, and Venetiis 1752.

[63] G. Bona, *Manuductio ad coelum continens medullam sanctorum Patrum et veterum philosophorum...* Rome 1658. This was translated into many languages during the following century; an Italian edition, *Guida al cielo*, was printed in Rome 1916.

[64] S. Pallavicino, *Istoria del concilio di Trento...* 2 vols, Romae 1656–57. There are many later editions: *Histoire du concile de Trente*, 3 vols, Paris 1845. Cf. H. Jedin, *Der Quellenapparat der Konzilsgeschichte Pallavicinos: Das Papsttum und die Wiederlegung Sarpis im Lichte neuerschlossener Archivalien*, (Pontificia Università Gregoriana: "Miscellanea Historiae Pontificiae", IV:6), Roma 1940.

[65] S. Pallavicino, *Della vita di Alessandro VII...* opera inedita, 2 vols, Prato 1839–40. By the same author, *Descrizione del primo viaggio fatto a Roma dalla regina di Svezia Cristina Maria...* opera inedita, Roma 1838.

[66] C. Reilly, *Athanasius Kircher S. J. Master of a Hundred Arts 1602–1680*, ("Studia Kircheriana", Schriftenreihe d. Internat. Athanasius Kircher Forschungsgesellschaft..., I), Wiesbaden & Roma 1974. V. Rivosecchi, *Esotismo in Roma barocca*, (*supra*, I, note 243).

[67] Reilly, *op. cit.*, 39.

[68] See chapter I, note 243. Later Kircher published *Oedipus aegyptiacus...*, 3 vols, Romae 1652–1654, and *Interpretatio hieroglyphica*, Romae 1666, and finally *Sphinx mystagoga...*, Amstelodami 1676.

[69] V. Rivosecchi, *op. cit.*, 139ff.

[70] F. Buonanni, *Musaeum Kircherianum...*, Romae 1709.

[71] F. M. Renazzi, *Storia dell'università degli studi a Roma detta comunemente la Sapienza*, III, Roma 1805, 156.

[72] *Ibid.*, 159.

[73] The manuscripts from Urbino, now in the Vatican Library, have been catalogued by C. Stornajoli, *Codices urbinatis graeci*, Roma 1905, and *Codices urbinatis latini*, Roma 1922. Cf. J. Bignami Odier, *La bibliothèque vaticane de Sixte IV à Pie XI*, ("Studi e testi", 272), Città del Vaticano 1973, *passim*.

[74] I. Giorgi, "Cenni sulla biblioteca Chigiana recentemente acquistata dallo Stato", *Rendiconti della R. Accad. dei Lincei, classe di scienze mor., stor. e filol.*, S. 5, XXVII (1918/19), 151–156. The library contained only 56 Greek manuscripts, but 190 Latin; there were also 254 medieval Italian manuscripts, and more than 1000 from the 16th and

17th centuries; the number of printed books was about 28000.

[75] G. Travaglini, *I papi cultori della poesia*, Lanciani 1887, 77f. The first edition of Chigi's poems, *Philomathi Musae iuveniles* were printed in Cologne 1645; later editions were printed in Antwerp 1654, Paris 1656 and Amsterdam 1660.

[76] G. Incisa della Rocchetta, "Gli appunti autobiografici d'Alessandro VII...", (*supra*, note 10), 439–457.

[77] *Ibid.*, 449: "...instrui l'occhio a quelle proportioni; onde non era opera di quella arte (architettura), che, subito, non giudicasse, se era a misura, havuto riguardo alla optica, et alla lontananza, o vicinanza della veduta, senza la quale non si può già mai architettar bene".

[78] *Ibid.*, *loc. cit.* P. Bacci, "L'elenco delle pitture, sculture e architetture di Siena compilato nel 1625–26 da Mons. Fabio Chigi poi Alessandro VII secondo il MS Chigiano I–I–11", *Bollettino Senese di Storia Patria*, N. S., X (1939), 197–213 and 297–337.

[79] For Flavio Chigi's patronage see V. Golzio, *Documenti artistici sul seicento nell'archivio Chigi*, Roma 1939, *passim*. Cf. F. Haskell, *Patrons and Painters*, London 1963, 139f., 154f. See also extensive article in *Dizionario biografico degli italiani*, XXIV, 750.

[80] G. Incisa della Rocchetta, "Il museo di curiosità del cardinale Flavio Chigi seniore", *Roma*, III (1925), 539–544. An inventory on twenty-five folio pages is said to have survived.

[81] For Flavio Chigi's collection of ancient sculpture see V. Golzio, *op. cit.*, 305ff., and *Die Dresdener Antiken und Winckelmann*, ed. K. Zimmermann, ("Schriften d. Winckelmann-Gesellschaft", IV), Berlin 1977, 15, 21ff., and *passim*. An inventory of the Chigi collection from 1705 is published in *Documenti inediti per servire alla storia dei musei d'Italia*, IV, Firenze & Roma 1880, 399–408.

[82] C. Rieci, "Il ritratto di Cristina Paleotti", *Bollettino d'Arte*, XI (1917), 3f.

[83] For Camillo de' Massimi see Haskell, *Patrons and Painters*, 115–119. The inventory of Massimi's collection in the Vatican Library, *Capponi lat. 260*, is published in J. A. F. Orbaan, *Documenti sul barocco in Roma*, Roma 1920, 515–522.

[84] On Camillo de' Massimi and Nicolas Poussin see A. Blunt, *Nicolas Poussin*, (*supra*, I, note 283).

[85] On Lorenzo Onofrio Colonna and Maria Mancini see P. Colonna, *I Colonna dalle origini all'inizio del secolo XIX*, Roma 1927, 271f.

[86] A. Neri, *Costumanze e sollazzi: Aneddoti romani nel pontificato di Alessandro VII*, Genova 1885, 35.

[87] The problems involved in Queen Christina's abdication of the Swedish crown and her conversion to Roman Catholicism have been discussed, mainly by Swedish scholars, for the last fifty years. One of the first to enter the field was Curt Weibull (*Drottning Christina: Studier och Forskningar*, Stockholm 1931, reprinted 1934 and 1962), who stressed that the queen's change of faith was her main reason for abdicating. S. I. Olofsson (*Drottning Christinas Tronavsägelse och Trosförändring*, Uppsala 1953) arrives at a different conclusion. He argues that Christina's reason for renouncing the crown was a combination of her dislike of ruling, her longing for the continent and the cultural life of Europe and her worry about growing financial problems. Sven Stolpe was the first to study Queen Christina's intellectual background and philosophical ideas (*Från Stoicism till Mystik: Studier i Drottning Kristinas Maximer*, Stockholm 1959), and he later wrote a more popular biography of the queen in which he summarised the problems and possible solutions, (*Drottning Kristina*, 2 vols, Stockholm 1960–61; English translation, somewhat abbreviated, *Queen Christina of Sweden*, London 1966). Stolpe points out that there is no sign of the queen going through any spiritual crises or inner conversion prior to her official conversion. Christina was a highly intelligent and well-read woman, and philosophy always remained her chief interest; her approach to the Christian Faith was that of a philosopher rather than a theologian. It has also been pointed out that in 1651, when the queen first announced

her intention of abdicating, the reason she gave was her aversion to marriage, and scholars have discussed the extent to which this was based on a Lesbian or bisexual disposition. However, it was after her first decision to abdicate, that she got in touch with the Catholic Church and wrote her first letter to the pope asking him to send a priest to give her instruction in matters of the Faith. The letter has survived, as has the pope's instructions to the two Jesuit fathers who went to Stockholm at risk to their lives. Christina may at some point have belived that she could remain in Sweden while secretly becoming a catholic, but she soon abandoned that idea. (P. Negri, "Lettera inedita del Padre Malines sulla conversione di Christina di Svezia", *Archivio d. Società Romana di Storia Patria*, XXXIII, 1910). It is probably impossible for us today to judge the depth of Christina's faith: more than one scholar has described the extreme complexity of her character; thus the deeper motives for her abdication and conversion cannot be explained by any simple formula. (Stolpe, *Från Stoicism till Mystik*, 15–20 and *passim*; cf. *Queen Christina of Sweden*, 96ff., and 141ff.)

[88] For Queen Christina's journey from Stockholm to Rome in 1655 there are two important contemporary accounts: G. Gualdo Priorato, *Historia della sacra Real Maestà di Christina Alessandra regina di Svetia...* Roma 1656, and S. Pallavicino, *Descrizione del primo viaggio fatto a Roma dalla Regina di Svezia Christina*, Roma 1838.

[89] For Christina's reception and entry in to Rome see Gualdo Priorato *op. cit.*, 232ff.

[90] Detailed accounts regarding the carriage and the other papal gifts have survived. G. Masson, "Papal gifts and Roman entertainments in honour of Queen Christina's arrival", in *Queen Christina of Sweden: Documents and Studies*, ("Analecta reginensia", I), Stockholm 1966, 245.

[91] Gualdo Priorato, *op. cit.*, 234f. Bernini is reported as saying "if there is anything ugly in this, it is mine", to which the queen promptly replied, "Then there is nothing of yours".

[92] For the following see Gualdo Priorato's description of the *cavalcata*, *op. cit.*, 236–252.

[93] Gigli, *Diario*, (*supra*, note 6), 474.

[94] The decoration of St. Peter's on this occasion is described by Gualdo Priorato, *op. cit.*, 255. Cf. *Christina Queen of Sweden: a Personality of European Civilisation*, ("Nationalmusei utställningskatalog", 305), Stockholm 1966, No 620, 275.

[95] This banquet is described by Gualdo Priorato, *op. cit.*, 258ff.

[96] G. Masson, *Queen Christina*, London 1968, 253; the documents found by Georgina Masson are unfortunately not cited in her biography.

[97] *Christina Queen of Sweden*, No 622f. P. Bjurström, *Feast and Theatre in Queen Christina's Rome*, ("Nationalmusei skriftserie", 14), Stockholm 1966., 17ff., with illustration.

[98] For these decorations see M. Fagiolo Dell'Arco & S. Carandini, *L'effimero barocco*, 2 vols, ("Biblioteca di storia dell'arte", X–XI), Roma 1977–78, *passim*, with numerous illustrations.

[99] On the decorations for the so-called *Quarantore* see M. S. Weil, "The decorations of the Fourty Hours and Roman Baroque illusions", *Journal of the Warburg and Courtauld Institutes*, XXXVII (1974), 218–248.

[100] Gualdo Priorato, *op. cit.*, 294.

[101] *Ibid.*, 295f., cf. F. Clementi, *Il carnevale romano*, (*supra*, I, note 74), 534f., and A. Ademollo, *I teatri di Roma*, (*supra*, I, note 78), 74.

[102] Clementi, *op. cit.*, II, 532f. Cf. P. Bjurström, *Feast and Theatre*, 23ff.

[103] On Barberini's theatre and the stage sets for *Trionfo della Pietà* see G. Masson, "Papal gifts and Roman entertainments...", 253f. Cf. Bjurström, *Feast and Theatre*, 23–30, and *Christina Queen of Sweden*, Cat. No 980, 984ff.

[104] Ademollo, *op. cit.*, 76; cf. *Christina Queen of Sweden*, Cat. No 979.

[105] Gualdo Priorato, *op. cit.*, 297ff.

[106] *Ibid.*, 301.

[107] *Ibid*, 302–310. Cf. Clementi, *op. cit.*, 525–532.

[108] Detailed accounts, discovered by Georgina Masson, have survived in the Barberini archives, "Papal gifts...", 258.

[109] C. de Bildt, *Christine de Suède et le cardinal Azzolino: Lettres inédites...*, Paris 1899. The friendship between Queen Christina and Cardinal Azzolino is also discussed by Sven Stolpe, *Drottning Kristina efter tronavsägelsen*, Stockholm 1961, 106–119; cf. Stolpe, *Queen Christina*, 253–263.

[110] For the Monaldeschi affair see C. Weibull, *Drottning Christina och Monaldesco*, Stockholm 1936, and by the same author, *Monaldescos död: Aktstycken och berättelser*, Göteborg 1937. Cf., Stolpe, *Queen Christina*, 228–245.

[111] *Relazioni ambasciatori veneti*, II, 216.

[112] P. B. Romanelli, "Etichetta e precedenze a Roma durante il soggiorno di Christina di Svezia", *Il Giornale di Politica e di Letteratura*, VII (1931), *passim*.

[113] O. Sirén, *Nicodemus Tessin d.y:s studieresor..., anteckningar, bref och ritningar.* Stockholm 1914, 182–186.

[114] For Queen Christina's collection of ancient sculpture see *Christina Queen of Sweden*, 573–579; cf. F. Haskell & N. Penny, *Taste and the Antique, passim* and for *Castor and Pollux* 173, for *Faun with Kid* 211.

[115] For Queen Christina's collection of paintings see O. Granberg, *Drottning Kristinas tafvelgalleri på Stockholms slott och i Rom*, Stockholm 1896. Cf. E. Waterhouse, "Queen Christina's Italian pictures in England", in *Christina Queen of Sweden*, 372–375.

[116] *Christina Queen of Sweden*, 488–504.

[117] C. Nordenfalk, "Queen Christina's Roman collection of tapestries", in "Analecta reginensia", I, (*supra*, note 90), 284f. Cf. *Christina Queen of Sweden*, 490f., 579f.

[118] Ch. Callmer, "Queen Christina's library of printed books in Rome", in "Analecta reginensia", I, 59–73. J. Bignami Odier, "Les manuscrits de la Reine Christine au Vatican...", in "Analecta reginensia", I, 33–43. About a quarter of the collection *Reginensia* in the Vatican Library comes from collections other than Christina's.

[119] J.-Q. Regteren Altena, van, "Les dessins italiens de la Reine Christine de Suède", in "Analecta reginensia", II, (Nationalmusei skriftserie, 13), Stockholm 1966.

[120] S. G. Lindberg, "Christina and the scholars", in *Christina Queen of Sweden*, 53.

[121] For Gian Domenico Cassini see article in *Dizionario biografico degli italiani*, XXI, 485. The treatise on the comets was entitled *Theoria motus cometae anni 1664 et 1665*, Romae 1665.

[122] R. Stephan, "A note on Christina and her academies", in "Analecta reginensia", I, 366; cf. *Christina Queen of Sweden*, 376.

[123] Domenico Bernini, *Vita del Cavalier Gio. Lorenzo Bernino...*, Roma 1713, 104.

[124] *Ibid.*, 94.

[125] *Ibid.*, 95f.

[126] R. Krautheimer & R. B. S. Jones, "The Diary of Alexander VII: Notes on art, artists and buildings", *Römisches Jahrbuch für Kunstgeschichte*, XV (1975), 199–233, *passim*: henceforth abbreviated *Diary of Alexander VII*.

[127] On the square of St. Peter's before Bernini's time and the prerequisites for his design see Ch. Thoenes, "Studien zur Geschichte des Petersplatzes", *Zeitschrift für Kunstgeschichte*, XXVI (1963), 97ff., 104f., 107–109. Bernini's design within the urban setting is discussed by M. Birindelli, *La Machina heroica: Il disegno di Gianlorenzo Bernini per piazza San Pietro*, ("Saggi di storia di architettura", IV), Roma 1980.

[128] F. Baldinucci, *Notizie dei professori del disegno*, V, Firenze 1847, 330. Brauer & Wittkower, 67.

[129] *Ibid., loc. cit.*, and F. Fasolo, *L'opera di Hieronimo e Carlo Rainaldi*, Roma s.a., 215f.

[130] F. Ehrle, "Dalle carte e dai disegni di Virgilio Spada", *Atti d. Pont. Accademia*

Romana di Archeologia, Serie III: *Memorie*, II (1927), 34 and note 155. Present were all the cardinals in the congregation and its *thesaurarius* Franzoni and Virgilio Spada.

[131] *Ibid.*, 34 and note 156. Three different comments written by Bernini regarding his designs for the piazza have survived in the Vatican Library (codex *Chig. H II 22*, fols 105–109); they are reproduced in Brauer & Wittkower, 70, note 1.

[132] Ehrle, *loc. cit.*, and S. Fraschetti, Bernini, (*supra*, I, note 197) 314, note 2; cf. Brauer & Wittkower, 69.

[133] On 13 August the pope noted in his diary (*supra*, note 126), that he had ordered Cardinal Barberini to summon the congregation of the *Reverenda Fabbrica* and that he wanted the loggias to be parallel, "Sian paralleli che si possi; senza fabrica sopra maco' balaustri e con statue ad ogni pilastrino..." i.e. single-storey loggias with balustrade and statues.

[134] Brauer & Wittkower, 71.

[135] Bernini's *giustificazione* in cod. *Chig. H II 22*, fol. 109r., cf. Brauer & Wittkoer, 70, note 1.

[136] Brauer & Wittkower, 72f., and fig. 161a–b.

[137] Ehrle, *op. cit.*, 35f., and note 158; Brauer & Wittkower, 71; the *giustificazione* in *Chig. H II 22*, fol. 105r., *ibid.*, 71, note 6.

[138] *Ibid.*, fig. 180c in the Vatican Library, cod. *Chig. VII 9*, fol. 40v–41r.

[139] On these drawings see R. Wittkower, "A counter-project to Bernini's Piazza di San Pietro", *Journal of the Warburg and Courtauld Institutes*, III (1939/40), 88–106.

[140] T. K. Kitao, *Circle and Oval in the Square of Saint Peter's*, New York 1974, 12f. On the inspiration from ancient architecture see M. Fagiolo, "arche-tipologia della piazza di S. Pietro", in *Immagini del Barocco: Bernini e la cultura del Seicento*, ("Biblioteca internazionale di cultura", VI), Roma 1982, 117–132.

[141] W. Lotz, "Die ovalen Kirchenräume des Cinquecento", *Römisches Jahrbuch f. Kunstgeschichte*, VII (1955), 7–99. On Bernini's *ovato tondo* in the square of St. Peter's see Brauer & Wittkower, 76f. Cf. Th. Thieme, "La geometria di Piazza San Pietro", *Palladio*, N. S., XXIII (1973), 129–144 and particularly 130 and fig. 2. See also Kitao, *op. cit.*, 31ff.

[142] Birindelli, *op. cit.*, (*supra*, note 127), 45–98.

[143] Brauer & Wittkower, 74. In the course of the following years three more medals were struck to commemorate the construction of the colonnades; all four show slight variations in the design. Medals I–IV are reproduced together by Kitao, *op. cit.*, figs 20–23.

[144] Bernini's corridor does not coincide with the one from the Ferrabosco tower to the façade; the difference is shown in a drawing reproduced by Brauer & Wittkower, fig. 164c.

[145] Already on 2 September 1657 Alexander VII wrote in his diary "Bernino col disegno ultimo di colonne piu grosse e no doppie" *Diary of Alexander VII*, No 130.

[146] Brauer & Wittkower, 81 and fig. 162a.

[147] Brauer & Wittkower, 81. In 1688 Nicodemus Tessin saw this model in the Vatican Library. Sirén, *op. cit.*, 161, (*supra*, note 113).

[148] *Relazioni ambasciatori veneti*, II, 218.

[149] In an interesting article Angela Guidoni Marino has tried to prove that Bernini in using oblique and rhombic forms in the colonnades of St. Peter's was inspired by certain architectural theories which were presented at about this time by a Spanish theologian, Juan Caramuel de Lobkowitz ("Il colonnato di Piazza S. Pietro: dall'architettura obliqua di Caramuel al classicismo Berniniano", *Palladio*, N. S., XXXIII (1973), 81–120). Alexander VII was acquainted with Caramuel, whom he had met in Germany, and in 1655 he invited him to Rome. However, Caramuel's work *Theologia moralis fundamentalis*, which was published in Frankfurt in 1655 and of which the pope owned a handwritten copy, had been put on the Index of forbidden books. Caramuel's ideas were certainly fascinating and very unusual for the time. Hypotheses and experi-

ments, he argued, must always be given priority, even in theology, and what was not explicitly forbidden should always be allowed. For this reason he was opposed to ecclesiastical censorship. Needless to say, such ideas caused a scandal among the theologians in Rome, but Alexander VII, who recognised Caramuel's intelligence, nevertheless made him *consultore* of the Sant' Uffizio. Caramuel also had a keen interest in architecture and, as we might expect, objected to Vitruvius whose great authority made him obstacle to free development. When it came to geometry, Caramuel was like one possessed, and he believed that geometry could solve any problems—even in theology. Thus, in architecture, he advocated the use of oblique lines and rhomboid forms. According to Angela Guidoni Marino, Caramuel took part in the discussion of Bernini's design for the colonnades of St. Peter's, but to the present writer her arguments do not seem conclusive. While it is true that Caramuel criticised the "errors" which he claimed could be found in Bernini's design, the book in which this criticism is presented, *Architecura civil*, was not published until 1678 in Vigevano; even his other very important work, *Mathesis biceps vetus et nova* was not printed until 1670.

[150] According to cod. *Chig. H II 22*, fol. 162r., quoted in Brauer & Wittkower, 81.

[151] According to documents in the Archivio della Reverenda Fabbrica di S. Pietro, quoted in Wittkower, *Bernini*, 245.

[152] Wittkower, *Bernini*, Cat. No 67. Alexander VII notes in his Diary on 10 August 1659 that Bernini had showed him the first statue for the colonnades. See also A. Haus, *Der Petersplatz in Rom und sein Statuenschmuck: Neue Beiträge*. Diss., Freiburg in Br. 1970 (typescript copy in the Bibliotheca Hertziana, Rome), 17f. For the iconography, *ibid.*, 28f.

[153] On the various designs for the *terzo braccio* see R. Wittkower, "Il Terzo Braccio del Bernini in Piazza S. Pietro", *Bollettino d'arte*, XXXIV (1949), 129–134; reprinted in English translation in R. Wittkower, *Studies in the Italian Baroque*, London 1975.

[154] Brauer & Wittkower, 86 and fig. 63a.

[155] *Ibid.*, 86; cf. Wittkower in *Bollettino d'arte*, 1949, 130f.

[156] Wittkower, in *Bollettino d'arte*, 132.

[157] Already in 1653, before Bernini had been invited to design his colonnades, Virgilio Spada had suggested to the *Reverenda Fabbrica* that all the buildings between the Borgo Nuovo and Borgo Santo Spirito, the so-called *spina*, should be demolished in order to open up the view from Castel Sant'Angelo to St. Peter's. Ehrle, *op. cit.*, (*supra*, note 130), 29. For a modern evaluation of the present Via della Conciliazione and the buildings between this avenue and the colonnades see R. Pane, *Bernino architetto*, Venezia 1953, 33f. According to Pane, the Via della Conciliazione is a complete failure, "...rappresenta oggi il più compiuto fallimento dell'architettura ufficiale italiana", and he advocates the construction, according to Bernini's design, of the *terzo braccio* in order to close the area of the piazza—which would simply mean completing an unfinished masterpiece. But cf. M. Birindelli, *op. cit.*, 126, who is against such a pastiche, also on aesthetic grounds.

[158] Strangely enough, this important relation between Bernini's colonnades and the façade of the basilica seems to have escaped all those scholars who had discussed Bernini's design, and was first presented by Theodor Hoppe, "Beobachtungen an Berninis St.-Peter-Kolonnaden", *Österreichische Zeitschrift f. Kunst und Denkmalpflege*, XXVI (1972), 160–165.

[159] See Bernini's *giustificazione*, Brauer & Wittkower, 70, note 1.

[160] In Bernini's *giustificazione*, (*ibid., loc. cit.*), it is said, "...the portico accurately expresses her act of maternally receiving in her open arms Catholics to be confirmed in faith, heretics to be reunited with the Church, and unbelievers to be enlightened by the true faith...", (Kitao's translation, *op. cit.*, 14). More on the *concetto* in Kitao, *op. cit.*, 22ff. Cf. V. Mariano, *Significato del Portico berniniano di San Pietro: prolusione*, Roma 1935.

[161] Kitao, *op. cit.*, 19ff.

[162] Brauer & Wittkower, 89 and fig. 164c. This drawing shows clearly the relation between the new and the old corridor and the original position of the Portone di Bronzo.

[163] *Ibid.*, 91.

[164] E. Panofsky, "Die Scala Regia im Vatikan und die Kunstanschauungen Berninis", *Jahrbuch d. Preuszischen Kunstsammlungen*, XL (1919), 242 ff. H. Voss, "Bernini als Architekt an der Scala Regia und an den Kolonnaden von S. Pietro", *Ibid.*, XLIII (1922), 16 ff.

[165] On the effects of perspective in the Scala Regia see Panofsky, *op. cit.*, 246. Recent contribution is M. Birindelli, *Il lato nord di Piazza San Pietro: Scala Regia*, Roma 1981, 5 ff.

[166] Domenico Bernini, *Vita*, 101.

[167] S. Fraschetti, *Bernini*, 317, note 1, and 318, note 3.

[168] Wittkower, *Bernini*, Cat. No 68.

[169] Fraschetti, *op. cit.*, 318, note 4.

[170] Wittkower, *Bernini*, Cat. No 73, fig. 108.

[171] For the dates, *Ibid.*, 251 f.

[172] A copy in Bernini's handwriting of Nikeforos of Constantinople, describing Constantine's features, is preserved in the Bibliothèque Nationale in Paris. K. Rossacher, "Berninis Reiterstatue des Konstantin an der Scala Regia", *Alte und Moderne Kunst*, XII (1967), 3. On the violent contemporary criticism of Bernini's *Constantine* see Wittkower, *Bernini*, 254.

[173] Wittkower, *Bernini*, 253 f. Hans Kauffmann on the other hand points out (*Giovanni Lorenzo Bernini: Die figürlichen Kompositionen*, 287), that the drapery was of old a traditional token of majesty often used in statues of heroes and *condottieri* in previous centuries.

[174] Domenico Bernino, *Vita*, 154. On August 27th Alexander VII notes in his Diary, … "habbiam ordinati i marmi pel nostro Sepolcro al Cav. Bernini…", *Diary of Alexander VII*, No 56.

[175] Ehrle, *op. cit.*, (*supra*, note 130), 71.

[176] The most important studies on the Cathedra of Bernini, on which the following is based, are: Brauer & Wittkower, *Die Zeichnungen des Gianlorenzo Bernini*, Berlin 1931; R. Battaglia, *La cattedra Berniniana di San Pietro*, ("Collectanea urbana", II), Roma 1943; H. von Einem, "Bemerkungen zur Cathedra Petri des Lorenzo Bernini", *Nachrichten von der Akademie der Wissenschaften in Göttingen*, I, Philolog.—Hist. Klasse, Jhrg. 1955, Nr 4; H. Kauffmann, *Giovanni Lorenzo Bernini: Die figürlichen Kompositionen*, Berlin 1970; R. Wittkower, *Gian Lorenzo Bernini: The Sculptor of the Roman Baroque*, 3rd ed., Oxford 1981, (first ed. 1955).

[177] Giovanni Battista De Rossi, "La chaire de S. Pierre au Vatican et celle du cimitière Ostien", *Bulletin d'archéologie chrétienne*, V (1867); a very thorough investigation by a team of scholars is published in *La cattedra lignea di S. Pietro in Vaticano*, (*Atti della Pontificia Accademia Romana di Archeologia*, Serie 3: Memorie, X), Città del Vaticano 1971; important for the history of the *cathedra* and its symbolic value during the Middle Ages is M. Maccarone, "Die Cathedra Sancti Petri im Hochmittelalter: Vom Symbol des päpstlichen Amtes zum Kultobjekt, I", *Römische Quartalschrift*, LXXV (1980), 171–207, and II, *ibid.*, LXXVI (1981), 137–72. The most recent contribution to the discussion of the *cathedra* in the Middle Ages is M. Guarducci, *La cattedra di San Pietro nella scienza e nella fede*, Roma 1982.

[178] On the symbolic meaning of the *cathedra* see H. von Einem, *op. cit.*, 108 ff., and Kauffmann, *Bernini*, 247 f., 251 f., and Maccarone, *op. cit.*, I, 187 f., and II, 137 ff.

[179] Biblioteca Apostolica Vaticana, cod. *Barberini lat.*, *4409*, fol. 18.

[180] Battaglia, *op. cit.*, 70 f.; Maccarone has shown (*op. cit.*, II, 172) that Alexander VII actually stressed the symbolic meaning of the papal throne rather than its value as a relic.

[181] Ehrle, "Dalle carte e dai disegni di Virgilio Spada" (*supra*, note 130), 35 and note 158; Ehrle quotes two versions of the protocol from this session. Cf. Battaglia, *op. cit.*, 154–233; for the chronology, see also Wittkower, *Bernini*, Cat. No 61.

[182] Royal Collection, Windsor, No 5614, reproduced in Brauer & Wittkower, fig. 166a.

[183] Brauer & Wittkower, fig. 166b, from C. M. Metz, *Imitations of Ancient and Modern Drawings*, London 1798; the original drawing was lost but was later found on the London Art Market and published by P. L. Grigaut, "A bozzetto for St. Peter's cattedra", *Art Quarterly*, XVI (1953), 130 and fig. 5.

[184] *Diary of Alexander VII*, No 188.

[185] Battaglia, *op. cit.*, 160ff.; cf. Wittkower, *Bernini*, 235f.

[186] Grigaut, *op. cit.*, 124f., and fig. 1f.

[187] Battaglia, *op. cit.*, 21; Wittkower, *Bernini*, 236.

[188] L. Pascoli, *Vite de' pittori, scultori, ed architetti moderni*, Roma 1730, (fac-simile, Roma 1933), I, 19–20. Cf. Kauffmann, *Bernini*, 264.

[189] Battaglia, *op. cit.*, 168.

[190] Vatican Library, cod. *Chig. a I 19*, fol. 42v., reproduced in Brauer & Wittkower, fig. 74b.

[191] Battaglia has shown that the Glory consists mainly of putti and angels made in stucco by various artists and that only a few of the bigger angels are of bronze, *op. cit.*, 25f., 121ff. and tav. XXIX–XXXIV.

[192] Battaglia, *op. cit.*, 28f.; for the casting of the other three and the discussion of chronology, *ibid.*, 29–33.

[193] The pope's keen interest in the progress of the work is shown by various entries in his Diary: for example, of 7 September 1662 he notes, "Questa mattina a 12 hore si e gettata la terza statua della Cattedra di bronzo... che è venuta forse meglio delle altre due, deo gratias!"—and on 2 October 1664 he notes, "...andiamo a s. Pietro, vediamo indorar la 2.a statua...", *Diary of Alexander VII, passim.*

[194] Battaglia, *op. cit.*, 41f., 48f., 196.

[195] *Ibid.*, 100ff.

[196] *Ibid.*, 187.

[197] The ceremony is described in the *Diaro* of the basilica of St. Peter's, Battaglia, *op. cit.*, 229ff.

[198] Battaglia (*op. cit.*, 70f.) rightly warns against going too far in this interpretation, "...si rischierebbe di perdere il valore più duraturo dell'opera nei motivi contingenti della polemica".

[199] According to Bordini, the Pantheon was considered the symbol of the triumph of the Roman Catholic Church over paganism and over any political authority. S. Bordini, "Bernini e il Pantheon: note sul classicismo berniniano", *Quaderni dell'Istituto di Storia dell'Architettura*, Serie XIV, fasc. 79–84 (1967), 81.

[200] Bordini, *op. cit.*, 54.

[201] The design for the stucco decoration has survived in two drawings in the Vatican Library (*Chig. P VII 9*, fols 111–112 and 114), and both are reproduced by Bordini, *op. cit.*, figs 53 and 55.

[202] For the church S. Tommaso da Villanova at Castel Gandolfo and the dates of construction see Brauer & Wittkower, 115ff. Cf. T. K. Kitao, "Bernini's church façades: method of design and the contrapposti", *Journal of the Society of Architectural Historians*, XXIV (1965), 263–284. Also Golzio, *Documenti artistici sul seicento nell'archivio Chigi*, Roma 1939, 379–391, and documents 392–407.

[203] According to documents in the Chigi archives (Brauer & Wittkower, 119, note 4), Antonio Raggi was paid for his stuccoes in 1660.

[204] Brauer & Wittkower, 125. Golzio, *op. cit.*, 389, 402. In St. Peter's the medallions had been hung under the arches in the nave; a drawing of this arrangement is reproduced by M. Fagiolo Dell'Arco & S. Carandini, *L'Effimero barocco*, II, ("Biblioteca di Storia dell'arte", 11), Roma 1978, fig. 149.

[205] Originally the cornice and entablature of the interior were the colour of travertine and the rest of the church was whitewashed with marble powder (Golzio, *op. cit.*, 385, 400). The last restoration in the 1960s does not seem to have gone back to the original colour scheme.

[206] A drawing for the main altar from Bernini's workshop is reproduced in Brauer & Wittkower, fig. 169d.

[207] For the church at Ariccia see G. Incisa della Rocchetta, "Notizie sulla fabbrica della chiesa collegiata di Ariccia", *Rivista del R. Istituto d'Archeologia e Storia dell'Arte*, I (1929), 349–392. Cf. Golzio, *op. cit.*, 239–253 and Brauer & Wittkower, 122 ff., and figs 94 ff.

[208] Incisa della Rocchetta, *op. cit.*, 369.

[209] *Ibid.*, 371. Cf. D. Graf, "Guglielmo Cortese's painting of the Assumption and some preliminary drawings", *Burlington Magazine*, CXV (1973), 24–31.

[210] A contemporary report, *Racconto della Fabrica della Chiesa di S. Andrea a M.te Cavallo della Comp.a di Gesù*, has survived in the Archivio della Provincia Romana della Compagnia di Gesù. Ch. L. Frommel is preparing its publication, "S. Andrea al Quirinale: genesi e struttura", in *Atti del Convegno su Gianlorenzo Bernini* which at the time of writing is still in the press. S. Andrea al Quirinale has been more carefully studied than any other of Bernini's churches; the essential dates can be found in Brauer & Wittkower, I, 110 ff. Later studies are, F. Borsi, *La chiesa di S. Andrea al Quirinale*, Roma 1967, and J. Connors, "Bernini's S. Andrea al Quirinale: payment and planning", *Journal of the Society of Architectural Historians*, XLI (1982), 15–37.

[211] In september 1658 Camillo Pamphili declared that he wanted to give a huge sum of money to the church "per sua devozione". G. Eimer, *La Fabbrica di S. Agnese in Navona*, (*supra*, I, note 153), 527 and note 28.

[212] *Ibid.*, 528.

[213] Connors, *op. cit.*, 17 ff.

[214] Discussed in detail by Borsi, *op. cit.*, 46–51. Cf. Connors, *op. cit.*, 25.

[215] Connors, *op. cit.*, 21 and appendix, 37.

[216] *Ibid.*, 20.

[217] U. Donati, "Gli autori degli stucchi in S. Andrea al Quirinale", *Rivista del R. Istituto d'Archeologia e Storia dell'Arte*, VIII (1941), 144–150.

[218] Wittkower, *Art and Architecture*, 120.

[219] There is no evidence, however, that Bernini designed these stuccoes by Raggi. Brauer & Wittkower reproduced only his drawings for the angels over the altar, figs 84 f. See also Wittkower, *Bernini*, 239 and U. Donati, *op. cit., passim*.

[220] H. Hibbard, *Bernini*, Harmondsworth 1965, 144. The façade is also discussed by T. K. Kitao, "Bernini's church façades", (*supra*, note 202), 278.

[221] Domenico Bernini, *Vita*, 108.

[222] H. Hibbard, *Carlo Maderno*, ("Studies in Architecture", ed. A. Blunt & R. Wittkower, X), London 1971, 213 f.

[223] Golzio, *op. cit.*, 25 ff.

[224] P. Askew, "The relation of Bernini's architecture to the architecture of the High Renaissance", *Marsyas*, V (1947/49), 39–61.

[225] On the Louvre façade see R. Josephson, "Les maquettes du Bernin pour le Louvre", *Gazette des Beaux-Arts*, XVII (1928), 77–92. Cf. Brauer & Wittkower, 129 ff.

[226] On the negotiations leading to Bernini's journey to France see A. Schiavo, "Il viaggio del Bernini in Francia nei documenti dell'Archivio segreto vaticano", *Bollettino del Centro di Studi per la Storia dell'Architettura*, X (1956), 23–80. On Bernini's journey to France, the negotiations leading up to it and Bernini's artistic activities at the court of Louis XIV, there is a recent and comprehensive study by Cecil Gould, *Bernini in France. An Episode in Sixteenth-Century History*, London 1981.

[227] There are many editions of Paul Fréart de Chantelou, *Journal de Voyage du Cavalier Bernin en France*, and it has also been translated into other languages; one of

the latest is a handsome volume printed in Aix en Provence in 1981. However, it lacks an index, which the present writer has found only in the German edition by Hans Rose, München 1919.

[228] See vol. I, 312f.

[229] Document in *Ragguagli borrominiani: Mostra documentaria*, catalogo a cura di Marcello del Piazzo, (Ministero dell'Interno: "Pubblicazioni degli Archivi di Stato", XLI), Roma 1968, 114. For the following dates see also P. Portoghesi, *Borromini: Architettura come linguaggio*, Milano 1967, 277.

[230] The plan has survived in a drawing in the Albertina in Vienna (No 887), E. Hempel, *Francesco Borromini*, Wien 1924, 158f. and figs 55ff. Cf. G. Antonazzi, *Il Palazzo di Propaganda*, Roma 1979, 27f., fig. 22.

[231] Antonazzi, *op. cit.*, 59.

[232] *Ibid.*, 62f., and figs 40–41.

[233] See vol. I, 307.

[234] L. Montalto, "Il drammatico licenziamento di Francesco Borromini dalla fabbrica di Sant'Agnese in Agone", *Palladio*, N. S., VIII (1958), 139–188. Cf. Eimer, *op. cit.*, (*supra*, I, note 153), 430ff.

[235] Eimer, *op. cit.*, 456–518.

[236] Portoghesi, *Borromini*, 291f.

[237] Hempel, *Borromini*, 61ff. Cf. P. Portoghesi, "I monumenti borrominiani della basilica lateranense", *Quaderni dell'Istituto di Storia dell'Architettura*, N. 11 (1955).

[238] Hempel, *op. cit.*, 167f. Cf. Portoghesi, *Borromini*, 287.

[239] R. Wittkower, "Francesco Borromini: personalità e destino", in *Studi sul Borromini*, (*supra*, I, note 133), I, 13–33 and *passim*. On Borromini's death see Pascoli, *Vite*, I, 302ff.

[240] H. Ost, "Studien zu Pietro da Cortonas Umbau von S. Maria della Pace", *Römisches Jahrbuch f. Kunstgeschichte*, XIII (1971), 269f., 278. On Pietro da Cortona as architect see also forthcoming publication by A. Blunt, (at the time of writing not yet published).

[241] A plan in the Vatican Library (cod. *Chig. P VII 9*, fol. 74) shows the piazza that was opened up and the demolished properties around it. See also H. Ost, *op. cit.*, 234, 236, note 13.

[242] *Diary of Alexander VII, passim*. Cf. Ost, *op. cit.*, 241 and *passim*.

[243] *Diary of Alexander VII*, Nos 60f., 14 December 1656.

[244] Ost, *op. cit.*, 268f.

[245] *Diary of Alexander VII*, No 54.

[246] P. Portoghesi, *Roma barocca: storia di una civiltà architettonica*, Roma 1966, 234.

[247] Wittkower, *Art and Architecture*, 350, note 15, and 353, note 32.

[248] K. Noehles, "Architekturprojekte Cortonas", *Münchner Jahrbuch d. bildenden Kunst*, 3. F., XX (1969), 197. The drawing of the façade in the Vatican Library, cod. *Chig. P VII 10*, fol. 11.

[249] For the dates of this church see G. Drago & L. Salerno, *Ss. Ambrogio e Carlo al Corso*, ("Le chiese di Roma illustrate", ed. C. G. Paluzzi, No 96), Roma 1967, 62f. Cf. Wittkower, *Art and Architecture*, 161.

[250] Wittkower, *Art and Architecture*, 181.

[251] On the old church of S. Maria in Campitelli see L. Marracci, *Memorie di S. Maria in Portico*, 2nd ed. 1675, 107ff. Cf. R. Wittkower, "Carlo Rainaldi and the Roman Architecture of the full Baroque", *Art Bulletin*, XIX (1937), 282f.

[252] Cod. *Chig., P VII 10*, 104r, 107. Cf. Wittkower, in *Art Bulletin*, 283.

[253] H. Hager, "Zur Planungs- und Baugeschichte der Zwillingkirchen auf der Piazza del Popolo: S. Maria di Monte Santo und S. Maria dei Miracoli in Rom", *Römisches Jahrbuch f. Kunstgeschichte*, XI (1967/68). Wittkower (in *Art Bulletin*, 286) believed these were the plans of a later project, but Hager (*op. cit.*, 297) has proved that they can be no later than 1658.

[254] Pastor, XIV:1, 520.

[255] L. Marracci, *op. cit.*, 117. Cf. Hager, *op. cit.*, 298.

[256] Wittkower, in *Art Bulletin*, fig. 45.

[257] *Ibid.*, fig. 46.

[258] Marracci, *op. cit.*, 122; Wittkower, in *Art Bulletin*, 289.

[259] Wittkower, *Art and Architecture*, 183.

[260] *Ibid., loc. cit.* Also discussed in *Art Bulletin*, 290.

[261] Wittkower, in *Art Bulletin*, 258ff., see also F. Fasolo, "Carlo Rainaldi e il prospetto di S. Andrea della Valle in Roma", *Palladio*, N. S., I (1951), 34–38.

[262] Wittkower, in *Art Bulletin*, 262 and note 44.

[263] Documents regarding the two churches in Hager, *op. cit.*, 299–306.

[264] Hager, *op. cit.*, 200f., and fig. 136.

[265] *Ibid.*, 207, 214.

[266] *Ibid.*, 212f., and fig. 144.

[267] On the evolution of this oval plan and the contribution of Carlo Fontana see Hager, *op. cit.*, 220ff.

[268] Golzio, *op. cit.*, (*supra*, note 202), 122. For Bernini's influence on Fontana's design see Wittkower, *Art and Architecture*, 185.

[269] For Antonio del Grande see O. Pollak, "Antonio del Grande: ein unbekannter römischer Architekt des XVII. Jahrhunderts", *Kunsthistorisches Jahrbuch der K. K. Zentral-Kommission*, III (1909), 133–161.

[270] *Ibid.*, 139f.

[271] R. Lefevre, *Palazzo Chigi*, Roma 1972, 130, 134, 145; on Vincenzo Della Greca, *ibid.*, 130.

[272] "Il Papa ha tutta Roma di legname in camera distintissima e curiosissima, come quello che non ha maggior sfera che di abellire la città." *Rivista Europea*, V (1878), 676, quoted from Pastor, XIV:1, 524, note 2.

[273] For the following see *Diary of Alexander VII, passim.* On the activities and projects of this pope for the benefit of Roman urban development and the embellishment of the City see also recent study by Richard Krautheimer, *Roma Alessandrina. The remapping of Rome under Alexander VII 1655–1667*, (Vassar College: "The Agnes Rindge Claflin Endowment"), Poughkeepsie N.Y. 1982.

[274] S. Stucchi, "L'arco detto di Portogallo sulla Via Flaminia", *Bullettino della Commissione Archeol. Comunale di Roma*, LXXIII (1949/50), 101–122.

[275] The document in the Vatican Library is *Chig. R VIII c*, fol. 13r. It was first mentioned by Krautheimer in *Roma Alessandrina*, 20, and is more extensively discussed in an article, "Roma verde nel seicento" in a forthcoming publication in honour of Giulio Carlo Argan. I am indebted to Richard Krautheimer for kindly allowing me to read his manuscript.

[276] Krautheimer argues that with the planting of trees along many streets Alexander VII was carrying on a specific Roman tradition that goes back to the beginning of the seventeenth century, ("Roma verde...", *passim*). He also points out that, more than his predecessors, the pope consciously wanted to integrate the *disabitato* with the *abitato* of Rome.

[277] M. Zocca, "L'ambiente urbanistico delle chiese di Roma", *Capitolium*, XVII (1942), 33–45. See also *Topografia e urbanistica di Roma*, (Istituto di Studi Romani: "Storia di Roma", XXII), Bologna 1958, 440f. A drawing by Pietro da Cortona, probably a copy, published by Portoghesi (*Roma barocca*, Roma 1966, 235 and fig. 201) shows a wide avenue with porticoes on either side leading up to a church which can be identified as Il Gesù. Portoghesi believes this to be a project produced by Pietro da Cortona for Alexander VII; the avenue would have occupied approximately the space between Il Gesù and the present Largo Argentina. However, nothing is mentioned in any other source about such an enormous project, neither that the pope cherished such an idea, nor that Pietro da Cortona produced any other projects of this kind or on this scale. In

fact the drawing is very probably no more than a design for a stage set.

[278] Golzio, *op. cit.*, 336. Brauer & Wittkower, 120f., and Pls 89 a–b and 90a–b. Cf. Bordini, "Bernini e il Pantheon", (*supra*, note 199), 53–84.

[279] Photo montage of the piazza as planned with the two columns in M. & M. Fagiolo Dell'Arco, *Bernini: una introduzione al gran teatro barocco*, Roma 1967, No 201. For these projects see also R. Krautheimer, "Alexander VII and Piazza Colonna", *Römisches Jahrbuch f. Kunstgeschichte*, XX (1983), 193–208.

[280] *Diary of Alexander VII*, 9 September 1665. The drawing from Bernini's workshop in Brauer & Wittkower, fig. 171b; also reproduced and enlarged in *Palazzo del Quirinale*, Roma 1973, Tav. 47.

[281] Drawings after Bernini's model, which has not survived, are preserved in the Vatican Library (*Chigi, P VII 10*, fols 30v.–31r.) and in Nationalmuseum, Stockholm (*Cronstedt, CC 790*, and *THC 4444* and *THC 2226*). Cf. Elling, *Rom*, 294ff. For the negotiations regarding the project between the French court and Rome see M. Laurain-Portemer, "Mazarin, Benedetti et l'escalier de la Trinité des monts", *Gazette des Beaux-Arts*, LXXII (1968), 273–294; cf. W. Lotz, "Die spanische Treppe. Architektur als Mittel der Diplomatie", *Römisches Jahrbuch f. Kunstgeschichte*, XII (1969), 39–94, and C. D'Onofrio, *Scalinate di Roma*, Roma 1973, 277ff. For the various drawings connected with the project and the problem of their attribution see also a more recent study by T. A. Marder, "Bernini and Benedetti at Trinità dei Monti, *Art Bulletin*, LXII (1980), 286–289; cf. M. Worsdale, "Bernini and Benedetti", *Art Bulletin*, LXIII (1981), 315.

[282] On the history of the chapel and its iconography as built and decorated by Agostino Chigi see J. Shearman, "The Chigi Chapel in S. Maria del Popolo", *Journal of the Warburg and Courtauld Institutes*, XXIV (1961), 129–160.

[283] For the dates of these decorations and sculptures see Wittkower, *Bernini*, Cat. No 58.

[284] H. Kauffmann, *Bernini*, (*supra*, note 176), 222.

[285] Brauer & Wittkower, 57, and Pls 42–46. On the classical models see R. Wittkower, "The role of classical models in Bernini's and Poussin's preparatory work" in *Studies in Western Art*, (*Acts of the twentieth International Congress of the History of Art*, III), Princeton 1963, 48f.

[286] I. Faldi, "Ercole Ferrata: un bozzetto della pala della Santa Emerenziana", *Paragone, Arte*, VIII (1957), N° 87, 69ff. For the dates of the reliefs see Eimer, *La Fabbrica di S. Agnese*, (*Supra*, I, note 153), 449ff.

[287] Faldi, *op. cit.*, 69.

[288] R. H. Westin, "Antonio Raggi's Death of St. Cecilia", *Art Bulletin*, LVI (1974), 422–429.

[289] On the date of Melchiorre Caffà's death see J. Fleming, "A note on Melchiorre Caffà", *Burlington Magazine*, LXXXIX (1947), 85ff.

[290] *Ibid.*, 87; Wittkower, *Art and Architecture*, 202, 362, note 11.

[291] Wittkower, *Bernini*, Cat. No 71. Drawings for the monument, some of them originals by Bernini, in Brauer & Wittkower, 144f., Pls 176ff. Cf. *Bernini in Vaticano*, Roma 1981, No 199ff.

[292] On this obelisk see C. D'Onofrio, *Gli obelischi di Roma*, Roma 1967, 230–237. Cf. E. Iversen, *Obelisks in Exile*, I, Copenhagen 1968, 91–100. D'Onofrio argues against Bernini's authorship and attributes the design of the monument to one of the Dominican fathers, Giuseppe Paglia.

[293] W. S. Heckscher, "Bernini's elephant and obelisk", *Art Bulletin*, XXIX (1947), 178.

[294] *Ibid.*, 155–182. The *concetto* of this monument is also discussed by Iversen, *op. cit.*, 99f.

[295] Pietro da Cortona was working on these cartoons 1652–1663 and received the last payment in 1668. G. Briganti, *Pietro da Cortona*, Firenze 1962, 252f.

[296] On the frescoes in the Quirinal gallery see L. Ozzola, "L'arte alla corte di Alessan-

dro VII", *Archivio d. Società Romana di Storia Patria*, XXXI (1908), 41 ff., with quotations from old literary sources. Cf. Briganti, *op. cit.*, 107. The most important study is N. Wibiral, "Contributi alle ricerche sul cortonismo in Roma: i pittori della galleria di Alessandro VII nel Palazzo del Quirinale", *Bollettino d'Arte*, XLV (1960), 123–165.

[297] Passeri, *Vite*, ed. Hess, 369.

[298] Wibiral, *op. cit.*, 143; G. Briganti, *Il Palazzo del Quirinale*, Roma 1962, 47.

[299] A. Mezzetti, "Contributi a Carlo Maratti", *Rivista dell'Istituto Nazionale d'Archeol. e Storia dell'Arte*, N. S., IV (1955), 266.

[300] Bellori, *Vite*, ed. E. Borea, 582.

[301] Briganti, *Palazzo del Quirinale*, 49.

[302] Briganti, *Pietro da Cortona*, 261.

[303] *Ibid.*, 267.

[304] *Ibid., loc. cit.*

[305] On the frescoes in Valmontone see L. Montalto, "Gli affreschi del Palazzo Pamphilj in Valmontone", *Commentari*, VI (1955), 217–302.

[306] Passeri, *Vite*, ed. Hess, 371. R. Cocke, *Pier Francesco Mola*, Oxford 1972, 5 f., 35.

[307] N. Pevsner, "Die Wandlung um 1650 in der italienischen Malerei", *Wiener Jahrbuch f. Kunstgeschichte*, VIII (1932), 69–92.

[308] On Poussin's last phase see A. Blunt, *Nicolas Poussin*, London & New York 1958, 302 ff.

[309] For the dating of Poussin's *Diogenes* and on its extraordinary light see D. Mahon in *L'Ideale classico*, (*supra*, I, note 285), 215 f., Cat. No 85. For the variations in mood in Poussin's paintings see the same author, "Poussiniana: afterthoughts arising from the exhibition", *Gazette des Beaux-Arts*, LX (1962), 121 ff.

[310] Blunt, *op. cit.*, 332. Cf. in *L'ideale classico*, Nos 86, 87, *Summer* and *Autumn*.

[311] M. Röthlisberger, *Claude Lorrain: The Paintings*, I, New York 1979, 311 f.

[312] *Ibid.*, 369.

[313] L. Salerno, *Salvator Rosa*, Firenze 1963.

[314] On Claude's influence on Salvator Rosa see H. Langdon, "Salvator Rosa and Claude", *Burlington Magazine*, CXV (1973), 779–785. Cf. H. W. Schmidt, *Die Landschaftsmalerei Salvator Rosas*, Halle 1930.

[315] W. W. Roworth, *Pictor Succensor: A Study of Salvator Rosa as Satirist, Cynic and Painter*, (phil. Diss., 1977, Bryn Mawr College, Outstanding Diss. in the Fine Arts), New York & London 1978.

[316] For the following see Wittkower, *Art and Architecture*, 213 ff., and L. Salerno, "La pittura del seicento in Italia", in *Il Seicento Europeo*, (catalogue), Rome 1956, 19–28.

[317] G. Montenovesi, "Il pittore Mario de' Fiori", *Archivio d. Società Romana di Storia Patria*, LXXIII (1950), 225–235. Mario de' Fiori painted so much for the Chigi that he was given a monthly salary of 30 scudi, Golzio, *Documenti artistici*, 267.

[318] Gérin, *op. cit.*, (*supra*, note 44), 116 ff.

[319] For the last days of Alexander VII and his death see Pastor, XIV:1, 385–388.

CHAPTER III

[1] For the conclave of 1667 see Pastor XIV:1, 527–530.

[2] On the personality of Clement IX see G. Beani, *Clemente IX (Giulio Rospigliosi): Notizie storiche*, Prato 1893, *passim*. Cf. article by R. Meloncelli in *Dizionario biografico degli italiani*, XXVI, 1982, 282–293.

[3] *Relazioni ambasciatori veneti*, II, 328.

[4] The *maestro di camera*, the head of the pope's anticamera, was one of the highest officials of the papal court: one of his functions was to introduce ambassadors and princes visiting the pope: he also assisted the pope when he was travelling outside

Rome. The office was abolished in 1962. The office of the *datarius* dated back to the Middle Ages. Originally this official put the dates under papal letters and documents, but later it came within his competence to assign certain benefices and pensions and even dispensations from ecclesiastical law. This office was abolished in 1967.

[5] Beani, *op. cit.*, 56; cf. Pastor, XIV:1, 534.

[6] Pastor, XIV:1, 535, note 2.

[7] *Relazioni ambasciatori veneti*, II, 328 f.

[8] Pastor, XIV:1, 536.

[9] Beani, *op. cit.*, 59.

[10] M. Petrocchi, *Roma nel Seicento*, (*supra*, II, note 34), 36.

[11] *Relazioni ambasciatori veneti*, II, 360.

[12] On the Jansenist controversy during this pontificate see Pastor, XIV:1, 553–593.

[13] *Ibid.*, 597.

[14] For the following see Pastor, XIV:1, 602 ff., and M. Petrocchi, *La politica della Santa Sede di fronte all'invasione ottomana*, (*supra*, II, note 42), *passim*.

[15] Pastor, XIV:1, 602–608.

[16] M. Fagiolo & S. Carandini, *L'effimero barocco*, I, ("Biblioteca di storia dell'arte", 10), Roma 1977, fig. p. 240. Cf. description of the *possesso* in F. G. Cancellieri, *Possessi*, (*supra*, II, note 7), 275 ff.

[17] H. M. Von Erffa, "Die Ehrenpforten für den Possess der Päpste im 17. und 18. Jahrhundert", in *Festschrift für Harald Keller*, Darmstadt 1963, 348 f., Abb. 7–8.

[18] Clementi, *Il carnevale romano*, (*supra*, I, note 74), 556.

[19] Extensive account of this carnival in Clementi, *op. cit.*, 578 ff. The drawings of these floats by P. P. Sevin in the Stockholm National Museum have been discussed by P. Bjurström, *Feast and Theatre in Queen Christina's Rome*, Stockholm 1966, 78 ff.

[20] On Clement IX as a playwright see G. Canevazzi, *Papa Clemente IX poeta*, Modena 1900, 145 ff., and 186 ff.

[21] A drawing by Sevin, representing the fireworks at this occasion is reproduced in Bjurström, *op. cit.*, 51; cf. Ch. Gérin, *Louis XIV et le Saint-Siège*, Paris 1894, II, 227.

[22] Bjurström, *op. cit.*, 53 f., with reproduction of Sevin's drawing in the Stockholm National Museum.

[23] C. de Bildt, *Christine de Suède et le cardinal Azzolino*, (*supra*, II, note 109), 199.

[24] Clementi, *op. cit.*, 579.

[25] Bjurström, *op. cit.*, 74 f.

[26] Clementi, *op. cit.*, 579; cf. Bjurström, *op. cit.*, 81 ff.

[27] Clementi, *op. cit.*, 578.

[28] *Ibid.*, 577.

[29] On Leone Allacci see article in *Dizionario biografico degli italiani*, II, 467 ff.

[30] Pastor, XIV:1, 548 f.

[31] Brauer & Wittkower, 88.

[32] *Ibid.*, 87.

[33] For Bernini's work on the Ponte Sant'Angelo see H. G. Evers, *Die Engelsbrücke in Rom*, Berlin 1932; H. Kauffmann, *Bernini*, 290–311; L. Grassi, "Disegni inediti del Bernini e la decorazione di ponte S. Angelo", *Arti figurative*, II (1946), 186–199; Wittkower, *Bernini*, Cat. No 72; M. S. Weil, *The History and Decoration of the Ponte S. Angelo*, University Park & London, 1974 which is the most thorough and extensive work on these sculptures; the most recent contribution is C. D'Onofrio, *Gian Lorenzo Bernini e gli angeli di ponte S. Angelo: storia di un ponte*, Roma 1981.

[34] Brauer & Wittkower, 160.

[35] On the iconography of the angels see E. Mâle, *L'art religieuse après le concile de Trente*, 2nd ed., Paris 1951, 19–104 and 72–86. Cf. Weil, *op. cit.*, 92 ff. At this time several books with meditations on the Passion were published, such as Jacopo Salviati, *Fiori dell'orto di gessemani e del Calvario...*, Firenze 1667, with a dedication to Pope Clement IX.

[36] For the symbolic meaning of the bridge see Kauffmann, *Bernini*, 350 ff. Cf. H.-W. Kruft & L. O. Larsson, "Entwürfe Berninis für die Engelsbrücke in Rom", *Münchner Jahrbuch d. Bildenden Kunst*, 3. Folge, XVII (1966), 156. On the iconography of Bernini's angels see Weil, *op. cit.*, 89–103. Rudolf Kuhn links the iconography of the angels to the iconography of the interior of St. Peter's: The pilgrim contemplating the Instruments of the Passion is prepared to meet the celestial court of saints on the colonnades and to procede into the basilica where he will participate in the Eucharist; the angels on the bridge are thus a kind of parallel to the first stage in the *Spiritual Exercises* of St. Ignatius on whose teaching Bernini had based the iconographic programme for his angels. However, to the present writer, Kuhns arguments seem inconclusive. R. Kuhn, "Gian Lorenzo Bernini and Ignatius von Loyola", in *Argo: Festschrift für Kurt Badt*, Köln 1970, 299 ff.

[37] On the discussion regarding the chronology see Wittkower, *Bernini*, 248 f., and Weil, *op. cit.*, 90 f.

[38] Kruft & Larsson, *op. cit.*, 145 ff., and Kauffmann, *Bernini*, 298.

[39] Kruft and Larsson (*op. cit.*, 158) remark that this ambiguity corresponds to what certain German scholars in discussing the history of literature have called *Ausdruck antithetischen Lebensgefühls*.

[40] The stylistic differences between the angels are discussed in detail by Weil, *op. cit.*, 71–88. Cf. L. Grassi in *Arti figurative*, II (1946), 186–199.

[41] See above, vol. I, 136.

[42] E. Hempel, *Carlo Rainaldi*, München 1919, 59 ff. All dates regarding this project in Brauer & Wittkower, 163 ff.

[43] Bellori mentions in his *Vite* (ed. Borea, 594), that the foundations were laid and that Bernini had begun to quarry the travertine which was needed and that the pope had entrusted Carlo Maratti with painting the new *tribuna*; possibly, the mediaeval mosaics were to be moved to the new apse.

[44] Gérin, *op. cit.*, II, 388.

[45] Gigli, *Diario romano*, ed. Ricciotti, Roma 1958, 487.

[46] For this correspondence see C. de Bildt, *op. cit.*, *passim*.

[47] Pastor, XIV:1, 611–615.

[48] *Ibid.*, 616.

[49] C. de Bildt, *op. cit.*, p. II.

[50] For Clement X and his personality see Pastor, XIV:1, 618. Cf. article by L. Osbat in *Dizionario biografico degli italiani*, XXVI, 1982, 293–302.

[51] Pastor, XIV:1, 621.

[52] *Relazioni ambasciatori veneti*, II, 360.

[53] Petrocchi, *op. cit.*, *passim*.

[54] Pastor, XIV:1, 622 f.

[55] *Ibid.*, 628 f.

[56] *Ibid.*, 660.

[57] *Ibid.*, 662.

[58] *Ibid.*, 644.

[59] For the conclave 1676 see Pastor, XIV:2, 669–676.

[60] For Pope Innocent XI see Pastor, XIV:2, 676 ff. Innocent died with the reputation of holiness and the cause of his beatification was introduced in 1714 but was abandoned some fourty years later only to be reopened in 1944; the beatification took place in 1956. The acts used in the process of his beatification were published in 1713 under the title *Romana beatificationis & canonizationis ven. servi Dei Innocentij Undecimi…*, and again in the twentieth century, *Beatificationis et canonizationis… Innocentii papae XI. Disputatio Rev.mi Relatoris generalis super causae statu et super quibusdam difficultatibus*. Typis pol. vaticanis 1953. Modern biography by G. Papasogli, *Il beato Innocenzo XI*, Como 1957.

[61] Pastor, XIV:2, 678 f.

[62] G. B. Scapinelli, "Il memoriale del p. Oliva S. J. al card. Cybo sul nepotismo", *Rivista di Storia della Chiesa in Italia*, II (1948), 262–273.

[63] Pastor, XIV:2, 961 f.

[64] *Ibid.*, 683 f.; cf. Petrocchi, *op. cit.*, 78 and *passim*.

[65] *Ibid.*, 780 f.

[66] Petrocchi, *op. cit.*, 84.

[67] Pastor, XIV:2, 779.

[68] Petrocchi, *op. cit.*, 38 f.

[69] Cipolla, (*supra*, II, note 1), 178–185.

[70] Petrocchi, *op. cit.*, 104.

[71] *Ibid.*, 106.

[72] The spiritual life in Rome during the 17th century is extensively treated by Petrocchi, *op. cit.*, 91–118, with ample bibliography in "Appendix", 183–201.

[73] On Innocent XI and France see Pastor, XIV:2, 902–911.

[74] Pastor, XIV:2, 912 ff.

[75] On Queen Christina and Pope Innocent XI see Pastor, XIV:2, *passim*. Cf. S. Stolpe, *Queen Christina of Sweden*, London 1966.

[76] On Quietism see Pastor, XIV:2, 983–993, and Petrocchi, *op. cit.*, 125–129 with extensive bibliography. Cf. article in *Dictionnaire de théologie catholique*, XIII:2, Paris 1936, cols 1561–1574.

[77] Petrocchi, *op. cit.*, 127 ff.

[78] On Christina and Molinos see Stolpe, *op. cit.*, 314–326.

[79] Pastor, XIV:2, 985 f.

[80] *Ibid., loc. cit.*

[81] R. Stephan, "A note on Christina and her Academies", in *Queen Christina of Sweden*, (*supra*, II, note 90), 367 ff.

[82] *Ibidem* and S. G. Lindberg, "Christina and the scholars", in *Christina Queen of Sweden*, (*supra*, II, note 94), 52 f.

[83] Giovanni Pietro Bellori was born in Rome although not in 1615 as often stated but on 15 January 1613. *Dizionario biografico degli italiani*, VII, 781.

[84] J. von Schlosser, *Die Kunstliteratur: Ein Handbuch zur Quellenkunde der neueren Kunstgeschichte*, Wien 1924, 416.

[85] On Massimo (also Massimi) and his patronage see Moroni, *Dizionario di erudizione storico-ecclesiastica*, XLIII, 239 f.; cf. Haskell, *Patrons and Painters*, 114–119.

[86] For this theatre see A. Cametti, *Il teatro di Tor di Nona poi di Apollo*, I, Tivoli 1938, 37, 49 f., 61, and fig. 6.

[87] For the following operas see Cametti, *op. cit.*, 62–69 and 323 ff., 336, 241. On Queen Christina as patron of this theatre see P. Bjurström, *Den romerska barockens scenografi*, ("Svenska Humanistiska Förbundet", 88), Lund 1977, 67–81; cf. P. Bjurström, *Feast and Theatre*, (*supra*, note 97), *passim*.

[88] A number of drawings by P. Sevin have survived, now in the Nationalmuseum in Stockholm, showing some unidentified scenes for the Tor di Nona theatre, Bjurström, *Den romerska barockens scenografi*, 76 ff.

[89] Bjurström, *Feast and Theatre*, 104.

[90] For the following see C.-A. Moberg, "Christina and music", in *Christina Queen of Sweden*, 65–69; cf. Bjurström, *Feast and Theatre*, 100 ff.

[91] G. Hilleström, "Alessandro Scarlatti et son opéra L'Honestà negli amori, dediée à la Reine Christine", *Queen Christina of Sweden*, (*supra*, II, note 90), 137.

[92] Cametti, *op. cit.*, 9.

[93] Moberg, *op. cit.*, 68 f.

[94] On Benedetto Pamphili and his patronage see L. Montalto, *Un mecenate in Roma barocca: Il cardinale Benedetto Pamphilj (1653–1730)*, Firenze 1955.

[95] *Ibid.*, 311.

[96] *Ibid.*, 137, 311 f.

[97] *Ibid.*, 348, 355.

[98] A. Mercati, "Nuove notizie sulla tribuna di Clemente IX a S. Maria Maggiore", *Roma*, XXII (1944), 18–22.

[99] Pastor, XIV:1, 543, 624.

[100] C. D'Onofrio, *Scalinate di Roma*, Roma 1974, 44.

[101] For De Rossi see G. Spagnesi, *Giovanni Antonio De Rossi architetto romano*, Roma 1964. For the old Palazzo Altieri, *ibid* 66–72. Cf. A. Blunt, "Roman baroque architecture: the other side of the medal", *Art History*, III (1980), 72 ff.

[102] Spagnesi, *op. cit.*, 151–158. Cf. A. Schiavo, *Il Palazzo Altieri*, Roma s.a., fig. 18.

[103] Ch. Elling, *Rom: Arkitekturens Liv fra Bernini til Thorvaldsen*, København 1956, 241 f.

[104] Schiavo, *op. cit.*, 65.

[105] E. Rossi, "Palazzo Altieri", *Roma*, XVIII (1940), 57.

[106] Whether or not the attic windows in the cornice belong to the old palace from the middle of the century is not quite clear. However, they recall the attic windows of the Palazzo d'Aste which De Rossi had built before he rebuilt the Altieri palace. The window pediments are 16th century in style also on the new wing and Blunt says of this palace that "though the conception has a certain grandeur the detail is defiantly archaic", *op. cit.*, in *Art History*, III (1980), 72.

[107] Spagnesi, *op. cit.*, 157. Schiavo points out (*op. cit.*, 75), that according to Giuseppe Vasi (*Delle magnificenze di Roma*, 1754) several of the stuccoes in the interior are by Ercole Ferrata. See Schiavo, *op. cit.*, figs 53–57, with reproductions of drawings by Tessin now in the Stockholm National Museum. The neoclassical decorations in some of the rooms are of great interest and quite unique in Rome, see Schiavo, *op. cit.*, tav. XXI–XXXVI.

[108] Haskell, *Patrons and Painters*, 114–119.

[109] Pastor, XIV:1, 625.

[110] H. Hager, "La facciata di San Marcello al Corso: Contributo alla storia della costruzione", *Commentari*, N. S., XXIV (1973), 58–74; an earlier project for this façade by Carlo Rainaldi is reproduced in fig. 2.

[111] H. Hager, "La cappella del cardinale Alderano Cybo in Santa Maria del Popolo", *Commentari*, N. S., XXV (1974), 47–61. A project by Bernini (Brauer & Wittkower, 171, Tav. 185a) was abandoned on the death of the architect.

[112] Wittkower, *Bernini*, Cat. No 66.

[113] *Ibid.*, Cat. No 75, and p. 257.

[114] Kuhn, *op. cit.*, (*supra*, note 35), 310 f.

[115] On Bernini's *Beata Lodovica Albertoni* see Kauffmann, *Bernini*, 328–335. Cf. Wittkower, *Bernini*, Cat. No 76.

[116] The iconography of this sculpture has been debated: Wittkower believes that Bernini represents the *beata* as dying; so too, does Hibbard (*Bernini*, 222). Kauffmann, on the other hand, suggests that the sculpture shows the ecstasy of the blessed Lodovica. F. Sommer is also of this opinion. "The iconography of action: Bernini's Ludovica Albertoni", *Art Quarterly*, XXIII (1970), 30–38.

[117] For the Tomb of Alexander VII see Brauer & Wittkower, 168–171 and figs 129a–b, 130 with the earliest projects for the tomb. Wittkower, *Bernini*, Cat. No 77, quoting documents from Fraschetti, *Bernini*, (*supra*, I, note 92), 384–391, and Golzio, *Documenti artistici*, (*supra*, II, note 202), 117–147. The monument is also discussed by Kauffmann, *Bernini*, 312–327.

[118] Fraschetti, *op. cit.*, 384 f.

[119] E. Panofsky, *Tomb Sculpture: Its Changing Aspects from Ancient Egypt to Bernini*, London 1964, 95. Some notes in *Diary of Alexander VII* show that the pope already at an early stage discussed the iconography of the tomb with Bernini and imparted his own ideas on the allegories to be represented.

[120] Documents, in Golzio, *op. cit.*, 117–147.

[121] The documents connected with the tomb give us a clear idea how the work was distributed among Bernini's assistants. The *Veritas* was first prepared by Santi but was chiselled by Lazzaro Morelli and finished by Giulio Cartari. The statue of the pope was sculptured by Michel Maille but the ornaments on the pluvial and tiara were made by Giulio Cartari and Domenico Baciadonna. The *Prudentia* was started by Giuseppe Baratta but when his work was found to be unsatisfactory it was given to Cartari instead. The *Caritas* was first prepared by Santi and was then chiselled by Giuseppe Mazzuoli. The *Death* caused many problems: a model made by Morelli was tried out on the monument before it was moulded in bronze by Girolamo Lucenti and then finished and gild by Carlo Mattei. The large drapery was made in travertine by Morelli and covered with Sicilian jasper by Gabriele Renzi; it was actually finished before the sculptures were made. Some lesser known artists were responsible for certain details on the monument: Filippo Carcani, for example, made the drapery which covers *Veritas*, and this was then executed in bronze by Lucenti. Cf. Wittkower, *Bernini*, 259 f.

[122] Wittkower, *Bernini*, Cat. No 78.

[123] Drawings related to the Tabernacle were published by Brauer & Wittkower (131b–136b), who also gave an extensive account of its construction (*ibid.*, I, 172–175). The drawing in the Hermitage was first published by Wittkower, *Bernini*, fig. 116.

[124] For the statuette of Christ see M. S. Weil, "A statuette of the Risen Christ designed by Gian Lorenzo Bernini", *Journal of the Walters Art Gallery*, XXIX–XXX (1966/67), 6–15.

[125] F. Trevisani, "Carlo Rainaldi nella chiesa di Gesù e Maria", *Storia dell'Arte*, XI (1971), 163–171.

[126] *Ibidem.* Cf. Wittkower, *Art and Architecture*, 2nd ed., 208.

[127] The tombs of the bishop and the knight are both by Francesco Cavallini; the first tomb to the left is by Maille and the one on the right by Aprile, Wittkower, *Art and Architecture*, 370, note 29.

[128] N. Pevsner, "Die Wandlung um 1650 in der italienischen Malerei", *Wiener Jahrbuch f. Kunstgeschichte*, VIII (1932), 69–92.

[129] L. Montalto, "Francesco Cozza nella Libreria Pamphilj a Piazza Navona", *Commentari*, VIII (1956), 44. On Cozza see recent biography, L. Trezzani, *Francesco Cozza (1605–1682)*, Roma 1981.

[130] E. K. Waterhouse, *Italian Baroque Painting*, London 1962, 69.

[131] On this painter see R. Enggass, *The Painting of Baciccio: Giovanni Battista Gaulli 1639–1709*, University Park 1964. Baciccio, or Baciccia, is a nickname, a familiar form common in Genova for the name Giovanni Battista.

[132] Enggass, *op. cit.*, 9, 140. Gaulli also made a project for decorating the dome of S. Agnese; a *bozzetto* in the Düsseldorf Kunstmuseum has been identified with this project dated 1689, U. Fischer Pace, "Un bozzetto di G. B. Gaulli per la progettata cupola di Sant'Agnese in Agone", *Commentari*, N. S., XXV (1974), 71–72.

[133] The *concetti* of these paintings are not quite clear. The interpretation given by Enggass (*op. cit.*, 10 ff.) does not convince the present writer.

[134] L. Pascoli, *Vite...*, (*supra*, II, 188), I, 200; cf. Enggass, *op. cit.*, 31, who also reproduces the contract, 176 f.

[135] P. Tacchi Venturi, "Le convenzioni tra Gio. Battista Gaulli e il generale dei gesuiti Gian Paolo Oliva per le pitture della cupola e della volta del tempio farnesiano", *Roma*, XIII (1935), 149 f.

[136] For the frescoes in the dome see Enggass, *op. cit.*, 135 f.

[137] Tacchi Venturi, *op. cit.*, 152.

[138] For these frescoes see Enggass, *op. cit.*, 136.

[139] Enggass, *op. cit.*, 43 ff., and 136 f. A *bozzetto* for the paintings in the vault has survived in the Galleria Spada in Rome.

[140] Weil has in fact shown that the iconography of the ceiling was influenced by *apparati* for the Forty Hours Devotion designed by a little-known artist, Giovanni

Maria Mariani, for Il Gesù in 1665, 1671 and 1675, Weil, *op. cit.*, (*supra*, II, note 99), 235–240.

[141] Pascoli, *Vite...*, I, 200f; Nicodemus Tessin mentions Gaulli's ceiling in Il Gesù in his Roman diary, (*Nicodemus Tessin d.y:s studieresor...*, utg. af Osvald Sirén, Stockholm, s.a. /1914/, 161): "Al Gesù siehet man die sehr herliche Pencée vom Cav. Bernin im gantzen Gewelbe der Kirchen durch Sig:r Bazziggi exeqviret, wass den mahlereijen angehet."

[142] F. Titi, *Nuovo studio di pittura, scoltura ed architettura nelle chiese di Roma*, Roma 1721, 190.

[143] Pascoli, *Vite...*, 202.

[144] Queen Christina's visit is mentioned in a diary by P. Ottolino, quoted by Tacchi Venturi, *op. cit.*, 153. Enggass *op. cit.*, *doc.* 20.

[145] *Ibid.*, 155f.; Enggass, *op. cit.*, 67, 137f. and 178. This fresco is badly damaged, but two *bozzetti* which have survived give a good idea of its original condition. The *bozzetto* in the Young Museum, San Francisco, is a preparatory study, while the definitive *bozzetto* is in the sacristy of Il Gesù. It seems that Father Oliva had first asked Borgognone to decorate the choir and had also received money from the Duke of Parma, but when the artist died in 1676 nothing had yet been done. P. Pecchiai, *Il Gesù di Roma*, Roma 1952, 108.

[146] Pascoli, *Vite...*, I, 200f.

[147] *Ibid.*, 202.

[148] On Gaulli as a portrait painter see Enggass, *op. cit.*, 75–87.

[149] *Ibid.*, 142.

[150] E. Schaar, "Carlo Marattas Tod des heiligen Franz von Xaver im Gesù", in *Munuscula discipulorum: Kunsthistorische Studien Hans Kauffmann zum 70. Geburtstag 1966*, 250.

[151] Enggass, *op. cit.*, 141. The two lateral paintings in this chapel, *St. Francis Xavier Preaching*, and *St. Francis Xavier Baptising*, belong to Gaulli's latest works; they were not executed until 1706.

[152] Schaar, *op. cit.*, 262, 265.

[153] Apart from the princes only the marchesi Costaguti, Patrizi, Theodoli and Sacchetti had the privilege of showing their coat of arms in this way, and, for this reason, they were called *marchesi del baldacchino*.

[154] Haskell, *op. cit.*, 161; Bellori, *Vite*, ed. Borea, 159. Cf. below, note 158.

[155] A. Schiavo, *op. cit.*, (*supra*, note 102), 92f.

[156] *Ibid.*, Tav. XL and XLI.

[157] Bellori, *Vite*, ed. Borea, 597.

[158] On Maratti's drawings for the frescoes that were never made for the Altieri palace see W. Vitzthum, "Drawings by Carlo Maratta for the Altieri palace in Rome", *Burlington Magazine*, CV (1963), 367–369. Later contribution with discussion of the iconography, J. Montagu, "Bellori, Maratti and the Palazzo Altieri", *Journal of the Warburg and Courtauld Institutes*, XLI (1978), 334–340; note 3 in this article gives bibliography for the drawings in question.

[159] On Lorenzo Onofrio Colonna as patron and collector of art see Haskell, *Patrons and Painters*, 155f.

[160] These landscapes are Nos 158, 162, 167, 175, 178, 186, 190 and 193 in the *Liber Veritatis*; Röthlisberger, *op. cit.*, (*supra*, II, note 311), *passim*.

[161] For these frescoes see S. Bandes, "Gaspard Dughet's frescoes in Palazzo Colonna in Rome", *Burlington Magazine*, CXXIII (1981), 77–91.

[162] On Giovanni Coli (1636–1681) and Filippo Gherardi (1643–1704) see N. Dunn-Czak, "Coli and Gherardi, two little-known painters of the Roman baroque", *Apollo*, CII (1975), 110–114. From 1669 they painted the dome in S. Nicola da Tolentino under the patronage of the Pamphili famili, and the ceiling in S. Croce dei Lucchesi, their countrymen's church, completed in 1675.

[163] P. M. Ehrlich, *Giovanni Paolo Schor*, (diss., Columbia University, 1975), microfilm-xerography, Ann Arbor, Mich. 1977, 38ff. According to documents in the Colonna archives the decorative framework was painted by Schor and his workshop 1665–67. I am indebted to Hans Lepp for this information.

[164] For Antonio Gherardi (1644–1702) see E. Waterhouse, *Roman Baroque Painting*, Oxford 1976, 80. Cf. M. Lange, "Between Mola and Cortona: Origins and development of Antonio Gherardi's pictorial style and religious imagery", in Institutum Romanum Norvegiae: *Acta ad archeologiam et artium historiam pertinentia*, Serie altera in 8°, I (1981), 275–380.

[165] On Canuti see E. Feinblatt, "The Roman work of Domenico Maria Canuti", *Art Quarterly*, XV (1952), 45–65. The iconography of the ceiling in Ss. Domenico e Sisto has not yet been seriously studied and many of its allegories are extremely complex and difficult to decipher; cf. Th. Poensgen, *Die Deckenmalerei in italienischen Kirchen*, Berlin 1969, 92.

[166] Wittkower, *Art and Architecture*, 220.

[167] E. Feinblatt, *op. cit.*, 53; for the iconography see Th. Poensgen, "Some unknown drawings by Domenico Maria Canuti", *Master Drawings*, V (1967), 167.

[168] On Giacinto Brandi see A. Pampalone, "Per Giacinto Brandi", *Bollettino d'Arte*, Ser. V, LVIII (1973), 123–166. Brandi had studied in Lanfranco's workshop between 1646 and 47, he also admired Mattia Preti, Mola and Guercino. On the date of the S. Silvestro ceiling, *ibid.*, 150, 152.

[169] A. Paolucci, "La pittura della volta della chiesa di S. Pantaleo in Roma rivendicata al suo autore F. Gherardi, detto il Lucchesino", *Roma*, VIII (1930), 49–54.

[170] B. Kerber, *Andrea Pozzo*, ("Beiträge zur Kunstgeschichte", VI), Berlin & New York 1971; for the ceiling in S. Ignazio, 54–74.

[171] The *apparato* in Il Gesù 1685 was reproduced in Pozzo's own treatise on perspective, *Perspectiva pictorum et architectorum, pars prima*, Romae 1693, fig. 71 with a description. The treatise had great impact and during the 18th century was translated into many languages including New-Greek (1720) and Chinese (1721–29), Kerber, *op. cit.*, 267. Cf. P. Bjurström, *Den romerska barockens scenografi*, 90–95 and fig. 33.

[172] Domenico Bernini, *Vita*, (*supra*, II, note 123), 171.

[173] *Ibid.*, 170f., and I, Lavin, "Bernini's death", *Art Bulletin*, LIV (1972), 163f.

[174] Lavin, *op. cit.*, 159f.

[175] Domenico Bernini, *Vita*, 173. Cf. C. D'Onofrio, *Scalinate di Roma*, Roma 1974, 51ff.

[176] Lavin, *op. cit.*, 165f.

[177] D'Onofrio has shown that Bernini's *Sangue di Cristo* which can be found as an illustration in Marchese, *Unica speranza*, was not originally meant to illustrate this book (*Scalinate di Roma*, 48f.), and D'Onofrio argues, partly in opposition to Lavin, that the etching Sangue di Cristo was published by Bernini in order to make Clement X interested in his activity. This can be understood as a kind of flattery, and D'Onofrio believes that Bernini never seriously thought of Death until he was on his own deathbed. However, the present writer finds D'Onofrio's arguments inconclusive in this case.

[178] *Tessin*, ed. Sirén, (*supra*, note 141), 184.

[179] Lavin, in *Art Bulletin*, LIV (1972), 176.

[180] *Ibid.*, 172 and fig. 10. Also I. Lavin, "Afterthoughts on Bernini's death", *Art Bulletin*, LV (1973), 429–436.

[181] Domenico Bernini, *Vita*, 171.

[182] Quoted by S. Stolpe, *Christina of Sweden*, ed. Sir Alec Randall, London 1966, 272.

[183] Domenico Bernini, *Vita*, 176.

[184] *Ibid.*, 174f.

[185] S. Stolpe, *Från Stoicism till Mystik*, (*supra*, II, note 87), *passim*.

[186] Haskell, *Patrons and Painters*, 158.

[187] Wittkower points out (*Art and Architecture*, 237) that Maratti had a considerable influence also on sculpture: drawings by his hand have survived for the Tomb of Innocent XI by Monnot and for the statues that were to be placed in Borromini's aedicules in the Lateran Basilica etc.

Index
for Rome in the Age of Bernini, Vol. I and II

Numbers in italics refer to pictures.
References to the two volumes paged consecutively as follows:
I: xxx, II: xxx

A: PERSONS

B: PLACES AND SUBJECTS